P9-DXF-783

Where the Nights Are Twice as Long

CALGARY PUBLIC LIBRARY

MAR   2015

Where the nights are twice as long

Love Letters *of* Canadian Poets
1883-2014

Edited by DAVID ESO and JEANETTE LYNES

GOOSE LANE

Preface copyright © 2015 by David Eso.
Introduction copyright © 2015 by Jeanette Lynes.
Copyright in all other materials held by the authors, except where noted.

All rights reserved. No part of this work may be reproduced or used in any form or by any means, electronic or mechanical, including photocopying, recording or any retrieval system, without the prior written permission of the publisher or a licence from the Canadian Copyright Licensing Agency (Access Copyright). To contact Access Copyright, visit www.accesscopyright.ca or call 1-800-893-5777.

Edited by Katia Grubisic.
Cover and page design by Julie Scriver.
Cover image detailed from "Chasing Galaxies" copyright © 2012 by Oliver Charles, www.olivercstudio.co.uk

Printed in Canada.
10 9 8 7 6 5 4 3 2 1

Library and Archives Canada Cataloguing in Publication

Where the Nights Are Twice as Long : love letters of Canadian poets 1883-2014 / edited by David Eso and Jeanette Lynes.

Includes index.
Issued in print and electronic formats.
ISBN 978-0-86492-384-4 (pbk.). — ISBN 978-0-86492-829-0 (epub). — ISBN 978-0-86492-832-0 (mobi)

1. Love-letters — Canada. 2. Poets, Canadian (English) — Correspondence.
I. Lynes, Jeanette, editor II. Eso, David, 1982-, editor

PS8351.L6S84 2015   C816'.00803543   C2014-906874-3
C2014-906875-1

Goose Lane Editions acknowledges the generous support of the Canada Council for the Arts, the Government of Canada through the Canada Book Fund (CBF), and the Government of New Brunswick through the Department of Tourism, Heritage and Culture.

Goose Lane Editions
500 Beaverbrook Court, Suite 330
Fredericton, New Brunswick
CANADA E3B 5X4
www.gooselane.com

Contents

ONE
No Road Back to the Old Life
Poets in their Teens and Twenties

TWO

A Minute is Too Long

Poets in their Thirties

THREE
from the Bottom of My Spongiform Heart
Poets in their Forties

FOUR
Hiring Omniscient Narrators
Poets in their Fifties

FIVE
I Promise Not to Philosophize
Poets in their Sixties, Seventies, and Beyond

PrefАce

"love is an abbreviashun uv reality" — bill bissett

In the spring of 2010, five thousand kilometres from home, I waited out a day-long Atlantic rain in the Bathurst Public Library. I came across "Desire in Poetry" by Michael Brian Oliver in the *Fiddlehead*'s fiftieth anniversary issue. "Love poetry," Oliver writes, "is not personal; it repeats a cosmic dialogue." Travelling alone through northern New Brunswick, my understanding of love shifted.

That day, I wrote to an old flame and asked if she still had the last letter I had sent, years earlier. She replied (instantly, O Internet!) that the letter was indeed retrievable. But why did I want a copy? Deleting as I typed, I gave up my attempt to articulate my new understanding of love and my sudden nostalgia for the woman who had inspired my first experiences of love and heartache. Instead, I told her that an editor I knew was compiling a collection of love letters by Canadian poets. A white lie, a poetic truth.

The trunk which held my letter would have to be sent from her grandparents' home in India to England, and she would then forward my letter on to me. It took six months to arrive, but when it did, I did not open the envelope. Instead, I set about the project I had intended as alibi.

The dialogue of love follows an irregular chronology. The letters and letter-poems in *Where the Nights Are Twice as Long* follow not an historic timeline but are presented according to the poets' ages at their times of writing. We begin with novice lovers: Malcolm Lowry, Gwendolyn MacEwen, and Robert Kroetsch at sixteen, nineteen, and twenty respectively. A single lifeline set in motion, we follow an amalgam of the Poet, year by year, through life's slow process of maturation. Telegram and text, e-mail and handwritten letter collide as the years, decades, and centuries shuffle according to our poets' biographical progression. We end with figures in their sixties, seventies, and eighties (including Susan Musgrave, Leonard Cohen, and Al Purdy) reflecting on loves lost or rediscovered. The compilation reads as if these elder figures had gained their wisdom by enduring the joys and strife of those poets who occupy the earlier sections — or as if those still tangled in their heart's drama had not read closely enough. Our collection, then, contains not only letters of courtship but representations of the endless variety of romance: remembered love, enduring love, unrequited love, unwanted love, erotic love, violent love, regretful love; odes and lyric ecstasies, tirades and tantrums, pastoral comforts and urban horrors, all delivered with the vibrant erudition of Canada's finest poets.

If relationships and love are explored in depth in this volume, many other themes dart in and out of the periphery. Historical events, personal philosophies, daily life, geography, and the literary landscape all seep into the letters gathered here. Our national character, above all, rises to the surface — in distance, winter, and our understated trench humour.

Where the Nights Are Twice as Long cannot reproduce many of the charms of typed or handwritten letters — rips and stains, corrections and stamps. As Duncan Campbell Scott wrote in 1930, "one charm of a written letter is the difficulty of reading it." The collection does, however, preserve the poets' fraught relationships with the laws of grammar, though errors in spelling and punctuation have been silently corrected where deemed a product of haste rather than a matter of style. In most cases, diacritical and typographical marks, as well as spacing and indentation, have been standardized for readability.

The editors have resisted the temptation to offer introductions to the relationships represented here. Rather, the letters speak for themselves, gestures to larger realities and to the Letter as literary form. *Where the Nights Are Twice as Long* has brought Jeanette Lynes and me, at times, closer to the lives of poets and their families than anticipated. In a mercifully small number of instances, individuals have been unsettled by our research. In at least one case, however, our project has led to the reunion of a separated couple. Permission to reprint many personally revealing letters discovered in the course of our research was not granted; in response to our requests for romantic epistles from our nation's living poets, we received at least as many refusals as submissions. Poets most commonly declined by stating that our project defied their (sensible) sensibilities; and secondly, by claiming to have no copies of such items available. Only one poet claimed to have "never been in love." As in any anthology, difficult lines had to be drawn. Though we included Lindsay Zier-Vogel's pilgrimage letters to Amelia Earhart, excellent letters have been omitted — Ivan E. Coyote's letter to a breast lost to an operation, or David McGimpsey's correspondence with Doritos México, a product he Truly Loves.

In drawing on the published correspondence of Lowry, Glassco, Layton, Carman, Roberts, Grove, and Kiyooka, the present volume repeats redactions enacted by editors of those collections. Redacted passages in these and other correspondence are identified with [...], while ellipses not contained within brackets appear in the original letters. In the interest of protecting privacy and copyrights, as well as with our readers' patience in mind, passages from certain correspondences have been excised (Kiyooka, Lowry, MacEwen, Waddington, Garton, Hansen, Webb-Campbell, Haley, Livesay, and Carman).

The editors took care to reach out to various poetic camps, from spoken word to conceptual literature. Some figures also (or better) known for vocations other than poetry appear in this collection: Louis Riel as revolutionary leader, Duncan Campbell Scott as deputy superintendent of the Department of Indian Affairs, George Woodcock as scholar, Roy Kiyooka as visual artist, and F.P. Grove, Malcolm Lowry, and Brian Fawcett as prose writers. While the representation favours writers with a notable or iconic national presence, we have also included younger poets. Female poets seem more reluctant to publicize private correspondence than their male counterparts and also suffer underrepresentation in collections of correspondence, both published and archived. Epistolary love poems were originally admitted into the collection to correct the resultant gender inequality. However, as the work continued, we came to see these verses undeniably as letters. Aspects of form illuminated by the study of poets writing variously in epistolary prose and poetry contribute greatly to this anthology and especially to its usefulness in classrooms. Finally, the editors' distance from French poetry in Canada results in a dearth of these poets (with the exception of Riel's letters, which have been translated for inclusion here). We must leave it to some other intrepid editor to present a corresponding anthology that focuses on our French-language poets.

We thank the poets and their family members, executors, agents, and publishers who granted us permission or facilitated rights to the material gathered in this collection. Thanks also to the special collections and archival staff who assisted us in our search at the University of British Columbia, Simon Fraser University, the University of Calgary, the University of Manitoba, Queen's University, McMaster University, and the National Archives of Canada. Our gratitude must be expressed to those who assisted with deciphering difficult handwriting: Colette Colligan for Archibald Lampman, Jennifer Bobrovitz for D.C. Scott, Barbara Eso for Robert Service, and Donna Kynaston for Dorothy Livesay and William Wilfred Campbell. As well, we extend our appreciation to Irving Layton and John Robert Colombo for inspiring our title. My personal thanks to Jeanette Lynes for her courage, hospitality, and verve. Lastly, thanks to Daphne Marlatt, Linda Rogers, Heather Haley, Weyman Chan, and Judith Fitzgerald for their support. The camaraderie of our lively correspondences kept me inspired at times when the enormity of this project caused my enthusiasm to falter. In fact, NightsAreTwiceAsLong@gmail.com contains its own fascinating archive of the letters of Canadian poets, correspondence that we hope will continue to grow.

DAVID ESO
Calgary, Alberta, October 2014

Introduction

"It surely is a mystery how a letter, mere scrawled words, can elicit profound sympathies and inexhaustibly bind two people together."
— Roy Kiyooka to Monica Dealtry Barker, 1955

"Poets need to write love letters," wrote one of Bliss Carman's correspondents in 1927. This observation captures much about this volume: the sheer compulsive *urgency* of writers to express their desire, hope, fear, and disappointment through the materials of their art — *words*. Given that this volume spans over a century of romantic correspondence, these expressions take a variety of forms, tracking changes in the technologies of epistolary discourse, and in the material conditions of writing letters. Some of us remember a time before e-mail, as do, or would, many of these poets. If twenty-first-century technology facilitates accelerated connection and the potential for nearly instantaneous response, as reflected in the text-message exchanges reproduced in these pages (Lausas–Atkings and others) or the e-mail exchanges between James Deahl and Norma West Linder, pre-digital-era correspondence often felt like, as Charles G.D. Roberts puts it, "an arrow shot into the void." The letters sent through traditional post, subject to the vicissitudes of mail delivery, often occupy a skewed, discontinuous kind of world where two or even three letters might arrive on the same day after a prolonged gap — famine or feast. As P.K. Page laments in a 1944 letter to F.R. Scott, "Letters seem to take centuries to go to and from." There is a strong sense of ritual here, too, in the posting of letters, down to an erotics of stamp-licking (Musgrave). Irving Layton tells Sandra Beaudin, in 1979, "Red ink is so sexy." The material conditions of letter-writing — type of paper, colour of ink, the walk to the post box, the licking of the stamp — is front and centre until the onset of digital technology in the 1990s. Even then, the keyboard remains foregrounded as a medium, as reflected in Gregory Betts's keyboarding rampage-on-repeat — a frenetic technology for frenetic emotions. Sometimes the medium is *more* than the message, bringing comfort in and of itself, as John Newlove tells Susan Newlove: "Just typing to talk to you." Among the most poignant moments in this collection is Louis Riel having to end a letter to his wife because he has used up the sheet of paper allotted to him in prison.

We typically think of love letters as intensely private documents, the baring of one soul to another. To be sure, an epistle of such a personal nature is a document of vulnerability. Yet because the correspondents in this volume are writers, their letters are also texts, literary artifacts that often signal their own awareness as such, that critique their own styles and reveal a sense of their status as dramatic performances — for surely love and all its iterations, including anti-love, is nothing if not a dramatic performance. The writers herein are sometimes brutal self-editors, as when Gwendolyn MacEwen refers slightingly to her own "insane little letter," which, when she "read[s] it over [is] tempted to throw [her] career in writing out the window entirely and become a missionary instead." Bliss Carman accuses Gladys Baldwin of sabotaging his ability to write, in his postscript: "These lines are not good at all. I cannot write. I can only love you." In other words, these letters and epistolary poems are dramatizations with often, as Lowry also writes, a "touch of bathos." Often documenting their own missteps, flaws, violations of prohibitions and proprieties — "But I forgot: I must not call you that," writes Archibald Lampman — the authors of these letters adopt various personae to negotiate the flux of their relationships during different stages of their lives. In the arena of love, which Ivan E. Coyote quite rightly calls "a tricky bastard," age doesn't necessarily equal wisdom.

Not surprisingly, these poets are inventive in their romantic expression, using, in addition to more traditional modes of letters sent in sealed envelopes through the post, visual poems (Beaulieu), musical notations (Rogers), and other graphic elements. Alden Nowlan's self-portrait doodle drawn in his love letter to Claudine Nowlan is a standout. Letters are written on "scraps of paper" (Garton), exam booklets (Priddle), hotel stationery. Some of these exchanges remind us that digital communication is not the panacea it's sometimes billed as — the correspondence between Jane Eaton Hamilton and Julia Balén, reproduced from an on-line dating site, for example, reveals, albeit often through humour, the shyness, vulnerability, and fear of rejection that is part of meeting a potential lover. Sometimes the letters are hallucinations, dream-like fantasies, speculative narratives, such as Lindsay Zier-Vogel's letters to Amelia Earhart — dabblings in theosophy, spirituality.

While at times these letters reflect a grounded, meditative mood, they are more often imbued with an essential restlessness, a pacing-the-floor manic energy. Not surprisingly, distance is a key trope, as is travel. Our poets write from trains, buses, ocean steamers, hotel rooms, hospitals, prisons. They write from the road, from home, from landscapes relived through memory, from dreamscapes, from the tops of mountains. The reader will find in these letters a full gamut of emotion ranging from eloquence to rancour, from adoring ode to scathing tirade, flights of lyric ecstasy, tantrums, testimonies of hope, renewal and healing (Barton); a poetics of absolution (Heighton) but also despair, hatred, anger (Acorn, Layton, and Service, among others); gratitude, remorse, hung-over-ness, and drug-induced expansiveness (Trower). Drama, melodrama. The cerebral. The courtly. The carnal. The mystical. Apologies, pleas for forgiveness, for second chances, third chances. Stories. Anecdotes. Jokes. Dirty talk. Brief goodbyes. Long goodbyes. A strong penchant for postscripts, which suggests the difficulty of signing off. Serial epistles set aside and resumed over a course of days. The reader will also find politics — socialism, feminism. Anti-establishment indignity over pot laws and societal taboos. Critiques of patriarchy, of oppressive regimes always too ready to incarcerate. George Elliott Clarke's piece explores the decolonizing agency of love.

These letters often exude a sense of occasion, marking anniversaries, birthdays, Valentine's Day (Norris and others). The act of composition often constitutes its own occasion. Sometimes our poets revel in a sense of play, particularly in salutary pet names such as "My dear Atom," "Dearest Pussypants," "Lambie-pie," "Dearest Duck." As dramatic personae, the poet lovers in this volume construct themselves and their beloveds variously as muse, teacher, mentor, cruel torturer, repentant sinner, prodigal, literary collaborator (Warland–Marlatt) and, not least, the lover-as-clown. The anguish and angst of love notwithstanding, humour is present in these letters. Against a quintessentially Canadian winter backdrop of minus twenty-eight, Ross Priddle writes: "Hades, I had Chinese food and chocolate cookies (out of a metal box) for breakfast and then danced Corybantically to OAO by the Golden Palominos (with John Zorn plying duck calls). I think I am suffering from Tartanism. I needed to sweat (I lied when I said I only liked to sweat for money) and it was too damned cold to step outside."

Jane Eaton Hamilton writes to Julia Balén, on an on-line dating site: "I... have mucked around with dating but am not really attuned to it, being, you know, old and flabby of body and brain (see above, sitting in chair as the fit jog past), and seem to very quickly make a botch of it. It is not really helpful to spend a date thinking: I could be gardening." The humour in these letters is often enough of a self-deprecating cast, as if the poet-lover were aware of her or his clownishness or, at times, of the essential absurdity of her or his plight and the cosmos in general.

William Blake's proposition that "without contraries is no progression" is germane to romantic correspondence, for often enough in the trajectories of relationships mapped, across time, in these pages, desire is shadowed by doubt, love by hate. Extremes, oppositions, and contrary states are frequent motifs in these letters. Documentary details like the price of wheat (Grove) and a day spent hauling manure (Knister) are set against the heart's longings. The letters in this volume delineate love as a humanizing force, as well as love as a dehumanizing force. Christine Lowther writes "We move: toward and away. Burning and consumed." The lover as muse but also anti-muse. Irving Layton writes to Harriet Bernstein that the poems he had written for her, "poems of great affection and tenderness," have turned into "poems of hate and despair." Some poets examine the aftermath of love, its wreckage, what gets left behind. Wilted flowers. Wigs on bathroom floors. "Aftermath is a place" writes Renée Sarojini Saklikar. A notable example, among many, of this after-place is the postscript to the poem, "letter to a former lover from a young drag queen on the threshold of manhood":

> p.s. could you send me those encrusted pumps
> the ones with eight inch heels and zirconed ankle straps
> that gave me all the hope you mocked, adored
>
> I think I left them on the kitchen floor
> > Those lush imported tiles and the harsh synthetic
> > colours of those gorgeous cupboard drawers.

The signifiers of romance are at times embraced and at other times turned on their heads, into anti-romance — for example, Weyman Chan's deconstruction of the supreme love signifier, roses "red as bald assholes."

Along with these deconstructed turns, readers will find many of the traditional devices of love in these pages: the lover as one who suffers acute agonies (the old courtly love tradition), who cannot sleep or eat, who would sacrifice life and limb — driving over icy highways in northern British Columbia, to cite only one example — to see the beloved. John Newlove documents, in his letters to Susan Newlove, a pain caused by separation that is almost unbearable. Robert Service's letters plumb the depths of melodrama in their expressions of love's attendant suffering. bill bissett captures the destructive aspect of love and the need to recover as well as anyone: "ium kinduv / fukd up again but iul / keep on trucking / I will."

In keeping with their poetic vocations, the writers in this volume mobilize their literary skills, often creating vivid scenes and sensory landscapes in their letters and epistolary poems, and tapping into figurative language, imagery, and other literary devices to express their feelings; astronomy is a popular topos — comets, moons, stars — along with food, fire, mirrors, glass, and textiles/clothing/shoes. Ronna Bloom writes: "I wanted you like a rug." Heather Haley goes for broke — at least in my woman's opinion — when she tells her lover "you can wear my Fluevogs." That's intense. "Love is depicted as strawberry cheesecake, also as "the tiniest of briskets, and hardest to view, / mangle and chew, and absorb in lechery's saliva" (Rosenblatt, "Phantom Dog"). Bliss Carman conceptualizes romance's vertigo as a natural hazard: "A dangerous whirlpool, which ought to be marked 'Danger!' but isn't." Pathetic fallacy appears in more than one letter, the alignment of climate and weather with the poet-lover's mood; as Pearl Luke puts it, "it's a cold, grey day, greyer because you're not here." A recurring theme throughout these letters is the desire on the part of poet-lovers to forge their own mythology, their own creation myth, to write their own story with, hopefully, a happy ending — in Ronna Bloom's terms, a "real" myth: "Here is my creation story…This one is no myth. No names have been changed. The locations are all true, the transplants and transatlantic losses." Robert Kroetsch tells Martann he is "searching for a story that will end happily." Ivan E. Coyote writes, "I really do love a good story…We wrote some really good stories, you and I." In his poem, "Flames, at the Beginning," Douglas LePan evokes a phoenix rising from its ashes:

> I am burning your letter, as you asked me to.
> In the light through the window it flames up like a great
> gold chrysanthemum.
> Our love will flourish like that, extravagant and secret.

LePan's simile — or perhaps more accurately, metaphysical conceit, comparing the burning letter to a flower — in turn likens the loop of destruction and creation to the clandestine love relationship.

The older poets in these pages treat aftermath rather differently, as revealed, for example, in the near-obsessive inventory-taking (of the past) in Earle Birney's letters. Later life, for Linda Rogers and her beloved, is "our season of unrelenting/vigilance." The inevitability of impending death exerts a sombre presence in this terminal season, and hard questions must be confronted: *Who will come for / us when the morphine kicks in?*" (Rogers; italics in original). While tough questions such as this demand tough minds and hearts, poets in later life also demonstrate that age does not necessarily bring fewer feelings of vulnerability. What experience and time perhaps do bring, as Al Purdy suggests in his late-period poem "To –," is a learned ability to embrace the contraries, the essential paradox at the heart of love:

> And the mind that is both fearful of nothing
> and fearless of everything has grown and become
> lovely and earthly and yet beyond our soiled planet
> its innocence the wisdom of things newborn
> before corruption has entered their minds and bodies
> and directed them to walk toward their death
>
> — to see everything and to realize the best and worst
> of everything
> is to love and not forget

The romantic letters and epistolary poems in this volume reflect just this — "the best and worst / of everything" along with the courage and essential humanity of our poets. For baring their souls and wearing their hearts on their ink-stained sleeves, we owe them much gratitude. To my co-editor and the founding captain of this extreme epistolary marathon, David Eso, thank you. I am grateful to have had the opportunity to ride on the coattails of a fearless romantic, renegade thinker, and compassionate collaborator. I am also grateful for Roger Dorey's constant support and original love songs, and for the diligent talents of my graduate student assistant and budding graphic novelist Courtney Loberg.

JEANETTE LYNES
Saskatoon, Saskatchewan, October 2014

ONE

No Road Back
to the Old Life

Poets in their Teens and Twenties

Malcolm Lowry to Carol Brown
Inglewood, Caldy, Cheshire, England
9.45 am, Saturday, April 1926
age 16

Carol: I am about to otter hunt. Ottiturhunturus sum. I didn't sleep last night at all: I didn't try, as a matter of fact — I paced up and down the room like a loon, half-blubbering: Then I swore for three quarters of an hour using a different word every time. Then I tried to read "The Way of All Flesh." Then I drank some cold coffee Russell had shoved in my room. Then I swore for half an hour further using a different word every time. Then I went on trying to read "The Way of All Flesh."

Then I paced up and down, laughing and swearing. Then I tried to go to sleep in a chair: I couldn't bear to get into bed, and finally, having dozed for about half-an-hour, till roughly 4.40 am — I climbed out of the window, on to a balcony, let myself down on to our unused tennis lawn, and walked to Heswall. At Heswall I smoked three* (this * on second thought is an exaggeration — I smoked only two) pipes: then I walked back again in time for breakfast. (I had a cold bath before this: detail is the essence of art oh artist) And now I am going to otter hunt. Ottihunturus sum.

{7 pm.} I've just got in (not the bath) — from the otterhunt: naturally, you will see, the first thing I do is to continue this. It's been on my mind all day — not the letter — you: apologies for "it."

Now. Bachelor. I must apologize. There was much truth in what you said so far as concerns yourself: I can see that it must be dashed annoying to tell people cheerfully every other day that they're paying you a superlative compliment but (dot), and (dot), if (dot). But as for me, did I tell you to your face that I loved you? I didn't? I do, of course, but ça va: wait a minute: I gave you a note telling you as much, a note which had it not been for a combination of ridiculous circumstances, I would never have given you. Of course I meant every word and much more: but let me say to my credit that if I have written one note to you I have written fifty, or five hundred is perhaps nearer, which I hadn't the cheek to deliver, of course, then: I tore them up sadly railing at the irony of…the strength of note-paper. Wait a moment. I've got to browse upon a chop with considerable gusto. Then on with the dance.

{11.30 p.m.} [...] I'm writing this in bed so excuse the pencil. Now talking about this letter — here was I dying of love for you taking a walk before lunch for no purpose other than just to see the house you live in, and (sentimental blighter) as I walked I dreamed a little dream: I would meet you on the moor, and you would be looking sweeter than ever: you would rate me sardonically-playfully for ill treating the dog, and the dog would look at me so adoringly that you couldn't help but believe that here was the perfect master: the wind would play about with your hair, you would accompany me on my walk, or I on yours, and in a secluded spot I would say "My God, Carol, I love you." Just like that. No more, no less. { I would give you the letter to read later.} And you were going to be so impressed, but not impressed enough to make me believe that you hadn't thought I loved you all along, and you would be just discouraging enough for me to see that you not only didn't mind but were as braced as anything. And in the stage of my mind, a pretty little romance featuring yourself, myself, the dog, and wind (off) — with ripping scenery — was playing its two thousandth performance to an empty house.

{12-2am} So far so good. And then suddenly my seat in an ethereal upper circle became heather: You were there, a scarf was blowing about. My hat, but didn't you look sweet, not 'arf you didn't: You were there, Carol dear, I was there, the dog was there. You looked so fair. Chaucer would have said you were fayre Shakespeare that you were fair. I have said fair. What indeed could be fairer than that? And I came along to you, and I swallowed and looked a complete smidgett, the dog ran away, and as a last resort I gave you the letter as though to convince myself that the dream, had, in a fashion, come true. And it had for you were there, and it was the most deliriously happy moment of my life when I saw you. I walked to Greasby looking for the dog which had gone in the other direction — but I sang all the way. Thanks, dear Carol, for whatever you may have done in the ultimate restoration of that canine — awfully. I sang my way into lunch. I sang my way into Hillthorpe to play tennis. I sang my way silently into the drawing room: and sang discordantly into vile drivel I strained out of a wonderful piano, but a piano which must just hate the sight of me in future — poor piano. I sang my way down the drive: but at the bottom — "You were flattered," You were a member of a worthy club, You were horrid and you were bitten and you didn't encourage me in the least: (really you made me love you more {12.30} than ever.) There were others. So with me — but all vanished in the wind. I'd die for you, Carol. I'd sell my soul for you. If you were bitten — I'd sail round the world to make the fellow who bit you apologize to you for it again. Or if you love him, I'd make him marry, you, somehow — dunno how, damn him! I know I'm the sincerest: I'll love you still when you haven't a tooth or hair in your head: for you, if I'm in your way, I'll chuck up all my material ambition, such as it is, run away from home, school, toil, kindred (see hymn?), and become an assistant bar tender in Honduras or somewhere without a 1/2 sou if necessary — I'm not trying to appeal to your sense of romance: I'm endeavoring to be desperately (you will say, {12.45} comically, or pathetically or something — "the child Malcolm isn't old enough," isn't he though!) sincere.

I'll wait as many years as you like if you'll offer me only hope: I can't believe that I have it in me to write a letter so consistently unappealing and bad as this. Carol, I'm beastly sleepy, you're seeing Raffles to-night aren't you, hope you have a good time.

Oh Carol will you try and manage to see me *alone* again to-day: if you disdain to dream of me as a too youthful lover, can't you effect a compromise between the idea of a friend and a lover. More than friend — less than lover, a lie — : but a lie of advancement; a sort of frover, not be confused with plover. Carol, if you won't wait, I'll swear that I'll never marry anybody else, and I'll die of love for you anyhow, before I could think of such a thing. Carol I'm going to sleep with the light on I'm too tired to turn it off

{2am} Light's still on. I did go to sleep, Carol, but my brain's clear now. I — love — you. A word in eight letters beginning with I and ending with u. Will you write some sort of note just telling me the worst, telling me to go to blazes or something, though don't say anything you don't mean because you're so kind to everything you might easily Am I a rotter talking like this?

How can I possibly stop loving you when it's sort of predestined. I know I'm rather a smidgett: but I play the average games as averagely badly as the average public school boy: and there's always one chance in 1 million, twenty thousand, five hundred that I might win the amateur (pronounced *amater* {I've just learned that}) Championships. I'll die of sorrow at school if you don't say something.

Tell me your address at the Art School and I'll write you there from school if it's only friendly, "unaccomplished unaccomplishment." But I accomplished something to-day. I went to an Otterhunt. I have otterhunted. Otterhuntavi. Oh my hat, there is nothing like adding the last touch of bathos.

Yours

"Mr. If not exactly right not altogether wrong"

•

Malcolm Lowry to Carol Brown
C.B. Leys School, Cambridge, England
June Night, 1926

Dear old Carol,
    You have that inestimable treasure, a sense of humour. I hope that
I too,   "   "   "   "   , "   "   "   "   .
    xxx
You, yourself, are an   "   "   ; you silhouette excellently, dance price-lessly, play tennis comme un cherubim: in fact you are everything, and no doubt can analyze everything in your own way, but strictly between you, me, and the O. Cedar mop, you are entirely inaccurate on the psychology stunt.

    If you knew, woman, how I read and reread your letters; how I'm thinking of you all the while; in short, how passionately fond I am of you; how this, and how that; you would see how hopelessly you fail to put your creed over the footlights. (Wait a mo, a cove has got the "Fascinating Rhythm" on the gramophone, and the record has just reached that piano solo part, and I can't keep still). Where have I got to — oh — I see. Well — believe me. What I mean to say is this, without for a moment growing sentimental (because you hate me when I'm being sentimental), that in accordance with the Coué system of Arithmetical progression — I love you more & more. And dash it — your letters are ripping, and I frenziedly (spelling very doubtful) look every gift postman in the mouth every time he doesn't bring one of your letters. I dart to and fro to the porter's lodge — every post, and come away with a grin or a groan, as the case mebbe. And if you really mean that ingenuous remark about my being a man in a hundred if I can still care for you, well, I raise my Stetson to myself, I am a man in a hundred. What — ho!

    Yes, and talking about laughing behind people's backs — we had an inspection to-day, you know, a sodden beribboned old field marshal with an eye glass swerved about and looked generally cynical, (have I made that remark before; I'm fond of nursing metaphors), and told us, after 4 pints of Bissekers Italian Vermouth, that we were the world's best corps. West were fifth in the house competition, which is distinctly good considering there were, I believe at least five entries. However.

Your actor friends, your description, and your photographs (for which thanks very much: I can't bear to send them back the one of you, but I suppose it's a point of honour, not that I have an honour or anything, but you know what I mean) are most interesting. I'd love to meet them; however conflicting circumstances conflict and all that [...].

I hope that for the promotion of admirability of character, you will never either see or hear my play "Traffic" — which is a drunken soliloquy; which I am assured would run for years in the Fiji Islands as a curtain raiser, but here would not get within three feet of the Lord Chamberlain, who would have to use ink with a spray. However it is quite sincere, but will, I'm afraid, have to be buried quietly, although it means well. Monsieur Émile Zola, and William Shakespeare, confrères of mine — have the same trouble. What?

My dearest old thing; it takes seven forwards all stamping on my neck in the scrum to hurt me, so don't be alarmed; and talking about Thomas Meighan — I can do that sort of thing.

> (herewith)
> (lover)
> Absolutely yours, Malcolm

•••

Gwendolyn MacEwen to Milton Acorn
December 28, 1960
age 19

Dear Milt –

Probably the most beautiful and honest thing that I've ever received was your little letter. I can't match it.

Sincerity like this staggers me; I've seen too little and too much of it one way and another; I've valued it so highly that when someone hands it to me as directly as you have, I'm not sure whether I should jump for joy or burst into tears. (In a way I'm much more a child than you'd like to believe)

I'm going to say many things here — not to be long-winded, not to give the impression of point where there isn't any — But because I want to tell you things somehow. I think if I could paint out one long _me_ through all the different tones and shades and intensities I'd truly be an achievement...

Milt, don't ever write a novel — or two — or three...after a while you become unable to condense thoughts, feelings. I'm so over-conscious of words now that I can't (as you so beautifully can) imply and mean so very much in so very little.

Sincerity. This is what my dear father named the Number One Virtue in life. (Why couldn't you be just a little insincere and make it easy for me?) But then I think that's what drew me to you really — one enormous plus sign —

And insincerity — insincerity to oneself — probably the most deadly thing that can happen to a person — I've seen that in action too...and its outcome

So much for the background of those words — all I've done (and not too well, I'm afraid) is given you a glimpse of the reason honesty has such an impact on me

Love. Again I've had too little and too much of it. Probably too much (if that is possible). So much, in fact, that I'm convinced I'll eventually be swallowed up in it, completely. Horrible fate!

I believe everything I do, think, or feel is touched off by love. And I have such a capacity for it I don't know how to focus it in any one direction. I might go out tomorrow morning and kiss a dozen butterflies! (This is not a piece of imagery from a poem — this is a fact)

A love for people. (I'm still young enough not to have this fact of love shattered. If it will be then I'm determined not to grow any older. Not the least little bit

This idea, Milt, is what I call my blissful ignorance, and will remain so until life forces me to alter it — if ever. Although I believe in some ways that what I've experienced thus far — would make some people become absolute cynics, or failing that, prompt them to take a long neat dive from a tall bridge.

No, no — I'm not bemoaning it at all. Somewhere along the line I developed one terrific resistance — which I'm grateful for. But what is more important I retained a whole big chunk of that initial love, trust, and joy of life that we are born with. And along with it, an immense and overwhelming delight and sensitivity in, yes — almost anything. This has made me something of a poet (am I permitted to be so presumptuous?)

I didn't mean to ramble on so, really I didn't. So much for SONG OF MYSELF!

Of course I love you! But I am neither capable nor ready for the kind of love you offer me. I don't even have a half-decent letter to give you, let alone myself!

Milt, my love is not the same as yours...you're a mature man, and I'm (and I'll defend this to my dying day) still in a sense a little girl poking my head out the window at the world. Existence? I'm still establishing it to myself. At this point I need no proof for it — I feel no need to <u>find</u> myself physically, sensually, emotionally in another person — I'm still laying the foundations! I'm still getting acquainted with life, with myself...

I don't want that song of yours to end, to be completed; to me there is no expectancy, no conception of fulfillment. There is today and tomorrow and tomorrow and tomorrow and me listening to you and you listening to me (though I don't say much) and gaining what I can from you (you've taught me so much already, you know) and feeling myself wonderfully diminished with you (because sometimes I get O so big)

But beyond this rather endless list — nothing more. Your "completeness" can't find a place in all this for me, I know it...as I see our relationship, this is not a natural outcome at all. I feel this way, Milt — because as I said before — your feelings are those of a mature man, while mine...well you know the rest

Because you fit another sort of niche in my life altogether, one which I know and understand — one of the few things I do understand — you'll never quite realize just what you've <u>already</u> given me

Completion, fulfillment in themselves — I'm aware of the need for it as I possibly can be at this stage. When I eventually find this particular need in myself, however, I'll try not to worry

Milt — I can't possibly give you back a fraction of what you've given me — I mean this. So when you're suddenly loaded down with droves of little fluffy animals and things, please take pity on me, because it's the best I can do —

I want, I wish so much for you — because your life, your happiness, your desires truly matter to me. I want to see a hundred more little miltons going out and damning us with their honesty

but most of all I want you just now to understand what I've said, what I've tried to say in this insane little letter (when I read it over I'm tempted to throw my career in writing out the window entirely and become a missionary instead)

because my father's "Number One Virtue" is the most difficult thing for me to use — only because I value it so highly. Each word, each phrase must be just as I mean it, or it won't do at all...

But believe it or not, I can't remember when I've been able to open up like this for anyone. It's confused, it's contrary, yes but it's also me. Please accept it; please don't be hurt or angry — I wouldn't have been able to tell you even this much if your feelings hadn't meant enough to me to warrant my giving you the best, the most truthful answer to what you've asked that I am capable of

Gwen

•••

Robert Kroetsch to Martann ———
Heisler, Alberta
August 25, 1947
age 20

Dear Martann,

You have probably forgotten the sad young fool who bid you farewell on the cloudy morning of the 23rd, but he, a victim of youth's idealism, has not forgotten you. You are hard to forget.

It is not raining today. It is not raining as it rained the day we parted, but the melancholy of rain is not gone. You are hard to forget, and when something is gone but not forgotten, melancholy must linger on, especially when the dreamer does not want to forget.

After your train disappeared into the mountains, Geoff and I went back to the cabin and finished packing. After lunch we took our baggage to the station and went down town. There were no familiar faces in the Quaker. They were all gone; replaced by strange, older, more serious faces. There were no students sitting and gossiping on the auditorium steps. They were all gone, and the steps were bare. The school was silent and baggage was piled in front of the girls' dorm. Then we realized what the end of school meant. We were no longer two groups of gay students, living and laughing together; we were two bored tourists, gazing curiously at the town of Banff and wondering where the happiness of the past six weeks had gone. We went to the Quaker and each had a turkey burger and a chocolate milkshake, and then we went to the station.

We saw Pat, Ro and Charlotte at the station. Charlotte's friend was there, perfectly sober and saying good-bye to everyone. Jackie was there, and after a sweet embrace, she took leave of Alex. Their engagement, if they are engaged, will have to endure a temporary separation.

Geoff and I boarded the 5:45 train together. Soon we were rolling eastward, talking about the pleasant past and reviewing our regrets. The mountains shrank to foothills, the foothills flattened out to become prairies, and then we were at Calgary. Geoff went east and I went north, each sorry to leave the other, and hoping to meet again.

I slept through a show, "The Hucksters," in Calgary and caught a train at 11:45. By 6:30 I was in Edmonton.

It was Sunday and there wasn't much to do, but George (He caricatured you in your autograph, remember?) was spending a few days in Edmonton on his way to Toronto, so I phoned him and we went for a long walk in the Alberta sunshine.

We walked and talked. Like all masculine conversations, our conversation soon had a feminine topic. Two feminine topics I should say, for he talked of Dat. and I talked of you. You will forgive me, I hope, but it is relieving to get such things off one's mind. It was a delightful conversation, centered on a very delightful subject, and we walked a long ways.

We walked around the university campus, and I was disappointed to find its traditionally calm and scholarly atmosphere disturbed by the sights and sounds of feverish mechanical activity. But I shouldn't really complain, for they are building a new library, and what more could a student dream of? (A wonderful girl, far away!) George and I parted late in the afternoon when I boarded a bus bound for Heisler. George was a great pal. He would do a friend any favor, and everyone was his friend. He spends an enviable life, traveling and painting.

Heisler and home had not changed. Heisler was still a little town; home was still a nice place at which to be.

It has been raining for four days, the fields are wet, so I have nothing to do but to read and to write. I am reading Hutchison's "The Unknown Country." It is a most interesting book on Canada. I hope to read MacLennan's "Two

Solitudes" anon. The wheat is ripe, so as soon as the fields are dry, I shall have only the evenings free for reading and writing.

I rather like to turn on the radio and work, or pretend to work, as I listen to good music. But this evening all is quiet as I write.

My sisters (I have four of them, and no brothers) are all gone to visit a lady who has just returned from the hospital with a baby girl. Poor lady! Four girls, all younger than I, can make a lot of noise. Silence is truly golden.

The sunset was beautiful tonight; more beautiful than any I saw in the mountains, for it was a masterpiece, painted by a free and boundless painter; a painter who had all the sky for a canvas; a painter who covered the blue sky of the west with a jumble of orange and red and purple clouds.

You are probably engulfed in a charming little fog now. How fortunate you are! Or I should say, how fortunate the fog is! If I were a fog I too would engulf you in my misty arms.

But I am a mortal being; too well aware of the limitations created by 900 mountainous miles, so all I can do is send this letter. If it should inspire a response, as I hope it will, please address your letter to me at Heisler. Heisler, Alberta; that's all; no more, no less. I shall not be in Edmonton until the end of September, and that is a long, long ways in the future.

I am going to start my story about the artist now. It is going to be a tragedy. It is going to be a tragedy because life is so full of tragedy, and it is the writer's task to portray a phase of life as he sees it. Someday, yes, someday, perhaps, I shall have a reason for writing happy endings!

•

Robert Kroetsch to Martann ———
St. Joseph's College, University of Alberta
Edmonton, Alberta
September 29, 1947

Dear Martann,

You have converted me. I am going to write a story with a happy ending. My tale about the artist has become a short short story and I'm now engaged in the tragic task of searching for a story that will end happily.

I hope you will forgive me for not sending a snap of myself, but it has rained almost continually for three weeks (worse than Victoria), and I can't get a camera, the sun, and myself together at one time. But I promise to have one for you the next time I write, for the traditional Alberta sunshine has returned in all its glory to rule supreme for the next few weeks. Besides, I can't understand why you would want a picture of me when you've got the excellent sketch which you made the night we met at the new chalet. No camera could ever rival the hand of so illustrious an artist!

I have a few pictures of Geoff, and am willing to part with one. I fear that you have misinterpreted Geoff's attitude concerning you. Everything he said about you was complimentary, and I'm sure that he didn't want to leave the impression that he disliked you.

Please tell me more about the art school. I'm very much in on institutions which endeavor to spread and develop the fine arts.

Last Thursday I registered for my third and last year in Arts at the U. of Alberta. I am taking Philosophy 51 (The history of ideas), Psychology 58 (Psychology in relation to social and economic problems), English 57 (The Romantic Movement) and Political Economy 63 (The theory of government). Sounds interesting, doesn't it? I have a terrific stack of textbooks to read, so instead of facing the brutal fact, I'm reading "The Robe" by Lloyd C. Douglas. It's great fun being an escapist.

There was a dance for freshman last Saturday night, so I, a mighty senior, disguised as a humble freshman, crept in unnoticed (after paying 50¢). Who did I meet there, but Alexandria, who used to live in the new chalet.

She said she writes to you. I danced with her twice, trying to get up enough courage to talk about you, but only succeeded in talking about everyone else. You see, I felt that I would be betraying a sacred secret if I, a hard-hearted man, revealed the fact that a woman, a mere woman, a very pretty, charming and talented woman, would be my favorite topic. And so, as I danced with Alexandria and suffered in silence, I talked of art and professors, and thought of Banff and you! Still I hope to write a happy ending. Young writers are vain creatures!

The story I wrote at Banff is, I hope, no reflection on my character or my past. I have never been a squatter's son living in a cabin by a creek, I have never been in an embarrassing predicament with a rancher's daughter, and I have never frozen to death in a snow storm. The story was a fictitious story, based on observations rather than experiences.

I received a letter from George a few days ago. He sees Ro and Chris a lot at art school in Toronto.

Have you any brothers or sisters, or are you a spoiled only child? My sisters are all in school now, and I'm one hundred miles from home, so I have escaped from the noise and gossip. In fact I miss the noise and gossip a little. Tell me more about your family, the wonders of Vancouver, and the life of a painter in general.

My two snaps of you are masterpieces in the study of feminine beauty!
With love,
Bob

...

Gwendolyn MacEwen to Milton Acorn
Ward's Island, Toronto, Ontario
January 16, 1963
age 21

Dear Milton,

I moved my things over today, am finally settled.

No, I don't believe my actions indicate any need to care for someone… any more than I married to care for you…if the cards look that way on the surface, it is because circumstance has flung them in one direction; I don't, for instance, want to "care for" Mallory…only two men have been <u>strong</u> enough to draw out the depths of <u>me</u> — you and he. You may not understand the last, but it is so.

Please remember that for you…many experiences were <u>behind</u> you, trials and errors, that you had had your time of discoveries in love, and wanted most to be settled with one. I thought I too wanted that…but realized quickly that I hadn't had <u>my</u> time, that you were the first, and even the bonds we had were not sufficient to stop me from loving another. My concern for your welfare now consists of praying that you realize it was not whim or wildness which made me go, but a sudden clear realization that tho you were the first man of importance to me, you could not be the last.

Of course I am a socialist (with much to yet learn of it). But you seem to think that by being able to love one who is not, that makes me not one…I don't understand your reasoning here (if that is your reasoning, I'm surmising mainly)…was Vikki a socialist? Does it matter? Does that make you less one? Mallory was a communist…but, dwarves, you say? Only when you see giants can dwarves be implied. Only when you have seen the beauty of the potential man can you fiercely laugh at our littleness — the impatient wild loving laughter of a dwarf looking at himself and knowing he is potentially more. Mallory is also a dwarf. What do you think drives him to sickness? Think on it. No need to say more here.

> And I'm a dwarf, and you...
> But we are also giants...
>
> Knowing it drives us to the poem...
> It drives some beyond the poem...one should never have to see
>   what is beyond that...

[...] My supreme wish has always been to be of benefit to man. It is greatly idealistic, and I must work until I can work no longer; I don't know when that will be.

Yes, I did break the promise of marriage; only because I made it not knowing many things of myself, made it for all the wrong reasons...Now I am out of it. I would not have it any other way. My wish is that you will begin things again for yourself...yet you say you can't...surely it was more than me that has emptied you like this...somehow it is terrible and frightening for me to think that I could hold that size of life-meaning for another human being; it is heavy; it does not make me proud. Yet for you it was a settling, a surety, after you had had experiences...whereas for me it was a beginning, a growth of myself...in spite of our bonds, which were rare and beautiful... we cannot pull those two ends together...

> gwen

•••

A.M. Klein to Bessie Kozlov
October, 1931
age 22

To Bessie:

> Here they are — all those sunny April days!
> The sticky buds upon the maple-trees;

The dawns; the dewdrops juggling the sun's rays;
The robins prim, and the swashbuckling bees.
And more than that. Here June, and dog roses —
Do you recall the bush we plucked ours from?
The tall grass bent where lovers hid to kiss;
Unchristened fieldflies, and their heathen hum.
I cannot bring a forest on my back;
Nor pull the lining of my pockets out,
Dropping a sun or moon; nor can I crack
A whip, and have trees leap and mountains shout.
But what I can do, failing such magic bright,
Is bring these, as I do, in black and white.

— Abbie

Think not, my dear, because I do not call
You darling names over the tea and cakes,
Nor sigh, nor stroke your fingers, nor speak small,
Nor point to show the parlour my heart aches,
Think not I love you less. Not I the man
To wait until the sewing-circle hoves
In sight, then love according to a plan,
And set the gossips talking of two doves.
Too much the mine to show it to the mob,
Or tattoo it upon my arm, or wear
It dangling public from my watch's fob,
Your first-name, which is ours, and not to share.
It is enough the sparrow on your sill
Already knows our love, as others will.

•••

Kai Cheng Thom to ———
Montreal, Quebec
July 15, 2013
age 22

I want to ask if you know what it feels like to be queer and Chinese and working class and sleeping with a rich, pretty White boy, but of course you don't, and you never will. Well, boys like me spend their whole lives waiting to be chosen and fucked and dumped by boys like you. That isn't your intention, of course. You don't really know what you want. You want to just try things out, experiment, have fun, see where it goes. Well, I want that too. But it doesn't work that way for people like me. We don't get to experiment, just have fun, without consequences. We don't know what it's like to not be in love with you. We loved you the moment you looked at us, held our hand, danced dirty, kissed us. We were lost in you way before we even met, before the thought crossed your mind that you were bored and we were vaguely good-looking, interesting, exotic, fuckable. While you were weighing options, we were just hoping that it wouldn't hurt too much — the fucking, or the falling in love, or the rejection. We didn't get to choose.

Yes, I know that you have problems too. Coming out is hard, social anxiety is hard, relationships are hard, figuring out who you are in life is hard. I don't want to belittle your hardships. But we are different, and I am frankly too old to be afraid of naming our differences. You were afraid of being gay and getting cut off by your parents, so you waited until you were in your teens or twenties to go to a bar, get hit on, go on a date. You had the thrill of first eye contact when some other pretty, white college student looked at you from across the room. You had the exhilaration and terror of first touch, first sex, first boyfriend home for Thanksgiving. You never knew what was going to happen, how things were going to turn out, and yes, I sympathize, that must have been really scary for you.

I had being outed at 12 before I knew what the word faggot meant. I have a whole community that believes queerness is a white people's disease. I had illicit touching by my camp counsellor at age 14. I had the belief that this was the best gay loving I would ever get. I had being the only Asian in the gay bar on any given night. I had knowing that the only men who would find this attractive found only my being Asian attractive, not me for myself. I had rape after rape after rape and no words to say slow down this is wrong please stop I am not okay. I had the strangely calm, detached knowledge that all of this was going to happen before it did. This horrible weakness, like some invisible, incredible weight pulling me through the motions of touching you, trying to please you, falling in love with you, swallowing all of your bullshit. This skin cripples me. It always has.

•••

Chris Masson to "Moana"
Montreal, Quebec
2006
age 22

our lady of many voyages,
how were the rails?
i miss yr ringtone alrdy.
come back yestrday
sent 11:13pm Fri Jun23

met up with j and jo
soccer was a no go
supper was yum, yo
miss u like gong shows
luv u like god knows
cant wait till we touch toes
sent 8:50pm Sat Jun24

we luv like hyper psychic luaus
u are my dynamite cherry pie
i luv u 2 bits
<3 <3 <3
sent 1:03am Sun Jun25

the street fair is on.
st laurnt is all tents and mangos
ppl r out in 2s.
i hve leftovr chow mein
but no1 2 leave it ovr with.
sent 9:22pm Sun Jun25

yr train is in my dreams of u.
it blows blond smke
and has big round wndows.
it gets in at 110
and has a rugby team of me waitng
c u at 111
sent 12:57pm Mon Jun26

•••

A.J.M. Smith, 1925
age 23

What Strange Enchantment

What strange enchantment
Out of Faery
Or the land of flowers
Have you woven over me three times
That the shy glances of your eyes
Are the meshes of a net
For my limbs
And the dark sheen of your hair
Candle light
For my moth thoughts
And your white breasts
Twin moons
To draw my tides?

•••

Priscila Uppal to Christopher Doda
mid-October, 1997
age 23

Dear Chris,
    It is funny how I can't find time to mail my bills but when I'm trying to
keep myself from phoning you I make my way to a pen or a keyboard and

greedily lick the stamps and find the time to mail these little lines to you, pretending you are here, with your long comforting arms around me, and my words (oh so many words) rattling off as if you were listening. I think I hear you sometimes while I sleep, I think I see you by the light in the hallway, your grey robe draped slightly over your shoulders, your head hunched down, taking off your black socks and your belt, getting ready to startle me with your icy toes and steal all the heat I managed to cocoon myself into by the time you finish brushing your teeth. I know I'm being sentimental and gooey but you must expect such sucky behaviour out of me by now.

I burnt my toast thinking of you today, I nearly missed the crosswalk, I told you I loved you out loud, and I pet the cats as if my fingernails were long and welcome as yours are. I even think of the conversation we will have tomorrow so I include none of it here knowing I will tell you myself about my test, and my visit from my fairy godmother. This note is just pure love. Isn't that what letters are for? And if words could kiss each one is my lips upon yours, or on your forehead, or on your back, knees, fingertips, I could go on, as you probably know…

I hope your thoughts are less desperate than these, but it is midnight and though I couldn't sleep last night and can barely keep my eyes open, some nights I find it really hard to sleep in our christened bed alone and tonight is one of them, and though I spoke at school, and had Gabby over, I feel as if I haven't had human contact because I've been denied of yours. Halloween awaits us, I suppose. In costumes and make-up the two Scorpios will meet again. I invited another girl to the party and told her that myself, you, and Shannon were Scorpios all in the same week — her reaction was "God! There must be so much sex going on!" At least astrology has given us a good and true calling. I miss your body on mine, and Shannon's of course. My two soul mates are elsewhere, but always in my thoughts. I hope there will be room for all these people, and I hope that it won't be too cold out, though today was awfully cold and windy too.

Prof, who was asleep, is now of course jealous of the computer, probably thinks I'm eating. He's giving me dirty looks and is still being a grump-a-lump since yesterday. I think he's getting old and weary. He has taken every opportunity in the last two days to sit on any book I've touched and to push his little face against a book if I'm reading in bed. Not allowed: must give full attention to the divine creature he is. He must think I'm so boring. Speaking of which, I hope you're not, by the letter or by your own readings. I will let you go now and may you have a good day after reading this or a pleasant night (depending on when you open your mailbox). I love you darling. I hope you don't mind typed letters. I'm trying to get practice on the computer, and it goes faster, and you don't have to deal with my handwriting. Anyway, love, goodnight, and don't worry I hear your sweet messages over the miles somehow.

Love,
Pris

•••

C. Isa Lausas and Tyson John Atkings
Across Saskatoon, Saskatchewan
January 23-27, 2014
ages 23 and 24

01/23/2014

12:27pm Do you remember the room
     where you almost fell apart?

12:29pm   *It was white...I think.*
12:47pm   *Have you seen it?*

12:50pm Likely. I remember water stains
     on the roof. I remember the
     floor. I remember spending a lot
     of time looking at the corner of
     the room.
12:55pm I remember twisted orgasms and
     watching the dustbunnies float
     across the floor.
12:56pm I remember flaccid dick and
     thanking the sun for a window.

1:05pm   *Visual details are blurred for me. I*
             remember the dark. The moulded smell.
             A silent scream. I thought I was alone.

1:05pm Were you?

1:50pm   Be careful what you say...
speaking of ghosts will bring
them to life...

1:59pm   (Apparently i summoned one, ha)

2:18pm   (I dont believe in God but I am
starting to believe in coincidence
less and less every day)

3:12pm   *I do not speak of loss. Anonymity and
an apparent need of touch. I saw a faceless
figure, far in the street, when I closed my
eyes to the experience of a muted sense of
shame.*

3:22pm   (Keep going, lady)

3:26pm   *(I'm in class)*

3:36pm   *The white walls seemed too high for
humans. First object of attraction: blood
on the rags on the floor. Body away from
itself.*

3:48pm   *Be quiet I was told. A threatening breath
and a silent scream. I thought I was alone.*

4:07pm   *Was the door unlocked?*

4:16pm   Questions are natures way of
making fire.

4:17pm   *No-one ever believed it.*

4:20pm   *But I was there.*

4:23pm   *I thought I was alone...*

4:33pm   (I would believe it)

4:34pm   Locks are natures way of causing
break-ins.

4:38pm   *How can you remember?*

4:39pm   How do you talk to an alien?

4:40pm   Slowly.

4:40pm   Remembering is natures way of
forgetting.

4:41pm		*I thought I was alone.*
4:42pm		*No-one should remember.*
4:44pm		*Unless you will.*

| 4:46pm | (My heart is bleeding from today. Can we be together tonight?) | |
| 4:51pm | (We don't have to talk or anything I'd just like your company) | |

5:11pm		*(Perhaps. I am going to —— around 7 for a launch, I can let you know when i'm done there)*
5:12pm		*(This one took a lot out of me, I think I deserve my wine tonight, haha)*
5:18pm		*(No worries though, I'm actually quite happy about it)*

| 5:18pm | (I wasn't worried) | |

| 5:19pm | | *(Good)* |

01/26/2014

| 7:12pm | | *There is no air in my lungs today.* |

| 7:16pm | Suck it up. *cough* | |

| 7:16pm | | *Lack of oxygen. Dysfunction.* |

| 7:18pm | I tried to write something beautiful; flat. | |

| 7:27pm | | *I wonder if acid rain means poison air.* |

| 7:36pm | (Fuck it's cold) | |

| 7:36pm | | *Flat writing. Watery signature on letters.* |
| 7:38pm | | *Bubbles in brain. Black hole in air.* |

| 7:41pm | The divine vacuum hums into the night. | |

8:53pm   The post-poets hang & swing &
          distribute leaflets. I just hang.

8:57pm   *My teeth are fallingofffallingoff people are*
                                    eating nachos with their hands my head
                                    is elsewhere they talk they speak I can't
                                    breathe lack of air
8:57pm   *If I disappear who'll miss me? Not me.*

8:59pm   I will miss you.
9:09pm   The wind blows and hanging is
          not
          always bad.

9:16pm   *Hang on hang on hang on. You're so small*
                                    that the wind will take you away. I've
                                    always been floating. I've never learned the
                                    art of flying. I keep falling.

9:20pm   We both read that flying is falling
          and missing the ground.

9:31pm   *When falling you're waiting for the ground.*
                                    It stops the falling. I fall and float in water
                                    deeper and deeper looking for the ground.
                                    How can you fly under water?

9:38pm   Did you know that Einstein said
          the ground falls towards you?
          Underwater is flying, no?
9:54pm   (Seriously are you ok?)

10:16pm   *It's floatingfloatingfloating and hoping to*
                                    be falling. Magnetic trauma. Blue and black
                                    electroshocks. Watching for the red ones.
10:16pm   *(Don't worry. I'm always ok.)*

10:31pm   Red is heat hot warm love pain
          and
          stop. Keep hanging.

10:48pm   *Blue is the warmest colour I know.*

11:06pm   Blue is a hellish friend

11:47pm   *I stick with a mixture of black and white.*
                           Grey is reliable concrete.   Catching and
                           swallowing the bubbles of silent screams.
                           The thick ld air will keep me still.

01/27/2014

12:07am   *(Where the fuck are you?)*

12:11am   Fresh cold air keeps us moving
          and our hands keep typing.

12:14am   *(Fuck you)*

12:15am   (im just walking dont worry)

12:16am   *(Where?? We're all worried.)*

12:17am   (just go home don't worry)

12:18am   *(FUCK YOU)*

12:19am   (isa im fine calm down)
12:27am   (im sorry i didnt mean to scare
          you)
12:37am   (hey im downstairs please let me
          in for a second)
1:26pm   Cold makes the colours sharper.
          Especially blue.
1:26pm   It can take your breath right from
          your chest.

2:47pm   *Blue has the deepest smile. Red always*
                           fades away. Yellow has no soul. Green can
                           be trusted though. Within grey it calms
                           down.

4:34pm   How do you feel about grey skies
          and their wet, wet winds?

5:47pm		*Rain is relieving, wind is confusing. Together they are a mess. Grey is neutral. The sky should always smile.*

5:47pm *Rain is relieving, wind is confusing. Together they are a mess. Grey is neutral. The sky should always smile.*

6:53pm I wonder if it can rain underwater.

6:54pm *Underwater storms do exist.*

01/25/2014

8:47am Lately i've been living on the smell about your neck

8:51am *A good smell can sometimes cover a bitter taste.*

9:22am Focus. Focus. My hands are running wild.

12:44pm *Can you read what is written on the body?*

12:57pm Once, i learned to read scars like braille. I would run my fingers over their seismographic secrets

12:57pm I read very few languages.

1:07pm *Visible scars are hypocrite secrets. Can you decrypt the skeletal pattern on the chest?*

1:10pm I can play ribcage piano.

1:31pm I've drunk the shaking fear and made it my own. I've penned invisible wings on the backs of the insane.

1:32pm I tend to eat more than i write; i smell sweet vanilla.

2:48pm *Overeating causes abdominal pain.*

3:00pm *Vanilla is a heavy smell. In small rooms it makes me nauseous.*

11:28am   *What is your favourite smell? Mine is bleach. Clean. Aggressive on skin. White beauty and perfection of a boiled egg.*

11:30am   I've smelled skin on fire before, it is not a nice smell

11:51pm   *Things we like are not always nice.*

12:05pm   I saw my father with his hand inside a ribcage once or twice. Blood up to his elbows.

1:50pm   I have smelled so many putrid smells. I like them best because they tell me when to pay attention.

1:51pm   They tell me when to be suspicious. They tell me when to be worried.

1:54pm   The best & worst are the ones i will   later taste

2:00pm   *I like the absence of smells. A floating empty space. Feeling of acid gnawing through flesh to clean, pure bones. Water in the lungs.*

2:32pm   What else do you like?

2:44pm   *Silence. It always talks to me.*

2:45pm   Can you see him?

2:47pm   *Shapeless. A sublime transparency.*

2:48pm   Sounds like a drinking buddy.

2:49pm   *I like my wine alone.*

2:50pm   In silence?

2:52pm	*In noisy observation. Silence is hiding in my head.*
2:54pm.	I saw him in your eyes last night.
2:55pm	*How did he look like?*
3:03pm	*(I think I'm going for a walk. Wanna join?)*
3:03pm	Sure come get me plz
3:04pm	(Oops)
3:04pm	*Ok, I'll come get you*
3:04pm	*(Oups)*
6:31pm	He looked like a twinkle on an indifferent face. Like darkness in the eyes of a beaming one. Like winter blues on a summer face.
6:34pm	*Have you ever met him personally?*

01/26/2014

1:33pm	I have faced his many faces. I often turn away, his stare is endless.
2:54pm	*Most dangerous poisons are translucent. Tasteless. Shapeless. They can be diluted to anything in secrecy. Did you sense it? Runrunrunrungowhileyoucan.*
3:42pm	I feel faceless. He knows us all. We have friends like shields and swords. Why fear becoming? We are always becoming.
5:15pm	*Fear hides behind a mask. A mask is faceless. It is a lie.*
5:22pm	Do you like fear?

5:31pm		*I don't know fear. We've stepped on the*

5:31pm   *I don't know fear. We've stepped on the same stairs occasionally. Do you know him?*

5:42pm   *I've seen him crawling in hospital corridors. In the head of a hammer. In a hand. Running in the streets. Haunting heads. I've always refused to talk to him.*

5:17pm   He is a slave who owns the master. I wouldn't say i know him. What does he smell like?

6:33pm   *Like a running rabbit on concrete. Only rubber can reveal it.*

6:33pm   *How do you smell like?*

6:36pm   Some say I smell like poison.

6:39pm   I think i am beginning to smell like you.

•••

Archibald Lampman to Maud Emma Playter
40 Grove Avenue, Toronto, Ontario
July 27, 1885
age 23

My Sweetest Darling

I received your letter this morning — in fact just 10 minutes ago. I was so glad to get it. I read it over two or three times and thanked you many more times as I did so.

I have been in your house I think twice since you left, and it seems to me to be dead for the soul is gone out of it and fled away to Toronto. Ah!, I hope it will soon come back. Dear Maud I am trying to work; I keep to my room very nearly altogether now in the evenings; but I do not succeed very well. It will be some time before I can work myself into the mood, and then my thoughts go wandering off westward till they come to somebody who is very lovely and fair, and when they reach that person they find themselves so happy that they do not come back in a hurry: in fact after a long time I wake up out of the sweetest dream and find that the sheets of foolscap paper are lying in front of me still, but there is no writing on them. However I wrote some yesterday and maybe before long the inspiration will come. At any rate I have finished the Romance of a Drunkard. I ended the last chapter on Friday, and like it very well; much better than the first two.

How I should have liked to have been in a corner behind a curtain somewhere at that full-dress party of yours: just to have had a good gaze at my darling: how lovely she must have looked. Perhaps if I had come out from behind the curtain, she would have given me a few of those delightful dances, that others were so lucky to get.

If I am not with you in the flesh I am at any rate always so in the spirit. My dreams are with you more often than you can imagine. Whenever you turn your thoughts to me — which you must do often, dearest, you may be pretty sure that I am thinking of you. You may feel me stretching my arms in fancy over all that distance and drawing them round you, and pressing the sweet, sweet mouth with a hundred long soft kisses.

Forgive the abominable blots on this paper; my office desk is so spattered about with ink I could not prevent it.

Your loving,
Archie

•

Archibald Lampman to Maud Emma Playter
Sept 7, 1885

My Darling

I was very much delighted to get your letter this morning. It is nearly a week since I came home from camping, and you will say that I have neglected my Maud: not so. You know me so well and how much I love you that when I tell you that I have been so busy and worried with one thing or another, that I could not write you a good letter, you will believe me and, I know, forgive me. I did not get that letter you wrote me, when I was camping. I suppose it went astray. It was difficult out there both to get letters and to send them. I sent you two; I hope you got them.

You think that perhaps I would rather you didn't write to me either. Eh? What an idea, my Love, my beautiful. (But I forgot; I must not call you that). Yes I am so glad you wrote to me, & I am glad that you like to get letters from me. Ah, I want plenty from you, Dear. More than I get. Write whenever you can.

We had an excellent time in the camp, and got strong & brown and gluttonous — even quite fat — and I grew a <u>beard</u> which I have not yet shaved off and which has excited immense disgust at home. However it will come off today. We looked very wild and unkempt on the journey home. I had only one collar with me and that had got covered with mud in the camp; so I came back without one. The ticket agent at Buckingham wanted to sell me a <u>second</u> class fare: he didn't know what such a "tough" as I, could be wanting with a 1st class one.

Three or four days before we left the camp, we made an expedition to a beautiful lake a few miles north of us. We paddled up the river, carrying provisions with us, to the mouth of a creek. Then we bore the canoe on our shoulders across the country over a rough road to the Lake — Escalier Lake. We fished for a few hours and caught 25 pounds weight of fish — I caught one pike that weighed 13 pounds. When we got home we were very tired and dusty.

I wish you could have been with us for one thing on the way home — running the long rapids on the Lievre. We went down the rapids which are a mile long — in one of those long pointed rowboats, called pointers or buns. It was exciting — far ahead of tobogganing — only there wasn't enough of it — We rushed down so fast and furiously, that it was all over a good deal too soon. I thought that I would like to have hauled the pointer up and gone down again.

When I get you back again into my arms, dear, in some dusky corner as of old, I will tell you all about the camping down to the smallest detail. In the meantime with more love than I can tell, and so many soft, soft kisses
I remain
Your Archie

P.S. How did you like the <u>sonnet</u> I sent you? or did you get it?

I have all the no.s of the Current. Do you want to read them now or when you return? say which. I suppose there are candies in Thornhill. Buy some and eat them for my sake.

•••

Colin Morton to Mary Lee Bragg
The Great Boreal Forest
August, 1972
age 24

Mary Lee
Dear Sir:

I have some pennies in my pocket that feel like they want to be in your
cat. I also notice that pennies have gone out of circulation, then nickels, as
the price of pop from machines changes gradually from 15 cents to 20 to 25
as we move east.

You probably remembered about the travellers' cheques in your purse
just after getting on the bus I ran out to see pull away on sixth avenue.
Fortunately that's not the stupidest thing we've managed to accomplish. In
fact, it wasn't too late as I waited till 8:15 for the second bus to arrive for the
extras — which was alright because that one was air conditioned while the
first one wasn't. At first I thought it would be adventurous to see if I could
make it to Toronto on the $3 in my pocket, but my prudence got the better
of me and commerce overcame industry: I cashed a cheque in Kenora which
I haven't used yet (ie the money).

Melville could write with genuine awe about the oceanic vastness of
Lake Superior and the impenetrable boreal forest. But what about us? ("Well
it was just awful it took us two days to drive through it and the restaurants
and the radio stations! Just awful!") Despite those awful squirmishes last
April I still don't know, as I look out at the bush (just getting to the amethyst
highway) what this forest *smells* like, say, or what it sounds like, or what
infernal beasts lurk there or in the hearts of men, as you would if you spent
two months canoeing through it, or two years blazing a trail through it.
Mind you I know something about the rock formations under it since the
road has been blasted through hills to avoid those annoying curves. The
fact is, with McLuhan or without him, we are all eye-fixated — that is,
mesmerized — and the media of communication and transportation are
responsible. WE can always be somewhere else if present circumstances are
not to our liking — which they won't be since we don't have any respect for
them because we can always be somewhere else. And so divorce becomes
the norm.

You can't write too much when you're travelling faster than a speeding arrow, so I'm going to put this down in a minute. I assume and hope you put those cheques in the mail before 10:30 yesterday morning so they'll be there when I arrive. But I have some cash now so it's not necessary. Right now it's sunset. Maybe at sunrise in Sault Ste. Marie I'll pick this up again and wax romantical. Good Night

Saturday morning — Today and last night the moon is full at its perigee so it's the brightest night you will ever see. For some reason this coincides with eclipses. The moon rises at the same time the sun sets and sets as the sun rises, which is to say that it is at some time bound to be at the direct nadir of the world, with the earth's shadow covering the sun. The TV camera on the moon will show an eclipse of the sun, but if my layman's reason is not sidearmed there should, at the same time, be an eclipse of the moon (at its brightest visible from the earth). Now Keats believed in the lunar effect on poetry; ie that inspiration ebbs and flows like the tide or a period. He took seriously the confraternity of lunatic lover and poet. What happens I wonder when the moon at its brightest loses its sun and so is eclipsed? Death by consumption? And you thought astrology was weird. What animal was the moon to those Chaldeans?

We stopped in Regina for an hour for supper Thursday, so I phoned Cruickshank, who has moved into an apartment with his brother Ken. Neither of them was home, but I talked to their brother Chris, who is 5 years younger (ie one of Those People). He was expecting me to call because he was in a car that passed me on the road Tuesday and if it hadn't been full he would have had the driver stop. Apparently one of the kids Charlotte placed over the winter was his (it's "kickin around the states somewhere and is going to come along and shoot me when I'm the Establishment"). Then last night I tried to look up Andy in Thunder Bay, but he wasn't in The Book and I didn't have time to hunt around for Jean Street. Then two hours later I was positive I recognized him passing the bus with a group in Marathon. We were about to stop, so I went up to where they were standing and petted their dog for a while, but it wasn't Andy. Marathon is a strange town consisting mostly of big war-housing-type units with broad grassy quads going up the hill from the lake. A very interesting town planning idea. Of course all the people that live on the quads work at the paper mill or work to keep the people who do.

I'll be arriving in Toronto at 7:15 tonight which should give me time to get to where I'm going at a reasonable hour. I bought a loaf of bread and some salami at Med Hat that with the lunch you packed me lasted until this morning, and I still have raisins & cookies to munch on.

We're starting off again now, not so depleted as you might expect. I might not get this mailed this morning, in which case I'll add to it when I arrive. I was going to say how are you taking it (?) but with Marilyn and Lorraine and Rachel and on etc. etc. and my people phoning you, you should hardly have time to consider the question.

How could I avoid, when I get the chance, writing about people on the bus, and of course the moon (people lost in outer space as well) everyone drawn into their own invisible selves and observing, like the moon, a pyramidical silence (these are Melvillean phrases), and also the delphian silence of talking on the bus etc. Well, more of that later. (Still though, isn't Melville less divertingly inventive than Barth and less delightfully pedantic than Sterne?)

Noon — Well look where an untamed imagination can get you. Here I am on the surface of the moon — or more precisely, Sudbury. Mining destroys forests, & what lives there; milling the water, & what lives there; smelting the air, and what lives there; driving the earth, & what lives there. Earth, air, water, food — aren't these the elementals.

Mary Lee — I'll write to you again right away. Starting when I mail this. If we can unburden ourselves to each other this way, as <u>always</u>, it won't be so far.

Love
Colin

•

Colin Morton to Mary Lee Bragg
99 Bogert Avenue, Willowdale, Ontario
1972

Dear Mary Lee,

Well, my arrival in Toronto was hardly auspicious, and I started to get the feeling that I really hadn't come anywhere in the past six years since I arrived before. It turns out that my Gramma is staying up at the lake all summer and didn't get my message. I don't know yet whether I'm going to be able to get hold of whatever you sent me at her place. I phoned the

Davidsons' place, and they were just leaving on holidays, so I walked down here to Ruth & Ken's even though I was getting no answer on the telephone. (I got a number for John who lives out by the York campus and hasn't been heard from for quite a while, but he wasn't home — I'm trying to locate him now.) When I got here the house was dark and I figured they'd gone away for the weekend too. But the neighbours across the street had heard about me in passing and took me in, gave me tea & sandwiches, phoned Ken's dad & found out they had just gone out for the evening. They arrived about midnight. Grampa Newton is staying with them, Craig sleeps in the dining room and I'm downstairs; so there are still problems about finding a place to stay — except that I have no money to speak of — especially if I still owe $10 on the course. There is the chance I can get uncle Lloyd to unlock Gramma's mail for me.

Well (this seems to do as well as indentation opening paragraphs) I just phoned John who is staying at his parents' while they're away and he says I can go up there and drive his father's car to the school. That sounds — I don't know about that but in any case I'll go up there now and talk to him, probably stay there tonight. I'll write you some more tonight and tomorrow and maybe get this straightened away.

Well then, this is Sunday night. Since the above I've talked to you on the phone, and it was such a relief to hear you that I'm sorry now I didn't talk longer. My phone paranoia somehow increases though with the distance — another of my irrational tics. Listen, if you'll write and tell me when you'll be home — and what time I can phone you again at the end of the week.

There's something I want to say in this space, but it's an emptiness where there's usually a hug.

...

All of a sudden I feel somehow defeated; as though I'm launched on a battle with less than half my forces. Please send some morale support. I'm sure I'll feel better about tomorrow — unless my works are the first to be discussed and then set aside as finished with. I'm going to go to sleep now, that will help. And I'm certain that it's not going to be a battle tomorrow — except if I have to fight the traffic four times every day, the pace could be a depletion instead of an exhilaration.

Well, it's going to be exhausting, I know that. Good night.

I am drifting between four walls — such a feeble space capsule —

stationary — amid the passing crowded void. My message to you is weak — as a radio beam at the far end of the band — late at night — scattered in the stratosphere. We locate one another only by triangulation — on the surface of the moon. But we see never the same moon — a pale spot among half-lit buildings — a face sadly twisted — the reflector of disjointed signals. And the moon — who is he — but an indifferent glow upon us — caught in the teeming action — of a drop — saying nothing — only — stop — there is time — there is room — there is nowhere — else to go. The moonlight rests — on the roofs of frantic cars — strung out — along the highway out — of sight — rests — on the quivering antennae — serene — as on the rolling water of a lake — saying nothing.

Sorry to give you something so heavy — like an anchor — but that is all I seem to be able to articulate of my feelings. The rest is something like a void, a glow, a hug that is not there. Say that the nothing the moon says is what I want to say to you — that hug articulated the only way it can be. Does that make it an auspicious moon, or only an aching one? (Here I am staying up all night again, but with not you to come to. Drop it for now. Look at the moon.) You know "I love you" in a way "that" doesn't say.

Love

Colin

•••

Jack Garton to Jennifer Hammer
2:52 p.m., Friday, October 10, 2008
age 24

hi jenn,

i read your letter yesterday evening beside the blue blue ocean. it was beautiful. then i embarked on a lot of walking, during which i did a lot of thinking. after the sunset turned into nightrise, i eventually turned up from the ocean and found a really cute cafe squeezed in between alleyways and old buildings, and i tried to remember my thoughts and write them down. so here is the letter that i wrote last night on scrap paper. the letter ended when i ran out of paper, not when i ran out of thoughts.

today is a whole other world of life. born again with the sun. I knew that this would have to face reality at some point the morning you left London.

My lips and eyes and heart were stinging when you kissed me in the dark. Today is a day of fantasies coming up against realities. collision. This is the first time i have been able to FEEL right in my bones the reality of our situation. Your proposal sounds wonderful, frightening, necessary, among other feelings that don't have names to represent them. i've been collecting all these thoughts while walking through Thessaloniki;

i'm at a critical point in my journey now. the fact of my time coming to an end is now very real, and i'm having to make choices about what i actually have time to do. Greece, the land of myths, is as i should have assumed also a land of logistics, actualities and things as mundane as catching boat and train connections on time. but what a strong magic here! the sunset tonight absolutely ripped my heart wide open. the greeks snickered at my short pants as i strolled along the ocean with tears rolling down my cheeks.

the tears that came prickling to my eyes when i read the last lines of your letter indicate to me the need for some kind of resolution. a space to acknowledge each other. so i say yes to that.

that's where i ran out of paper.

— and just so you know, i don't think you need any man in a stinky car to drive you anywhere. i hope i'm not missing the point, but my instinct says that you're not really trapped in the gilded cage either. anyway, i should get away from this dumb computer.

love

jack

ps — do you want to do the Thriller dance this Halloween? it seems that there may be multiple opportunities. i'm still negotiating fees, etc. but i'd like to propose something to you. it seems that Kat won't be able to dance with her foot broken. i'm not sure, but if that's the case, i'll need to find someone else to be Michael's "girl." interested?

•

Jack Garton to Jennifer Hammer
6:22 a.m., Wednesday, July 16, 2009

wow, i'm up late at the studio again. i just want to tell you about how much i love you all the time. i'm on my way home now and i'll crawl into bed with you and it will feel as always like i'm floating on a cloud holding

up you and me and malakai far above the world. or like we're lying on the
open pages of a love story, our bodies making the words.

        mmmmmmmmm
        see you soon
        jack

        •••

John Barton, 1982
age 25

Sixth Letter in Autumn

Since you left I have remembered
the minutiae of your face
and hands, lifted debris
from every pore as a smith would
dints from a silver cup.
You are constantly reborn.

Here we are, and were,
two men meeting for the first
time over coffee and talk,
watching leaves gracefully
snake to the earth;
and later, in a midnight cove,
hunched up on driftwood
one Christmas, the two of us
resting elbows on knees,
shivering, our two lives
opening like an iron gate,
shore mist blurring the waves;
and still later, in a bar,
flipsides of the same woman,
a game of hesitance and remorse,
jazz, laughter, the waitress
caught in our forced

lightness like a moth;
and still later, in your kitchen,
the day after she left me,
two months after she left you,
your hand on my shoulder,
your face dark against pale
morning light, your voice
exhausted, restrained,
smoke twisting from a flame;
and finally, the day you left,
your hand on my shoulder,
your foot one foot from the gas,
my face a contusion of loss,
anger, and tears as you held me,
thinking of the long climb
into the interior mountains,
coal towns and money to earn,
brook trout and distance.

I am not alone here healing.
A woman down the street
reads in a window on sun-marked
days drinking tea, and looking
away from her book, can spur
me to laughter, saying her last man
made himself an unwritten letter,
an unopened letter.
How often have her eyes
and mine illumined the rain,
the moon in its last crescent,
the two of us home from the sea?
And another, a friend I shelve
books with at work,
keeps shuffling his cards,
a royal flush yet to flesh out,
a full house of want —
both of us at times

so desperate for love
we open our lives
warmly near the windows,
shafts of light
falling, row after row,
between the dark
knowledge of books.

Such a gift this art
of healing, of growing still,
changing like a leaf
aware on an unfurling self.
Despite our words of anger
I have kept much —

your eyes quiet
each time we broke bread
in my kitchen
while outside the ivy
quaked in the wind;

your eyes holding mine
quietly, the eyes
of the woman ours followed,
spinning, talismanic with loss;

and though sometimes
you could not understand,
and sometimes, laughing,
would not admit to
the moon's recurrent circuit of pain,

your eyes quietening
each time you said my name.

• • •

Robert Priest, 1976
age 25

Come to Me

Come to me
I know we are out of sync
I know they will call it dying
but come to me anyway
I have tried to hate you with the strength
of many animals and I cannot hate you
so come to me burning
and I also will burn
come to me with ancient music and I will be a snake
writhing with my many wrists
each one more undulant than your long hair
o I still have nights and nights of you
all queued up in the thirst of a single slave
to work out
come to me with snow and I will promise
to be red in it
come to me unique and I will match you
stare for stare
come to me in greek in spanish in french in hebrew
and I will sing that I found you
because I overthrew reason
because I live in the wreck of my senses
by wish and magic
like a roc in the ruins of its egg
come to me dancing
that dark bacchanal of your kiss
so wet on my lips for days I will not want
drugs or water
just your own sea broken like a sheet of lightning
on your thigh so sensual
come to me because we will arrive
anyway at each other
because it has been many lives

and each time we touch
great forces
are again able to move
come to me cruel and lovely
because I am abandon
because I am silver
because a million years
you have suffered in slavery to men
and know at last how to be free

•••

Rhonda Batchelor to Charles Lillard
1978
age 25

The trouble with the flowers
you brought   is that
they remain   after you

•••

Raymond Souster, 1947
age 26

The Nest

It will have to be near some water
so there can be moonlight like a pool
to bathe our tired, sleep-returning eyes.

There must be a high, strong roof
so the rain children will not break
the step of their marching above us.

White sheets to lull our flesh asleep
after we've squeezed all the love from our bodies,

with God's hand on the door
so none can touch the slightest scattered hair
of your head on its pillow, that none
will hand me a gun again and say,
leave her, there's new blood to be spilled
in the name of our latest lie.

•••

Christopher Doda to Priscila Uppal
Early September, 1997
age 26

Dear Pris,

It is Wednesday night. I am alone writing you by the kitchen light, beer in hand. I have yet to purchase a living room lamp so after dark my apartment takes on the appearance of a morose twilight. With its white walls, I feel like I inhabit some sort of dismal asylum. I will have a phone and a phone number on Monday, so I can have contact with the outside world, and my "old world" (as the explorers would have called it.)

My things arrived this morning, which cheered me a little. For two nights I slept on a bare mattress underneath my leather overcoat. It will be nice to have a blanket again. And towels. I've been using a T-shirt for drying until now. How simple one's desires become when one is reduced to nothing.

I have had two classes thus far plus one session of the one I shall (hopefully) be teaching. The enrolment looked pretty good though but I am worried that Walt Whitman will scare people off. Professors at McGill don't get confirmed class lists until sometime in mid-October (!).

Renaissance Studies looks very difficult, consisting almost entirely of people I've never read before, save for My Personal Savior, Machiavelli. The Prof seems nice though she talks too fast and is one of those annoying people that opens her every sentence with "I think that..." like nothing could be possibly thought of unless it came from her head. If today was an example this tendency has rubbed off on her students already.

Romanticism seems more my speed. It would appear that the farther back we go, the less interested I become. Although something happened during that first class that I hope is not prophetic. I had a spontaneous, and as yet unaccounted for, bout of bleeding. I noticed a girl across the table from me pointing at my elbow and when I checked it, sure enough, it was covered in blood. As I tried to dab it out with my finger, she tossed me a Kleenex and, moments later, a Band-Aid. Why she had these things on her I have no idea.

Your observation about grad school being populated by gays seems borne out here too. Or, at the very least, a haven for beefy guys and short haired women.

[later]

I think I am in shock. I've tried to write you a letter from my public face, the one that people see in classes, to tell you about my first two days here. And I can't. I've grown too adept at concealing my loneliness from others but not from you. It still hasn't hit me that I'm gone. I keep expecting you to be at the door or something. When the delivery man buzzed my door this morning, my first thought was it was somehow you come to visit. Every night I spend some time pacing back and forth, crying. I don't even want to know what the next few months will be like. I can't believe that you and I aren't "us" and the more time goes by the less of an "us" there will be. I love you. I am afraid. Afraid that no amount of scholarship or alcohol can fill the void that my life became the moment I got into that taxi. I've been little more than a zombie. An inhabitant in the city of death. I walked home last night in the freezing, pouring rain and could not bear to get on the bus. I just wandered through the downpour for two hours and bawled out my misery to the uncaring sky (most of those early explorers were prisoners. I am beginning to understand how they felt). When I'm not raw, I just feel empty; dead. I love you. I miss you. I don't know what else to say.

I'll call as soon as I can.

Love,

Chris

•••

Shannon Webb-Campbell to ———
September 4, 2009
age 26

Dearest,

I just watched my first sunset over Paris. Two nearby lovers embrace, their silhouettes glow among the moment. I smiled to myself; remembering your lips on mine. I wish you were here to see the skyline fade, darken into night. When I close my eyes, I can still feel you on my skin, your hand in mine, your body on my bones.

Earlier today I wandered the streets feeling displaced. I was a freshly caught fish who only wanted to be put back in familiar waters. To nurse my fevers I got half litre of wine, a baguette and some blue cheese at the market and took to the park, changing spots every time a pigeon came near.

I'm feeling far away from Halifax, as if the rest of the world doesn't exist. I'm still orienting myself with this notion of travel, how just the other morning I woke up to the sun coming up over your Gottingen Street bed, and today the Eiffel Tower looms in the distance of my small shared room.

I've made friends with my top bunkmate; she's a doctor from Brazil. Immediately we carried on like old friends filling in the gaps — who makes your heart patter, why you are in Paris and what's next on the agenda. Yesterday we took the Metro and wandered up to the Eiffel Tower, playing the role of dutiful tourists we went all the way to the top.

The view is absolutely stunning. All you can see for miles and miles are rooftops, an endless sea of historic urbanization. It didn't matter how much I squinted, for the life of me I could not see the ocean. In views of the city, I remember our nights on the beach, meteor showers, red wine, and sand between our toes. What a beginning.

At the base of the Eiffel Tower, among the panhandlers and dumb-founded travellers, we found the antique carousel. Time blurred, and I became a child, twirling around with the artfully crafted horses. Up and down, up and down, up and down. Never going anywhere but round.

Dizziness and raindrops pushed us on, while the local hustlers changed their Eiffel Tower key chains to umbrellas for sale. We found our way back to the Latin Quarter to Rue de Gobelins and settled in for a late supper and bottle of red wine from Bordeaux. The restaurant was dimly lit with tea lights, red drapes hung in the doorway. I ordered a savoury crepe, and Manu, duck confit. After we licked our plates and had only small pools of wine left in our glass, a gentleman came over to introduce himself. Apparently his other male counterpart thought my Brazilian company was gorgeous and just had to come over. We entertained him for a moment before he returned to his table. Moments later the waiter informed us the two gentlemen in the corner wanted to treat us to another glass of wine.

They were both Parisian mathematicians, one a PhD student and the other in finance. Another drink in us and we all hopped in a cab to take in the city of lights at night. As two tourists it was great to have local eyes, ears and tales of Paris. Some true, others fabricated to impress us. I was paired off with the quiet academic, while my Brazilian friend got the drunken buffoon who had a hard time listening when she assured him she was already taken. We wandered the streets together, rowdy and boozy. Shortly after 3:00 a.m. we sent the boys on their way and stumbled into bed.

This morning I woke late and missed breakfast, Manu long gone. A patisserie around the corner fixed all hunger pains. Parisians are so casual about their food, walking to and from their destinations biting off chunks of baguettes and croissants. I love how the chairs face the street at the cafes; it's an interesting contrast to our North American ways. In Paris, you want to be seen.

I read your words before I hit the streets and took strength from your heartfelt sentiments. It was like you were with me walking hand-in-hand, thank you for these gentle nudges. Together, if only in my imagination, we made our way around the city, by foot and Metro.

The Louvre was the first stop today, and I wept in front of Venus de Milo, again later moved to tears by Botticelli's work. The art in Paris overwhelms, I had to sit down, sip water and contemplate every so often. I feel spoiled and in need of reflection.

Early evening I wandered around the Notre Damn, scribbling poems in my small fresh notebook. I am starting to feel the narrative building within me; I just need a room of my own and space to allow my thoughts to simmer. But the beginning is all about the living, the dirt under the nails and blistered feet from pounding the cobblestone streets.

As I was photographing the sunset over the Seine it finally hit me that I'm in Paris, I have arrived. Thank you for the most gorgeous send-off. Our night in the hotel overlooking Halifax harbour, I don't think of it as a goodbye but merely the birth of something beautiful. I do hope that you are feeling open, wistful and filled with curiosity.

You are within my thoughts, dear one.

With love,

SWC

•

Shannon Webb-Campbell to ———
September 15, 2009
age 26

Dearest,

[...] Oh Leonard Cohen, he certainly knows how to craft the perfect song, be it a serenade for lovers, a ballad of heartache or longing. He knows how to build an arc out of narratives that sails beyond the contingency of time and space. He is the keeper of love and heartbreak, and the lyrics in-between.

Many great thinkers and artisans have fled to Paris over the centuries, this is not new. They say each person takes a piece of Paris with them; it is only now that I can feel the city finding its way into my bones. I tossed and turned last night after we said our good nights. I couldn't give my body what it craves. My mind is riddled with questions — the hows and whys of love. I only want you.

I woke feeling less lethargic, I must finally be shaking the jet lag. I began the day at a nearby café. I've been writing letters, asking for guidance, praying for understanding and a welcoming hand.

An older couple beside me feasts on salad and some sort of chicken dish. I love the smell of the woman; she's a blend of lilacs, baby powder and my grandmother's skin. I can see the cook in the kitchen sampling his recipes as he pulls the orders down from the pegs. Two handsome waiters usher in patrons, shell out menus and eye me suspiciously. Something tells me it's rare for people to bring their laptops to restaurants in France.

I thought of you in the shower this morning. I can still feel your fingers within the very depths of me, each fold and layer opened and closed to the memory of our nights together. I remember the gold sheets, sand and unmade hotel bed. The thought of your body against mine, skin to skin, soul to soul, replenishes the ocean within me.

You have revived me, called my soul forth. I can feel the glacier of my being cracking. It has been months, years even that I have felt this sort of movement throughout me. There were moments in my small attic room that I believed I had lost the lover within me, I thought she died quietly somewhere along the way.

It's been so long since I've felt this alive. These words are more than sweet nothings, they are my truth. Perhaps they may land like rocks as distance has a way of making everything feel weighted, but know that I have no expectations of you, us, this. I feel deeply for you and very well could believe this may grow into a narrative. I know we are two souls still carving our own paths. I can give you love, care and respect unconditionally, only asking the same in return.

I don't have any questions about anything, we are unfolding at our own grace. There is no reason to rush the season. We are creating our own time, our own collection of memories. If we were in the same city perhaps our concerns would heighten. We'd rush into things, but distance and an ocean make our pace.

I know the universe has a plan for me, for you, for us. We must be brave and be kind. I love your words, as a writer there is nothing more romantic in my mind than the exchange of letters. Of my great loves, it has always been language that brought us together. With you it began differently — I was certain I wanted you before any words bubbled to the surface. I am intensely attracted to you without a pile of fears, questions, or concerns. It's plain and primal — pure, unhinged desire. You are the essence of poetics.

Regardless of where our tale may go know that I am invested in you, your soul, your character and well being. There is deep compassion and love growing roots between us; this is something I value more than any romance. I can assure you that I do not give love easily or quickly, this is new. I do know that my greatest love must be with myself right now in whatever shape or form that takes.

Over the course of my life I have struggled greatly with my sense of self. I've questioned everything, thought on existentialism and nearly gave in to suicide. My wounds are deep, my scars invisible, but I am mending. I am being careful with myself, cautious and loving.

Today I plan to take to the books. Language always reconnects me to myself, my purpose. When I write I feel similar. I'll head to Shakespeare and Company and spend the hours with old friends, both on the page and perhaps make some new ones within the surroundings. My first week in

Paris was filled with motion, now I'm looking to settle into a nook and travel without moving.

My darling, I do hope that this day finds you well, perhaps with a bounce in your step and thoughts of a girl wearing flowers in her hair. I'm thinking of you, loving you from Paris and beyond.

Yours,

SWC

xo

•••

Bliss Carman to Maude Mosher
Fredericton, New Brunswick
11 p.m., Wednesday, December 28, 1887
age 26

My dear Maude: Verily thou are a good creature; to-night when my fearful eye lit upon your hand I trembled for the wrath that was my due — and behold a renewal of kindliness and beautiful charity. And yet when I read through the letter I find that "something awful" is to happen to me if I do not write soon. When I see such words, and know that Berenson is your ally, I tremble for my safety even at this distance. Let me hide my ink-bottle, and anon come forth with an oblation.

[…] Fredericton, you would not know it is Winter. I came home — how beautiful winter weather, and it is not a bit better than Cambridge (pardon!). No snow at all, dull, overcast, and glowering most of the time. Christmas not exactly "green" as they say, but about whitey-brown. A few glorious days, though, and a good river of ice for skating. There stand up out of the river now six or seven great stone piers, part of the unfinished new railway bridge. The railway strikes the town just below the Cathedral and runs out toward college hill on one of the streets! Good-bye to the quiet of the place now.

Behold now it is changed to a country of snow. I should fail altogether if I tried to give you the least hint of the beauty of winter in the North here. Of a fine day after a storm there is something so wonderfully calm and sweet in the color of the air at sunrise and sunset. For you must know that sunrise comes at such a convenient hour it is no trouble to see it any morning. The whole country is covered with soft snow, and the sun seems to beam upon it and fill the river valley with a finer and more spiritual sort of day. It is full of romance and there is not a touch of it in literature. The nights with their stars and blue are simply beyond me. I only long for the able hand to come by this way and tell of it all.

New Brunswick to *you* means summering and canoeing. Well sir, that was a fine old paddle we had on the Nashwaak if I *did* try to make away with you in the watery depths. "Do you do anything but take little trips for pure country air?" Ah, that was a cruel cut. Maude, you know I never could bear to go out there after the evening you and I were there together. How we walked under the trees in an ecstasy of silence. It did not seem as if I *could* say anything. Just to feel your arm was enough, was *too, too* much! O my own fine fiddler! Can I ever forget that night? Ah, think of it in far off Paris. Almost I could give you a rhapsody of longing and despair thereon — but fear not, I will spare you this once. I will have nothing to tell you about myself particularly. Though I should very much like to see you and have a talk. I don't believe I will ever come quite to your point of view of life, but indeed sometimes the world is a foul-seeming place. But blues are not potent enough to deal death to the Muse.

Good-bye now, and forgive the sad folly of this too trifling letter.
Sincerely your friend, Carman

•••

Ross Priddle to Shannon Kastor
Edmonton, Alberta
RETURNED TO SENDER (unopened)
3 p.m., December 19, 1990
age 26

It's minus twenty-eight both outside and inside. The pathetic fallacy. As we got glowing, the world got glowing. As we got closer together the temperature rose. As we got confused the world got confused. As we melted together, the world melted with us. And now that we have been separated and solidified back into our "proper" places the world has frozen solid once again. As I walk out in the squeak and scrunch of that wind packed and blasted snow, with the distant cold sun below the roofs of the houses at noon, I feel in sympathy or harmony with the world. I think of you as soon as I step out the door and feel the first marrow seeking chill. I think of you as the sun ever present and giving illumination to the stark frozen world but too distant to shed any warmth. Three more days to the solstice and then things will turn around, more warmth on its way. Today there were two brilliant sundogs around noon. This city is a ghost town at this temperature, nobody is outside unless they absolutely have to be. Or maybe it is just your absence that makes it seem so deserted. The only part of themselves that people are showing on the streets are their eyes. One thing you very rarely see is an ugly pair of eyes. Everyone looks very beautiful as they walk swiftly by. Eyes meet and twinkle and say "we must be crazy to be here, but we're crazy together." I think of your eyes. So big, and wide and round sometimes. If I can catch you off guard they seem surprised and frightened like a deer caught by headlights on the side of the highway, well maybe not exactly on the side but close enough, assuming it can collect itself in time, to leap in the right direction. Metaphors have a tendency to get away on me. Sometimes your eyes take on this distant, aloof, invulnerable, unaffected look as if nothing I could say or do would make any difference to you. It is a frightening look. And then there is your pained look that involves a partial closing of the eyes and tries to say "I don't want this" "I didn't ask for this" but although it may have spoken true once, now it whispers at the corners with tiny filigree wrinkles "life is whisking me away, maybe this is now or never." I am thinking of the moment after I asked if you wanted to go out again. You jumped from eighteen to twenty-four just by closing your eyes a little. And then you said you were "booked up," like a dentist's office or something and made it sound like you were a relieved to be "booked up." And so you went to see <u>Mermaids</u> on Friday night and while you were sitting in the theatre trying to lose yourself in the movie time was howling up and down the colding streets; while you were sitting quiet, still and alone (I know you were with someone but you were alone) trying to squeeze a little pleasure out of watching someone else's life, yours was ticking and slipping away silently. Slowly, but oh so swiftly. This is the same "talking to" (as in "I'm gonna give you a good talking to" or "what you need is a good talking to") that I gave myself the night of Timothy Findley. I was guilty of exactly the same thing: of running away from life. After that class we stood up, you said "so, are you guys going to that thing tonight?" and I said "I don't know, I was thinking about it. What about you?" and you said "I don't know, I was thinking about it. What time does it start?" etc. and the next thing I knew I was outside the door, and after taking a drink from the fountain I looked back and you weren't coming out yet and I knew if I waited you would come out and agree to go, but instead I turned and ran towards my Chaucer class which was even cancelled that day so I went and sat under a tree and wrote a few notes with all my hair standing on end and the sun seemed to be alive and warm and in sympathy that day. I tried to convince myself that you would be there if I went and eventually I walked over and walked past the door but I could feel your absence so I didn't even go in. And while I sat at my friend's watching T.V., I heard the howl of time. The mingled sensation of lost opportunity and disaster avoided. For, of course that is a part of it, the feeling that maybe it was a good choice after all. I'm sure you try and tell yourself the same. And maybe you're right. Maybe you're doing both of us a favour. And yet, here I am writing this letter.

(Dec. 20-28)

Hades, I had Chinese food and chocolate cookies (out of a metal box) for breakfast and then danced Corybantically to OAO by the Golden Palominos (with John Zorn playing duck calls). I think I am suffering from Tarantism. I needed to sweat (I lied when I said I only liked to sweat for money) and it was too damn cold to step outside. The frost is creeping in around the door and the windows as if it were going to take over the house.

Is your dad the "Chirptr"? Douse the flames. Does "Chirptr" stand for "chiroperan"? And what is all this nonsense about a cervicide? How about this little nugget from the O.E.D?:

"Shannon: An artificial salmon fly used on the river Shannon in Ireland... The large heavy water Shannon flies are very showy affairs...The Shannon... Tag, gold tinsel and lemon-yellow floss." [...]

I hate the thought that all this is just wasted effort. If I expended this much effort on my courses I would get nines. If you write me back I won't think that you have fallen in love with me but I'd like to hear from you to see what you think of all this.

•

Ross Priddle to Shannon Kastor
Edmonton, Alberta
RETURNED TO SENDER (unopened)
December 25, 1990

The nice thing about getting a letter from someone you don't want to hear from is that you don't have to read it if you don't want to. Unlike a phone call which requires at least a little crudeness or cunning to get rid of

quickly a letter can be cast aside without the slightest regard for feelings or
decorum. And even more unlike a coffee, lunch or dinner date which might
involve anywhere from an hour to an evening to escape, a letter can be dis-
regarded without even being opened. But human curiosity and boredom
being what they are, chances are fairly high that an unwanted letter will be
read quite thoroughly, eventually.

Dear Shannon,

   Merry Christmas! Happy Holidays! Holy Hannah! I'd like the opportunity to thank you for helping me finish my exams and to apologize for
seeking you out when you thought you were home free. It is a great relief
having so much distance between us (I'm sure you'd probably agree).
Although I am still thinking of you, I am not troubled by an unconquerable
desire to call you. I'm terribly sorry for any inconvenience my childish
outburst may have caused you and I beg for your forgiveness. As you already
have discovered, I am not too proud to beg. I think I'll write a pamphlet
called "The Art of Grovelling." I just looked that word up and it has another
meaning: "To give oneself over to base pleasures." Which reminds me of
Strawberry Cheesecake. You've already grovelled with me once (or twice).
Maybe we can grovel together sometime in the future.

   Let me describe the pleasure I took in eating that piece of cheesecake that
you forced me to take. The container itself (which I now have before me)
was/is an amazing artifact. It sat in the back of the refrigerator for a couple
of days and every time I opened the door, it reminded me of you. It is a Becel
Light Diet (I had a certain radiance or sunniness that reminded me of you.
A sort of golden aura. Chryso — Or — Aur — Glimmer — Glamour glow
although I have to admit that I don't believe you're quiet or "Scandinavian"
as you'd like me to believe) Margarine. 87% Sunflower oil. (In case you have
forgotten or didn't notice) with a golden sun pattern on it. Finally I decided
to eat it. As I opened the container the trapped air (from your apartment)
escaped and surrounded me. Could I really smell you or did I only imagine
it? The bright red strawberries and the smell of the cheesecake touched off
strong memories of your presence. In some strange way you seemed to be
present in my kitchen, there in my peripheral vision as I contemplated the
cheesecake. I imagined you putting the cheesecake into the container. If
you remember, I was around the corner and although I could hear that you
were having troubles I could not see you. So I imagined you with a knife in

one hand trying to lift that piece of cake, (it's wobbling) steadying it with your other, licking your fingers, finally getting it all in (it's too big!). So you see, perhaps, the extra pleasure I took in eating the already delissious (I can never spell this word) cheesecake. "Her fingers were probably on this, is that a finger print? Perhaps even a little of her saliva, (Heaven forbid!)"

I've been thinking about your nebulous "boyfriend in Hannah." And, well, I guess I feel sorry for the poor guy (assuming he exists) waiting patiently and faithfully for you back home while you're up in the big city flirting with the fringe element from your English class. Poor guy, stuck in Hannah. A palindrome, and there's no escaping that.

I may not always be nice, but at least I'm honest.

I hope getting this letter doesn't annoy you too much. Imagine if I turned up on your doorstep in Hannah, in person and said "Howdy, I was in the neighbourhood, so I thought I'd drop in and wish you and the folks a Merry Christmas!" That would bug you a lot more, so be thankful for small mercies.

It's quite amazing how well I feel knowing that I can call you when you get back even if it is almost a month away. Maybe if you let me have coffee with you once a month I wouldn't feel like bothering you more. OR I could just write all my feelings down and send them to you and you could drop them (unopened) one by one down the garbage chute until I was cured of this ridiculous love-sickness, or whatever it is.

I've been turning a couple of things over in my mind, one being that you switched out of the feminist lecture of 398. In one way that is a great relief for me as a male, but in another way it shows a certain aspect of your personality that is not conducive to my desire and that is (please don't take offence) your certain fear of the different, the unusual, of the not strictly normal. Dare I say, of the new? The same feeling that chased you out of that class, chased you out of my life. But then, I consider my appearance, and think that there must also be a part of you that desires the different, the unusual, the new, because if you didn't have that curiosity, you wouldn't have gone out with me in the first place. Two other things that displayed your curiosity and willingness to learn were your close inspection of my tapes and the fact that you took the time to look up "cloying." I hope this doesn't sound condescending, I don't mean to imply that I am looking down from some giddy height of experience but merely that I am looking across a bit of an abyss to where you are standing. I am trying to bridge that gap, not only so you can look at things from over here, but so that I can look at the world from over there, too.

The other thing that I have been turning over in my mind is the way you behaved when I was leafing through the blue book and babbling about Solomon and English 360. You allowed me to go on talking, etc. without correcting me and pointing out that it was actually 359 that you were enrolled in. You were obviously afraid I was going to take it just so I could be in the same class as you.

Isn't this an imaginative use of an exam booklet? Just in case you should get the overpowering urge (haha) to write me back, my address is 10635 – 84th Ave, Edm. T6E 2H7

Ross

P.S. I'm not sure why my desire to write you gets greater as the temperature goes lower but it seems to. It's pretty amazing that I haven't gone down to Hannah to visit you by now. I hope you appreciate the amount of restraint I am exercising for your benefit. Anyways, I'm going to Montreal in a couple of days to ski with my Dad and Brother and their partners so you don't have to worry. It seems crazy to fly to Montreal to ski when the Rockies are only a few hours away but what can you do? Maybe by the time I get back I will have forgotten about you completely.

•••

Phyllis Webb, 1954
age 27

And in Our Time

A world flew in my mouth with our first kiss
and its wings were dipped in all the flavours of grief.
Oh my darling, tell me, what can love mean in such a world,
and what can we or any lovers hold in this immensity
of hate and broken things?
Now it is down, down, that's where your kiss travels me,
and, as a world tumbling shocks the theories of spheres,
so this love is like falling glass shaking with stars
the air which tomorrow, or even today, will be
a slow, terrible movement of scars.

...

P.K. Page to F.R. Scott
Thursday, June 15, 1944
age 27

All in all three nice letters from you to date. The last containing the report. So glad to get it. I feel miles away from everything and desperately out of touch. Do you think anything is going to come of it all? I half wish I had been there — but it was better not, wasn't it? Letters seem to take centuries to go to and from. You say you had only just had mine. The first I wrote on the train and posted at Bathurst. That you should have had by Saturday anyway. Since then have written thousands of little notes — some of which I have posted and some torn up. The ones I have posted I have wished to hell I had torn up once they had disappeared into the maw of the letter box. And I say to myself Hemingway's Cathy would not have done that. I even doubt if Brett would, and then I feel sick at heart and rationalize like mad and say, but if I can't write to him, I shall surely, surely go mad. Yesterday I made up my mind that I'd not write again until I got the news — but no news yet and here I am writing. So all in all I'm quite unreliable and you're well rid of me.

I've not written one word since I arrived, only don't tell anyone that. I feel a sweet cheat indeed. However I have been intensely practical. That is I got a letter off to Kit finding out what way the land lay in the event of an emergency and got a wire back from her. That way the land is a southern exposure of the very best type. Please _pretend_ to understand all this for the time being at least. Bawl me out for all you're worth afterwards if you wish, but not _now_.

It's an arid place this. Conversation blows about like sand and only gets in your hair. When you post the picture send me a note also — the latter to this address so I will know when to go and call for it and there need be no strange telephone conversations. I am sending the address again and getting this off Air Mail in case the other letter takes weeks. So don't think I've lost my mind.

Mme. L. Richards
406 Tower Road.

Remember, all the things I don't say are the important ones, really. [...]

•

P.K. Page to F.R. Scott
June 22, 1944

Darling this is the sort of day we should take our lunch up to the cemetery. And I would be very quiet and shy and look at you in wonder. But perhaps I never could be shy with you again. That was many years ago that I used to have my shy spells.

I dreamed of you last night — but it was frustrating. Crowds and crowds of people were with us and wouldn't go and then they would disappear; but no sooner had we moved a step towards each other than they'd all be there again.

My rolling and billowing brother has blown in from the Panama. Is the colour of old brick and now a seasoned tar. It's fun having him here.

Mostly I want to tell you how much better I feel. I can't say I've never felt better in my life — but hope to be able to soon. Dizzy spells are fading and I can get by on 11 hours instead of 13 per night. Yesterday I went to the most awful party. The girl who was in the snap I showed you with me in the mud — and whom I had not seen since that time — was there, plus various others I had known years ago. It was ghastly. They talked of nothing but their maids. Saw Lady in the Dark last night with the brother and it was rotten. Could have been quite good too, which made it more annoying.

Today I go to a coffee party and this afternoon tea with my sweet Leoni. All these people who think themselves so war conscious and brave have banquets instead of teas. Never have I seen so much food and such fussy food. Jiminy! The person I like best so far, barring Leoni, is the char who is a perfect old pet and has a glorious sense of humour.

One day when you have time, please look the Henry Birks up in the telephone book for me and send me the number of that apartment. I promised to send Jo a card with my address on it and can't, having forgotten the number again.

Look after yourself, take your vitamins even though it is summer.

I have just finished a book about a drunkard & am certain now that C. did have something approximating D.T.'s.

What happens when you get to your sisters? Do I have any contact then at all?

<u>Later</u>.

Your note has just come.

You say you've just offered yourself to Hermes from the chin up. Even <u>that</u> makes me frightened. (I'm only teasing you really.) The thought of those 2 heads makes me want to die laughing. It's really too absurd. Have you sent your picture yet? And how many years is it since I left? Do you think it bearable for a whole summer? And the awful part is I can't remember what you looked like at the station. I felt so ill & used all my strength in refraining from flinging myself at you with the result that I remember only a strong light & heat & our shaking heads & the sensation of some great tidal wave rising in one which broke when I said Goodbye. Altogether whichever way I look I know you're the biggest thing that ever happened to me. Nothing can ever be mammother. I thought maybe when I got away things might look different — people always tell you they do — but they <u>don't</u>. Not these things anyway.

Maybe I shouldn't write that way. All your letters are "nice" — think they cannot help but be. I am the only one subject to moods.

Do you hate me writing so often? It's such an awfully nice thing for me to be able to do. But maybe I'd better slow up. Tell me if you think it wiser & I'll curb my cavorting pen.

<u>Later</u>.

Well tonight I really

<u>Later again</u>.

I don't know when I began this. Anyway, it got stopped partly by a prolonged depression & partly by what seemed like a prolonged silence from your end. It was actually only 3 days — but in the state I was in, it seemed interminable. Anyhow 2 letters came today. What I want to say first is that one of my letters to you is missing. I wrote it the day before the one about the picture & in it I said "I've never felt better in my life." But I made the fatal mistake of sending the damn thing airmail & that usually delays rather than speeds it up. So remember. You've probably got it now — this is just in case. Anyway I can say what I said twice over now.

This is really the nicest time of the day: Did I tell you that yesterday, because I thought it yesterday. I get myself to bed with hotwaterbottle, glassofwarmmilk & onemorecigarette & a t t e n d t o m y c o r r e s p o n d e n c e. The first of the above-mentioneds is almost a necessity. The second the family think a necessity. The third a lousy extravagance. The fourth ——— a LUXURY: i.e. an even more necessary necessity.

Well I Govt. Housed in the hat. All well. Then I returned home & was given a picture of my love by my Pappa. A dreadful one at that, so dreadful in fact that I didn't recognize the guy & only discovered who it was after reading the cap.

Mr. G. after asking me out tonight found he'd got his wires crossed & had to cancel the date.

Darling don't go & get a mump. And if you do for pity's sake look after yourself. <u>Don't</u> get up too soon. It's almost conceit to feel I'm the only person who can look after you, but of course I feel it anyway.

Last night I had dinner with Mr. G. & returned to his place & yapped & listened to music with him. He <u>is</u> an extremely nice lad. I liked him a lot & apparently will be seeing a fair amount of him in the future. He seems anxious to give me the keys of the city.

Tonight I'm going to Dartmouth to have dinner with an old beau & his wife & children. How I shall smile with delight as I make my mental comparisons!

Thank you for Joe's address.

Everything is very quiet here. Your letters burst like bombs into the silence & the air is not still yet.

It seems very important to repeat the statement. which is always waiting to be spoken; which <u>is</u> spoken beneath the roar of the bath water, or into the pillow at night — & echoes of which & shades of which wander all over the letters I send you. Sometimes I want to get somewhere I [could] yell it.

Darling if you don't like your face then Hermes has botched you. And yes, how well I remember what you asked me — if you remember the question you did ask.

•

P.K. Page to F.R. Scott
June 24, 1944

I guess you've got to be tough to take this world — a whole lot tougher than I am & I'd better start learning right away. But how do I learn? Do I cut you out of me with a scalpel & pretend you never existed? I begin to think love is a bad thing. It doesn't make you strong. I seem to be going through some dreadful crisis that is worse than anything yet. It is partly you & partly other things — the other things are what have made me start thinking this way about you. It's a bit ironical, isn't it, that the thing that matters most to me is, through no fault of his own, the thing that makes me weakest. That is <u>my</u> fault, I know it.

If it were possible just to get the hell out with you — I'd do it without thinking twice.

Last night I went to Dartmouth for dinner. The ride in the ferry in the fog was wonderful & the smells got me very excited. Coming back it had cleared & the lights of Halifax were very bright & beautiful against the night. Lovers were all about the decks & I turned up my coat collar against the wind & felt very single & told myself I was a writer.

I found my old beau a beautifully reactionary Major & he & his wife called each other "dear" every minute & it all seemed rather odd. They talked about the younger generation having grown old before its time & how it was necessary to set a Jew to catch a Jew etc. We drank apricot brandy with our after dinner coffee & I felt very glad when I said goodbye & got on the toy bus to return.

In fact, there is no road back to the old life at all, at all.

This letter goes in stops & starts. Page 2 written yesterday. Then today 2 letters from you — one to L. with Poetry. And Mr. McGrath writes at the end of one of his poems "And love is never love — that cannot give love up." And I weigh his remark & try to get it down finer than that. That cannot give love up — for love? And if I <u>can</u> give it up would it be <u>for</u> love? No. Then do I not love? And who the hell is McGrath anyway?

I can't properly explain to you the condition I'm in — & perhaps that's just as well. Dear heart, I <u>do</u> miss you so. And I hate you being invaded by bugs of any kind — major or minor.

I wish I knew what had happened to the letter telling you how well I felt. Are you <u>sure </u>you didn't get it?

Don't let me ever doubt, will you. Not even if the worst has to be told. I get ragged & wretched as a dog with worms. And smack me hard for all this nonsense & tell me to grow up & be sensible. When I look at you you are very sane & tender. Are you when you read this?

I had a sort of feeling of a poem nosing about this afternoon. Tried it not very tentatively with one finger. (Block that metaphor!)

Am on the verge of going out with Myron again.

Prevailing conditions have made it impossible to get away before July

15th. Oh & by the way, don't bother sending mail to L. anymore. Its O.K. coming here.

•

P.K. Page to F.R. Scott
Monday, June 26, 1944

Hello. There is no news. Everything seems to be held at standstill. Atmospherics have something to do with it.

I spent yesterday at the "pin-money farm" of some of the city's richest. Really it was a fantastic day. About 20 of us were cooped up in front of a fire from about 11 until 6-ish. There was one good interlude when we went & saw the animals — bulls bigger than I knew they could grow — gargantuan beasts with horns you could hang a whole week's wash on. Pigs as big as ponies. A whole lot of gossiping chickens & some lovely gazelle-like horses.

I put them in a state of consternation by wanting to walk. They went everywhere by car. (not the animals!) Anyhow I walked & got very wet — everything smelled heavenly & I picked an armful of wild daisies.

Inside however it was ungodly. Yatter, yatter & only the mingiest drink to make us brighten up. They kept on at me about my writing — did I write wonderful books like Lloyd Douglas? Tell them the stories etc. Then came the visitors' book. Visiting author must write a poem for them. Visiting author could think of nothing except this which visiting author didn't write:

> The size of your house
> your pigs & your cows
> your turkeys & chickens
> were as big as the dickens.
> Even your wife
> was larger than life.
> Only the rye
> was a little shy.

Really it was a ludicrous day.
Went out with Myron again on Saturday. Funny lad, but very likeable.
No letter this mail. Had hardly expected it but am the most incorrigible hoper.

Beneath all these pigs & cows & things I'm fighting some kind of a big battle. If sometimes it spreads itself on to your territory you can always evacuate the battle area & remain strictly neutral. I think it overlapped rather nastily in my last letter. But there is a reason & that is that we've never marked our boundary line very carefully & there seems to be a largish area that we own jointly. I don't think I approached the remotest outskirts of your principal city! If I ever do you'll doubtless open fire & then I'll probably know I've trespassed & retreat.

Do you think maybe I could be a case of arrested development? <u>Seriously</u>.

D'you remember the poem that goes: (& I do not know who wrote it or part of the middle section)

When the small rain down does rain
...
Christ that my love were in my arms
And I in my bed again.

Vicarious living is a stinky thing isn't it? There must be thousands of people involved in it too. How can one expect masses of people to appreciate anything but identification movies when society makes such a mess of private lives.

What has happened to <u>Unit of Five</u> I can't imagine. No proofs even. I'm disgusted — have gone suddenly quite furious about it. "Now I really <u>am</u> mad," in fact. What's more there's nothing remotely about you among the poems included. Blast! But you're so difficult to write about. You go too deep for me to write nice lilting lyrics. If the day comes when I can write about you every word will have to be mined. I'll have to go right down into those terrific pits & bring the words up one by one. Darling darling you'll either make or break me. And that still hangs in the balance. I do so want not to be broken — even by you.

<u>Morning</u>.

It is nice today. Incredible! Also I feel I am approaching that almost mythical land of creative work. God if I could only write.

And now I want to talk to you — there are a lot of things I could tell you, one way or another.

•

P.K. Page to F.R. Scott
Wednesday, June 28, 1944

Wednesday.

darling, darling. Your wonderful red-letter letter has just arrived, all outflowingness & now I am a mass of you — veins full, head full. There is hardly any me left. And that is happiness. I would willingly be all you. If I had Kristin's chance I'd take it. She was just another escapist!

I am lying in my bathing suit on the porch wallowing in sun & writing — squint-eyed with it. There is nothing in the world I want at the moment but the all-clamouring, ever-present want. How I loved your windfall.

A letter from May today wanting to know all about that dreadful night. I don't know what to tell her. I feel I failed her terribly & its not a good feeling.

I went to a party with Myron again last night. I find a certain amount of comfort in Myron for some reason. He is a sensitive lad & very honest. He is off to the famous Peggy's Cove this week-end & wants me to join him. I'd quite like to go but doubt if I do. Next time I see him I shall ask him if he has any Scarlatti.

I can't understand about that letter. What goes on? It's hardly likely to be lost, is it? Anyhow I shall begin to number them.

I hold my face up to the sun & pretend its you. Sometimes my mouth seems to jut out with the need to kiss you, & it almost embarrasses me — for I feel it must be so apparent to everyone.

I had to stop this bango as the phone went & we were informed 2 Russian officers were arriving immediately. I dragged a sticky me into clothes at a terrible clip only to be reinformed that they weren't coming. It is now after dinner. Myron has just phoned to say he's going to drop some books in.

Its funny that there should be gaps at the end of the week. Your gaps are at the beginning. Mondays & Tuesdays are horrors. Specially as they follow up Sundays.

I have on your what-nots & they tell me I have gained weight. Inevitable I suppose, but unpleasant. The family simply pump milk into me & I must say my strange ferris wheel inside seems better for it.

I am writing a little again, but as if for the first time. It is very, very different. There is nothing I do or say or think that doesn't seem to stem from you.*

How many more sittings for the head? I wish I could see it. Wouldn't H. be surprised if she knew.

I believe people could die of loneliness & broken hearts & such-like fancy things.

*There is no virtue in that & no stability. Somehow I must learn the dreadful lesson of independence. But once learned then what? Is it possible for any relationship to exist between 2 completely independent people? Or am I talking in absolutes? I must be, of course. For biologically complete independence is impossible.

I'm sorry to write rot.

•

P.K. Page to F.R. Scott
Friday, June 30, 1944

Friday
<u>1x1</u> has just arrived. Lambie-pie how swell of you. I have been gobbling it up & not understanding but getting the feeling & going back & regobbling & understanding better & all in all feeling it's my birth day or yours or something. Cummings seems to be a sort of carrier pigeon flying back & forth between us.

I have decided to leave here on the 14th & that is definite. Will arrive at New River the same day — or night rather — if I can connect with a bus. I'm quite excited about it. From now on I'm going to try to work like stink on the histories to make enough money to coast for the rest of the summer. Have made 45 bucks to date without much effort. All I need to see me for the entire summer is about $200 so it ought to be easy. God how nice it is not to be at an office!

It would be wonderful if work was bringing you East instead of taking you West.

Do you think you look a little like mr. e.e. cummings because I do. He's a sort of rougher-tougher version.

Today I have cocktail party which fills me with cold dread. I deserve it — shouldn't get in these situations. I shall drink 2 drinks if I get chance & leave. One for you & one for me & the departure for us both.

Mr. Galloway is a very unpolitical young man who believes in ART. He tells me my ideas are very young. He says individuals are what matter & I agree with him, but he can't see how its possible for me to agree on that point & still contend that a social awareness is vital. He has a sense of intellectual superiority which almost completely isolates him. He refuses to allow that anyone who can not appreciate Beethoven is worth keeping alive. We drive rapiers into each other but neither winces — neither is convinced. It's easy to see what has made him as he is & he's at least honest about it.

e.e. cummings' name on the book is almost a reverse of your signature inside. In fact there are a lot of strange things about that book!

This, at this sitting won't be much more than a goodnight. Today I had mail from Hermes & Bruce, both of whom gave me little tiny bits of news about you, which made their letters more important than they knew.

I have just walked miles around the Park & I really mean miles. The sea smelled of the sea & the pines of the pines & now I am weary. But weary or no I could do with the good solid reality of you — your sweetness & your funny remoteness which was sometimes almost an agonizing inaccessibility & such a terrific contrast to the other you which was, as I think I told you once, only comparable to being enclosed in a swarm of warm, live almost imaginary birds — imaginary, because super-birds — & completely protected by them. Magnify that feeling & then you are the seraph I told you of. How silly this all sounds & how inadequate. Nowhere near as adequate in fact as the letters on fences spelling MARY LOVES ERIC.

•••

Dorothy Livesay to Duncan Macnair
Wednesday, May 12, 1937
age 27

Good Morning Dearest,

You may thank his majesty for this letter — mainly being written to drown out the sound of other people's radios!

The front line is holding its own. I haven't a minute what with doing all your work plus mine…or did I ever have any? Jack M and I have finally got the Green Apple Pie for T. to speak in (that's a restaurant, not a symbol) and are, you can guess how busy, telling people. And George has written a very funny radio play which the CBC would never use — so the NF Club is putting it on as a curtain raiser to T's talk.

Which points out that George is still with us. Though we had a good turnout last night, with some new material, those absent were conspicuous — Vernon, James and John. Prentice and I got locked in the building, as I was persuading him to take on the subs, which he has agreed to — but Pete to the rescue for your sake and then King turned up or rather down from the top floor with the necessary keys. (Hope you follow the sequence of events). Anyhow I was home at 12, and just nicely in bed when there was a tap on the door. The foolish virgin thought it was DCM — and leaped to open. There stood James and John, very bashfully holding out an armful of books of mine, from Vernon. James was completely floored when I told him, in answer to his question, that we had had a good meeting and that George was there and was made a member of the Ed. Board. In fact they both shouted "George was there?" incredulously. So there must have been some dirty working going on. I left them still gaping and anxious to come down to T's meeting…

Mr Newman is taking over the lumber co's for us and I believe will do the job speedily. Pete came to dinner and told me his life history…i.e. about the kids not being his etc. That explains, to me, why there is such a curious relationship between them and him — apparently an unconscious one. That also gives me another example of your broad capacity for keeping things dark…Ah yes, my dear, I see there is some rankling in me still.

Perhaps there isn't enough sunshine here. It rained old bones all week-end, and now today is cloudy. Speak to me of the sun!

Am going to Madge's for lunch, then on to Pete's. They send their commiserations to you. Pete says you have to have worked three days before getting compensation…but can't they cook it up?

The YMCA think that job you mentioned in your first letter might be a good thing to hang on to, and suggest that you keep up a correspondence, implying that you might consider the offer. They are keenly interested to hear of your success.

As for me, even T., whom I met yesterday, asked after my writing, and congratulated me on the articles I had sent to the paper last year, on my way out here. He is a darling, with an impish humour which is most attractive. Sorry you seem to miss everybody…Keep my address in your pocket in case you fall down unconscious somewhere — O my dear humorist, your most loving

Dee

Later. (8.30) Home to find two letters under my door. Dear, I miss you most painful…The month ahead seems interminable, now that the campfires and the singing of girls is gone. Now that I cannot talk to you, or touch...Oh, hurry, hurry, hurry, you old limping month of June!

The hills are full of your voice — but the city is empty. Tell me your full heart.

I have not real news, dear one. But Lon [Lawson] has sent me some excitement. He has found a new voice — Margaret Day from Montreal. Another woman — an Emily Dickinson in our midst? Listen?

Ode to Spring.....1937

Jackal, cormorant and kite,
You ranging in embraced division
Prevent effectively my flight.
No peace just now — bombs rain from heaven.

[...]

There are two others — equally, or more, metaphysical — too long to quote. It is not the sort of thing you like best, but it is right down my alley. She has an amazing piece of imagery about her "four-in-hand" — Marx, Engels, Blake and Lawrence...Duncan, loved one, I think we have found something!

And ALL RIGHT. Tim was born in England. But he was reared here and he considers himself a Canadian. I expect you are in league with Mecredy to prove that there can be no native born leaders rising in such a raw country. So be it.

Up in a rock crevice I spent most of my day. Shall we have Deep Coves again? All my love to you, heart's heart. Blessings on the work and the fingers.
Dearest, your own Dee

•

Duncan Macnair to Dorothy Livesay
Hedley, BC
May 14th, 1937

My Beloved One,
6:30 in the morning and the sun is barely peeping over the hill tops and here am I writing to you at this early hour. The method of operating your life

varies a bit as you get out into the wilderness, and at last I am conforming to medical advice and going to bed by 10 p.m. A slight but necessary variation of custom. We arise before 6 o'clock and accordingly the working man is ready to hop into his bunk at 10 p.m. and it would be unfair of me to keep a light burning after that hour — (even if the other occupants of the tent would permit it.)

Your fat letter cheered me up wonderfully yesterday. Father Livesay's Report doesn't faze me greatly — the process is a perfectly normal one in Capitalist Society, as you well know, but why don't these fellows follow through to the inevitable end, however far off that may be. Anyway, I get the impression that Father Livesay is tremendously proud of his accomplishments and his Report. Is that likely to be correct?

Am interested in all the details of T's meeting and am well acquainted with the Green Apple Pie, from the outsider's or spectator's viewpoint. Be sure to let me know who all turns up to the meeting and if possible send up George's playlet, together with the cast of the performing artists.

I'm willing to believe there was dirty work with Vernon and the other youths. Don't think it advisable to push James and John too hard – they will work away from V. in due course, but do treat them with every courtesy and consideration.

So Pete unveiled more of his life's history. When he told me of the children some 6 months ago he imposed silence which (in my opinion) included even yourself. It certainly clarifies the relationship between Pete and the kids. I understand the children don't know that Pete isn't their daddy. Your little pet Lamb, my Heart, is no monument of discretion, but you know the difficulties that Pete and Griffin can raise through their inordinate desire to tell everything they know. You know, my One, once or twice I've been tempted to mention Pete's family to you, because it would have helped to clear up a puzzling point, but strangely enough it never crossed my mind that the easiest way was for Pete himself to tell you. Was Pete surprised that I hadn't told you?

Certainly I'm willing to keep up my acquaintance with the Secret Service people, but I feel kind of puzzled as to what would happen when they start inquiring for references. Anyway, I shall jockey them along in the meantime but not too hurriedly.

Glad you had a word of commendation from T. but don't commiserate with me because I seem to miss everybody. Dear Heart, <u>I don't</u>. If you will refer to a poem called "The Outsider" you will discover (provided you happen to be sufficiently versed in philosophy) that it is sometimes necessary to send out scouts, and scouts are as necessary a post of the Army as even Field Marshals. Communication is not irrevocably broken because the outsider is out of touch with H.Q. for a few weeks.

Anent the opening up of a Bookstore in Victoria I strongly disagree with my impetuous friends Dee and Lon. The time is not ripe unless you are unconditionally prepared to lose money and spend enormous effort. You are much better carrying on with Social Service work. Some few days ago, you will recollect, George let a vociferous cat out of the voluminous bag when he asked you when the N.F. was going to pay for contributions. Apparently Lawson had visions of doing this within a year of starting publications. May I venture to enter a strong disclaimer? This sort of thing is on a par with Jim's perpetual promises that a world war will start next month. At the present time you are bloody well performing a bloody labour of love and you had better bloody well realise it. That's my poetic realism.

The possibility of merging with the Forum comes as rather a surprise. I don't think Lawson is capable of working in a subordinate capacity and it wouldn't be long before there was a display of pyrotechnics — with Lon on the outside.

If you don't agree with me, don't be afraid to say so — life is a dialectic process, and, as Homer sometimes nods — so does the Great Infallible occasionally nap. Remember my boners regarding Jack M. and his entry into the YMCA.

Already I'm losing my fine touch regarding the Political situation. I feel pessimistic about CCF chances. Don't see a sure thing anywhere, not even in Hastings E. Gretchen may make it, and possibly Colin Cameron and A.M. With regard to A.M., I am so biased that I have much more hope than knowledge. At the present moment I wouldn't bet on more than 3 seats.

Was in Hedley yesterday evening seeing the plumber and he won't let me work before Monday at the earliest and possibly Wednesday. The finger is healing splendidly but it would be folly to attempt work in a mass of oil and grease and foul water before the breach is closed.

These notes are pretty scrappy, My Love — evidently I'm not wearing my thinking cap these days — merely recording outside impressions. Am anxious to get to work.

Climbed to the top of the mountain yesterday afternoon and was overjoyed to see the new small flowers blossoming. I'm told this place will be a picture bye and bye. Glorious sunshine this morning again but still comparatively cool at this altitude.

The mail is going out now, so Cheerio! My Love,
                              Heart and Love to you, My
                                    Dorothy Beloved
                                        Aye Your
                                           Duncan

                              Keep a stiff upper lip !!
                                  Reiterate !
                                    Reiterate !!
                                      Reiterate !!!

...

Raymond Knister to Myrtle Gamble
Northwood, Ontario
December 3, 1927
age 28

Dear Myrtle:

Got your train letter yesterday morning (Fri). You do seem to be having a real holiday, all right. Astonishing to hear of riding in your grandfather's cutter. We've had no snow here to amount to anything, and the sleighs have laid in the yard in the mud for a month. Yesterday the mail man wasn't expected, but got here with two horses on a buggy, — and your letter. Hope he comes today. Did you get my letters and the parcels I mentioned?

Thursday afternoon we hauled manure, but the fields would be ruined now if we went on them with a wagon. Marjorie keeps hunting papers and listening to the radio in hopes of hearing of cold weather. If it turns cold Clarence may come today, but it can't now. She's to spend New Years with his people. Last night I told her to stop reading or C. would think her eyes were pink from weeping. She offered me the last of his 2-lb box of chocolates, first enquiring if her eyes were pink, I said no her nose. Then she asked if it was going to turn cold. I said yes. Then when I had the chocolate I said that her nose was not pink but red, and that it was turning to a cold rain with sleet, and strong east wind. She pretended great wrath. Anyway it's as mild and mucky as ever today (Sat).

I go to bed from 12 to 2:50 and rise about as late as usual. Have weird dreams, with you as one of the characters. Last night I was waiting for somebody and took a streetcar to have a jaunt around the city. Went out to a big depot, got off, tried to get a car to take me back to the city, and it was all flooded, and there was a river. I saw a big sedan with three boys in it scooting through the river, upheld by the balloon tires, though the water was up around the boys' necks. Finally I got over the river and through manifold barriers I reached the city again (Detroit, I think) and found you. A happy ending anyway. Expect to make it come true one of these times.

Yours ever, Raymond

x x x x X

PS — How's the money holding out? Shall I send some?

•

Raymond Knister to Myrtle Gamble
Northwood, Ontario
January 3, 1928

Darling Girl:

Your letters just arrived this morning, there was no mail yesterday, and it seemed a long time from Fri to Tues. I am sorry we couldn't have been together Christmas and New Year. I am getting along pretty well with the book. I have only four more authors to read. One of them is Roberts and he has a dozen books. May see him however and ask him what one he'd rather have in.

In regard to going to Toronto, I think I had better get my Introduction written and have the whole thing about ready to hand in when I go. That will make it about the first of next week. I don't think you had better come until I write or call you from Toronto. The first thing I'll have to do is raise some money, and then we'll know what we want to do. Perhaps take an apt. there, or perhaps return here and write a novel. I would prefer to be in Toronto, of course, or some place where we can have a place of our own.

Yes, you made me think of you New Year's Eve. I was sure of it. Did you know you dated one of your letters May 30? Your people seem to have no end of presents for you, and love with them. Wish I could have seen your grandfather and the other relatives. I surely appreciate the presents for me but of course they seem nothing compared to the marvellous soul which God caused to grow among them, and which they kept all those years — for me. Tell your dad I want to get some of those rum-running stories. I have a new idea. Perhaps my taxi novel might be split off in the middle — if the hero is adventurous, and he might take up rum-running.

Can't write a real letter, as we are in the throes of getting ready to go to town. Mail just arrived about eleven. As usual we are getting off about 12. I took the spark plugs out of the old bus, so hope it will be better. (May mention that I put the mail again too).

I hope we'll see each other in a few days. I'll write again tonight. Mail this in Chatham.

> Best and heartiest new years wishes to all your folks.
> Raymond
> x x X

•••

E. Pauline Johnson, 1889
age 28

Close By

So near at hand (our eyes o'erlooked its nearness
In search of distant things)
A dear dream lay — perchance to grow in dearness
Had we but felt its wings
Astir. The air our very breathing fanned
It was so near at hand.

Once, many days ago, we almost held it,
The love we so desired;
But our shut eyes saw not, and fate dispelled it
Before our pulses fired
To flame, and errant fortune bade us stand
Hand almost touching hand.

I sometimes think had we two been discerning,
The by-path hid away
From others' eyes had then revealed in its turning
To us, nor led astray
Our footsteps, guiding us into love's land
That lay so near at hand.

So near at hand, dear heart, could we have known it!
Throughout those dreamy hours,
Had either loved, or loving had we shown it,
Response had sure been ours;
We did not know that heart could heart command,
And love so near at hand!

What then availed the red wine's subtle glisten?
We passed it blindly by,
And now what profit that we wait and listen
Each for the other's heart beat? Ah! the cry
Of love o'erlooked still lingers, you and I
Sought heaven afar, we did not understand
'Twas — once so near at hand.

•••

Myna Wallin to Richard ⸻
November 26, 1988
age 28

Dear Richard,
    "...And after the summer if we get back together even though things might somehow be different I hope the happiness can continue, and you will remain the one and only love of my life."...words you wrote on May 14.
    I am still reeling over last Wednesday night. It was an incredibly bizarre, erotic, passionate-beyond-words-encounter. The sex was blazingly hot, fiercely loving. You see, no words could capture it. Well, you were there, certainly you felt it too.
    Where do we go from here? I can only say how I feel. I can't second guess what you want. I feel...I want to go out with you: I want to be with you. Like

a moth to a flame. I know it could be painful…that we might last two nights or two months…nothing matters.

There's something I want to explain. I was seeing someone over the last two months because I thought it was the best thing for me. I hoped I would forget you and heal from our breakup if I could fall in love with someone else. It backfired, though. It only made me miss you more toward the end. Anyway, it's over now.

Richard, you may need and want something different than what you wanted last May. But if it is still me that makes your heart jump, if it's still thoughts of me that make you cry, if it's still me that thrills you in bed… then don't let your pride or fear or even your confusion keep us apart. I love you in spite of all of it.

There is something between us that you also talked about in your May letter, that "kindred spirit of sorts that can be childlike in quality in its joy and needs in life." Believe it or not, I understand that, and feel it too.

Something inside me has shifted deeply. I no longer want to control fate, mine or yours. If we are meant to be together in the grand scheme of things… if our love is powerful enough to withstand all the pain and confusion.

It may sound awfully romantic, but I'm going to trust that our destinies will be fulfilled. No one has ever understood me when I told them how close you and I were, and I think that's because very few people ever glimpse that kind of a connection. It encompasses love and friendship and sexuality and a "spiritual" connectedness that is almost scary in its intensity. Maybe that's what you meant when you talked about "losing yourself."

Whatever happens, I want you to know I never really wanted to hurt you and I know you never meant to hurt me. (We both just got restimulated a lot, right?) If we could set aside our pride, our fear, our heaps of distress… perhaps we could well and truly love one another.

Was Wednesday night just one of those things, was it the almost-full moon, was it just lust, or maybe it was more. You tell me. Do you want to go out now and again? Do you want to give us another chance?

To quote (you!) from a sentiment close to my heart, "I hope that we are meant to get back together."

I have a hard time imagining my life without you.

I love you,

Myna

•••

Robert Service to Constance MacLean
December 10, 1902
age 28

My dear Miss Constance

What were you driving at anyway? Your letter gave me the greatest surprise and pleasure; but its contents completely mystified me. What ode do
you refer to? Has someone been sending you poetry? Lucky beggar to have
pleased you so, and lucky me to get the credit. Beastly jolly hard on the other
fellow, don't you know though. I think you had better make some more
inquires and find out who really is the perpetrator of the stuff. Meantime I
am grateful to him for your most delightful letter, the nicest, I assure you, I
have received for many a day.

All being well I am going to the Chemainus affair. I don't miss much, I'm
sorry to say. I swore I was not going out any more this winter; but I can't help
myself. You see I'm due to pass the medical matric. at McGill in June next
and at the rate I am studying I'm going to come an unholy Croppex. And
now I hear the dramatic club want me to take part in their theatricals of the
14th January — got a part they say that would suit me to perfection — some
vacuous individual I expect that gets kicked around. I am good at expressing
vacuity. By the way you do me the great honour in crediting me with brains.
They don't rise much beyond fishing and shooting, and apart from my enthusiasm for these, I am one of the dullest fellows imaginable. I am sure you
are clever, though — that "intangible indefinite something" fairly bowled
me over, by Jove. You have a certain quaint humour too which tickles me.
On Monday last in Duncan, I saw the <u>back only</u> of a girl as I came up behind
her. She wore a light fawn sacque jacket and was most neatly skirted and
booted, and looked so trim and nice. Was it you? I did not go to the King's
Daughter's jamboree. I felt bored, and was afraid I might yawn. Instead I
settled down to construe some Ovid (beastly muck) and ended up by playing ping pong and listening to a gramophone (I should like to play you at
ping pong). I heard the concert was very good. I was asking about your
playing — your classical masterpiece — and was informed you "had done
a <u>two step</u> or something." I am sure I would have appreciated it. I heard also

a lady recite "The Road to Heaven." I think I should have been much more interested if it had been The Road to — well, you know.

Many thanks for writing and telling me your Christian name. I shan't forget it. Meantime I will look forward to Friday evening and don't forget to reserve me some waltzes. So for the present: "auf wiedersehen."

From Yours most Cordially

Robert W. Service

By the way did someone (dash his cheek, anyway) really send you some verses or are you only fooling?

•

Robert Service to Constance MacLean
605 Cambie Street, Vancouver, British Columbia
August 15, 1903

My dearest Connie:

I accept the position and the penalty. I would have written to tell you this before but I have been kept on the strain with examinations and had little time. When I left you there was little doubt in my mind what course I should pursue. You have raised me one and it's up to me to cover. I will <u>never</u> give you up now — after you have spoken to me the way you did. You have given me what I badly wanted, a dressing down, and an ideal, and I believe by your words you have changed my whole character. I bless you for it and I worship you for it, and I will try to show by the best that's in me that it has gone deep. I mean to follow the path you indicated. I will do my utmost to work myself through the university. It may take a long time, and in the end I fear I may lose you; but I will have the ethical value of the struggle, and I will always hope, and if I succeed in retrieving myself in your eyes I will not have laboured in vain. You have taught me my lesson, dear, and I realize its value.

I have decided to go on with the Arts course here; the work is exactly the same as that at McGill and will keep me busy. Nothing I have ever heard or read impressed me more than your simple words on the Gospel of Work. No more pleasures, no more society; I mean to follow your ideal, and take it out of myself. Nothing can exceed the bitterness of my realization of the folly of my careless past. I suppose it is criminal to deliberately slay one's better self and my nemesis has overtaken me. But though I have been an easygoing spendthrift I have always kept certain ideals pure and one is my faith in the redeeming nature of romance. You say a woman should not influence a man's career. Love is the noblest incentive we have. You do not set a high enough value on yourself if you think a man who loves you should not weave you into the fabric of his life with every thread. I cannot help thinking of you more or less even when I am most busy; I cannot help thinking of you when I am talking to other women, and when I read a book the heroine somehow takes your image. I thought I saw you on the street the other day: my heart beat as though it would burst and I trembled all over. These physical manifestations are a painful evidence of my complete subjugation. I do not yet know my plan of action but it seems obvious that I had better keep on studying and let things develop. I may have to teach for a year or two, and I certainly expect to be up against it but I love you, I idealize you, and I will never give you up. I won't likely see you, and I won't try to speak to you till you wish; but I <u>must</u> write sometimes. Please suffer me.

I hope, dear, when you are assured of the sincerity of my endeavours and of my humility you will remove the excommunication. However long you see fit to punish me I will accept it as what I deserve but I hope patiently.

Yours with undying love
Robert W. Service

•

Robert Service to Constance MacLean
605 Cambie St.,Vancouver, British Columbia
September, 1903

My dear dear Love

Your <u>terrible</u> letter knocked the bottom out of my universe. You spent some time and trouble over that letter, Connie, and though it knocked me over I must admit it was <u>grand</u>. And it was true on the main and I deserved it all and a great deal more. Ever since, I have painfully been trying to look at things from your point of view, and I have succeeded so far that God knows how I despise myself. Now, I am not going to spare myself. I was a <u>cad</u> to write you that letter; and I am more sorry than ever I can say. Sorry! It seems late in the day to be sorry, doesn't it. I hope it isn't too late though.

Connie I've made a frightful hash of things between us two, and all through my own [illegible] priggish folly. I have deliberately undermined myself in your regard, and the result is an experience to which a surgical operation is a joke. However scathing your self-reproaches they cannot equal mine. You have handed me out my medicine, and it was no more than what was coming to me. You have given me the lesson of my life. Now, I think I will try to show you that I am worth my salt, that is if you will give me another chance. And I beg and plead for that chance as never I begged for anything before. Connie don't forget I have loved you deeply, truly, passionately and tenderly and I love you now so very, very much that you are all in all my life to me, as I have never loved anyone before and never will again. It was the most ghastly punishment for me to come here and receive that letter and you may imagine the state of mind I have been in ever since. My mind has been in a state of chaos. My dearest, don't say it is hopeless for pity's sake — have mercy and forgive. There is much to say that I will say when I see you. If it's utterly, utterly hopeless I think I will go home, and wipe B.C. and those miserable wasted years off the slate. But if you can throw out a ray of hope for me Connie I will try to show you I am worthy. You must not dream of [illegible] anything (if I could only blot out the stain on my manhood of that wretched letter). I would never, never touch anything I have once given you. If they are to be destroyed you must do it. You have talked awfully straight Connie and fancy will make me buck up your letter's will. I will come along on Thursday afternoon as soon as I can (I believe I have an exam on till 4). Remember I come penitent, humbled, and that you have already meted out a better punishment for me. So spare me, my Love and have pity. For I now only hold you dearer than ever and I cannot live without you. O my Queen, my fairest, forgive me, and give me another chance. I will be so different and I will show you that I can make myself worthy of you. I will come to take my medicine but don't make it bitter dear for already I have been half distracted.

      Yours
      Bob

•

Robert Service to Constance MacLean
605 Cambie Street, Vancouver, British Columbia
September 29, 1903

Dearest Connie

Remembering that tomorrow is your birthday I venture to wish you
many happy returns. I have always been expecting to see you sometimes
on the street but I have never had that luck. I saw Ethel at the "Burgomaster"
last night. It was <u>awfully</u> good. I am afraid that your method of punishing
me is going to put me in a bad way. You are never out of my mind. Good as
was the play last night it was you I was thinking of all the time, and the day
when I was privileged to sit there with you. I cannot read at all; I scarcely
eat anything; and though I do not show it half the time I am desperate with
misery. Shall I tell you what occurred this evening? Will it give you some
satisfaction to know how you are making me suffer? I came home feeling
terribly blue. Then I fell to thinking of you and by and by to reading over
some of your letters. I should not have done it. A queer feeling came over me,
an agony of loss. I could not help myself. I suppose it was want of nervous
control, but I broke down utterly. I threw myself down on my bed and cried
like a woman. It was an odd sort of cry, a sort of convulsive sobbing that
came from the chest and shook my whole body. I was afraid the landlady
would hear me so I buried my head deep in the pillow. It was a kind of
hysterics, I think. I remember a friend of mine once acting that way when I
broke the death of his father to him. It was painful to see and I think even
you would have pitied me just then. This fit lasted for nearly half an hour I
should fancy. It was a new experience. I have always boasted I did not know
how to cry but you have taught me. I expect you will despise me still more
for this manifestation of weakness; but it shows you the supreme success of
your course of [illegible]. O you girls know how to be cruel. I have already
suffered enough. I have repented in sack cloth and ashes for that letter. You
know how it was written. I was mad with jealousy at the time. Someone
had just told me you had been corresponding with two other [illegible]
fellows, and on the top of that last letter of yours I believed them. Besides
that awful road-work had got on my nerves. I was bluffing to you when I
pretended I liked that. I loathed it. The degradation of it ate into my soul.
So the letter came to be written and I would cut off my hand if I could recall
it. Well, I suppose it's all over now. I have wrecked myself as far as you are

concerned. I feel so heartsick discouraged and desperate. And yet I know I'll never give you up, for I waited so long for you. What I wanted to write about particularly is this: I have had bad news from home. My mother is ill and if she gets much worse I will be obliged to return, possibly in about three weeks' time. I hope it won't be necessary but fear it will. However I will let you know about a week before I go, and I trust in the Goodness of your heart you will allow me to spend a few hours in your society.

> Meantime Goodbye dear Connie
> Yours with undying love
> Robert Service

•

Robert Service to Constance MacLean
Undated

I think your letter was a <u>mistake</u>. Did you really mean it? Because if you did you have <u>hurt me</u> dreadfully. I would have answered it before but I have been ill a week with Lagrippe. I never thought you would so <u>humiliate</u> me as to ask me to explain what are <u>palpably falsehoods</u>. I <u>disdain</u> to do it. I think I know how to act like a gentleman. But you might tell your correspondents with their "very personal" they are <u>mean</u> <u>hearted liars</u> and <u>stupid</u>, to boot. And refer them to <u>me</u>. O the baseness of it! To try and poison a girl's mind towards the man who loves her more than life — and with <u>lies</u>. How I loathe such despicable machinations. Your allegations filled me with amazed contempt. And <u>you</u> — how could you <u>credit</u> them? I don't know what's getting into you but there's something strange, different about you lately. What is the matter? As for talk — it seems to me any talk is about you and [illegible] — I am supposed to be thrown over. How <u>providentially</u> [illegible] happened to be in Vancouver last week. How is it I hear all about you from <u>outside sources</u>? Why can't <u>you</u> tell me? Everyone has his rights and one of mine is to believe in the girl you love and trust her — <u>till the blow falls</u>. So <u>I believe in you and trust you</u>. Because if the blow ever does fall it will <u>crush</u> us badly. I'm different from most men you see. Love is all in all to me. Did you ever realize what it would be to break a man's heart, ruin his life, and damn his soul? Would your own be very happy? If you did that, Connie, God forgive you. There's a drawing back for me now; you should have checked me long ago if you wanted to. You say my last letter made you cry. You women are lucky in being able to cry. Sometimes during the past week, between the mental misery <u>you</u> have caused me, and the physical misery of the suffering, <u>I have wished myself dead</u>. I <u>must see</u> you. I can't very well afford it just now and the trip will likely cause a fresh attack of Lagrippe, but I can't get any satisfaction from your letters, so I'm coming over. When you get this I'll be in Victoria. I'll see you on <u>Saturday afternoon</u>. Till then — Goodbye —

The enclosed photo may interest you. I set some value on it as it is all I have left to remind me of California days. I got it taken in San Diego for a quarter, finished and mounted in five minutes. My inside pockets are bulging with books and papers. It is a tough looking case. My face is almost black with the sun and has a hard-bitten look; but I had real grit in those days and I was game for anything — my great idea was to get to the South Seas and marry a native princess. After you have seen this you might just shove it away among my other papers.

...

Roy Kiyooka to Monica Dealtry Barker
Calgary, Alberta
Feb 28, 1955
age 29

Dearest Monica:
    A bonus today! Two letters from you waiting for me when I got home. By now, nearly 12 p.m., they have been read many times. In between I have been finishing up a largish painting begun a few days ago. Mother and child theme, which comes closest to the real thing of any painting yet of this theme. It's terribly difficult to talk about it though.
    It surely is a mystery how a letter, mere scrawled words, can elicit such profound sympathies and inexhaustibly bind two people together.
    Sending along the small painting and the rest, hose, radio etc to follow. Will attend to them Wednesday afternoon.
    You mention you find my printing very hard to read, well my writing is no damn better so I will continue with printing because it is much easier to me, besides, part of the charm of my printing is its incomprehensiveness. My banality would be exposed if I were lucid in writing and thought.

I shall have to cut this letter short, it is nearly one a.m. and work plus school plus painting have just about drained me. There are only 2 more classes left, hooray! Know that I am impatient to be with you and only loiter til the moment is more opportune. I should have eight hundred plus at the end of March and already am planning my departure. Intend to go home about the 15th of March to pick up my brother's car.

All my love, Good night

Roy

•

Roy Kiyooka to Monica Dealtry Barker
Calgary, Alberta
March 1, 1955

Dearest Monica:

Radio, plus stockings, plus ashtrays, hope they reach you intact. Though I listened to it infrequently it served me well and should do the same for you. The only programs I heard with any regularity were: Anthology, Tuesday 10.30 P.M; Nocturne, 11.30 P.M., Thursday; and N.Y. Symphony, Sunday at 1 P.M. all over C.B.C., of course. Only one pair of hose (you just can't get two pairs for a dollar anywhere) instead of the two you asked for because you did not state size nor shade and I just took a guess, will send more if you give me data. Hope they fit! And the ashtrays, just try and find ordinary functional ashtrays without some crude joke or corny decor on them. Anyhow they are the nicest I could find, such a wonderful green! I expect you to decorate your room around them! As for other things you mentioned, I shall do some investigating for them and let you know.

Those colour samples you enclosed, did you want some paint or what?

I should think $35.00 per. reasonable for the suite you have, very much so when you consider I pay the same for my dingy room. I just mention this because you mentioned the rent twice, as though it may be extravagant.

As for painting, I think you should by all means. Try using a high back chair on which to prop your canvas. It works quite satisfactorily though it may require some hunching over. [...]

The painting in process I mentioned last time (mother & child) is nagging at me, won't let me be. There is something wrong with it and I just can't put my finger on it.

Heaven knows how many times I have read and reread your letter in which you speak of us and your parents. I thank you from the bottom of my heart for your utter frankness and am humbled that you should think so well of me. I hope that you shall always think of me the same light though fully realizing the difficulty of constancy. It seems to me that you are overly concerned about your relationship to your parents and blame yourself too much. This is altogether more admirable than blaming them or others for the tragedy of it all, but a breach was inevitable and there is always the hope of eventual reconciliation. So keep in touch with them, know that they will get along, but put them aside periodically and immerse yourself completely in the moment's activity.

And you love me because of my strength and I love you because of God knows what. It is a mystery quite impenetrable but beautiful. If there is a simple explanation, I suppose it is because you are a woman. Know that strength is, I believe, an inherent characteristic and not acquired, though completely relative and like many things prone at times to fluctuate. There is no need to assert our wants, a sensitivity arising out of mutual affection should make us aware of each other's desires & needs, is this not so rather than what you mention? You know that I have never presumed other than the fact that we would live in equality, it never occurred to me that it should be otherwise. I hope I do not sound as though I wish to make an issue of things. I really do not and couldn't care less for I am completely happy in the knowledge that you are waiting for me and I, I am so impatient to be with you.

All my Love
Roy

•

Roy Kiyooka to Monica Dealtry Barker
Calgary, Alberta,
March 6, 1955

Dearest Monica:
Saturday was "Bay Day"! Now generally I avoid sales like the plague. It is because I know that there are very few so called bargains and all the effort and crush to attain them are not worth the bother. But this day I was tempted to venture into the crushing mass with but one view in mind, that I

should purchase for you a suitable garment to keep your bottom warm. Thus the pyjamas, men's to be sure and not at all figure flattering, but I thought none the less suitable for the purpose. Do you agree? If not you could write me a suitably indignant letter telling me why. I was tempted to wander into the lingerie dept for something more akin to what you asked for, but upon noting the density of wildly gesticulating women, I lost courage and turned away. You will understand I hope!

Most every where one turns we are warned of the possible conflicts inherent in a marriage of two people both intent upon a career as a necessary adjunct to fulfilling their respective lives. There is possibly a certain amount of truth in this and not to be denied. This, so we are told, is all the more so if the interests and careers are divergent and the whole can be catastrophic if the wife makes more than her husband. (Dollars is what they are referring to). All well and good and fraught with danger if a much larger scope and significance is not bore in mind. I am certain that we possess common sympathies and there is a common ground from which our respective interests spring. Each should interpenetrate and give nourishment to the other. I long ago assumed in our relationship that due to the nature of your interests you will as a result, make more dough than I and I should surely be barking up the wrong tree if I tried to compete economic-wise in this respect.

However, in this regard I know you are as aware of these things as I. I merely mention them because they should be faced squarely and viewed as hard cold facts. In the larger sense I initially mentioned, anything is important and should be paramount to our mutual love for each other and making the most of our potentialities and in this way enhancing our relationship. Someone once wisely noted that to a woman life and herself are an unfolding (you open always petal by petal myself as Spring opens — E.E. cummings) whereas a man it is discovering, the seeking out of his elusive other self. You do understand? though somehow I have not expressed myself too well in the above. You could mention if I might be wrong here or if you are in accord! [...]

All my Love
Roy

•

Roy Kiyooka to Monica Dealtry Barker
Calgary, Alberta
March 8, 1955

Dearest Monica:

What is the position of an artist passionately fond of his art, his girl and life, confronted by a society alien to his ways (he has not met them half ways probably), incapable of refuting the lie of security though aware that it cannot be bought, whose generalities about love bring the wrath of the almighty down upon his head, though the awesome mystery of the thing is quite beyond his mere comprehension and thus could not be specified. Who is told to look for his beloved's individuality, to root it out, as inexplicable as it may be, to him and herself though full well knowing that this quality was the first impact, and the reason for all that has happened. Well, "there is only one position for an artist anywhere, and that is upright" (to quote the late great Welsh poet Dylan Thomas).

It has been hanging fire, though we had many times over talked about it and I had taken it for granted that it should be thus. So I shall show you how we can do it with neither of us capitulating, though it should be bore in mind, that our love will require for sustenance some selflessness. Now you know that Nelson meant architecture and must perceive that I surely have been completely aware of what it means to you. This I mention because you insist so much on the job and its importance to you as though I wish to usurp it and you know this is truly not so — I do love you very much and I shall come to Nelson sometime early April in spite of slippery roads, poor pay etc. I wait this long because I wish to have the majority of the money I require and will make up the small difference in the Summer months there. We will marry in Nelson and stay there, you at your beloved job and I whatever it may be.

We will be together and love and laugh & cry and get to know & understand, to share in common interests & menial chores and all the other things and in the early Autumn, late July or early August I shall head for Mexico. You could join me there at Xmas for a long holiday. In the Spring of the following year I will come back and together we could seek our fortune (nonmonetary) there or here or any what place we choose. So this is my plan, crudely wrought and wanting in adequate expression. You will have your job and I my trip and both: each other. We will be fulfilling promises to ourselves and to the greater cause of our love. It occurs to me suddenly, that is in the nature of a bona fide proposal, is it not? and lamentably unequal to the job. I shall wait humbly for your answer and anything pro or con you have to say.

You are right, so right. You talk of love with an ardour that strikes to the core and bespeaks aliveness whereas I am dumb, inarticulate about it and talk of life, merely embroider (pardon the metaphor). But really my dear, such exquisite embroidery!

Know truly you are with me
always and everywhere

Love,
Roy

I await your letter and hesitate not an instant if you need something I can get.

•

Roy Kiyooka to Monica Dealtry Barker
Calgary, Alberta
March 11, 1955

My Dearest Monica:
Look, honey you just can't buy a decent looking dressing gown for $3. Oh, I looked around, strolled as nonchalantly as I could into & through various Lingerie depts., fingered this & that, noting colour, prices, etc. but anything short of nine or ten bucks was just plain lousy. So you find the enclosed article, bought for half-price (though I'm suspect) plus discount at the Parisian. The price? was six-fifty and I thought it compared favourably with d.g. seen elsewhere. Anyhow I wanted to get it off to you as quickly as possible. I have visions of you freezing in your coal-heated flat and this will never do. Hope you like it, tell me if you don't.

Now I ask you why send me a money-order? Oh, practical Monica: you must know I think it inconsequential and that buying whatever it maybe for you is but a small token of my esteem for my girl. Unless? Well never mind.

So there is a profusion of articles these past few weeks on the various aspects of dilemmas of the H. Bomb. Oh, ominous shape, suspended by handfuls of fearful anticipation in this apparently hell bent earth of 1955!

God knows one has quite a time cleaning and keeping in trim one's own house, never mind the world at large. Well let's begin at home I say. I read about murders, robberies, hoodlums & thugs, delinquents and all sorts of violence erupting out of the apparent equilibrium of this civilized country so called and I wonder that there is not more, that something is going to go bang! And in the beginning there was man and there was woman and they looked upon each other and knew that this was truly good. They looked about and saw the heavens & earth and all their manifestations and knew that this also was truly good. So let's go back to the beginning or rather apprehend the beginning in the present.

But I'm getting carried away.

Recipe for cooking rice, why surely. The secret (found by experiment) is the right proportion of water to a given quantity of rice. The desired result is light, dry, fluffiness and not the usually soggy kind one is often faced with. Begin by rinsing in cold water, stirring vigorously by hand three or four times. To this add cold water (for obvious reasons) so it covers the rice plus an inch or so more. Not too strong a flame and keep tightly covered. Upon extracting the secret and to retain consistency in cooking, use always the same quantity of rice to the necessary amount of water.

Now Saturday. Yes it is 12.30 a.m. and time to forego this nonsense.

All my love, my dearest one

Roy

•

Roy Kiyooka to Monica Dealtry Barker
Calgary, Alberta
March 13, 1955

Dearest Monica:

Oh! Where shall I begin? Well I'll just plunge ahead at random come what may. After a lengthy dissertation on philosophy you conclude that religion should be a way of life (which is just right and damn the after life), then you mention that you lack direction: so merely revel in being and becoming. This also is good, truly good and to me is as positive a direction as any. ("You must come out of the measurable house of doing, into the immeasurable house of being,") so exhorts e.e. cummings to would-be poets and people at large. To be and to become bespeaks development, the very words are indicative of a organicness as opposed to "well that is the way I am and nothing can be done about it," an oft overheard remark meant to belittle oneself but in fact very vain. So take heart! We all tread the very fine line that has on one side, conventionality & the other x, the dynamic and the unknown. Like the drunk who to prove his soberness, we walk this line and lean one way or the other.

I have almost come to believe that this conflict between solid terra firma & the precipice just beyond is one of the inherent conflicts in everyone. However as you mention, revelling in being & becoming, in this perhaps the solution will surely make itself known?

Nelson must surely be a beautiful spot. I am willingly deceived by the too glamorous post-card you sent me. I can't imagine it could be otherwise, for wherever my girl is, there it must be beautiful! I look forward eagerly & with anticipation to the change of scenery.

You mention most love-poems are from men to women and thus you can't quote any. This is true to a great extent but there are exceptions. And the exceptions prove the rule. I have noticed in love-poems from women to men that they are much more passionate, more naked in the completeness of their revelations. Some poetesses that come to mind: Dickinson, Brontës, Millay, Elizabeth Barrett etc. These I know incidentally, I have much more familiarity with an architect, prose writer by name of Barker.

[...] Well I've come to the end of my letter, plumb worn-out.
Goodnight

Love

Roy

•

Roy Kiyooka to Monica Dealtry Barker
Calgary, Alberta
March 19, 1955

My dearest Monica:
Irresistible imitations of Spring! Today Spring was in the air (whatever it might be) and permeated all things. Some bold few could be seen in their Summer finery, blobs of red, green & yellow moving in & out among the drab greys of Winter wear and the browns of assorted furs. Unduly optimistic these, wishing to hurry the season along, probably well-knowing the

temperament of Calgary's climate. Others caught without their galoshes, skirting puddles & slush and giving vent to their anger at the impossibility of our wonderful climate. These and all were caressed by a lusty yet warm & invigorating wind, oh! wonderful Chinook! and all was overlorded (such a word?) by a radiant yet fitful sun, often disguised by a lace of clouds. Chronologically it is but two days away (Spring will have sprung then) but of course we will not be deceived!

From Spring to you (my beloved) is but a small jump, from Spring to you & I and I insist they are (that is Spring & us) alike, for both signify the beginning or emergence, the stretching out to receive the light of the world, vague imitations of becoming & attaining and all things the symbol of Spring is noted for. And so I hope and pray you are happy as I am happy and that you do not fret overly much about some matters, known to myself also, that may be causing you anxiety, that you should be optimistic rather than otherwise (because it is fitful & negative) for surely there will be difficulties enough to be encountered. I mentioned that in letters I sound the pompous ass but I can't help it and do not put much store by words anyway (too much reading and a semi-consciousness of the literary). Know that I am irrevocably committed to our life together and there is naught else so important to me.

> All my love dearest
> P.S. And Write
> Roy

•••

John Newlove to Susan Newlove
Nova Scotia
March 1, 1968
age 29

Susan:

> What would you think or feel if I said I love you
> and miss you so much.
> John

John Newlove to Susan Newlove
Nova Scotia
March 3, 1968

Dear Susan:

This is after having telephoned you last night. It was so good to hear your voice again.

There really isn't very much to say, is there? except that I love you and I miss you so much I can hardly bear it. It seems to get worse. I can't think now why I would ever have wanted us to be apart. I don't think that I could live with anyone else but you.

Perhaps I'm being paranoid. You sounded very quiet on the telephone, resigned. Please don't think that you must live with me; you haven't any obligation to me at all, but to yourself. You deserve to be happy. You must decide if you want to live with me again, if you can stand it, if you will be happy.

What will your family do? I expect that they will be very much against it, as they seem to have always been. Perhaps it will be worse this time.

Oh Jesus, I'm assuming that you do want us to be together again. I'm hoping.

I love you, Susan.

John

TWO

A Minute is Too Long

Poets in their Thirties

Brian Fawcett to Sharon Thesen
448 West 18th Avenue, Vancouver, British Columbia
4:00 a.m., May 13, 1974
OFFICIAL NOTICE
age 30

Awoke at this hour to a strange light in the back yard, southern exposure to a shrouded moon and 60 watts of the backporch light, thinking ah, I slept, and now I'm 30 years old.

Persian carpets and dark paneled rooms, orange tree bright green leaves under the growlight, Silver Lady on blue dais, water in a green glass, paintings & sculpture by various women, rosecolored hyacinth vase empty on oak table, adolescent expectations tell me I'm supposed to be dead, of suicide, this morning.

Into the bathroom, look in the mirror, hair to my shoulders and hooked nose broken several times beneath round wire-rimmed glasses, some grey hair, vanity, vanity, and a tear from sleep in the corner of left eye. Washed away, wash away my face, and hands dirty from working in the garden yesterday, brush my hair, how is it I've lived this long?

Ah well, straighten the apartment, my son's bed where he visited on the weekend, collect his soiled clothes, pull out my slippers from the box which he filled with the things in the house that attracted him, a glass, T.V. guide, bottle of shampoo, book, coffee spoon, some toys which I leave in the box under his bed.

Only a little milk in the house, enough for tea, boil water in kettle, make tea, sit at the table in the kitchen, smoking, alone.

All the women have come and gone, are absent, and will never come again in the old ways, to keep order, the canary sleeps in his cage, quivering on his perch with his head beneath a pale yellow wing, ancient singer — No longer birth of life but splendid life of mind and body. The sky from this west window is a deep purple, lightening, and outside the birds begin to sing, a houseful of plants awaits my care, sweet songs beyond in the world, and another decade.

Yrs faithfully
love
B.

...

Robert Kroetsch to Jane Lewis
1957
age 30

Reflections while half asleep alone in a cold bed in a
Strange room on a cloudy morning

i have walked the streets of the city thinking remembering have felt the
ache of a bursting heart the size of a vermont moon have dreamed of what
can ail thee knight at arms alone and palely loitering the girl is across the
continent and no birds sing...sore in a cool dry place...this way please but a
blossom fell and so i remembered other things a haircut in a subway station
a sudden response outside a room in a new york hotel mr and mrs kroetsch
and three bags remembered again the touch of a hand while driving through
a long night tired on edge a million kisses uncounted and suddenly precious
and rare a hundred million glances inquiring warm angry i am glaring at you
soothing comforting forgiving teasing a glance filled with bantam rooster
defiance a caressing glance knowing ah knowing wondering...the sheep
in the meadow the cows in the corn...i have walked the streets of the city
while old men huddle against the nagging cold look wise you ancient men
you have wisdom keep it i have a voice remembered as it bridged the night
i was writing you a letter she said and i was glad she wanted to phone and I
was glad...skeleton rattle your mouldy bones i will dare to laugh...so stud
got himself into a bit of a jam beware of pity study or mary will have a little
lamb and she will be unfaithful first and some unsuspecting bastard will get
himself seduced ah sweet mystery of life at last alas...bess...those remarks re
her younger·brother left me slightly astounded yes i did not have her figured
for that reaction hmmm she reassures me about something about herself
but never asks me to explain and all the world might be a stage eh yeah that
is right but you are not awful unsympathetic selfish no...she is a pretty girl
with a big potential but for her illusions of independence needs a certain
kind of man and a certain type of relationship and has it but suffering blue
eyed christ i hope she does not foul up...I need to apply my hand firmly
and rapidly to her lovely bunkey and tell her what I am doing and what she
is going to do but goddammit I can't until christmas...merci a thousand

times beaucoup for the atlantic kazin is right and kroetsch loves the glimpse of the future and reaches out and likes to think he sees another hand…the sphinx of egypt stood on its head and madame bovary wet the bed…i have walked through the streets of the city remembering a hand that touched me touched me held gently and this was an aspect one aspect of love's many oh happiness return…please remember at all times that clothing does not dry overnight in maine cabins…oh cloudy morning and empty room give back that happiness transcending time love

•••

Tanya Evanson to the Beloved
Paris, France
2002
age 30

In the name of Paris in the springtime. In the name of the tears shed by the prophets of God. What do I do now that I've left my lover for a room with a view? I'm alone in this Paris hotel, drunk and waiting. Dervish, where is your arc of return? Where is the source of my flavour? The source of that which enriches. I remember the day when you first appeared to me in the tavern. All smooth and working a mean conga. Slim and dangerous. A grazing of your fingers on my right arm and the cooking began. You scooped me up in rituals I hadn't known before. Fed me meals of such divinity (and I'm known for my gluttony). The divorce made me ugly. It increased my waist size. Created arms that did nothing above my head. Served only to lift bread and chocolate and liquor to lips. Bread and chocolate and liquor to lips. I tried hard not to be at the mercy of fragments, food or yesterday's mental actions but

In the name of Paris in the springtime. In the name of the tears shed by the prophets of God. What do I do now that I am a solitary traveller and a poor one at that, hiding under a crust of cautionary sense? A woman in the possible violence of night in new countries. Even old churches here sport gargoyles projected from above to watch over you. But I've got no one to watch my back but my own tattoo. I'm a pilgrim in new landscapes. Travel is a good ritual, like prayer. They are both examples designed to calm the body, focus the heart. Rituals are reminders. Our movement from gross to subtle. *Inshallah,* we find the most beautiful ones.

In the name of Paris in the springtime. In the name of the tears shed by the prophets of God. What do I do now?! I will carry myself up from the ocean floor 'cause I got me energy since you closed the door! I will leave the city at full moon! Leave the mistrals, the columns of dog droppings on winding streets, gargoyles at every head thrown back! Gargoyles ain't all that! They are lost lovers jutting from memory with jaws open, ready to get fat. Keep the memory solid. Use as a tool to remove garbage from the Straight Path. Let the gargoyles keep their watch in all their uniqueness and wrath. This magic is real. It comes from my heart, it fills out my hands. Its stirs the spoon in the pot, the pencil on the page. It prevents the rot, burns the lead away. This burning is real. There is no end to it, and this burning does eventually become sweet.

In the name of Paris in the springtime. In the name of the tears shed by the prophets of God. I go round and round in this pot you threw me in, and I thought I could swim. Now you're no longer the chef and I look up to see who's stirring me and it's the hand of God working the spoon of me. I see now, this is the meal of me that I offer as alms. The more I get cooked, the tastier I become. And so I let myself be seized, none of this can be undone. I submit myself to True Love, so that the meal of me belongs to everyone.

•

Tanya Evanson to the Beloved
Fes, Morocco
2002

I travelled through three countries to escape sadness. Forgive me. *Estagh-firullah*, I have failed to keep the company of my beloved.

I've split myself all over this pavement. They're kicking my dust all over the place. The Seeing quickly abandon me. Even you left me for a hollow reed and a country. I hope they are both good lovers for you.

One truth is hidden inside all the events of the world. And now, I cannot separate from the company of Secrets. It is the company I sought all along.

What was freedom on my feet doing? Living a life for joy and poverty worse than any I could ever encounter or survive. Whether you paint your body or your palm, there is some human water lost somewhere. Freedom, my friend, is on this page. Take one step towards it and it runs towards you.

I walked the medina blind, touching walls to find my place, mouth open to receive racism and flies with more courage than I. What was I doing in the Valley of Roses looking for you? What will become of me should I see your face? All my features would fall into a slow *zikr*. The *zikr* of no end.

I remember. There is no way for me to forget. The weight of my Heart will always be heavier than my Art. The weight of my Heart will always be heavier than my Art.

O the sharp message of your flight. May this other blind man leave as well! I have others to tend to. My own listening to work on. Pray the Truth comes quickly. Though I have partial sight, it will take millennia for this eclipse to fully pass.

I came to the door of Love but you turned me away. And so I became a dervish in the axis of my heart. Now there is a dervish at the door, to whom no one can refuse entry.

...

Malcolm Lowry to Margerie Bonner
Hotel Georgia, Vancouver, British Columbia
July 30, 1939
age 30

Margie darling —

We got here in 2 1/2 days at an average speed of approximately 63 mph. Once we hit 97. The first night we spent in a place called Weed. Weed! I don't seem to be going so good on this letter so far: it is so long since I wrote one I have almost forgotten how. The second night we spent in a place called — Grizzly! There were birds in both these places: doves. Oregon I thought the most beautiful place I have ever seen & I have seen some. One day we shall go to Crater Lake & be so happy in one another.

I have quit drinking but Señor Barleycorn still shakes my hand either as though he were perpetually glad to see me still alive or were persistently taking leave.

I think of you all the time & your photograph is beside my bed. She talks to me.

I wish I could put all the words of tenderness & love in the world into this letter. But the one simple humble vocable "love" does as well.

I will move the Himalayas to see you again soon: somehow.

But we can never be far away from one another. Look after Jack: give him my love: I shall write. I will try & send some money when I have got rid of Parks. I hope Omar & Princess are well. Think of me & we will sleep in each other's arms just as before & it will be as though we are not away from each other. Nor are we.

I love you. May God keep you safe.

Your
Malcolm

•

Malcolm Lowry to Margerie Bonner
Vancouver, British Columbia
August, 1939

Margie my little love, my darling, — what can I say to make you happy? What I can do is another thing: I think I am doing it.

— I think war will be postponed for the time being: England seems to be pulling herself together.

I have become terribly sober & fit & am working, of all things, for the British Columbian Government. My job: to help other people get jobs. In short I am on the unemployment board. It is exciting. Vancouver seethes & the other day some labour agitators captured the post office for twenty-four hours.

I have quite got rid of the jitters but sorry if you have had them, my darling. I have also gotten rid of Parks, but have to wait a bit for money.

My god, I love you, Margie — what happened to us? I don't know how I can smile till I see you again, or exist without your love & nearness & compassion: the sensation of underground bleeding, of being torn up by the roots like a tree by a big wind — do you feel that? God, I do! With all one's tendrils & everything that joined one to life & nourishment & earth upturned & smashed & freezing. Gurr. You have spoiled me for ever for any other relationship & you have spoiled all women forever for me & I'm glad of it. Tell me all about yourself & send some white birds of love flying through the red forest of the post. Thank you for your last letter — please please write again! My god let's make it soon when we can be happy again on a tousled bed in peace in spite of the pain. Forgive this dead letter & the I I, my my, refrain: tell me all your troubles & let me share them & god bless you sweet lady, woman, child

Malcolm

P.S. I think of your saying: Now I'll just put on a face —

•

Malcolm Lowry to Margerie Bonner
August, 1939

My darling Marjorie:

Two letters from you, both at once, which take me all the way from petunias to the Pleiades, and from Jupiter to Jaguars. Yes, I love circuses, or are they circi? I went to a Norwegian one long ago — SPRINGBOAR-TOGTUMPLINAKT, is a word I remember. I remember also the sort of fairy ring that the circus left after they'd packed up, on Midsummer common in Cambridge: that was very sad. And the lion that wept too, in a cage, in New Brighton, Cheshire, Eng, where I was born. And two lion-faced ladies who wept, twice nightly, in another cage in the same place. They had come all the way from the hinterland or somewhere. You observe astutely, "sometimes I can't read my writing myself when it's cold," to which my only possible reply could be "and sometimes I feel I oughtn't to read it when it's hot…" I've been suffering slightly from the jealousies, just slightly, since your description of the circus: I'm not any longer though, I'm just glad you had a good time. However, it's just the sort of light-hearted gaiety we could enjoy together. I'm still waiting for the news, and the tension is getting unbearable: and I have a passion to share the things with you that make you laugh and gladden your heart. Your mention of your birthplace in a letter the other day made me want to go there and be near the soil and the green graces which shaped you. And somehow the very difference in our sex moves me deeply when I think of it, a sort of compassion gets mixed up with my desire, and I really do feel that I'm carrying you about in my heart; Lord knows where these feelings come from, it's just love, I guess. If the permission doesn't come I'm going to get down to you somehow, money or no money. I think I have enough contacts still to be able to raise some in California, & if not, I can sell some stories. It might be better, at that, to cut entirely loose from my income since, in spite of its advantages, it binds me & us cripplingly, as things stand.

How long the visa will last depends upon what they say at the border: and also, on news from England: but if the news is favourable this time, and I have played my cards wisely, I think we should have longer than we counted on having.

Please wait and be true to me, & us: the bottom has dropped out of the world of my generation: you and a love of the principle of beauty in all things are all that connects me to life: my god, what portentous rot that sounds! But it's true. Be with me tonight. I shall be with you.

Always, my beloved,
Malcolm

P.S. I'm sending you a poem written in a bleak moment. In a gay one, I'll write one about you, send it to you to-morrow.

•

Malcolm Lowry to Margerie Bonner
Vancouver, British Columbia
August, 1939

Darling sweetheart.

I think of you as wife sister mother mistress friend.

Please please take care of yourself until I can get to you. I'm so dreadfully anxious about & worried about you I can't sleep or think.

Damn & blast this cockeyed world not of our own making.

I'm going nuts waiting for news; & you there ill & needing me.

I can't find anybody going to Los Angeles as yet or I'd come news or no news & trust that I could clear up things with my attorney at the other end.

Meantime I think he is deliberately stalling, or England is stalling, with the idea that I shall enlist in this benighted country, which naturally I have no intention of doing now, since that is an irrevocable step & would knock things on the head so far as we are concerned.

Please look after yourself, darling, I shall be thinking of you all the time & praying that you are well & happy. Your

Malcolm

• • •

Penn Kemp, 1975
age 31

Dear Mentor/Tormentor.

This One's for you.

O

Men
Tore

Tore
Men
Tore:

Men tore
My art

Not my heart,

Pull ease,
Pull lease.

I imp
Lore

You too

Cease and

Desist

De siring
To Con

Core

Mon coeur.

It's not
For rent

For good
Nest Ache.

Till next we
meet, we part,

Yr Penn pal.

•••

Gregory Betts to Lisa Frith
July 31, 2006
age 31

„I „Lisa "„"„the waiting period („business („(and (on (is called (is called
(from left to right running (so (***** "to „A „the A "„"„, if „in „it „, that
is it „it, „it „is „it "„it „it "? „live. "mine „to business „speaking „„„uh-ah ")
„whoa "„„leave „„1. 1995, 2 there throw." S.A. agree over approximately
approximate confirm confirm announcement admission permit admittedly
ADS, afterwards afterwards after appropriate all all. "nearly also also also
always always to belong correspondences analytically? and and and and and
and and and and and and and and and and and and and and and and and
and and and and and and, anekdotische announcement another different
one, answer, "prehistory, anthropomorphically any all all everything? the
appositives attractive appositives approach approximation are are are are
are are are are article articles so like that as like so as like so as as as aspect
of aspect, accepts astonishment. On on on on on on at the attention. aural
attract, author: withdrawl is is is is is is is is is is because because because,
because bed bleeds before and bores beside ness between between boring
boring boring of the boredom boredom bored over the book.
    to preserve, cannot not cover, letter child of requirements can be able to
preserve both however however however however however past past past

past past past past past past by Cage, the campaign clearly close? closed reasoning, code collapse. Combination combination comma COMM on communication? weight complete distributed inventory part confirmed konfuses, regarded regard continuous contemporary content contradiction meeting meeting. Copy could circulate, present decoder decoding. Resetting demand did different: the discovered difficulty discovers that separation set clear do not do does does does doing do not draw to drops "disturb). Debt each colluding economic effect effect effect. eight. emerged, emptiness emptiness, terminated ends, cases of the substantial one of the Epigramms particularly even.

Finally exceed does each daily daily exactly example, exchange? the exclusive apology, which is express, explode, extension, the fact fact fact fact precipitate precipitates leaves rather falling wrong far fascinated fell few catch final round) discovery discovery discoveries followed followed for for for for for for form-form-form the form form form formal form. four. frequent of of of of the full full function function function function function splinter, which continues to work, generally gestural, gestikulieren that ghost image given going grammar, which led grammatical grammatical grammatical grammatical raster field assumption assumption debt debt, haiku haiku, haiku, haiku, haiku, to have coincidence has to have to have to have to have to have have to have having assistance to have here had?

is here it, as, how I I I I I I I I I I I I I I I I I I I I I I I I I I I I I I I I I I I I I I I I I I I I I I I I I I I me has, have if, if, if, if impersonal impersonal impersonal of the pictures implode inside inside inside inside inside inside inside inside in in in in in in in in in in in in in in in in in in in in in in in, instead of informs interesting interesting internal of the insoluble instrument in in investigation investigations, attractionable IS-IS IS-IS IS-IS IS-IS IS-IS IS-IS IS-IS IS-IS is, is, is, is, is not island not it it it it it it it it it it it it it it it it it, it, it. it. it? it is it is it is it is it is it is it is its its its its its its its jacket John straight fair Kaleidoskope, maintenance, which know friendly friendly kind know, knows knows, Man gelsprachensprachensprachensprachensprachensprachensprachensprache, language? last last inertia of the language) learns few few few few few from left to right running letters of the vacation, horizontally aligned level. Levels like as as as like probable Lisa and hear locate little logic logic logic, long long.

•••

Robert Service to Constance MacLean
1905
age 31

This is only a scrap, a fragment, a mood if you will, but one of those sacred, vital records of a moment when a man forgets everything else, thrusts aside the tawdry trappings of life, and stands in the sight of Her, a type, elemental, eternal, a Lover, and half a god. If I thought it was needful to make you read this seriously I would write it in my blood — as every drop of that blood is yours — but I only beg you once to mock me, and to read these few words, as the very best that is in my heart prompts you. I came home tired tonight, and I want to draw a pitcher of cool water from the well. The moon was brilliant, so I sat by the door and thought of you. (Where do I not think of you. I call your name a hundred times a day. Sometimes I think I am crazy to love you so. Sometimes I feel I will die if I do not see you soon). A long time I sat there alone in the moonlight just staring into the moon's face. Dearest if you had been there I could have made love to you as nobody else ever will, fierce, passionately, entreating, eloquent, tender, and so I may sometime if you will only let me. And then a reaction of intense sadness came over me and I sat for a long time with my face buried in my hands as I once told you I did in the early days after leaving you when you mocked me. Dearest, won't you lay aside, just for one moment that garment of flippancy in which you wrap yourself, and be your truest self — a woman not a girl, and capable of facing unflinchingly the starkest realities. You said once that one of my letters made you cry, and in these tears be my hope and my salvation. If you were to be very, very sick, Connie (perhaps with that chest trouble you had before) I would come over and would beg to see you, and I would throw myself on your bed and kiss your hand, and sob my heart out (but what a confession for a <u>man</u> to make). There is such a moment as that, with no false modesty between us, and only the evidence of my great love and pain, perhaps you would just whisper: "Dearest, I love you, too." O Connie, Connie, we are fellow travellers, and this world's not all gladness and sunshine and I just want to travel by your side always, always. And if the north wind blows I'll shield you; and I'll go on my knees and smooth away all the thorns and sharp stones from your little feet, and I'll try with the very best that is in me to make the shadows all sunshine, the sorrow all gladness. Just we two, dear, heart to heart, and the rest of the world — outside. O can't you trust me! I am not much more than a boy really, but I have a great deal of good in me, and it is you who can bring it out. I have utterly abandoned myself in my love for you and have thrown reserve to the winds. Why do you still keep it up in your letters? Your last was as mocking as ever. If I haven't won you now I never will. And sometimes, as tonight, I am despairful. We are young and love is never as sweet as now. Just think of it well, Connie, in your quiet hours, and test yourself. Could you give me up lightly? Would you feel any sense of loss in your life if you did? Tell me now. I am very serious tonight. Let us continue writing delightful nonsense to each other, but let us both understand what underlies it. You will not doubt now I love you and will not you too write these words to me just once — I love you.

•••

Fraser Sutherland, 1978
age 32

Here

I. *Driving Back*

Each pit, each pockmark of the road.
The shapes of night,
companionship.
The branches wave goodbye.
We have travelled great distances
inside each other's bodies,
slumped in the half-light,
a headless rider.
Once the engine kicked into overdrive.
The auxiliary's
activity of the spirit.
The chalice overflowed.
The moon enormous on the harbour.
I could drive into it,
pushed by the white line streaming past
while cormorants tuck into their wings and sleep.

The world is fleshed with dark.
The earth drinks me greedily.
Come home, it says.
Go back to her.

II. *Waiting Here*

This is not my room.
It's quiet, cool.
The cat has more right to be here.
The scotch is waiting.
Also the ice.
You haven't come home yet
but your smell remains from morning.
The bed's been made.
The place seems untenanted.
As if you were waiting for a
candidate from the day's heat.
Why expect the walls to beat like a heart
bringing you back?
Or a small pad
this writing's squeezed.
Now the cat has gone,
its place taken by the ticking minutes.
I would have been more at home
to have passed through the open window,
come to beg at the spread table.

III. *The Misty Heart*

Through the clouds of bedclothes
comes your face, a misty heart,
what beats with it
not the shallow muscle in my chest
but another deep within,
a tiny pulsing heart.

So the moon embraces night, her brother,
drained and sick of himself.
She has taken his strength from the day,
the moon in gauze,
now veils herself in white.
Odd that in this darkness
I should feel the white of your arms
as pink suffuses through your face.
Odd you should be living here with me.

•••

Lindsay Zier-Vogel to Amelia Earhart
August 1, 2013
Between Toronto, Ontario and St. John's, Newfoundland
age 33

Dear Amelia,

I always think I'm going to run into you at the airport, not that your airports were anything like the ones they have now. You'd take off from farmers' fields and country roads. Now, you can have brunch before your plane takes off, or go to a fake Irish pub for a hamburger. There's a place to get a ten-minute manicure and there are three stores that sell those beanbag neck pillows that never really work.

Now, you wouldn't be allowed to bring your thermos of soup on board with you, though maybe pilots are exempt from the no liquid rule. I'm not sure if you would think airports now are brilliant or ridiculous.

I didn't manage to get a window seat and the woman who did is not impressed when I lean over her, watching the runway tilt, then disappear, the sky rushing up to fill the window. The early morning streetlights are like pennies catching light.

It takes no time to climb through the clouds, the plane casting a smear of a shadow. Every now and then, there are gaps in the white, revealing green and brown squares. I have no idea what is growing down there.

I wonder how you managed to fly straight through clouds all the way to Europe, how you made yourself trust the numbers and needles over your own eyes. I don't think I'd ever be able to do that.

The woman with the window seat just pulled the plastic screen down and I want to ask her to open it again. Why bother getting a window seat if you're going to block out the sky for most of the flight? You should have to sign a waiver promising not to close the blind, even if there is glare on your Tom Hanks movie. Would you say something if you were here? I don't know the answer to that.

I fought sleep, knowing you'd never let your eyes close on a flight, even if you weren't flying it yourself, but ended up falling asleep, until we hit some turbulence and the captain's voice over the intercom woke me up. I wish you were here to tell me about turbulence — if it's like biking on gravel, or driving over potholes, or if you'd be just as surprised as the rest of us with our stomachs bottoming out?

The last time I flew was when I flew to the UK. I sat beside a pilot who wore a tie with silhouetted planes on it and pants with sharp creases. He had wings pinned to his jacket, even though it was his day off. He looked like a non-fighter jet version of Tom Cruise. He said he'd never flown a Vega, but told me that bigger planes just feel bigger, like the difference between driving a bus or driving a Cadillac. Then he said he didn't really like talking about flying on his days off. What kind of pilot doesn't like talking about flying? I wanted to ask him. I didn't though. I stayed polite.

The woman's movie is finally over and she's opened the blind. And there it is, the ocean. Its surface so evenly rippled it could be a cartoon of an ocean, instead of actually the Atlantic. And then the vertical drop of rock faces butted up against the water. And now a city, roofs jammed up against each other and fences separating backyards. But even with the roofs, it is still mostly trees and water.

Turns out, you didn't stop in St. John's, but in Saint John, in New Brunswick. I hate the authors and the editors who got it wrong, writing St. Johns, without the apostrophe, assuming there'd only be one town with the same name out here. You didn't ever pass the infamous coloured row houses and I feel ridiculous for thinking until a few days ago that you had been here too. But you were nearby, for both big Atlantic flights, so I'm going to try get a car and see if I can find your airstrip, or at least the place that your airstrip used to be.

I wish I could find the words to tell you how much I miss you, how much I wish you were here. I know you'd wave it off, but I just want you to know that I miss you. I do.

Love,
Lindsay

Lindsay Zier-Vogel to Amelia Earhart
August 3, 2013
Trepassey, Newfoundland
age 33

Dear Amelia,

The sun is so bright off the ocean, I can barely open my eyes. It feels silly now, to have thought the sun never shines here and leave my sunglasses at home, but I was expecting fog so thick, I wouldn't be able to see a few feet in front of me, the fog that kept you here.

I couldn't get a car for two days. I didn't think they'd run out and that would be that, but it's hard to imagine what an island is like until you're on one, I guess. I don't even know what I've been doing for the last two days, except walking up and down all these hills. Did you know St. John's is hilly? My calves burn all the time.

But I did manage to get a car and on the drive down here, I passed a million signs that said moose might wander onto highway. The caution signs alternated between aggressive silhouettes, and silhouettes that look more like the moose are grazing and I wonder if they really do wander onto the road, or if they charge onto it. On some stretches of the highway, there were lights that promised to flash if there were moose, but I didn't believe them and spent the whole drive scanning the forest. I could barely keep my eyes on the road and I wish you had been there to talk me down, to tell me that you would watch for moose while I drove. I wish you had been there next to me, even if you didn't say anything at all.

Eventually the trees disappeared and things got foggy and the only things on the side of the road were white stones and occasionally a tiny house that couldn't be more than two rooms with lace curtains. I sang along to Fleetwood Mac and tried not to be freaked out that there were no hydro lines, no telephone poles and my cell phone had no bars. Nothing. I passed another moose sign and panicked that I didn't get roadside insurance when they asked at the car rental place.

When I hit Trepassey, the sun started shining again and I passed a playground with a yellow twirly slide, a liquor store, a gas station and potted marigolds and I didn't have to worry about moose. I drove by the post office before seeing the long finger of ocean that pushes its way into the town.

That's the reason you were here all those years ago — that narrow stretch of blue.

Your French is better than mine, but the guy at the gas station said the name of this place comes from the French verb, trepasser, to die. It can't have felt very promising to be taking off from a place with such a dire name.

There's nothing here, really and I can't believe you were stuck here for almost two weeks, playing gin rummy with widows and trying to keep Bill from the screech. It's hard to imagine this place buried in fog, it was so sunny today.

Apparently, your curling iron is kept at the museum — did you know you left it behind? — but the door was locked and all I could see through the window was a glass case of teapots and silverware that washed ashore from the Titanic.

The woman at the post office told me they didn't bother opening the museum this summer, then introduced me to the guy behind me in line. I didn't feel like being friendly or chatty, but the man stood between me and the door and I couldn't leave. But then I was glad I was stuck in that unair-conditioned post office because his gran met you when the Friendship got fogged in. She went to the school up on the hill and he said the nuns were furious that you showed up wearing pants.

And he said you used to walk along the top of picket fences with your arms outstretched. Do you remember that? You're quite the legend in Trepassey because of it. They still talk about you like you were the tallest woman anyone had ever seen. I didn't have the heart to tell him you're only 5'8".

I pulled the car over to the side of the road, where I have a good view of the lighthouse. This beach isn't sandy, but made up of tiny smooth stones that look like black sesame seeds. It's hard to imagine your plane bobbing on the surface of the ocean, here, though this narrow stretch of water would make the perfect runway for the Friendship and its enormous pontoons.

I should pack up and head back soon, though I'm dreading doing that stretch of road without cell service again. I wish you were here to put your hand on back of my headrest and leave it there until we make it back to the city.

I'm off to Harbour Grace later this week.

Love,
Lindsay

P.S.: I wish you were here with me to listen to the Fisheries Broadcast. It's on every afternoon at 5:30. I don't really understand anything they're talking about, but the best part is where they sign off, "Wishing you calm seas and tight lines." Hilarious, right?

•

Lindsay Zier-Vogel to Amelia Earhart
August 9, 2013
St. John's, Newfoundland

Dear Amelia,

I'm back in St. John's now. I drove back before it got dark, but I don't feel like going out to find dinner, so I'm eating almonds and an apple I got back at the Toronto airport. I've also opened a lukewarm bottle of white I tried to chill in the bathroom sink.

I spent the afternoon in Harbour Grace and watched a man in coveralls spin the propeller of your Vega. You stood there; bluish and tall, your cheekbones smoothed out by the film. I've never seen you shift your weight when you stand. I've never seen you touch your lips with your fingers — were they dry or were you nervous? The VHS tape chugged forwards and I was so afraid it would catch and you would disappear.

The wind must've picked up, licking the edge of your shirt, turning the collar of your coat in on itself. Your curls were blown back from your forehead, and you looked so much younger than you were.

Had you already packed maps of the Atlantic? Was your thermos of tomato soup already in the cockpit?

The propeller spun so fast it became a circle instead of a blade, and the video skipped ahead to a bobbing landscape — the ground a dark blue, the sky a few shades lighter. Your plane, the Vega, cut through the reflection of the window, passing through my shoulder. The camera stayed trained on its tail until there was no plane, only sky, and the scratch and dust marks of old film passing across the reflection of my T-shirt.

I wish you were here, even if you might not approve of the wine, so you could tell me if maybe your fingers weren't nervous, but impatient — the sun sinking, the weather so changeable here. I know you wouldn't have wanted to get stuck here the way you had in Trepassey.

I'm leaving tomorrow, but I'm debating waking up early to walk by the water one last time, but we'll have to see. I haven't really been sleeping well.

I got on the shared computer to check into my flight when I got in and got an email from Rhys about someone finding your freckle cream at the bottom of the Pacific. The glass jar had been broken into five or six pieces, but someone put it back together and set it next to the original jar of Dr. Berry's Freckle Ointment for a photograph. I know I shouldn't have been checking my email and I wish I hadn't, because ever since I clicked on that link, I can't stop thinking about your cheeks, your nose, the tops of your ears, the parts of you you couldn't stand.

I miss you.

Love,
Lindsay

•••

Frank Davey, 1973
age 33

The Tower

I had known before
of time, seen the snow
blacken, cold flesh turn

to scars. My finger
where the saw
bit, is not

as it was, all this
I knew, yet
when you told me of your love

I would have erased time,
would have murdered:
him, you —

But revenge too, I saw
moves onward. Troy burns
& only

is as lost as Helen's chastity
or all the bathwater
of Agamemnon's reign.

& his tower fell.
Was there then lightning from the sky?
This crown of a king we shall not

wear again.
Did I love you?
I mourn Paris and Hitler.

I write this fucking pretentious poem.

•••

Stephen Pender to ———
January, 2000
age 33

A memorandum to the aforementioned lover, with salt,

There is a name for the way in which we settle into our fictions: it is lust, desire and, even in that haughty masculinity boys take for engagement, the longing for the everyday. You're right, too, that last night was all about boys: sinister little boys plotting and comparing sizes, all the while engaged in the same conspiracies they blithely condemn. In several senses, it was a test of my political mettle. The doubts I refused to loose amongst our carefully constructed moorings, the ruses of assurance folded into a laugh or some ritual, the rust in one's voice and the laughter in another's. I agree: I went along and I thought, precision does not make ideas precise; politics here is politics there. Everyone luxuriates in their roles and that, my dear, is the fiction.

I write now, after the morning has settled into forgiveness. Your anger was lenitive. We have taken reading to depths, you know, where seeing is no longer important. The restless sleep is out of my eyes but my heart was fast into it: the sense that I had acted — conforming to another fiction — was wandering in me, looking for a place (politics mixed with so much boy-pleasure, so little acuity, so well). When I am dead and doctors know not why, my friends' curiosity will have me cut up to survey each part, when they shall find a picture in my heart: a field in the middle of the city, a rare place where the sky is exposed, me reading — incunabula, maps, architectural drawings — straining next to a small fire. I see this now and hear a wan, insistent voice.

These moments are those I chose not to explain; pulling up the pegs makes the shelter fragile. I think, without them, without it, the secrets escape — history, how I have lived, how the world builds itself in us. Don't generalize from the moment, I used to say, meaning I will outlive this, it is only one part of the story, an open field at night with no shelter and the maps, glorious in their detail, finally set to burn. What I truly meant was, in the calculus of moments, nothing is lost, not even explanation.

My duties have weighed heavily on me in the last two months, as I'm sure you understand, and I have tried to lose them with drink, fucking and lies about progress and calm. At the centre of this tissue is you: the ways in which I thought our interaction either clarified the world or was infected with its disorder, the ways I thought about distance, about not thinking, and tried to live it in small brocade: experience woven with nostalgia, hope with fear, sex with love. Everything "boy" about that. I should explain, to make this reluctance to falter absolutely clear, but that we falter makes us feel.

With all best wishes,
Stephen

•••

David Helwig to Judy Yeo
October 31, 1972
age 34

Dear Judy,

No, no, no, that's not what I meant at all. Not at all. Do you like Jane Austen? Do you like Elizabeth Bennet's father? Do you agree when he says "For what do we exist, but to make sport for our neighbours, and laugh at them in our turn?"

Do you agree with the narrator of *The Watch that Ends...*when he says he can't describe Catherine's character because he loved her?

Will John marry Alice?

Does she or doesn't she?

Did you vote?

Did you listen to the results?

Were you happy?

Did you know I'm doing the Diefenbaker poem on TV for Weekend for November 12?

Does the sun shine on the unjust?

Will Leonard Cohen find God at the bottom of a urinal?

Will God find Leonard Cohen at the top of a urinal?

Did you know the series on Canadian prose writers begins on Anthology on November 8?

Is music the food of love?

What is truth?

Who is Sylvia?

Was Holofernes an innocent victim?

Is God unfair to monsters?

Did you read the patronizing review of Billie in the Globe?

Will I kick Bill French in the balls?

      Shall we dance?

      D.

      •••

Christian Bök

2000

age 34

Vowels

loveless vessels

we vow
solo love

we see
love solve loss

else we see
love sow woe

selves we woo
we lose

losses we levee
we owe

we sell
loose vows

so we love
less well

so low
so level

wolves evolve

•••

Robert Service to Constance McLean
Thursday evening, March 6, 1908
The Canadian Bank of Commerce
age 34

My own beloved:

I am so consumed with love and longing for you that it seems a relief to
sit down and write to you. I cannot find relief like you in tears but oh I feel
simply suffocated with wretchedness. I feel quite insane with love as if I
could give up everything and fly again to your side. That would be folly and
no doubt in a few days I will be all right but oh now I am quite <u>mad</u> for you.

However I am going to leave off lamenting and tell you about the trip
so far. When I left you on Tuesday afternoon (oh if we had only known) I
looked back <u>but you had gone in</u>. Then I had to wait a long time for a car
and it was a quarter to seven by the time I got into town. Then when I had

a hurried dinner it was quarter past. I had to hustle round to get an ex-press and just got down to the boat a few moments before eight. I never doubted for a moment but that I would find the boat wouldn't set sail till eleven, but imagine my horror when I found it was going to sail in a few minutes. I rushed to the phone in the freight shed and got you. How sick you must have felt, my darling. What had you been doing? You seemed so matter-of-fact speaking over the phone. Then people kept coming in and I couldn't say the things I wanted to and of course you couldn't either. Oh it was hell. I went back to the boat but they were loading horses and no sign of going that made it worse. If we had sailed sharp it would have consoled me but as it turned out I could easily have come up and spent a full hour with you. I hate the galling part of it all. Then I'd phoned you a second time just to hear your voice once more. It seemed so <u>cheerful</u>. About ten we started. I cannot describe the feelings of despair with which I watched the lights of Vancouver disappear. I certainly left my heart there. I tried to trace out Broughton Street too. If ever I felt the pathos of anything I did that moment. I stood on deck till the last light vanished then went below feeling chilled and dispirited. Oh my heart's dearest treasure where will this all end? We seem to be the sport of fate. Can you not realize now how much it means to us, our Love, and how little anything else means? Don't you feel the bond beyond all words or sense that holds us? Pour out your heart to me, my darling, as I do to you. It will help us both to bear.

> Your adoring
> Bob

•

Robert Service to Constance McLean
Wednesday, March 25, 1908
The Canadian Bank of Commerce

Oh my darling, my darling, my darling — what Hell it's been since I left you last night. I never realized so poignantly before how <u>impossible</u> life would be without you. It seems as if it <u>can't</u> be true that I'm not to see you tomorrow and feel your kisses — not for many tomorrows. I said once that when I got away my three months would seem like a dream — instead I find that <u>this</u> is the dream and the <u>great reality</u>. What a fool I was ever to agree to go back to the North. I feel like throwing myself over the side and trying to swim back to you. Oh I'm just crazy, crazy, crazy my dearest dearest dear. I suppose I will get back my sanity in a little while but this is the most awful yet. I hate to think of your feelings when you heard I wouldn't be able to say good-bye. How I was <u>reserving</u> myself for that. I had a dozen things to say to you, very very deep serious things that I could only say by word and look. I wanted to crystallize into some divine moments all our rapture and passion of the past weeks — make a climax of <u>our splendid love</u>. You, too, must have left things unsaid. There are very few moments in life when our hearts are torn open and all our souls are laid bare. That would have been <u>ours</u> and we have been cheated of it. Honestly, dearest, I think I should have <u>broken down</u>. Even now I feel a misery too deep for tears. I can't bear to <u>think</u> of <u>your</u> misery, my adored. How much we have learnt, haven't we? We've learned how happy we could be together and how miserable we will always be apart. I always feel now as if we were really married in a <u>spiritual</u> sense. Never will I forget your tender caressing ways — small exquisite touches of sentiment and grace. It seems to me now we never appreciated our moments as we should. I know I didn't. I never seem to have realized the finality of them. Now what would I give for just <u>ten passionate minutes</u> with your arms tight around me and your lips to mine nestling close like a child. Oh we never valued our moments enough. And to think we never said Goodbye — that was the bitterest. I've never felt so steeped in misery, so full of longing for you, my Priceless one. Will you write and tell me all you have felt — all you are feeling? Just pour out your whole soul to me without reserve. You know <u>nothing</u> matters now but us two. Life would be worthless without you, my Treasure, and my Hope. Oh if I even had a photo of you… never got that picture. Couldn't you send it to me? I can't help comparing this trip to my happy one on the way down, when every minute was bringing me nearer to you. Now every moment is increasing the distance between us my poor dear love. I hope you haven't cried very much. Why care if they do notice it in the house. Let them see you do care and do feel bad. They will respect your feelings. Tell them anything you like only <u>assert</u> yourself. You have me behind you. If it weren't for the Bank regulation against marrying under thirteen hundred I would marry you now and we would take a chance. But we must wait. But what a joy it is to know you would take me anyway for richer or poorer, for better or worse. Now we are partners, and I want you to make all your interests my interests, and my interests your interests. We belong to each other and are no longer two but one. I will tell you frankly all of my affairs. It was for your dear sake I bought the house and I will devote my life to you. Only I want love from you, great absorbing devotion, that's all I ask. Things have developed during the past few weeks beyond my dearest hopes. We love each other a hundred times <u>more</u> than we did and we will love far more than that yet. I was wishing till the last to tell you all you represented in my life my looks and words would have been a dear memory to you — but alas! Well please the lord the time may pass quickly. After all it will likely only be 18 months as I shall likely come out in October. I <u>will</u> come out then. I <u>must</u>. I can't stand it, my beloved. I keep wondering how you are feeling. I hope you are not taking it as bad as I am. When will I get a letter? My darling, my beloved, my precious priceless one, the bursting love of my heart to you

    Your own Bob.

•••

Charles Lillard, 1978
age 34

Roughing the Words

Wounded lives; lovers and ghosts —
shadows refusing to stay on the ground;
this midnight clutch of nights,
sleep mid-stride between illusion
and you waiting, awaiting
until I woke to find that daybreak's edge
a sheen of Sitkan roses
awash on your breasts;
and I sick with the poverty of my mind,
sick, having lost an old passion

•••

Ronna Bloom to Daniel Molloy
May 30, 1995
age 34

Dear Daniel,

I've been wanting to write you a letter for at least two years. How are you?

I need to ask that first to remind myself that you're still in the world, even though you can't answer just yet. Yesterday, I called directory inquiries (you see, even as I begin to talk to you, my language slips into Irish versions of Canadian life.) Yesterday I called information. That's what we say here, for Daniel Molloy in Rossport.

I spoke to the operator for a minute, I think he was in Dublin, and asked for your number, not knowing where you were. "There are two Daniel Molloys," I said, thinking of your father. He gave me a number and then the Canadian operator disconnected us. I didn't have a chance to check if it was you. I didn't call.

So hello. What have I wanted to say all these years? Start with the present. In two days a friend of mine, in fact, the one other real relationship I've had since you, is coming to Ireland with his new wife. He is coming to Ireland. I thought of giving him your number, if I had it, your name, your address, if I knew it. I thought of finding someone to connect him to you. Why? I supposed to reach you myself. Sending someone else is close. But it's not what I want. Two old boyfriends meeting each other is not a great fantasy. But part of me goes with him to Ireland. Whether he sees you or not, I am on my way back, in two days. I'm almost there now.

I am living in an apartment north of Toronto. In a suburb. Near the highway. I've been here six years and the hum of the highway has gotten louder each summer I open the windows again. You wouldn't like it. The smell is bad. The apple tree outside doesn't bloom, in fact, it's dead. And the evergreens — so common here and so rare there — are shedding. The winters have been merciless on the one I can see from my window.

Once I woke up to find it bent into my balcony, pinned under the weight of ice like an old man with a backbreaking load. I ran out of my house with a broom and hit the ice till it cracked and the tree sprang back. Tall, but barer than before. Thin but still there. That is something you'd have done I think: that icebreaking urgency. Flat-line panic. Rushing out to save trees.

Here in North York the cars are fancier than in Rossport. They're new. A banger is rare. It's a quiet neighbourhood with families and money. The kind we'd have choked on ten years ago: its distance from gritty and real, or glitzy and fake, or just plain land. Maybe that's why I had that frantic need to run out and protect that tree. Some reminder of land. Believe it or not, I like it here. The semi-quiet, the proximity to noise.

What I really want to tell you is how you are here. I look around my apartment and you are apparent. Not to anyone else, not even to me most of the time, but when I stop, I can see you, shining through. The mobile of the toy cars you gave me is hanging from the window, their stuffed little red car bodies fading from the light. That's an obvious one. Mostly you are less obvious than that.

There is the painting that Anthony did which I traded for one of my photographs when we ran the art gallery that summer. "The Red Pillow" he called it. A woman's face in such a blue, such an aubergine. The fluid strokes of her cheeks. Those strong lines. And it is the colours I carry with me.

Not that I have painted this apartment any cobalt or cerulean blues, but I know them. They are the powders in those jars in that store in Galway where we stood and gaped. Shelves full of them. Concentrated coral and salmon. All you need is to see the colour really hard once and it is yours. I love them, even their names excite me. You with the shade charts deciding how to paint your father's shop front. The Hunter Green gloss. The creamy trim. E. Molloy and Sons, Ironmonger.

The other day I was in a Victorian house downtown. It was grand, with wood floors and a fireplace. I remembered the names for things. The picture rail: that bit of moulding one third of the way down from the ceiling that runs around the room for hanging pictures on. The ceiling rose, a floral carving in the centre of the ceiling where once a chandelier hung. Decorative flashes. The names for a room's architectural details you taught me, came back, were revived in this house. As you had done: carefully lifting them out with grace and paint, to revive the shop front. Any shop front. I think wherever there was a wall you would have been there painting it, if you could. As though that is what walls were meant for: to hold up paint.

The other day I stripped the paint off a round table that has been on my balcony since I moved here. Once it had been the green of your father's shop. The high gloss. But all those winters killed it, chipped it, chewed it up. I went out with some chisels, no scraper, but found an awl — something you'd used to poke holes in the wood of picture frames for hanging — were they your chisels too? I don't know where they came from, but using the wrong tool, I went at the table with slowness in my hands. Small islands of green floated in the exposed sea of wood, emerging and disappearing with the scrapes. I wanted to save them, each time, to hold each one before carving it out, sanding it down, before erasing it. You would have known what I meant. Would have looked at this waxing green moon with your hands. I could have said nothing.

It's out there now, patch-faced table getting shiny in the rain. Darkening. I went to get paint chips for it. Found the green, the Hunter Green, I think. Here they call it — wait I'll check — they call it "Irish Beauty." Number 34-B-6. No joke. Belle Irlandaise. Among all the colours I could have picked: Poplar Grove, Green Pool, Banker Green, Mountain Grass, the one I picked was that one, without cheating. So this is my Casablanca: of all the paint chips in the world, etc…

Anyway, let me come back. To the table. The one in the rain. To this one inside, dry, where I'm writing to you. And why am I writing? If I knew it would be a shorter letter, less circuitous. I would just say it instead of touring through the city my apartment, talking about the furniture. But then it would also end.

I will need to go soon. I work as a therapist now. Your eyebrows arch up in that temple they make toward your forehead in disbelief. But this is what I do when I'm not writing or taking pictures or scraping tables. I listen. I see a few clients from my apartment, it has an extra room for this, for the stories. I am sitting here now. Mostly, I'm not working at all. In fact, one woman meant to come today at noon, which is now, did not turn up. Though I worry about the money, I am grateful for the chance to write this letter.

To write this letter I seem to need a clear space ahead of me, like a field with no people in it, like summer. This is where I am while writing to you, inside my North York apartment, at my wooden table and inside myself: the summer field. To get to you at all, I need to get there. This is where we lived.

Dear Daniel, again, here is the urgency. The summer is coming and is here and this friend of mine is leaving for Ireland in two days and I must get to you before he goes or get him or get him to get to you. What a circus. A maze. Reaching back and forward at the same time trying to pull it all in, the past is here already, see, I'm unravelling it for you. It's been here all along, I just never told myself how much, never told you, never took stock, the inventory.

Reeling it in like fish lines, like the lines of your brother's mussel farm. Ropes hanging down from rafts into the bay, the black shells clinging and spawning into full grown edible beasts. The long lines that tangled in the winter weather, dangle now, in the growing season. Or so I imagine them. Romantic thought, never having swum under the rafts, getting it from the sketches you drew to explain, your fish-farming diagrams. The concept was strange to me, not from the sea, of planting fish seed, a crop like wheat or corn. And so vulnerable to the storms. The family I come from is indifferent to weather. Working in offices with nothing to hold or pass between us, nothing that grows or smells.

Something happened to me when I got to Ireland. At twenty-two, my whole life in Canada, I felt like I'd never seen a tree before. "But Canada," you said, "you come from Canada!" Oh yeah trees. Forests and forests, vast arm wide spaces of trees, but not *a* tree. Not a single one in a field leaning against the wind. One. And I saw one there. First time.

As though eyes were given to me at Shannon airport, stamp your passport and hand out a pair of eyes. "These are your eyes," he may as well have said, "you can keep them."

But really they got fitted to my head, when I met you. My own original eyes always crossing and googly, all those operations as a kid to straighten them didn't work.

But the adjustment made was not in the eyes themselves, but in what was being seen and who else was looking. And it was you. You saw it too. Saying nothing but *look*, and pointing. We'd see the tree and the same pair of eyes would blink from each of our faces. First time for me, first time seeing a tree and someone else saying: "yes, I see it too."

This is what you did. Did you know? It started with the land. Walking into it. Rolling downhill. Putting your hand in a tide-pool on Achill Island. Just the tips of your fingers. Letting me see.

Then we did it together like a dance. The photographer's two-step. Silent on a walk, me with my camera and seeing some turfed-up tree, its roots exposed. And stopping to frame it, to hold it in my arms my lens, you'd enter, move in knowing when to move, how, and begin to be part of the holding. Lying down on the ground beneath the window where my eye is aiming. Silent. Held.

I am lying on the kitchen floor in the house in Kilmeena asking you to lie on me. We are fully clothed and I don't want your sex or your love, just your weight. Give me your weight, I'd say. Feeling sparks of myself flying off, I need gathering. Be a body, I'd ask, not person. I wanted you like a rug. I'm remembering this because of something I heard last night about an autistic boy who could not bear to be held. But when he'd fling himself against the porcelain sink, threatening his own single self, his nanny would wrap him in a sheet tucking in the ends tightly, and lay him on the bed. Sometimes, he would pat his chest when he needed the wrapping, when his exposure felt bare and unbearable, needing to be held in.

I'm remembering this because in those days, I was meant to be living the life of an artist, apparently perpetually on holiday and blissful. My father would call to ask if I was having fun, was I happy. And I had been when I arrived and opened my eyes. But then I couldn't bear the open.

Shards of me were flying off, molecules of panic, no words but needing you to lie on me, give me your weight, and you did. We didn't discuss it or understand it, just lived through it. "Thank you," I'd say, once I could feel my breath in the wall of my chest, once I could feel the edges of myself. You would get up and make a pot of tea.

I'm writing towards something now, can feel myself veer in the direction of the core when I started talking about the tree and you seeing you too. About seeing together. But I can't seem to get to it now, feel too close, too held back

Veering in the direction like a car on the road to Louisburg, passing Crough Patrick on the left and the sea on the right, passing the house with the red statues and it's yard, passing virgin after virgin, blue cloak, ring of lights. *Turn left at the lady.* Keep going fast. Driving fast on these roads is dangerous. The curves are sudden, as are the sheep, and you miss things. Miss the brambles full to bursting with blackberries and little ditches for falling into, miss the ruins of houses and rolls of potato beds grown over, miss turnoffs to piers with names driven by too fast to catch. But it's hard to slow down, to get out and walk the road. I might never get back, the story of each path is so long and thorny, I want to get past it quick. Sketch it out, but don't go in too far, just point: there's the road to Roonagh pier, and that one goes to Murrisk Abbey, and there's where we ate dinner one night at a fancy pub. But not go down any, just skitter past. I end up with nothing much but driving, the destinations all littered behind.

I want to stop. Not this writing, but the skittering. The little vignettes. I'm sick of their charm. I need to tell you something.

A woman once told me that people entered her through her eyes, could get inside and no way to protect herself but to close her eyes or look away. I didn't understand. I was looking out. But what I'm getting now is how they also take whatever is seen, absorbing like two sponges. And what did she see? I imagine all kinds of horror. Witnessing violence or death or pain. But what she meant was the look of someone you trust and see every day, looking back in disgust or indifference, reflecting back a thinly veiled disappointment while asking casually what you'd like for breakfast. How can you not take that in? It gets in through your eyes and stays. It becomes the world. It becomes you.

Then when someone arrives with a face of compassion, with eyes that shine for you, you have no choice but to shield. The brilliance of that look is like staring at the sun. Hurts. All the images your eyes remained open to, violently tooth-picked open, you now see like a screen. It makes you cringe. The love itself makes you cringe. It burns its way in, if you let it. Burn the veils of hate that feel like layers of your skin, layers of skin on your eyes. But first you have to see them, see the hate and feel it and feel what it does to you, how it tears everything soft apart and leaves a core of hard hate inside that you think is you. It must be. That's what you saw. But you don't let it in yet, not yet. There's no velcro in your body for this shine to stick to. The only stuff you know is the scratchy bitter look that feels like home. And you close your eyes and run.

You are building a shelf for my kitchen. Painting the brackets yellow, shelf red. The shelf has fancy curves on it. For me, the fact of you building is strange. Men in my family don't touch wood, except for luck. I tell you not to bother painting the curves "it's only a shelf." But you love it and care and don't stop. Watching you swear as you fit the dovetailed joints together that won't go. Swearing at the joints. My kitchen. You on the ladder up over the cooker. The finely joined joints. Red and yellow gloss. You look at me, proud. I look at the shelf.

It feels like I'm telling the story of us according to me but don't know it except in the telling. As though we made films I couldn't see then, which I'm playing here reel after reel. Keep trying to find the one that contains the sequence where the transition happens, where the editing changed. You know the way they do it in slow motion, back and forth back and forth, back and forth and point. There. There's where the cut is, that's where the car went off the road, or the train went off the tracks. It looks seamless but now we have it, the exact moment of derailment.

I'm finding that now, rewinding the film that hasn't been played for anyone, my own dingy screening room here. Only you know the story too, you were there. I suppose that's why it's you I'm playing it to; you were the only one who saw it. Back forth. Back and forth. Rewind. There.

The image of the trees, their skinny dark lines against the white sky, fat red bird resting on them, us taking it all in through our eyes, wordless and smiling. The shelf you made for me, its carved curves. You in the darkroom staring down at my pictures emerging in their chemical baths, rubbing your thighs, flapping your arms when you liked what you saw. It wasn't what you said but that body in action, rubbing your hands together, your face in the red light, quick gasps of air, then rubbing your sides, a small orgasm of recognition. No matter the words, your body told the truth and I knew it. Your eyes trained on these things, the things were us and then you turned and looked at me. With all the same excitement, small hoots of joy, breathing in and in and in, and for a minute, I was beheld.

Expecting your look to shatter, your eyes to sink back and disappear, turn towards other things — it didn't. Kept looking straight at me the way the sun shines because that's its job and nothing between it and the plants. You shone with love and I went black, burnt, turned away.

That's where the train went off, there. That's where the trees turned up. Where the screen went dark. Where I left. This is the exact image:

We are in Delphi Wood behind the lodge where all those farmers drowned one famine here. We were walking among the trees. The ones upturned by storms were most magnetic for us. I stop with my camera, finding within the frame three trees, two fallen and one standing, to hold, compose, to save. And in you come, into the frame naked and climb into the one standing tree, a hole in its trunk. Climb into the hole as if the womb of the tree. And ruined it. "Get out," I yelled. "Get out." And you did. I could not stand to look at you. Wanted my emptiness back, my bleak black hollow trees. Not your face, your body, your fullness. I cut you out. "I want it empty," I said. "I like the bare bones of the trees. Leafless." I took the picture. I have it hanging here. Stark.

You were a weaver bringing the language of the woods into your pictures, painting in their thronging colors, the grass screaming its green, the rowanberries popping red and the birds with all their names crowing. You were a meal too big for me. My stomach wanted its own bare walls. I hated you for loving me richly, for in that love I could see those who hadn't. And easier to live in the emptiness calling it the world than to see it from a distance as a place you'd been stranded, and that there were other worlds older and newer. You were a storyteller, a colour wheel spinner, telling of time before time. Shocking my narrow-shelved mind with stories of goddesses before God, of couples before Adam and Eve, stories no one told me. You could trace your family back four centuries to this very spot. You brought me worlds and worlds steaming and fragrant on heavy platters. Fed me.

And I have saved everything. Stored it up. Somewhere behind all that undigested shit I called myself there was this glorious gift I called Ireland I called Daniel Molloy. Separate. Unprocessed like film, like food. You said it once so clearly, how I saw myself a sea of shit I projected onto the world and swimming in it. How desperately you tried to get me to see it wasn't me. Literally holding up a full-length mirror so I could see myself from the back. Calling me beauty. I couldn't see it, couldn't see it, couldn't. Wanted to shatter you for saying it, tear at you shouting, "who are you seeing? Who?" Not wanting the layers to burn off my eyes. Not wanting to see.

Shit. In this writing I am wading into it, turning it over and over to look. The film rewound and projected is not retouched, just slowed down to see the moments, the tracks of sound and image and when they split or fit, the jumps, the missing frames, and found them. Cinematic archive of shit and technicolor, so many years of files, filing a life, with you in the booth right now, quietly rubbing your thighs, urging me on: "do it, I want to see it."

Here in the summer field, turning over and over the crap, breaking down each image, the mulch, heaping. The way compost is made. It begins to stink as I turn. Heat comes off, the steam and stink of change. Even my hands smell. Makes my eyes stream and want to leave, but keep working it. Releasing the compounds under sun-blasted, rain-stroked sky. Somehow, coming back as earth, the rich gloss. Ivory Black. Like paint, like eyes. There are flecks of shell in it, of egg and bone. There is beauty in this shit and I begin again.

Here is my creation story. I wrote for you, creator of creation stories. This one is no myth. The locations are true, the transplants and transatlantic losses. The finds. The pond and the pigment and the furniture. The trees: they live both in their soil on your side and in their photographs on mine.

The name "Beauty." The shit. The paint chips on this table. Green. All true. There is nothing left to say except I'm sorry I ran. I love you. And how I thank you.

Goodbye.
Ronna

•••

Brandon Marlon to ———
December, 2013
age 34

When I first laid eyes on you, you seemed so elegant (it was your coiffed hair). You reminded me of Mrs. Whittle from elementary school, whose white blouses I admired as a schoolboy.

For you, I ached and burned. Did you hear the crackle of my fire?

All at once, in an instant, I desired for you to let me be your reason why; to hallow me with your embrace, consecrate me with your smile, sanctify me with your touch.

At first disoriented, I soon became disillusioned. After that first week of my wishful imagining, your true colours were vividly displayed, and my blissful hallucinations dissipated like morning dew.

Pardon me; I thought you were someone else.

Post Scriptum: Why weren't you that person?

•••

Richard Harrison to Lisa ———
January 4, 1991
age 34

Dearest Lisa,

It's nearly noon, and I've spent the entire morning cleaning up the apartment. What a mess. It started when I figured I could easily find the two Findley books I know I have in boxes in my closet. That was three hours ago. No books (I gave up hauling boxes) but a tidier place. Now all my unfinished work is in a file box beside this table. IF put together it makes a stack of paper over two feet high. It's nice that I finally got it together, don't you think?

I missed you last night and I miss you now. I mailed a letter yesterday, but it may be sent back to me; I didn't know postage was up: 40 cents now.

I don't really have anything to say today. I just wanted in this way, these words, to touch you. This letter will go to your house. You'll hold it in your hands. You'll be happy to have received it, and you can think of me smiling as I put it in the mailbox.

I couldn't find the calendar I wanted, so I adapted the one from the Radio Centre. The calendar part of it, the ongoing "top ten" from me. It's a nice piece of work, and I can change the pictures whenever I want.

I can put my bluestone bracelet on now, you'll be glad to hear.

This is a funny letter, isn't it? I'm reaching for you in these words, and I'm reaching for words, too. I haven't yet found the calm place where poems are, or rather, when I find it, it quickly vanishes again. Maybe I'm forcing things. I need to learn to relax into that mode. But from where I am right now, there is something heavy about it, too. When do I write? When I am doing nothing else but playing, watching TV, checking the stats. Yet those things themselves seem unappealing. They don't bring me closer to me, at least not now, not in the pitch I am in. But then, there's a trap, too: thinking that the other things I do are forms of writing or necessary correlates. I've written under all sorts of conditions. No, it isn't the correlates, it's the core. I'm not yet back to me, back inside, in touch with my enthusiasm for the words, the game. Maybe my upcoming Blockbuster Trade will do it.

I hunger for you. Things have changed so much, so deeply, I'm still finding differences between before and now. I used to tire of sexual love; I guess my fears caught up with my desires, overtook them. That was before. Now I can't wait to touch you again, smell you, taste you, fill my mouth with your skin, your sweet, powerful juices (is it only an accident that juice and jouissance sound so close? It is, but it is not.) I want the feeling of the whole of you again and again. And I love anticipating you, us, too, our thinking together, talking, growing closer and closer, when we make love, our breath in each other's mouths, sometimes so close we make each other's throats sing. Ah, our naked, beautiful skin.

Here's the key. I must surround myself again, surround myself unashamed of what I truly love in all the ways I love it. Words reaching for you. Our bodies. Our sexual love, my need for you (in the book "Love" you gave me (which I read over and over) Erich Fromm says, "Mature love says, 'I need you because I love you.'" It is a good need.

And my need for play, right now, is still the intense competitive play of the pools, the games. I'm not out of that yet (no surprise there) and though I see through it, I am still in it, like a surfacing swimmer. Which means I must continue to swim. For now.

Well, it's 12:30 now, and I have to go to Concordia again. I'm setting the final disk for the thesis to be printed. I'll make a couple of changes, too, the italics in "I wanted to be a soldier" and the "After December 6" poem. I'll have a look at the "Soldiers sleeping." We'll see. What I also need to do is re-read the "91 Season" poems, to get back into them. I can't expect to get back into it at the level I reached (and I had to reach it) of a poem like "Ice."

It was good to talk to you. You are very much with me, you know. I send you me.

> all my love
> Richard

P.S. It's 4:30 now. I ended up walking all over the place getting my last books, talking to the people at Concordia. I'm at the Grad Students' Building, but somehow I just can't get into working on the thesis. I enclose two new Hockey Pool Poems with the set I made, maybe more like "beginning" poems. They're still with me. Funny how that works.

I love you. I'll talk to you on the weekend.

·

Richard Harrison to Lisa ———
March 16, 1991

My dearest Lisa,

There are places I'll remember
all my life

like the Dupont Subway station: I found a transfer in my wallet and thought of you, going to the station, seeing you off to work, or arriving at your door. Good memories. I like it when everyday places ring with us. I was down at the Alexis Nihon plaza this morning; I got tickets for D (arriving here on the 5th, I think now; I got to get stuff for him to do — he's not a convenient friend, so needy. I need to do something to set that relationship aright) and I for the playoffs, got a photocopy of the "Bobby pitching hay, topless for photographers" photo that M from my Creative Writing workshop sent me because of my poem — it looks great, and now I can send the original back before school ends, and I was feeling kind of lost and down about missing you and how much work I have to do, so I bought myself a treat — a t-shirt with the logo for the San Jose Sharks, the newest team in the NHL. They haven't even played yet, but their logo is cool — black and grey and a blue that looks really good on me — a big black shark putting the bite on a hockey stick, the way those mailman-biting dogs have a piece of pants in their teeth and laugh the way you and my father do sometimes, a laugh I love.

So here I am in Montreal approaching Spring with the windows open and a fresh Bodum of coffee and a shirt for a team that hasn't played a game, thinking of my dearest love and writing to you to boot. It'll be OK because much of it already is. Even if I don't get the Reverón, the Batman looks good. But even R likes the Reverón — the Deconstructed Man, he said. Oh well. Batman is both man and mask, the illusion/allusion won't be lost. I love you.

R and I had an interesting talk yesterday. He treated me to lunch. I really think he likes me, but something in me still holds back. Maybe it's the fixity of his smile. I wanted to apologize to him about that remark about B I made I told you about in my last letter, but I didn't. I didn't want to reveal to him that B and I had any connection under the surface. Likewise, I wanted to ask him to add a blurb to my book jacket, but I held back. I don't want to ask him unless I'm sure I want to use it, and something tells me I'm not sure. Yet he was immensely generous (though he said to me that he was less generous than he wanted to be) about it. What is it? I might even get a job teaching poetry next year because of him. And there is something of power in him that I don't want to give in to. Is it just me? Is it just me with men?

We talked about recognition, about there never being enough. He said he fretted once a week about it; he was much more worried about (someone like, but it became) W who has no recognition in any contemporary anthologies and the like. But he does worry about himself. There's something in him when he talks of L's success, and too many of our discussions centre on awards and reviews and on what he has never got. Do I fear he will call a debt? I'll probably talk about this with you tomorrow over the phone, now that I've pondered it for so long through my fingertips. Perhaps I still feel guilty about the way my manuscript went to G and then I had to pull it away. Perhaps I feel I made the wrong choice.

So much of what I feel now is drawn back to the travails of the book, the cover, the blurbs, the impending doom of recognition, or joy. How many confrontations lie within that book — E and K and the kids and Y, who knew me then, with all of them I am still unfinished. And C, too, the treachery of that gossipy line that that put you with knowledge against me. I'm glad you told me, you know. That was exactly the sort of thing to say that divides couples because with it they are forced into different enthusiasms about the same thing. And if my enjoyment of C's call is lessened, I'd rather that than an illusion on my part and a cheap shot laid at your door on yours. Shitty timing, too, on his part (or great timing depending on how you think about it) just when I'm on the verge of a new book, when my own sense of what I'm doing comes under such doubt. As you can see, I'm still dealing with this.

Ah well, Bobby is still pitching hay. Brett is waiting for a pass. You and I are kissing, four cats are peering from the long grass, an ornate horned frog is keeping her wisdom to herself, a red heart says I L Y. I have a nice desk. I think of you always. Talk to you soon.

with the love of my whole heart,
Richard.

•••

Evelyn Lau, 2005
age 34

I Love You

Fifty times a day you said it.
Anyone else would have died of boredom,
but for me it was the hook that slid under skin,
buried itself in bone.
Each time I tried to leave,
the line stretched taut
so I stumbled in the open doorway.
You said it in your sleep

and woke me from dreaming about you,
your father-face gazing down
upon my child face.
You wrote it on my back
with a finger dipped in acid,
substituting the words
with a heart and a horseshoe.
You left love notes in every room,
so many stacked around me I gasped
for breath like an asthmatic.
I'd waited my whole life for you,
a man with mirrors instead of eyes,
and arms like lifelines for the drowning.
But your love couldn't be traded for milk or eggs.
I couldn't weigh its worth,
calculate its market value.
I couldn't spend it in the stores,
or build a big house with it in a good neighbourhood.
No, not even a small house.
In the end it was too much, yet not enough —
it was beyond measure, like the soul,
so light that when the body gives it up
it vanishes like it never was.

•••

Nathan Dueck to Sharon ———
Calgary, Alberta
June 5, 2014
age 35

for Sharon, who understands.

With that line, I dedicated my book to you. I really mean those words, and I wrote them to say how much your commitment, your enduring compassion means to me, but they can't speak to the real meaning of your understanding. You listened to so many so-so ideas, you heard so, so many okay poems, and you read so, so, so many "good enough" drafts. When I griped about "good" not being "enough," you busted chops: "enough is enough." Then, after a few publishers rejected the manuscript, you encouraged me to send it out again, saying it's "too good to throw out." For those reasons, and the feelings I don't have words for, I know you love me. Only, I can't say that I get why. It would probably take more than a single line on one dedication page for me to come to terms with how understanding you are. Although it's a little maudlin to write, and I'm not quite sure how to put it plainly, I want to be just as understanding. I want to become more sympathetic towards you and less self-conscious, more aware of your needs and less concerned for my own. Who knows, I may learn to believe my intuition as well as my intellect. Maybe I'll even take myself a little less seriously. Let's call this letter another dedication — or, better, a renewal of vows. After all, I wrote the whole book wearing a ring you gave me.

Here's what I know: I've loved you since the day you asked me, "just what does this all mean, anyway?" You were leafing through a chapter of my grad school frustration. "I. have. no. idea," I whined. "I. can't. make. up. anything. anymore." You lifted my "poet" fingers from the keyboard. (I can't help but see you putting euphemistic, but not cynical, air quotes around "poet.") Once we pored over several pages, line-by-line, you flashed chops: "get writing, Dueck. Do it, or I'll never love you." That moment, and many others like it, lead me to think our relationship is the reality — really, it's a reality we make up, or the series of realities we're making up in real time — that helps ease my anxiety and isolation. I used to worry those feelings of loneliness would make me illegible to everyone else. Now, I worry that you're probably the only person with any hope of interpreting me. That said, I also hope to interpret you, and to care for your worries, even though I know that I'll never feel what you fear. Because of that insecurity, maybe, we make up realities to confess our needs with each other, together, even though we know words just aren't good enough. And, I'm beginning to believe that you're more at ease than I am with the uncertainty between words and meaning, between confession and understanding. You're better at relationship make-em-ups than I am. At least, that's what I get about how you understand.

So, I dedicate myself to you, here, before the witnesses who read these words: I'll try to be understanding, to become more sympathetic towards you and aware of your needs, attending to each moment we have together.

When you're feeling discouraged, intimidated, or overwhelmed, I'll understand. I'll be attentive to how those feelings change, anticipate a few of those changes, and try to accept them all. While we age, I want us to mature in understanding, which I take to mean I have to be less sullen. (I can't help but hear you say "good luck, smartypants" with emphasis, but no sarcasm.) When I write, I want to imagine you, or some part of your personality, understanding. By seeing you that way, by thinking about your compassionate endurance, I might be able to turn away from my worries. That is to say, I'll dedicate more than one line to you.

•••

Peter Trower to Jill Wright
Gibsons Landing, British Columbia
Spring, 1966
age 35

Dear little Jill:

After long silence and many vague rumours, it was strange and good to see your handwriting again. That sad, confused period when our lives became entangled has remained very clear in my mind and despite the inevitable changes I've gone through, I still get fond and nostalgic when I think of you. Two years of freaky experiences, poetry, pot smoke, publication, rejection-slips, several bewildered girls in the erratic orbit of my own bewilderment and you never came back to the coast.

I don't know if you heard about my bust last year. It was somewhat of a bummer as you might imagine but it certainly taught me a few things such as the necessity for keeping a scrupulously clean pad. The whole business resulted from an influx of heads into this area that is still going on and the inevitable mushrooming — magic, of course — of the dope scene. It was all super groovy at first — a lot of musicians moved up here and we had some fantastic parties with live sounds and a resident dealer. Things rapidly got out of control of course — someone started selling to the high-school kids in the unvarying way that pot always spreads and there was the usual panic-reaction among the straights. Apparently a number of students were interrogated and some attention-hungry little chick gave them a list of people she thought smoked grass. She also said that she figured I was the dealer. I wasn't but I guess I must have seemed the most logical suspect. Anyhow, they called in the Vancouver narcs who arrived by plane one Monday morning and proceeded to raid and search all the pads under suspicion. By sheer chance, a head who wasn't on their list drove into the middle of the first shakedown. They frisked him and let him go, a real goof on their part as he immediately warned all the rest of us to get our shit outside. So all our shit was outside and they really should have drawn a blank on the whole scene. I was at a friend's place when they tracked me down and, while pretty paranoid at their mere presence, I really didn't think they could nail me for anything. How wrong I was. I guess I'd lived in that goddamn place too long to be careful enough. When they started sniffing around, they discovered enough traces — mostly seeds — to bust me for possession. As you may well imagine, I was pretty drug behind the whole business.

I was the only person to get charged as a result of the raid and I figured they would really try to sock it to me. The trial was remanded for five weeks during which time, I sweat a good deal of blood. The Crown brought the narcotics prosecutor — a real witch-burning bastard — up from Vancouver for the occasion and I had the foremost pot lawyer defending me. They were pushing for six months but I ended up with a month and a $1,000 fine. Fortunately, I was able to get the fine paid out of my English trust-fund. The month in Oakalla was really very interesting and I filled two notebooks with observations and poems. I was assigned as a cleaner to the South Wing where the gallows is located and where the most hardcase cons are housed pending appeal. There were at least eight murderers in the building, a couple of them in death-row under constant surveillance. It was a bit of a mind-shaker for the first couple of days. I would visualize them pulling a desperate break and being trapped in the middle of it. Then I quit fighting it and let it take me much as you have to do with acid. After that it wasn't too bad except for the clanging, ferocious monotony. I rapped with a lot of fellow-losers including one real kindred soul, a good, gentle cat who had just been supplying a few friends with weed and through bum reassurances of an infiltrated friend, sold to an undercover agent and got hit with five years — later reduced to three. Sure is a fucked-up world we got stuck in. There were more cats doing time for bum beefs in there than I ever imagined. The Criminal Code is so overloaded with narrow, anti-human laws. May it burn brightly in the eventual bonfire of millennium.

Since that chastening and extremely expensive episode, I have been playing it fairly cool, staying away from potentially dangerous people and scenes, working at my steady part-time surveying gig, not drinking very much and attempting to become a better poet. I've been publishing a bit, mostly in underground papers and the local rag until I got busted. My most class or literary appearance has been in two consecutive issues of POETRY AUSTRALIA. This came about in a rather curious way. Early last year, I received a form letter announcing a special issue featuring Canadian poets and inviting me to submit. How they ever got hold of my name is a real puzzle unless it was from the WRITER'S DIGEST contest when I won $5.00 for thirtieth prize and had my name and address printed. Anyway, I sent them about eight poems and got a personal reply from the editor — a chick or, probably elderly lady — that she was considering one of the poems. The issue came out however with most of the winners being established poets like LAYTON and NEWLOVE — I wasn't in it. Giving a stoic shrug, I wrote the thing off as one more bum break and proceeded to forget about it. My subscription copies still came in however and a couple of issues later, I was amazed to see one of my poems on the contents page. I also got into the next issue — the last I've received — along with Robert Graves. Too much! Spurred on by this mad acclaim, I hastily mailed her some better poems and also sent verses to ATLANTIC and TAMARACK. Both the latter came back, somewhat dampening my hopes but to hell with it, I've tasted a little blood now and will keep banging on those venerable doors till they let me in. I'm a bit zonked at the moment and have just finished my first decent poem in weeks which accounts for over-optimistic foregoing but bear with me. I'm getting several poems in the first issue of an as yet-unnamed journal emanating from L.A. I'll send you a copy when it comes out. The same people intend to issue a series of chapbooks featuring new Canadian and American poets including me. I hope the deal comes off.

I'm spending a lonesome Saturday night by preference, getting high, digging all my latest sounds of which I have many and choice and tripping out on the Past and the fiery joy of communication. I sure did love you once, little girl in the lapwinged past several forevers ago. You have escaped the muddy, tenacious scene for lake islands and the inevitable truce with straight values but so have I and so have all the worthy people for the most part out of the concrete coffins to the where-it's-at wilderness. I no longer have my pad incidentally. I gave the bloody thing up after it was despoiled by the fascist badgers. I now have my own trip-shack on my mother's property where I can keep my visitors down to a cool minimum and get my head together. Just got DYLAN THOMAS' NOTEBOOKS plus his biography and have been really getting hung up on the whole myth all over again. I don't know if you knew that my stepfather died last year of a malignant brain-tumour. It was a grim business but he didn't suffer too much. Anyway, Marty and I are living at home again as befits perpetual children. It's not an ideal situation and we wrangle periodically but I can always escape to the sanctuary of my shack-office-womb.

Wow, this is the longest letter I've written for months. I always enjoyed copping out to you though. How about doing me a favour, phoning my sister-in-law again and telling her to write as she owes me a letter. Must split now as I'm expecting visitors. Flattered that you wrote an essay on me. How about letting me read it? Chow for now, little Jill, you will walk in my thoughts.

Lots of Love,
Pete

•

Peter Trower to Jill Wright
Gibsons Landing, British Columbia
June 9, 1966

Jill, honey,

Sorry I've been so long in answering. I seem to have been unusually busy the last while. I have a lot of exciting relationships happening at once plus I'm writing quite a bit of poetry, drawing cartoons again and still doing the survey gig. I've also started doing a music trip with Marty and Sandy Lemon, singing and reading poems. We had a really groovy thing going last year that I think I touched on in my previous letter. Two freaked-out tenor-players from San Francisco, a local trumpet man, two guitars and drums all out of their skulls and blowing up a storm every weekend. It was a far-out time that more-or-less fell apart after my bust as all went their separate ways. Lately, Marty and Sandy have got the thing together again with an organ and different musicians. They have a big studio in a very cool part of Kerrisdale and I took part in a couple of trippy sessions there last week. Singing is a whole other experience…it's such a good release. Also, since I'm going to have to break down and give readings before long, it's good practice for loosening up on a stage. Anyhow, it's a groove.

Had an incredible stroke of poetic good-fortune a couple of weeks ago. One of the poems I had published in POETRY AUSTRALIA was picked for inclusion in an international anthology called THE BEST POEMS OF 1967 and published by an outfit in California called the BORESTONE MOUNTAIN FOUNDATION. I don't know if you ever saw the poem but it's called THE SEA RUNS DIAGONALLY and will be reprinted in the next BLEW OINTMENT out of Vancouver along with some other poems of mine and a cartoon. Bill Bissett who puts the book out, is sending some copies to the HEAD SHOP so tell Yvonne to look out for it. It should be out in a couple of weeks. Bissett incidentally, is out on bail for four counts of possession at the moment. They busted him, his old lady and three other chicks at an embryonic colony past Powell River which is some distance upcoast from here. The fuzz in that area are particularly militant toward hippies and gave them a fucking hard time. Poor Bill has a previous pot conviction and will get a year at the very least. I feel a real sympathy for him, having gone through a roughly similar experience although my position was a little better than his. Also, I recently found out that it was Bissett who sent my name to POETRY AUSTRALIA in the first place. It's really sickening, the number of good, gentle people who are getting shot down by the Gestapo bastards. A person can only hope that Pierre Trudeau in his apparent enlightenment will do something positive about the screaming injustice of the pot laws.

Jonny Newlove just arrived back in town having achieved total recognition with the publication of his new, hardcover collection. Remember when I first introduced you to John at that party? I really used to act like an idiot around him, always forcing poems on him. I've outgrown that kind of bullshit anyway and we had a good talk. He finally read a thing of mine called WET TESTAMENT which is quite long and sort of a super cop-out on my juicing days. He apparently dug it as he said he would send it along to TAMARACK REVIEW with a covering letter. This is damn good of him really and he is also going to be one of my sponsors for a CANADA COUNCIL GRANT. Winning that award has done me a lot of good as people seem to take me more seriously now. Self-confidence is a good trip.

Enough of these ego freak-outs. I'd really dig to see you in the flesh again, little Jill. A little chick was over to see me the other night who is exactly your age and reminds me very much of you. As a matter of fact, I told her all about you and how it was in the learning turmoil of once upon a time. She didn't have your writing talent however or your understanding and our communication was and is on a shallower level. It's about 3 a.m. as I write and I'm smoking dope by myself, unable to sleep, and thinking about you. How about coming out here this summer and consoling the confused poet on the verge of becoming famous and older?

Anyhow, what else? Oh yeah, you were asking me what sounds I was digging these days. Well, of course I dig most of the psychedelic stuff which is truly the head's hit-parade but I also love stone soul like OTIS REDDING and ARETHA FRANKLIN. Saw the CREAM in person last week…their sound is absolutely incredible due in part to the way they exploit their amps which are the largest and most expensive-looking I've ever seen. Ginger Baker, the drummer is fantastically proficient as are the other two really. A truly tough group. Still trip out on RAY CHARLES of course. Just got his new album which contains a very groovy arrangement of ELEANOR RIGBY among other goodies. Also listen to my old idol, FRANKIE LAINE whom I also saw in person a few month ago and rapped with backstage. I get somewhat put-down by the hip purists for this little indulgence but I don't care. LAINE keeps me in close touch with the mad past that I must mine for all it's worth.

I think I'll send you a copy of my drunken saga that I mentioned earlier. It's not among my prettier items but I think it contains some fairly strong writing. It's hard to believe sometimes that I actually did all those insane things and survived. I drink only in moderation now…except for the occasional lapse…and feel much the better for it both mentally and physically. I acknowledge my dept to certain benign chemicals for this transformation. The search for enlightenment is much happier than the search for oblivion.

Well, little girl, I've got to crash out so will end here. Be cool, write soon or better, make it out here.

Love,
Pete

•••

Ivan E. Coyote to ———
Prince George, British Columbia
August 11, 2004
age 35

Dear F:

The thing is, I came to you. I found you. You were pretty honest about being a sadist, in fact, that was precisely what attracted me to you, right from the beginning. Whether I knew it or not, I was looking for you. A mean but sweet femme top in five inch heels.

Love is a tricky bastard. By the time I figured out that it was when you stopped hurting me, *that* was when I was really truly in danger, it was too late.

You try getting any sympathy when you tell your best friends how much the self-avowed sadist broke your heart, how much pain she put you through.

Even a year and something later, the thought of the smell of your neck will bring me to tears in a corner of a crowded coffee shop. But I don't miss you. That tricky old bastard, he makes no sense.

Even still, I regret nothing, and I wouldn't change a thing. Not a minute of it. Not even that night in that basement in Brooklyn. I can almost laugh about that now, and I really do love a good story. We wrote some really good stories, you and I. I am grateful to have all of them with me still.

love,
She

•••

Susan Musgrave and Stephen Reid
mid-1980s
age 35

Dear Susan: I finished working. Served 128 breaded pork cutlets, green breaded pork cutlets. Ran four miles. I just came in, had a shower, and I'm sitting here in baby powder and pyjama bottoms. Would you like to have an oil-fondue party?

Strange day. A friend of mine died last night. An Indian kid, Danny, I used to give the blues to on the hockey rink. I had to rack him up a few times — he was too fast, scored too much. I liked him. He was 24.

•

Dear Stephen: I'm feeling vulnerable, too. I wonder where vulnerable comes from, what's the original meaning of the word. I should have studied linguistics. The art of tonguing things? Once, in France, I was in a post office and I was licking stamps and the postmaster told my friend, who lived in the village, he'd like to hire me because I had such a beautiful tongue. When you get out I will only lick stamps in the privacy of our own bedroom.

I walked out of the prison last night, it was snowing, getting dark. One of the guards, walking behind me, said, "I'll trade you coats." I had on my raccoon coat, I said, "Even this one isn't warm enough for me." He put his arm around me, hugged me tight. He was older, looked Irish. He said, "Maybe you need a drink."

I said, "You are Irish." He said, "My parents were." He suddenly looking ashamed for letting a little of himself be known. Another man, walking slightly behind him, was shackled, in leg irons and a chain around his waist. He carried his belongings in a cardboard box.

The guard said, "I'm looking after him." I nodded. He became distant and we passed through the gates that lock us out, lock us in, lock us everywhere away. I got in my car and thought of you doing three years chained in the hole having bean cake slapped on your face three times a day, breakfast, lunch and dinner, and I thought that's the saddest thing I know.

[...]

There is nothing one man will not do to another.

Slipping into your cell, I wander around lost. I love listening to your breathing. Each night I lie awake imagining it to be my own.

My heart's a rag. It's a rag in the wind. It's a soggy bean cake, a man carrying his only belongings in a box, it's leg irons for one and Danny being poisoned by cyanide.

There is nothing one person will not do to another.

And out of these nothings, all beginnings come.

•

Dear Susan: I love you. All things begin there. Last night on T.V. a woman said she wanted two men. One to be her friend — tolerant, giving, someone to share her life with — then she wanted a more dangerous one, unpredictable, moody, a male animal. She said more. She was articulate and very intelligent — the only thing that bothered me was the impression I got that she wanted the two men in one — and to choose when he would be what.

·

Dear Stephen: I'm exhausted. My brother and I went shopping with Charlotte. We bought an axe. I spent the rest of the day in the computer room at the University working on The Joy of Sexual Failure, the chapter called "Total Failure," where sex leads to death. It's distasteful, after awhile, to be writing about men who only get off when they eat the toenail clippings of cadavers. Put me off my lunch, rather. One man, who used to close his penis in the toilet until it turned black and dropped off, believed that erections were caused by poor muscle control. I would think it was the contrary, but then I'm not a man. I just went into the kitchen and Bill Deverell was there playing Mr. Potato Head with Charlotte and Matt Cohen.

·

Dear Susan: My cell was ransacked this morning. I took my writing with me. We're still locked down. They're still searching. Why is it that every time someone gets killed they take all my extra underwear? They came up here looking for murder weapons and left with all the shelves and hangers and seven television sets. Maybe the guy was killed by multiple television reruns. Poor Eddy. Heard he was coming in off the rink. He's a goalie — it's like a fish out of water, a goalie off the ice. Too cold. Why did I let you leave?

·

Dear Stephen: I left, but I didn't leave you. How can I leave you, even for sleep? A minute is too long. For the rest of my life I want to write to you. I want to sit like this and write. Nothing more but letters to you. And nothing less.

·

Dear Susan: Someone tried to escape last night so we were locked down. Breakfast was a luke-cold cup of coffee, slice of plain bread. Then they announced they had found the guy, so our doors would be opening at noon, but there would be no lunch. I asked if they could leave my door closed and feed me instead. I got a dirty look.

I watched an authors' conference in Toronto last night. Ken Kesey, James Baldwin, Margaret Atwood. Will we go to authors' conventions? Writer's meetings? The HIS and HER sides of the wild side of Canadian writing. A poet and an outlaw. Which do you want to be?

I'll write you again this evening. Tell Charlotte she looks like a Vegetable Head.

•••

Shane Neilson to Janet Sunohara-Neilson
February 14, 2011
age 35

Dear Janet,

It's Valentine's Day. I think I may have told you this, but perhaps you've forgotten: I'm readying a manuscript of love poems for publication. Every one of them was inspired by you, by the love I have for you. I have about fifty poems written over the ten years we've been together, but I've been whittling them down — until I fell ill. Anyway, I'm sure production and editing will resume soon. I think I'll end up with about fifteen. I haven't shown you them for a few reasons:

(1) You used to be openly hostile to my writing,
(2) criticizing me for putting difficult feelings in the writing.

The funny thing is: unlike in life, I've always been honest in poetry. The love poems you've read from the past often contain dark elements because they reflect real life. In that life I always wanted us to be better, and these poems were signals that we were having difficulty. Looking back, I know a more effective strategy would have been taking the risk of sitting down and telling you what I was thinking. Maybe I resorted to poetry as the last means to tell you I was hurting, and when you didn't respond, or seem to care, I felt like shutting down even further.

This is in the past. The important thing is, I have a small (and unseen) sheaf of poems that are comprised of love. The working title of the manuscript is *Reclaim*. The narrative is one of despair moving towards redemption and renewal. Such is the narrative I've always wanted; such is the way I wanted the story of us to end. So, even though I wordlessly endured rejection and control, beginning to think that my previous behaviour had doomed us — to the point of contemplating ending the relationship — the best and truest part of me was hopeful that we would remain together, that our family would continue to develop. Though I wondered for years *if* we could transcend the past, I nevertheless wrote poems the whole time with a happy ending. The reasons are more than wishful thinking: writing this way honoured how I thought (and still think) of you. Even if the happy ending doesn't work out in real life, I want these poems to document what I intended. This is how I cherish you!

I'm a love poet and the poems I love best are, naturally, love poems. Milton Acorn wrote a fraternal love poem called "Letter to Al Purdy" that begins (after an opening salutation to Purdy) with the lines, "One defends that tangle of roots / at the heart." It's always been tangled in that vicinity for me, and you're deepest in that briar patch — what Acorn once referred to as "heartmuscle." The poem continues, "I've / reached the point where every human contact / brings pain: worst of all, any touch / of what's most human in me /…my poetry." Pain, poetry, and human contact — I know that Bermuda triangle well. In fact, I've been institutionalized there! Acorn, of course, wrote his poem while in the mental hospital. Where else.

More importantly, though, Acorn wrote in "Letter to Al Purdy" about how poetry is where his life is understood, where the true meaning can be found. When you read *Reclaim* after it's published in the summer (before we take the second honeymoon in Croatia), I hope you see how profoundly I care for you. Poetry is the greatest expression of feeling, and I'll never write something in a poem that isn't true. I can't do it, never could.

And you know what? Poetry takes care of me. I wrote the poems, and it seems like the narrative arc is coming true as indeed I wrote it. At least I am taking the baby steps of belief — it's early. So, below is the frame fragmentary poem from *Reclaim* that, like all the poems inside, has this dual message: you are loved; I know what I have. In discussions with my friend Jim, whom I've greatly shared with about my concerns and difficulties, he's said two things that have been in my head for the past few months. The first was said after meeting you. He said, "I can see why you love her." The second is, "I know that you love her."

A pox on contamination!

Sincerely,

Your husband

To the Elysian fields, to a grand skyway,
to a far distant busy, to a remove,
to the last heart's outpost, to sentry duty,
to a foreign language, to pain,
to the view of the point, to a mantelpiece with your photograph,
to the flung and hanging feeling, to the old mistake,
to the not your fault, to the sorry,
to the until, to the broken,
to not here, to not with you,
away,
where my arms gather you up and into strange development,
into a love addressed to always.

•••

Andrew Suknaski, 1978
age 36

The Last Letter

in your last letter you ask
"how are you?"
i still stubbornly smoke my pipe
though it's suicidal in my condition
i've grown a moustache and full beard
wear glasses now
and no longer comb my hair funny
but part it letting it fall sideways
knowing there's nothing left to hide

sometimes i'm still cruel
to those who love me most
even though i've grown gentler
i can still bring the toughest woman to her knees
beyond the tears where she lives
and i am not proud of this sickness
"nothing hurts more than a kind man
who's turned cruel"

said my new love one evening
seated in a dark alcove where she cried
while the rain fell on a distant street

sometimes a small animal
still leaves its hutch in my brain
to burrow on the lower edge of my ribcage
four years after you
i've learned to say
"i love you..." to another woman
but the stars do not dance
when i speak

•••

Roo Borson, 1988
age 36

You Leave the City...

You leave the city and I'm free,
i.e. for nothing, to get drunk with friends.
And stumble home late, asking
the Important Questions. Such as:
Why did you go?
What are you that I love you?
What's so important in Poughkeepsie
that it deserves you, even for a night?
Strangeness; loose ends; my body on the far side of the bed
desiring me.
Is this how it will be?
If you would help me, John Donne, help me —
prescribe a metaphysic
for when in Rome, Atlantis, all the wronged cities —
and they send for him, and he's gone.

•••

...

Derek Beaulieu to Kristen Ingram
July 11, 2009
age 36

Steve McCaffery, 1984
age 37

K as in Sleep
for Karen

Should find it hard
to relocate between these losses,
veils,
which isn't history.

The primary bigamist sits pointing
to canonical attributes
where a body comes undone
conflictual in the mirror's dispossessed
aggressions.

Can't understand
as immobility
the sign
which is
or the hair amongst others
which authorizes
definition.

To turn aphasic.
Frequent language
only when it troubles us.

One is never sure here
of the voice of passion
the televised desire to stay
the child in duty
as a recollection ordered, since
hatred agonized is different
to a scene possessed
then rearranged.

...

Alden Nowlan to Claudine Nowlan
Fall, 1971
Charlottetown, Prince Edward Island
age 38

Reply

> Love is coming
> home at the end
> of the day and
> finding you here

> > Love Forever,
> > Claudine

•••

Kim Maltman, 1988
age 36

Installation #67

Someone across the subway car is lost in reverie. The
      machine of the soul lies idle.
      Goodday, sir.

Gentle creatures up above, no doubt, cast quizzically about
      amidst the blaze of yellows and
      of greens.

The last weekends of the season are filled with chores,
      and melancholy. Still, there are a few
      we do not wish occasionally

to crush lightly under our wheels. On the streets the
      crowds swirl past, intent
      on anything!

Like Mohammed, intent on passing through the eye of the
      needle, you are leaned against the bare
      magnolia in your red jacket.

Overhead a kite leaps from a child's hand,
                it
                        too is green!

I had not thought
        to
            come upon

                    such joy
                            so easily!

                    •••

Louis Riel to Marguerite Riel[1]
St. Vital, Manitoba
July 14th, 1883
age 38

My Dear Marguerite,
        Voilà, already a month since I left the mission. I'm thrilled to be returning
but I am troubled. Money is so rare here that I cannot sell anything. There
is at this moment a financial crisis in Manitoba and land sells very cheaply
or rather, it does not sell at all. After making a few arrangements, I think I
will leave from here next week.
        Mother and all the family send their love and wish you courage and
health.
        The Orangemen have tried to cause me harm. They have spoken of
my capture. But the celebrations of July 12th have passed and that frightful
day brought me no harm. I hope now to be in greater surety. But, have
the goodness to pray for me and make the sign of the Cross over our own
darling, little one in my absence.
        My sister Henriette has married Jean, one of the boys of your Grand-
father François Poitras. The nuptials lasted two days with a reasonable
assembly gathered which I think frightened the Orangemen. The vows were
taken the 11th and 12th of July. The scoundrels might have caused me trouble
on that day if there had not been such an assembly present. The ceremony
was performed on the 12th to that purpose.

---

1   All letters by Louis Riel in this collection were translated from the original French by David Eso.

Mother and all the family spoke continually of you. Mother often said: "if my little child were here" and she had tears in her eyes. Mother loves you greatly. Our uncle François, your uncle Jérémie, our aunt Louise and my little sister-in-law Magdeleine visit us from time to time. Magdeleine has already grown so big.

I think I will not be able to sell more than 2 or 3 scrips.

Give my respects to the Reverend Priests, to our dear uncle Swan and all his family. My compliments to all our parents and friends.

I am for life,
Your husband in Jesus and Mary,
Louis David Riel

•••

Pearl Luke to Robert Hilles
Feb. 14, 1997
aged 38

So Many Hands in One Week

Robert, last Friday your old man hands lay open on the table as if they had nothing to hide. Later, as we watched *The English Patient* for the first time, they rested and sometimes fumbled out of reach while your forearm and occasionally a knee nudged mine. I refused to claim any part of you, although I thought that even a finger might do. On Monday, you accepted my invitation to Victoria's and, although it took ten swipes to dry your nose with your knuckles, those surreptitious attempts charmed me as much as our hours of easy conversation in wine-coloured wingback chairs. When I offered you a story, you followed me home. There, in my darkened doorway shortly after midnight, your palms like rumpled paper smoothed over my back and around my breasts, passed them over just as I hoped and didn't hope you would. Tuesday, after you took me for Japanese and sake and roe, we sat in my loveseat and hinted at things so close to the surface they still scrape, but when your fingers brushed my jaw, I felt the angry verbs of earlier tales slip back to make way for a poet. Wednesday, you left lines that made me smile through the day at my desk, and I held you to me through the sting of your whiskers on my cheek, the heat of your hands tending breasts still fresh in my mind. On the telephone we talked fictions and before goodnight

I read you a passage of minutia you had the heart to love. On Thursday, I burned with a fever of 101, and a need to touch; I went home early to bed and you came. Your lips pressed until mine swelled past pleasure and still I fascinated at the crisscross wrinkles of your hands. You layered each sentence with kisses and drew me so close that your scent clung to my skin until, when you left, I slept with you after all. At eight o'clock this morning I entered my class with a pen that inked only in A's because you met me in the corridor with carnations and roses. At nine o'clock I read your card again and laughed aloud at how appreciatively you ordered the alphabet. At five o'clock I took your hand and led you to bed so you would be still. Fully dressed, on top of the covers, we found bits of flesh between buttons and exposed our underbellys. It is Friday the 14th of February and my heart feels red instead of blue.

Once again, thank you for making my day so memorable — you are a gentle & romantic man,

Pearl

•

Pearl Luke to Robert Hilles
12:41:58, June 17, 1997

What god hears in the privacy of our bedroom

god i love you
god i'm so happy happy
i've never been so happy god
you're great you're terrific
god i love you

i love your twiggy toes, your rumpled
paper hands god i love the way you slide
over me into me both of us rubbing in
excess like a lotion that softens until
there are no aches to smooth none just so
full in my chest that when i breathe out
i blow silly little puffed hearts
that flow toward the ceiling and never

pop but gather in bunches to nudge and nod
so happy together you for me and me for you

god I love you so much
i love you i love you i love you
i will forever and longer god
oh god you're the best

and god — the smallest object
in the room — listens and laughs

•••

bill bissett, 1977
age 38

from **Pomes for Yoshi**

none of us is

a saint   i cant make
 religion out uv yu
   it cuts off yr
     freedom
            lust baby
       thats wher its at
   how long ar yu in
     town for
        dew sumthing
        abt it

yu know i love
   yu   that shud
    b enuff for
     whn its
   happening
      with
        us

yoshi
ium thinkin uv
yu
nd i shudint
b doin that yu
know
what i shud
be doin
rite
now
is
screwin
like
yr probably
doin   n
thats
cool
but i
aint
screwin
nothing
xcept
my
hed

maybe yul
write me tho i
know its too
soon for yu
to b doin
that
hope my
love didint
disappoint yu
too much
whn i

was bitchy
     yr just
        goin
           thats
all
     seems like i
had to stay
     again for yu
     to go   but
     thats a
           narrow
           way
     to look at
     th changes
     i guess

     sumwhun cum in to
see my paintings coupul a
     daze ago   looks past like
     yu only oldr   he felt sum
        thing for th pictures
           like it was yu
              freeked me rite out   duz
it mean iul see yu again in
     five years or so   wow herd
        thats happend to othr
        frends we know
           seein sumwhun that
lookd like yu   ium kinduv
     fukd up again   but iul
        keep on trucking
        i will
           the models in th store
windows look like yu
     sumwhun tol me ium
        playin games

with my
mind
       what am i doin
       lovin yu like ths

whn yu cum
into my hed   is ths
yu doin it   to me
  or me lettin myself
  feel yr vibrashuns
  see yr face

        yu wantid to
        b alone   yr not
        i didint   i am

sure didint
want to b alone
but i have to
b coz thats
whats
         happening

              guess yu cudint
       miss my madness

now ive
written abt
yu

   ar yu gone

love is an
abbreviashun uv
reality

is a what   chestnut
        flowr   eye
        uv venus

    sure was
    great meeting

            agen

    i just thot i saw
    yu in th ally

            see yu soon
            ok

    see ya latr
on
      good times

    take care

                            •••

Rocco de Giacomo, 2011
age 38

I Need You to Know

Things you leave around the house
are my articles of faith. I never told you
that guests visit from time to time
when you are not here, and I say things to them
like "here is the cardigan that she wears when
she wants to relax" or "here is the mirror
she grooms with." Once, I almost told a couple
from San Diego about your book of crosswords
and your favourite coffee cup in the cupboard,

but seeing how they looked at me then,
like reluctant pilgrims, I decided against it;
instead we sat quietly — everyone to their own
thoughts — and listened to the buses that didn't
bring you home.

Things you leave around the house
are my articles of faith. I should tell you
more stuff like this, I know, about how often
I think of you, but these things I am talking about
(much like my social graces) are as delicate as
minnows or the quiet of those couples in cafes.
Old couples, sharing between them small piles
of unfinished crosswords.

That's it.
My love for you is that soft seeking focus.
My love for you is a half-jar of rare seeds.

Things you leave around the house
are my articles of faith. Now, if only
the rest could be sidelong and stoic, content
and beholden to a thousand shared secrets — but I have
stumbled already; there is something more: You are

with me now, in bed; you're doing your crosswords.
I've put my hand on your thigh and I'm pretending to sleep;
you've never known it, but by turning the possibilities
in your head, you occupy my spaces, giving them — at least
for the time being — the weight, the calm of all those
sweet things you are waiting to hear me say.

• • •

Miriam Waddington to Allan Donaldson
457 Dufferin Road, London, Ontario
Sunday, 10 p.m., 1957
age 39

Darling—you still are—in spite of all the phony romantic nonsense you constantly indulge in. You know all this desperation etc. is just an attitude—and though I admire romantic gestures, and romantic actions, to indulge in the phony attitude is a great waste of time. I am probably still arguing about the Thomases. No, this isn't going to be a nasty letter—not in the least. I came home very much out of sorts a couple of hours ago—we spent the weekend camping at a place called meacham lake south of Malone, in the adirondacks, and all should have been idyllic but was not. The sun was hot the wind hot, the water nice, the scenery all the eye could wish, but the children were impossible, whiny and demanding, having numerous minor accidents with cuts and burns, feeling ill done by, and refusing to go to bed at a reasonable hour, and I had a headache and a toothache and was on the threshold of a constant irritation. The only nice thing was that I read some poetry which I wanted to share with you—and will type some out if I have the time and the skill. It is called New British Poets—1947, New Directions, and very intelligently introduced by Kenneth Rexroth, the editor. Do read it if you can—it will surely stimulate your own writing. I particularly liked Keith Douglas, some of the Gaelic revival poets, Kathleen Raine, and Francis Scarfe—the last seems a kindred soul.

Anyway it was a miserable week-end—and this afternoon I was filled with black hatred of you (and hoped you were not feeling the same for me, but you probably were—) and I imagined the bitterest kind of dialogue between us, which might amuse you if I reproduced it—but the whole point of it was that I was making the most devastatingly revealing cruel remarks to you, very brilliant—illuminating all the realities with a sneer, so to speak. I wont reproduce this fantasy, which was as much self-tormenting as anything else, and the upshot of which was entirely unreasonable—to the effect that this is a very great love indeed which permits you to enjoy not one, but two women. But we wont discuss it, not in letters anyway, and it is really not good of me to mention it. And I did not intend to sound this continuous note of plaint and complaint. But darling, next time I cry in your presence, comfort me, and don't look for metaphysics. If you cried, I would comfort you and not choose that time to tell you some painful home truths. But all this is contentious, and I got your letter today, and wanted to say that in spite of everything I love you, and I don't want to be free of you — even if I could be at this point — and I don't feel we are ended. I do feel depressed, because in other separations at least the lovers can look forward to some time when they will be together and freely so — and we cannot. But the thing to do is not to look beyond the next meeting, and as you say, to try to work until then. That I have this same sense of paralyzing desire — not romantic at all — is beyond discussion. At least I don't want to discuss it except in poetry. I am sure I am far from being an accomplished mistress — as you know, that has never been my chief work in life. I don't even think I was cut out to be any kind of mistress, but I also know that our last meeting was an injustice all around. Anyway, let us not talk of this, it depresses me, because it touches on things that mean a lot to me. All the time I was to say while I type this — whatever I say or do, Allan, I do want you to love me as I love you — and let us not discuss or argue about it. That's why I get annoyed at your pessimistic references to predestination, a short life but an unhappy one, and your praise of Byron or Thomas. I think Thomas was a horror and his wife too — I am not judging them, but I would keep miles away from either of them and have no pleasure in such friendships. As you wrote, Milton and Shakespeare and many others were quite different, and also much greater, more complete artists. It is fine to dominate life through art — but to try to dominate life through life and living, is entirely foolish if not arrogant. There is more to one's life than oneself, and neither Byron or Thomas ever advanced beyond the stage of the world as self where they could trust life a little, and let things happen. So let us be more trusting, and neither defy life nor have to have it all go our own way. Because, believe me, I am no romantic poet in that sense, and would have no use for the romantic part played out either for me or around me; I am much too real for that, I simply wouldn't be satisfied with such literary suffering all to no purpose. And I know there is a part of you that wouldn't be either, a part that is not even put into words — the part I feel as your spirit — the part that you describe as energetic and optimistic — which is your emotional self, full of love and faith and probably not complicated by all that neo-romanticism. That's what I love, not all the phony desperation, which is just junk. You are going to hate me — I seem to be loving you for the wrong reasons, and again misinterpreting your slightest statement; anyway, please do something for me that will make me happy — happier than all your unhappiness at missing me or your happiness at my missing you — stop trying to write poetry. It is too tormenting — write instead a couple of short stories, which would be the dearest gift you could give me — because I am sure that you can write wonderful prose, and that any story you would write would be terrific. And that is serious. But then you'll feel that I am pushing you and be bound to resist me and go off and present your romanticism to some other woman who wont think it is phony, and who will encourage you to waste time writing poetry. Don't be hurt — but I know damn well that when someone has this much difficulty they aren't going to write whatever it is that is difficult. It is just a way of avoiding writing something else which you can write. And I don't want you to say of me years later that I ruined the summer of 1957 for you, no I don't. So how about skipping poetry for now, and if you like — read all the good love poetry you like — there is enough to make us both quite envious. The Rexroth collection is full of poems I wish I could write. And write those two stories.

You know, 75 percent of my depression is due to the pressure at the office. I have 5 days to do about 6 weeks work in, and it is killing me, the very thought. Also, I have little privacy — tonight Pat went to the Comptons' without me, at my insistence, but usually people come and waste my time and put upon me until I never want to hear a phone or see another acquaintance as long as I live — or at least not for two months. And I have a great pile of dishes to do, and when Pat sees them undone he will be justly annoyed and lecture at me for hours and hours. So I have to get going.

It was all right to tell Fred about the nightingale — I told Galloway and Pinsky and everyone else who would listen — but perhaps it isn't so important. I have almost given up about the book — McClelland & Stewart has had it for five months and then they'll have the nerve to refuse it — they needn't take so long. They haven't replied one way or another yet. Write what you like — how can I tell you? But I am not so worried about the law of averages as you are — I am not really ashamed of anything I am doing, and only feel wrong about one thing between you and me. I am not afraid that Pat will find out; I don't tell him because to be truthful, I can't or don't want to make a decision about a lot of things at this point — and more obviously, though I am not sure how true this old classic is — I don't want to hurt him by telling him something that really has nothing much to do with him, though I wouldn't feel it had nothing to do with me if the shoe were on the other foot.

It just isn't simple, but I can't bear to be reduced to the level of a mistress, nor can I indulge myself in just simply having a lover. For one reason or another I have to have it be more — and if all this worries you, I can only tell you that in this I cannot change, and I assure that I do not intend to act like Lucas and create a crisis in my or your life either. God knows, maybe this is all a grand rationalization for an unreasonable sex attraction — but it is more, always is. Maybe the religious people are right — Buber claims that sin is a process that man starts, but he cannot stop it by his own will — he is caught in it and must go on being enmeshed in it unless he turns towards the true life of the spirit. It is too hot, and I am too exhausted to think about it, and I long for you with every thought I have, and how can you doubt it when I wrote you that loving poem about poets and statues, and I still have fixed on you that unreasonable hope and emotional belief that you can at moments make my broken world whole? Maybe it is a naïve hope.

                     Miriam

P.S. And it strikes me also that you haven't been feeling so happy lately — I'm sorry darling — I wish I could be near you and then I would feel at peace and try to make you feel the same. I am sure that we will have something of this some Time or Times — so be patient. And I do look forward to seeing you at the end of July — even if briefly.

•

Miriam Waddington to Allan Donaldson
457 Dufferin Road, London, Ontario
Friday, June 14, 1957

Dear Allan,

    I just got a new ribbon and a new roller and ten dollars worth of repairs on my typewriter, and you will just be sitting down to supper, as it is exactly five o'clock, on the hottest muggiest day yet. Do you mind my typing you a letter? Sacrilege or something, is it? Or perhaps the last time I typed one it was not so sweet. However, it being hot and voluptuous this afternoon I haven't the energy to be nasty. Besides, I spent the whole day extravagantly thinking of you. My reactions are either delayed, repeated, or else stimulated by your poem. I really only missed you with senses on Monday and today — and today very intensely — I am not even going to write about it, though I could do so beautifully. I remembered every single thing about you, and all the things I did not say, and could only think in a completely idiotic way that if you were the most horrible character, the greatest evildoer on earth, and had a harem of a thousand wives, I would still be imbued with this primitive biological urge towards you. But don't get worried, or start feeling complacent, because if you were that kind of person I would not give in to my biological urge, but would be all restraint and transform everything into something else. Anyway, it must all be what you called the rut of summer in your poem.

[...] I shouldn't discuss my work with you — it is all something very much more deliberate, disciplined and channelized than any other part of me. Somehow I don't carry over its disciplines into my own emotional life, or at least I don't carry over its analyses. Above all I cant analyze either you or me at this point, except that I realize there are a great many paradoxes in both of us, and I do not understand what meaning you really have for me, or I for you; maybe because I don't want to, and at this point, don't feel that I need to. As I said before, somehow I feel and trust that whatever happens between us will have some kind of important meaning; I hope it wont be horror that I am innocently walking towards; maybe I need to tell myself this in order to rationalize a crude sex attraction, which a less complicated woman could accept at a more simple level. But then again, I know that human sexuality is infinitely complicated and hasn't been simple since we moved out of the caves. And I am also convinced that it has little or nothing to do with one's maturity; perhaps it simply has to remain mysterious, and one can only respond, like the xistentialists, to the present moment, as honestly as one knows how, and as completely.

But this is the kind of talk you don't like to hear. [...]

One thing you can look forward to — once we go on holiday you will have peace — no letters from me, and I will nicely fade from your thoughts and you'll do some terrific work.

Miriam

•••

John Newlove to Susan Newlove
666 Woodbine Avenue, Toronto, Ontario
1977
age 39

Susan:

It's now about five minutes after midnight, about to be Monday, less than four hours since you phoned me. A peculiar thing happens; after you phone me I don't like going to bed in our bed. Then I usually sleep downstairs. Between the voice and the bed I miss you too much, so I guess I cut it in half.

I think I've been reasonably good. Mrs. Zimmer asked when you would be back. I was stopped by that jerk Heather. She said, "Hello, John." I said, "Hello, Heather." She said, "Where are you going?" I said, "Shopping." She said, "And then you'll have a few drinks, eh?" Then she wanted to be remembered to you. There's no doubt the woman's a big loony; she was supposed to have been back at the bank in August; and she isn't.

I'm just typing this out of loneliness, so don't mind. I was proud of getting along alright for the first three weeks or so but now it's getting to me. Just typing to talk to you.

Nothing's really happened. Called in on the Birney another couple of times, so said (reasonably) that they owed me more as fees. They agreed. I took it out in books. A new Clark called Animals and Men, the Tom Thompson book, and Edward Gorey, and a novel Taylor recommended. I've put them aside instead of putting them in bookcases, so you can see which ones they are.

This is my usual standard of typing. Which explains why my letters are so valuable to archivists.

(love)

John

Also, I've promised Young to go to the meeting to vote for you.

Also, I've joined the Champlain Society, which I've been wanting to get into for years. I hope you don't mind. It's something like the Hudson's Bay Record Society — costs $15.00 a year.

My beard's growing. For the first ten days, no one would look at me.

•••

Pat Lowther, 1974
age 39

The Face

1. THE FACE

Always when I wake my first consciousness is of your face, inside me, as it were under my own, as if my features overlay yours. In those first moments the face is stylized, the hair and beard curled like those of statues. Only gradually, as I move, you move too, the face becomes individual.

I do not recall having dreamt of you. I cast back into sleep: a heavy vacancy, neither of us was there.

All faces change minute to minute. Aspects of your face accompany me, changing without waiting for my intention. I do not invent you. The photograph you sent me has an aspect which has occupied me less than others. I must bring it into balance with your other faces.

The face in the photograph is impressive, formidable in fact. The man with that face, I say to myself, can *cope*. That man will always have everything under control. I am perhaps intimidated.

Most often I remember your face close up, foolish-loving, looking much younger. Or with eyes closed kissing, the even tension of shut eyelids, a sheen like wing cases, a detail giving disproportionate pleasure.

But at my first waking I think we are both eyeless, with the brutal dignity of ancient masks. I imagine myself thin and gold, my hands locked at my sides, tongue locked to the roof of my mouth, each hair root locked in its pore. I imagine myself a sarcophagus carried to burial, an image of you static as a photograph locked under my face.

2. THE CLOTHING

You are so much more clothed than I am. Underwear top and bottom, everything tucked in. I could never touch your body by accident. I could never in a casual embrace slide my hand onto skin and body hair. You have to undress first.

And you carry your life like clothing too. It's very becoming, it suits you. Your relationships with the people around you look good, their textures are interesting. You are conscious of origins.

Maybe you have it all worked out: just enough pain and struggle to keep the nerve ends vibrating. Enough disorder to have let you fall in love with me.

I have a longing now to stare at your real face, to question, demand to know you. But you were the one who stared that way into my face. All the time we were together your eyes never left me, I couldn't eat or sleep. And when you asked me to tell you about my life, so that you could picture what I'd be doing at different hours of the day, I wouldn't answer you.

Listen: every morning I take a razor to the fabric of my life, I cut out a woman shape, I step into it, I go out, I perform, it works. But every morning it has to be done again.

Sometimes I can't get the blade sharp enough, the shape flat enough. I can't manage a protoplasm silhouette one molecule thick.

My shape takes exaggerated depth like those optical-illusion letters they use to advertise religious movies, where the edges go back and back into the page and come together at a point representing infinity. My continuum drags behind me, a rubble of dark and rough and glitter stretching back probably to the point of birth.

Then my whole life seems like the act of birth, as violent and difficult and inescapable. My clothing is bloody membrane and sea water, dragging at my body.

I can't even imagine what you feel like in your turtleneck sweater, checkered pants, tidy underwear.

3. THE MACHINERY

The machinery is, in abstract, like a space wheel in orbit. Stately precise turning into and out of sunlight. If we were separate from it, it would seem lovely. We would breathe in delight seeing it in a movie.

The machine is, of course, a centrifuge. We're locked on its outside walls by the magnetic soles of our feet, the veins branching downward. I think of a glass anatomical model of a man, with an erection.

As if the earth had gone transparent and its gross axis become visible, turning us. Like a drill-core spectrum, a blackened rainbow, the red orange yellow at the centre, further toward the ends roughness, jumble, glisten of oil and coal pools, moving capillaries of water. The ends themselves hard glossy white, ice that never melts. The effortless spin of the thing generating so much brute power.

Sometimes I think I can see you across the curvature of the walls. We might reach out, try to touch.

But the machine holds us motionless. Our muscles flatten, our veins and arteries spread out like maps. We are splayed, pinned down on separate beds, in separate cities.

I'm turning downward into sleep. I will not dream of you. Slowly, slowly, it's turning you toward your morning. You are beginning to remember me.

•••

Marjorie Pickthall, 1922
age 39

Going Home

Under the young moon's slender shield
With the wind's cool lips on mine,
I went home from the Rabitty Field
As the clocks were striking nine.

The yews were dark in the level light,
The thorn-trees dropped with gold,
And a partridge called where the dew was white
In the grass on the edge of the fold.

O, had your hand been in my hand
As the long chalk-road I trod,
The green hills of the lovely land
Had seemed the hills of God.

•••

Judith Fitzgerald, 1991
age 39

Harmony of Moonlight

I watch my plane ascend towards the jagged moon suspended
in its rectangular frame; west by mere degrees, the smouldering Everglades reminding me of a card, a relic signed and seared with phrases

from a permanent island of temporary refuge. "Neverending Love."
A flourishing epiphany inscribed on a page from the book of my heart.
I don't know. I believe I absorb you through my fingers until you tear
my future from the socket of your everlasting past. I remove a strand
of wool you pull over my neatly structured, sadly chaotic complimentary
closing. Yours unconditionally, indestructibly. The upside oblong view
of life above the Tropic of Cancer, trans/parallelogram, latitude of love.
I could not begin at the beginning at the best of times. Now, crenellated
indanthrone blue and carmine interplay south of this acute juncture
of flight. Yours infinitively, with various shades of chromium cerulean hue,
Everglades dissolving in a frame of smoke-red lead. A heart burns up
the atmosphere. The atmospheric camarilla. Infinitesimally yours,
chronicles rapturous and wild.

THREE

From the Bottom of My Spongiform Heart

Poets in their Forties

Vivian Hansen to Bruce ——————
October 3, 1998
age 40

Well thank God you're not a stranger yet…

On the topic of Wilfrid Laurier University, I am glad I didn't stumble over it in the first year after I graduated…I had delusions of grandeur and wanted to move right on to a graduate program. Real life has set in since. Now my writing provides me with a large part of all the fulfillments I need in my life right now. WLU seems small enough to do a grad program, though. I would be tempted to work with Ron Grimes, primarily because he has such an easy feminist focus that he has defended simply by "showing" how he chooses to live, not just talking about it…I cannot tell you what a relief this is for me, who has trusted him with my text — purely on blind faith. He has not let me down.

I guess that is similar to my relationship with you. Odd, really, that I am finding men to trust with my Creativity, my Self. A new journey for me.

My chapbook has come out, and I have sent you a copy. I am leery about the poetry, realizing that it is not my best stuff. (I may have told you this). I was at work at Chapters today, but I sent Alexis (my daughter) to sell my books at Judith Hall's art showing at the Nolan & Reid gallery. Both of "Nose Hill Park: reflections," and "Never Call It Bird" deal with location of Nose Hill, and Judith Hall's painting "the old fence" is my front cover for "Bird." Judith's paintings are breathtaking, but she didn't have a lot of action at the gallery, so she came home early. Now I am nervous about having 500 copies on my shelf that cannot be sold. Silly me. I'm still selling copies of "Reflections" and that came out two years ago.

Faith. Patience.

About that Patience thing. It's my weakest point. You may have noticed. Maybe I am attention-deficit or something.

Tomorrow the old Calgary General Hospital is being imploded. I was born there. Some of my friends live close to it. The police force are arranging a No Man's Land around it…interesting…the woman whose husband is doing the implosion is Catholic. There was an article in the paper about her sprinkling holy water on all the beams and praying for the "death" of the hospital…which is a symbol of Calgary, really.…I was very moved by this. What a fine and beautiful gesture, and so lovely, so womanish…she's running around wearing a hard hat and praying…now there's a ritual that Ron Grimes would appreciate. Maybe I'll contact her and ask her about her processes…I'm sure they don't include this stuff in any "Demolition 101" classes. Maybe they should.

My friend Carole Thorpe runs a glass-blowing studio with her husband. They call it Double-Struggle. She blows the finest, most beautiful glass… she has been writing something on the implosion, since she lives close to the General…says that you can implode colour into glass, too…I can't wait to read/see what she blows into this space-in-time.

In any case, I felt the Muse on my shoulder this morning…had an ache there that aspirin wouldn't remove…maybe I shelved a book that was too high or something, but I prefer to call her my Muse…she was positively leaning into me…then I looked outside and saw the gold of sun move like buttermilk through the colours in my hedge. Golden Morning….the one before the hospital implodes and tomorrow I will write my poetry into the implosion…some very fine ceremonies and rituals happening this weekend…glad I can tell you these things without fear that you read me as "nuts." I must tell Grimes all about this Ritual of Implosion.

I found E.D. Blodgett's new book of poetry, Apostrophes II, and read "Of Roses," which is really about you and I, writing in this cyberworld and how alphabet becomes/your presence […]: "it spells the rose that says our name."

Take care, sweetie. Hope you are resting, "drawing water into yourself," as Rumi would say.

{{{Bruce}}}} by the way, {{{ }}}} these are caresses combined with hugs, which can only occur when you are corresponding with a poet. [[ ]] are regular hugs, which I can give too, but do not want to be pigeon-holed into boring-kind-of-hugs.

@----<--- your Rose…xoxoxo you know what these are…

•••

Jane Eaton Hamilton to Joy Masuhara
February, 1995
age 40

When I breathe in, taking your exhaled breath back inside my lungs, I can feel our love physically, through the barrel of my chest, as if an angel has me down on the floor and is puffing bits of divinity into me, warm and rich and healing. The air I breathe is carrying spoors of pleasure. The sensation isn't quiet. It's big and rackety. This is no goody-two-shoes angel — my chest expands and churns until it feels like I have a mass of whirling stars under my ribs. I have you under my ribs.

Mom called from Key Largo. I said it was raining all the time here, but that I didn't mind. She said, "You don't need sunshine. You have Joy."

•••

Louis Riel to Marguerite Riel
Regina Prison
August 22nd, 1885
age 40

My very dear Marguerite,
You may wonder if I have heard news of your health and of our dear little children. I have done nothing but [text missing] our dear brother-in-law. The news he gave me was consoling. Be courageous. When you feel that tears wish to win you over, offer your pain to the Virgin Saint and our Lord.

Reflect upon, in your spirit, all that the Good Lord has done for us since we have been together. Fear not: take courage. The Good Lord who saw us through frightful dangers, unharmed, on the day of combat at Batoche remains unchangeable: he attends our prayers and our good deeds. And if we please sufficiently our Lord, he will aid and save us [text missing] as easily; [text missing] powerful [text missing] as on that day. He did not reveal all His power when he kept us with such charity at Batoche. The Good Lord's gifts have been constant though he can always provide further favours because his power is without limit. It is infinite. Let us not measure our obedience. And the blessing Our Father who is in the heavens bestows upon us, according to the visions of his Providence, are kind and without measure.

My very dear Marguerite, you know I set our dear little children to prayer, many times during the day. I counsel you to do the same. As often as you might, take them to chapel with you. Even small children benefit from a few moments before the Holy Sacrament.

The presence of the Good Lord in the tabernacle fills the entire church with grace. When little children [text missing] by the determined devotion of parents, enter a chapel or a church, where the Holy Sacrament is found, it seems to me that the graces of the sacred Eucharist enter their little spirits and their little innocent hearts like humidity enters our garments when walking through a fine, falling rain.

Dear Marguerite, I was to write a long letter but I see I have arrived already at the end of the paper, that is to say, my sheet of paper.

I wish you courage and the grace of God. Embrace our little children for me. Pray the day! Pray the night! Be well,

> Your husband in our Lord Jesus Christ
> Louis "David" Riel

•

Louis Riel to Marguerite Riel
Regina Prison
September 17th, 1885

My very dear Marguerite,

God in his greatness who has taken such care of you and I since we have been together, has granted a great happiness upon this day, September 17th, in delaying by an order of yesterday, the execution which would have taken place tomorrow. My little daughter Marie-Angélique, in her second year, may pronounce my name with a smiling joy of hope and happiness. Blessed be the 17th of September, birth day of our little Marie-Angélique. Blessed be this day whereupon God favours me with this grace He has provided charitably; this day which should have been the eve of my death has changed to a beautiful day of gratitude. And you, my dear Marguerite, pray to the Good Lord that he receive my thanks.

Now take communion, to render unto the savior the deeds of grace we owe him. The Good Lord is behind us, to see if we will place ourselves in good faith; and if we will place ourselves there, once and for all. If we commit ourselves to good deeds and live as real saints, I think he shall grant us all we ask of him but if we make pretty prayers with our lips, and if we pass our lives occupied with meaningless tasks, useless affairs crowding our spirits and our hearts, we will not have much luck, I believe.

I pray to the Good Lord to bless you; that your patron Saint Marguerite and the Virgin Saint shall steer you and keep you; by the grace of God, in long life.

I embrace my sisters and my step-sisters, my little nieces.

And my dear little Jean, my boy, I bless you. Pray for me, my boy. Because the Good Lord will hear you, I have faith in your little prayers, especially those made before the Holy Sacrament.

May the Good Lord be with you, my dear Marguerite,

I am your husband for life.

Your husband who loves you,

Louis "David" Riel

•

Louis Riel to Marguerite Riel
Regina Prison
October 5th, 1885

My very dear Marguerite,

I wanted to write you yesterday but I postponed until today and I do not wish to delay any further. I received almost immediately the letter that our dear Henriette wrote me on the 30th. She spoke of your health. I ask you again to heed our aunt Julie; and to not neglect sound advice.

Pray to the Good Lord that he keep accidents and misfortune from you.

Yesterday, in the afternoon, in prayer to the Virgin Saint, there came to me a grand hope and a strong assurance that your health will be fortified and that you will be protected. So take courage. Set your little children to prayer, have them recite all sorts of little prayers and often throughout the day address to God, for me, their pure and powerful supplications; hands clasped, upon their knees.

Recommend us well. And if the Good Lord is for us, his charity will shelter us from all pain and evil.

This grand morning, at daybreak, I saw Our Lady of Mercy. She held in her hand a length of rope. But it was no wider than the nail of my thumb. All in tatters.

She told me that it was with a feeling of pity that she had placed her hand upon the rope that was prepared for me.

Hope. I hope. But cease not your prayers. The Virgin Saint is powerful. It was she who saved my life, many times, on the Missouri. It is she, so close to God, who can perform a bounty of charitable wonders. Let us have faith. You who are free, please, go from time to time to take the Holy Sacrament for me.

Dear Marguerite, if you write to your father, give him all my compliments: that he should pray for me. My respects to the entire family, to Moïse August, my fond remembrance.

Embrace for me our dear little children. My deep, filial affections to mother; my good wishes to my brothers and sisters, to our brothers and sisters-in-law, to our parents, to our friends.

> Your affectionate Husband in
> Our Lord Jesus Christ,
> Louis "David" Riel

•

Louis Riel to Marguerite Riel
Regina Prison
November 16th, 1885

My very dear Marguerite,

I write you early this morning. It is around 1 o'clock. Today is the 16th: a very remarkable day.

I send you my fond remembrance. I advise you today by virtue of the charity you have inspired in me. Take good care of your little children. Your children are even more of God than of you. Try to provide them with all care consistent to our religion, have them pray for me.

Write often to your dear Papa. Tell him that I have not forgotten a single day. That he should take courage. Life seems sad at times, but times that seem to us the most sad are often the very same which are the most agreeable to God.

> Louis "David" Riel

•••

rob mclennan, 2011
age 41

Goldfish: studies in fine thread

1.

Martyred, green. Ceiling, red waves   smart, arranged, amend; these
goldfish made. The bedroom,   jaw-faced stern, a sleepy

decorative blue. Trio lingers, float. Sounds we recognize. Coated, crepe.
   Flecks

            silver, glisten. Window, polish.

Bait, constructed. Incongruous, light. We fish.

2.

Aquaria, an ornamental. Freshwater, answer. Carassius auratus auratus.
Studies, carve alight, attention, into   undercover, final.

Speculate, a cloud of. Sheared, shaved, exacto-measured. Cut. A
   threaded miracle.

            How fortunate we are. Observe: we fish,

inanimate. Could never answer.

3

Briefly, 1620: gifting, a tradition. The scarcity of goldfish, singled.

Married men to wives to celebrate   , anniversary
                     the first of many. Prosperity, a wish,

this coming year. Absence, or. Our human shape. Until more prevalent
in Southern Europe,

the excess gathered, stones
and moss.

4.

Strength of the adhesive, doctor blade. A corridor of slipping,
cellular.
Geometry, the paper gulp. It floats   on silent linen, thread.

A single pulpy sheet,

translucent, skin. Accumulate, twelve months: breath, a fishing
line, a lure.

Kiss, pendulum lips. Like I was, never. Nylon air.

5.

Blink breeds, sleek. Aquarium. Bedroom splinters,   plaster,
paint, the window-passage, framed. Once sticky-red. Spine, my instep.
Surface,

pulls, the subject: casement, white. Black tracery.

Back deck of our first year   foothills, furrows, wind. Someday,

will step, step off. A room gets smaller, breeds. Horizon, lines
the wooden slats. Below,

sidewalks remain, recycled. Spent, collision.

6.

A goldfish,   gifted. Narrative, interior. Trees. A cardboard box.
Coldwater hollows, commons,

comets,   create, this sizing. Tin mysteries of fishes, blossoms

tinged with colour, contradict   a hollow form.

    The paper; vellum,   tracery, a root. Parchment, curls

a scooping sound. Amid a crucial, sensitive criteria. An atmosphere
that slides like water,   uterine,

        an incognito gravity.

7.

These cognate, third-floor fisheries. Tissued, hot-air hood. High-
   pitched. Reversible,

        a sunset; orange fins

and gills. A room alone is rarely large. It shadows, red. Would allocate,
aquatic gravel, substrate, sand; such further,

filtered surfaces. Bite, and swallow-stroke. Fresh oxygen. Airstone, or
a pump.

8.

Beyond the body's aptitude. Biochemichal, a charge. These artifacts.
Tradition, goldfish bowls   unsuitable,

a rendered, mortared cloth. Clear, illuminate. A sparkled fin, moves
   forward.
Tupperware, enunciates a smooth-green, fathoms. Whistle,

        what's left, will-swept. Metaphor: the force

that holds down, atmosphere.

9.

Articulate, a second medium. Paraphyletic. Moonlit, sun. Would slowly
    bleach
the autumn bluster, leaves. Idemic, sameness. Replicate, we summon.
    Reproduce,

one duly-facts. Love, this splintered many-splendoured. Satellite,
a codex. Aquatic vertabrate. Uncorrected,   beauty-strewn,

            a handmade sky. We cast

the widest net.

•••

Milton Acorn to Gwendolyn MacEwen
1208 Granville, Vancouver, British Columbia
August 20, 1965
age 42

Dear Gwen;
    Write or wire me telling me how much money you'll require to get my
books and papers off the Island. Send them collect, freight, to Mrs. R.F.
Acorn, 205 north River Road, Charlottetown, Prince Edward Island. I think
I can raise all the money.
    I'm sorry I didn't write you sooner. I've been deeply troubled. I hope it's
not too late. Never mind the clothes.
    "Regards" you say. You're right in style there. Why conclude a letter with
"love" when there is no love? Nevertheless I always conclude a letter, even a
letter to an editor, with "love." It is my defiance, one of the ridiculous things
I insist on living for.
                    Love,
                    Milt

P.S. I've done a lot of writing in the last three years, tho little of it has gone
out to editors. There seems little point and little use in it when my own love
was cast off and thrown away, as if it was of no account or meaning. All my

life I've stood against the cheats, the kibitzers, the cynics. They won. They couldn't write poetry like me but they could steal my happiness…even tho they could make nothing of it themselves.

P.P.S. God how I loved you! How proud I was that you loved me. Yet I did little writing. I was entirely absorbed in you and what you were doing. I thought I was thru writing, but separation from you opened up entire new areas of experience. It also drove me crazy…perhaps the two are connected. Lying with you in bed at night I used to talk as I never talked to any person before or since. You understood me, and I was beginning to understand you more deeply. I couldn't tell you but I was beginning to know how to play your moods. It was people you needed, a relationship with real people doing real things. It is this real communication between human beings that is needed…not the dizzy bed-hopping game. I wished I could have told you that, but I couldn't. There are some things that just can't be said. Now I suppose you look on my love for people with an amused contempt, an unforgivable softness in a world where people need to be hard…where there is no honour, no justice, no truth; and those who believe in them are pitiful weaklings.

•••

Malcolm Lowry to Margerie Bonner Lowry
Dollarton, British Columbia,
October, 1951
age 42

My dear sweet wife:
    Please do not punish me by the silent or savage system or otherwise. I want things between us to be better as much as you do, and I have determined to make sacrifices to bring this about. Please do not say Bah! either: there is no "Bah" about it. The impasse is my fault, I am thoroughly aware of the fact, and if I don't pull us through you have every right to leave me. I am extremely aware of that and being aware of it doesn't make it any happier for me.
        Your devoted yet alas ill-natured — yet still determined to improve –
                Husband
                Malcolm

P.S. Please say dear duck at least and don't leave me with such a troubled heart in silence.

•

Malcolm Lowry to Margerie Bonner Lowry
Dollarton, British Columbia
October, 1951

Dearheart: I'm extremely sorry. I don't want to make excuses. But I wasn't being deliberately churlish. Nor was heart not in the right place. The mistake I made was more childish than anything else. I have been having a hell of a time with this section writing this defense and I was in fact so tired, that no drink would have pulled me together for very long. I did honestly want to "use" it to get over a large hump: witness 8 intricate pages this morning that didn't show any signs of alc. But I allowed myself foolishly — or perhaps it was due simply to strain — to feel hurt that you weren't "trusting" me, even if you were justified & that was for my good. I don't know if you've ever felt in the mood: "Anything is better than to feel like this." I imagined a big slug or two would help & of course it both did & didn't & then I was tight for awhile & lost my temper. That my heart was fundamentally in the right place is shown by the fact that I did eventually pull myself together even dress to take you out (even though you understandably didn't want to come by then) finally tucked you up in bed, put water by your side & tidied up. You are, of course, "right." But it wasn't deep dark treachery on my part or the usual kind of compulsion or even loss of self-control. I had felt myself heading all day for one of my gloomy & intolerable moods because of frustration in work & I had wanted to avoid that at all costs at your little Europa party. Then when I'd solved the problem & wanted to read – you thought that was just the "old kind of thing," & I got a kind of coitus interruptus. But oh dear duck things are so much better & I do want things to be happy for you & then for me: so will you out of the goodness of your heart at this season give me the ramshackle old boy the benefit of the doubt & allow him to make [amends].

With all love
Dear duck

P.S. Besides you hurt my [wouf] & dat's de truf.

Malcolm Lowry to Margerie Bonner Lowry
Dollarton, British Columbia,
February, 1952

My own sweet dearest wife:

I am sorry from the bottom of my heart. I don't know what beastly thing got into me, or has got into me on such occasions. I have no excuses. All I know is I'm going to do my absolute level best not to let such a filthy demon get hold of me again. And I mean starting *Now!* The thought of having hurt you just gratuitously when you have been doing everything in the world for me is unbearable. Believe me, I am suffering. About all I can do to-day is sit here & try & finish this task I set myself by this evening. Please try & forgive me, even if it is for the 70th time 7. The only difference is, I do not forgive myself this time. I know I can do something about it.

    With all my dearest love & remorse
              Your unworthy
              husband Malc

•••

Vivian Hansen to Angus ———
Thursday, May 27, 1999
RE: Leylines and other profundities
age 42

I read somewhere that York is an old Viking settlement. I got your "Dancer" in the mail last night. She is so perfectly shaped; her driftwood legs, breaching the gap of a ledge, her face so perfectly contemplative. Even in her misshapen driftwood she is EVER so pretty. She is a she because I want her to be.

I experimented with certain places for her in my house. The livingroom seemed too central. She is far too marginal of soul to be displayed so centrally. I finally decided she had to be with me in my bedroom. I placed her in one of my cubbyholes at the headboard so that if I happened to wake up, I could touch her. She has leylines in her wood-skin, trilled (I conjured that word early this morning) from salt water, swirled into knotholes. I love her hair — that nutbrown fantasy that quarters itself inside a walnut. She has a breast, I noticed. Only one. Like a true Amazon. I like that.

I have not named her yet, because you forewarned me that naming her would cause her soul to BE. So I must take care with this. Dancer is beautiful. And there, her driftwood, purposeful body has been named.

I hope you are not homesick, yet. I expected to have a lot of time to myself and to be able to work on my poetry, but I found that outside of my landscape, I created another kind of force, so to speak. Maybe you are finding the same thing. I did write some poetry, but I am not at all sure it is good stuff. Doesn't matter. It needed to be written.

I'm still struggling with Jack-the-Ripper and leylines while simultaneously snatching reading time with Dietrich Bonhoeffer. I think I am reading Bonhoeffer in order to offset the evil of the Ripper. I would rather NOT deal with the Ripper, but this is more poetry that must be written. Besides, I spent two really pleasant days in Ripper territory, so I think the souls of the women he murdered must have found some peace, or I would not have felt the need to write about angel wings.

But I digress. What are you working on? The Blip? A strange design of poetry? If you are working on the familial Blip that unites us, you may as well forget it. There. I not only look like my mother, I also sound like her. That is perhaps every woman's comeuppance. My mother recently sent me a letter (she likes writing letters) that told me what a rich, powerful WOMAN I had become. I think I've been a woman now for about 30 years, but it was the first time my MOTHER had called me that. I felt different. In charge.

But I digress again. I really wanted to talk to you about Leylines and Dragons. I lapsed into journaling. It's okay to cast your wishes into air, too.
Love, Vivian

•

Vivian Hansen to Angus ———
May 28, 1999
RE: Leylines and other profundities

I keep returning to this note, even fifteen years later, to re-vision that woman I was, the one you loved and lost your mind and heart to…because of The Great Orme — The Mighty Worm, the Vikings called it.

Worms are sensitive to sound and vibration. The Blackfoot used to chant to worms on bushes: *Comiosche!* With the emphasis on the final syllable; with the last clap of sound the worms fell off the bush. I asked you, *Why Chester?* when you responded about the strangeness here, the gateway to Wales and wonders. You wrote that you found me on Welsh soil.

On the mighty headlands over Llandudno the wind snapped at your coat-sleeves, tugged at the ragged hair of Kashmire goats. You wrote about St. Tudno and where he made his church, believing that God spoke from the white rocks below his feet. In time, I learned to read this as *white caps*, the ocean's thrill of wind, how we sacrifice ourselves to the sanctification of white — hoping, always hoping, for eternity between two.

The Great Orme — the Mighty Worm, you said, is right here in northern Wales where you find your dragon, nothing you either expected or dreamed. As I read these words so many years later, I remember that in that first read, I did not merge myself with the dragon you were speaking of. And yet, that was the peculiar whiplash of knowing; St. George, you said, with all his might and power could never slay a dragon such as this. The peculiar poetry of geological time: 300 million years ago, lava raging in her plutonic arteries, spread her copper nerves for miles, pushed them up into her flesh of dolomite.

Can a Giant Worm crouch? These words for a worm suggest stealth, and ambush. Looking across the Irish sea past the red sand shores of Anglesey, she never lost her crouch. When Spaniards came to cut her flesh and steal her copper veins, the Giant Worm waited. As I did then, not knowing I was being compared not to a Giant Worm, but a Dragon you feared and worshiped. You walked, crouched, slid, and climbed 200 feet within her dark and sweating gut. You felt her spleen, her viscera stretch on for endless miles beneath the headland and the sea, never to be encompassed. Not by tourist boards, not by avaricious man, nor governments.

Henri Nouwen tells us to watch for signs to complete our discernments. It is biblical to make these connections; spiritual knowing. And you saw your sign; almost missed your sign. It spoke of a shaft made in centuries past, which plunged straight down 450 feet through rock and vein. When you read the name your breathing stopped. They called it: Vivian's shaft.

Here lives my dragon, and you.

•••

Louise Bak, 2014
age 42

Restlessness
    to Guang Lu

*air smell washed, sidewalk's shipping crate's uncollected newspaper's
high-ranking officials. a forecourt photo's tousled abbey blouse in the
cart's overstretched stocking of uncollected tea. a news portal's picked
out simpler juk syun for "disgusting," zip maai, broke up with slowed
forward, fingers indenting flat yoke of a dress, at palm molding's atta,
at x eyes, worsted on lops around its hem. 5:15 a.m. cheep from leaf-
crumbled clump, green "pass" certificate more rigidly vertical than a
sandwich board's "destiny reform" skill. stripped up sleeve as part of
sock runs down from knee, wind's whup of glass panel set in wall, at
a cricket in a see-through tube, crosses into wet dab of cotton, where
it drinks. glancing across small hexagonal mirrors, i-ching coins, the
dry-pivot needle at centre of a diviner's board, its line for north-south
dire, hooded by a lock charm. inscription of tian chang's perpetuality*

*is worn, as waxing moon, flat-bottomed clouds rolled, when lurched
off, a watch's claymore sword style hands, to inside of hand by egely
wheel, glass-boxed. surrounded with more of palm, sighed sensation
to clockwise flit, tensed legs respread at quavered turn, to more brisk
mincing on a redox ring. slid at fifth finger's dip joint, cocked doubt-
fully, at contrition and defiance of a mayor, caught by cp24 reporter's
"but...i...i..." appallingly told to newsroom, while uhn shrugged,
that at least not toronto sensible, to pieds-à-terre towers underway, to
go up to 915 ft, perks of built-in speakers, forced-air heating, but the
scratches on some velux windows to overlook side elevation deemed
"those grandmas, thinned by the first week." bumptious timbre on ga
yull, to hurt the sale of units, remarking the walked direction at a few
khata scarves, that the ring musn't stay on a finger without movement.*

*advancing warm front curdled the surface pitting of pomes, in swelter
formed within packages. separated husks of roasted watermelon seeds
from seizes of gold premolars, that handed over from long bus back, a*

bottle's semi-cola-colored water swished, bent stiffly, in heard versing
a younger generation's "can give just 10 (or whatever) hours for free."
by a stairwell's tarpaulin, slither of alu foil paper, where the extension
ladder weighted it, leaking "hiraeth," at blown sauveteur sticker, stuck
on cigarette butts on steps, to more metallic candy wrappers, cornering
the entrance. tpl tee still draped on boxes stacked against the wall, from
hardly picked detritus of a branch's vhs titles. lust for life's outstretched
razor on cobbled path, in static-lined chase. sticking drawer opened for
twist-tied villous amomum fruit, pericarps' longitudinal cracks marked,
in which negatives were under such compression, that some coursed to

floor and off a bowl of liang pi's starch paste formed at the bottom of it,
water risen to the top, cupped with a polymer note of 100 yuan, china's
century temple on its backside dampened more, from lain on boxed rice
and in way of slammed gemel bottle, blots ambroxan, like pervading of
men's aisles. tongue's stagger to inside of cheek, to noodles-thickness as
a pen's coating, braided and lashed on a table, without arresting forward
motion, ungained run skips. cordoned outside, steps' cascading of blood,
after stabbed female, without vital signs taken to hospital, relayed by the
entering of road restrictions and area resurfacing on a keyboard. the okay
asked in writing, so it could be known what to be meted, while a queased
quiet, ambled crossing a tank's sanddab. its maxillary reaching below the
anterior part of a lower eye, reported borne franticly, splashes from cloth.
bony ridge mid eyes, twained on one side, cam border's hanged seriatum

zip maai, conceal, bury (Cantonese)
tian chang in phrase tian chang di jiu, everlasting
ga yull, (to add oil) — to cheer someone on by saying "go, go go"!
hiraeth, homesickness (Welsh)
liang pi, literally "cold skin," a noodle like Chinese dish

•••

Jane Eaton Hamilton to Joy Masuhara
November 1, 1996
age 42

The last thing I should be doing is writing to you, Joy, when I am only in the break between novels and it's nearly two. But I can't stop thinking about you…

Why I think about you, of course, is the plethora of gifts you've given me these couple of weeks. The dozen white roses, the bagel chips pinned to my bulletin board, the books, the angel sconce, the mirror — which, by the way, is absolutely exquisite — and I think about how happy I am to be with you and I think about the great good fortune involved in the simple, complicated act that was falling in love with you, and I am left speechless. Lucky, lucky me. And no one knows. No one else is inside this good and nurturing relationship. No one can know. I think of K — and B — probably on the rocky shores and what good women they both are and how still they're on the rocky shores and I think, oh God, why? Why me? But then why not, for once?

Thank you, thank you, from the bottom of my spongiform heart, Joy, just for being the woman you are, and looking after me while I do this intensive work, and just for the being yummy. I feel spoiled and like I'd like to spend the (sunny) day curled up in bed with you. just relaxing into what we feel.

But alas.

J.

•••

Fred Cogswell, 1960
age 43

Lost Dimension

I from my myness
must a you create
for your yourness
is inviolate.

Likewise your yourness
makes the me you have known,
for my myness
is all my own.

Hard spheres are we
whose edges join,
seeking to grasp
an illusion,

that lost dimension
whose laws are such
not circumference
but centres touch.

•••

Miriam Waddington to Allan Donaldson
11 Flanders Road, Toronto, Ontario
May 7, 1961
age 43

Dearest Allan,

forgive the typewriter; I am a terrible correspondent. I have a horrible
sinking feeling that I am living in a kind of nightmare, and only when I
am dead will I finally wake up. It is as though I am not really myself, and
am called upon to act all the time, and I go through certain motions,
occasionally hoping something will come of them, and generally finding
that nothing does. The world and people stay hopelessly the same. Including
myself I suppose. I think I suffer from the delusion of hope. Anyway, I
should not complain; yesterday I cleaned all the floors upstairs and today
washed heaps of clothes, and eventually I will iron them. The labors of
Hercula. So something was accomplished. The dragon's teeth they multiply
a hundredfold.

[…] I have been re-reading WEB AND THE ROCK — it is young, but
so full of truth and of passion that goes beyond just being young. I hope to
get to work as soon as I am settled. I listen often to music and think of you.

I hesitate to buy opera tickets as they are 12.50 each, if still available. I would pay for my own, but doesn't it sound extravagant? Not for nothing do they call Toronto hogtown.

I am discouraged about my poetry — I'll explain why when I see you. My book wasn't in the exhibit at the Arts Conference for one thing. However, I will still go on writing it or something else, only because I can't do anything else but. Good enough reason I suppose. Some of my poems will be on CBC ANTHOLOGY Friday May 26 — they are all old poems by now of course.

Mostly, dear Allan, it is the inanimate objects and the plain practical difficulties which beset me and leave little peace. One by one I will free myself from them, and then, hopefully, emerge serene and better than ever. Do forgive me my sadness, won't you? I am not always like this — especially when the flowers come out and the cardinals fly past. I mourn for alder trees on Dufferin road, for my humming birds and rock plants. Well, onwards to the new and to some sort of new yorker type story called making a new life for oneself. Fortunately you are one of the bright things in this landscape — and there are good other ones too —. my dearest love,

Miriam

•••

Roy Kiyooka to Monica Dealtry Barker
Montreal, Quebec
April 8, 1969
age 43

Dear Monica
    ...this is the 3rd letter I've started and goddammit I'm going to get this one off to you. I've had my last classes. There'll be the end of the year meetings, the markings and other matters to tidy up. Then, because we won't be coming back there's all my belongings (in the office) that have to be packt. Etcetera. The York U. fibreglass mural nearly complete — Chris and I intend to hire a truck and take it to Toronto Sunday the 20th. — If you get back in time you should be able to see it before we pack it.
    Carole the babysitter and a former student has taken pictures of the children rehearsing their fashion show. Yesterday she gave me the prints to take home and show them. I had a long hard look at each print and thought

my gawd how they have grown even more beautiful — as they become more and more singular: I have always wanted to let them "be" and though I have been irresponsible towards them, that thought remains constant. I want to let them be more than anything else. And the same goes for you my dear wife. Even you should "be."

About the House: I need a more precise figure of how much it's going to cost, within a thousand dollars say. And I want a written agreement from Harry that he will hold to that price before we go ahead. It would be useful to know how long it will take to build as we can't afford to build and pay rent at the same time. (Ideally) we want to move from here in the late summer straight into the new house. (p/s it's gonna cost a thousand plus to get our goods and chattel back to the westcoast.) As for the strip of land the Copithornes want figure out how much it cost as per square foot then measure of their piece and charge them the same plus the costs of surveying. I suppose all this will have to go through the city hall for it to be legitimate — will you look after it?

As for the Expo '70 commission and the Winnipeg Ballet commission, I've not had a contract from either so it's all still up in the air. There's been no time to worry about it anyhow with so much to do.

Anne one of our other babysitters has a luvly head. She tells me about her acid-trips. She is a friend of the children and very gentle. I would say she was one of the tribe Marcuse talks about in the Georgia Straight vol. 3/no. 51 (March 28/April 3rd 69 issue). If you have time read it, it will enable you to grasp my stance.

Now I am beginning to see more clearly the issues involved in the Sir George Williams U. racial/computer BUST and I am glad that I stood against those whose anger turned into ugliness. Racial prejudice is the stirrings of hypocrites whatever their colour. I am really clear at this moment this turning point in our lives. How many many times have "I"/"we" turned to go off in other directions? How many circuits have we closed and how many open ones have we left? This is getting altogether too abstract — more concretely when you get home. And yes do fly bugger the expenses WE ARE ALL WAITING FOR YOU COME WHAT MAY.

Love to Carole and Brian
tell em we will see them come May

•••

Jane Eaton Hamilton to Joy Masuhara
February, 1998
age 43

I know Feb. is a long, tough month for you, made worse this year. But I want you to know, if it helps, how much I care for you. Not just the love part, which is extreme, but the regular, everyday admiration. Because you're such a good woman — intelligent, funny, generous, thoughtful, kind. A good partner. No matter what happens, Joy, know that these five years with you have been the most invigorating and satisfying of my life. You've taught me the meaning of partnership — of love.

All my love now and forever,

J.

•••

Charles G.D. Roberts to Mary Fanton
The Rectory, Fredericton, New Brunswick
September 19, 1904
age 44

Dear Mary

I am glad to get your letter this morning.

My attitude was all along just exactly what I told you before I left for Europe, and what I wrote to you from the dock before sailing and also from Cherbourg just before landing. I think it will not surprise you to learn that the attitude changed somewhat when I learned, on authority which could not well [be discredited], of the way you had talked to my sister of your being so ardently and devotedly in love with Will,[2] at the time you were in Fredericton last spring — and while I had every right to believe that you were in love with me. My confidence in you was at that time, in spite of everything, absolutely unquestioning. The discovery, which was so at variance with the explanations which you had given me, was a severe shock to me, — or whatever my *own* faults, I treasured fervently my utter confidence in you. I did not wish to say anything about it at the time, intending to make absolutely sure when I got to Fredericton. A talk with Janie (during

---

2   William Roberts, Charles' brother.

which, *needless to assure you*, she had no suspicion of my purpose, and heard nothing from me but what would confirm her more & more in her affection and admiration for you!) set my mind clear, and made it easier for me to reconcile myself to the complete and final loss of you. Do not think I am blaming you. I am only letting you know honestly my attitude in accepting your decisive dismissal. It is the simple truth, and only fair to you to say it frankly, that no other woman I have known could be so great a loss to me, and no other woman ever filled so great a place in my life. I was not angry, only overwhelmingly sorry and heart-sick, when I found out that you had been in love with Will at the time you were assuring me otherwise. And even now, my predominant feeling is that of the greatness of my loss, and the empty, unadorned condition it gives my life. However I may have failed you in this or that detail, I had been for the past two years in no doubt as to my own attitude toward you. Your place in my heart was absolutely alone and supreme, and with all my heart I desired to make you my wife. Having frankly stated my complaint against you, I must not let you think I overestimate it. I know that I value your friendship beyond words, and shall strive to hold it, in every way that is consistent with Will's perfect peace of mind. If he marries you, I shall feel that, in spite of every possible argument to the contrary he has won the most desirable and most worth while woman whom I have ever known. And it will be a happiness to me if I can, now and always, be a help to the situation, a background of support in emergency of any kind. I shall certainly spare no pains to obliterate from Will's mind any soreness over the past.

> yours always
> C.

I ought to say that if you marry Will it will give unqualified delight to the whole family here, from whose minds I have, I think, removed all possible suspicions in regards to myself. It is for you to use your own judgement as to how much or how little of this letter, if any, you show to Will or tell him about. Your wishes in the matter are mine.

•••

Jeevan Bhagwat to Anna ———
March 2, 2012
age 44

Anna my love, it is now midnight, the hour of starlight and dreams. Under the canopy of night's ebon cheek, my thoughts turn to you, the glimmering girl of my heart. Yes, we will walk together on your father's farm and I will kiss you a thousand times. I am sleepy but the memory of your eyes' light haunts me so. My love for you glitters like a comet that burns through the darkness of night. I will hold you again!

Anna, I will always send you poetry because I love you and want you to smile. I will always bring you flowers because you remind me of springtime. And, I will always keep you in my heart because it dances with joy when you are in it. You will forever be my beautiful girl with sun kissed hair and crushed starlight in your eyes!

Your Jeevan, who loves you tremendously.

•••

Miriam Waddington to Allan Donaldson
August 3, 1962
age 44

Dearest Allan,

Forgive my practice paper — I'm impatient with writing and so I am typing to you — unusual for me. I loved your long letter, its cheerful advice — your wonderful metaphor of striking a match, finding it isn't the street you want to be on anyway. My trouble is I haven't yet established my vision or intention — or the most clamorous one. But you are right — talk will do no good — one must write. And I hope and know it is true — whatever happens for writers actually happens in and through the writing. I haven't given up hope. I wrote some poems, felt pleased with myself — I am sending you two — what do you make of them? Gardeners has a very good self-portrait, where perhaps I made use of my self-deprecatory tendencies poetically. Vigorously anyway.

And I saw the proofs of my four Toronto poems in Tamarack — and felt good, because I know that no one else could possibly, can possibly do what

I can and did do in **Saints and Others**. Modest or not — what images, what effortless originality.

But that never lasts long. I quickly revert to my more usual feelings and broodings. Did you know — you must have — that I feel like some kind of monster, but I can't discover what is my secret wickedness, my terrible flaw? All because I am condemned to live alone, (don't tell me thousands would love it; they wouldn't) because my husband left me for another woman. The humiliation — since then so often relived, repeated in other experiences (just in case I might forget) is just about the most ever present thing in my emotional life. No, I don't believe that this is the hand of the almighty sent to smite me down for my sins. But I guess I do believe, or have until now, that such psychological havoc, chaos, events, must have its origin in some flaw of mine. Why mine? Well, everyone seems to think so — Pat is so manifestly a nice guy — like Vronsky in Anna Karenina. We can't <u>all</u> be honies and have things turn out so destructively for so many. There's the big riddle.

Of course I know that I have no natural aptitude for sex; you know I was hurt when you indicated this to me, but all the same, I had suspected it was true for the past two years or so. Before that I used to think I was as good as anyone, and more healthy, less sick that way than most. But somehow I am not sure that I care about that — or else I care too deeply to have any hope of changing it — changing it to what? That's really what I don't know — the secret of the world.

That isn't really what's so crippling; people make out somehow, and everyone has to be a little different; what is crippling is living unnaturally alone; I feel that once I had some sweetness in my nature; though it doesn't feel as if replaced by bitterness, the sweetness is all gone, I don't feel myself that way any longer; I feel myself only as a grieving hurting creature, and wonder if this is the natural state of all humanity.

Maybe these were some of the things on my mind when I saw you — they are in my mind always, but I can't often speak of them. Or do you think I speak too often of them? Well, do forgive me — I know that you accept me even with my weaknesses, but with you so far away, you can't help me to live through all the short spaces and little difficulties.

Well, to be more cheery. I ordered and had sent to you a very interesting new novel (and expensive like crazy!) James Baldwin's <u>Another Country</u>. I think you will find it worthwhile — I hope so. It is the most serious and detailed exploration of sexuality and love — really the connection between them — that I have ever read; It is far more sub rosa than anything Lawrence ever wrote — Baldwin doesn't feel the biological good sense of things the way Lawrence seemed to — also he writes of a disordered world — biologically and socially — and with Lawrence you got a clear sense of the order of species and genuses and sexes and things. I've just finished it myself — I had very ambivalent reactions — on the one hand I did not believe (but had to, he convinced me) that sex had to be so hostile — (another aspect of my cluelessness I suppose), on the other, some of his characters are dim and shadowy for me — wooden too — but he writes with great gravity and solemnity about sex, and he cares to explore it, and does so with fantastic variety and beauty and believability — and not sentimentality. Read and see. Nothing is resolved — just as in all good novels — I get now such a strong sense of the life in and for itself that a real novel has. What you feel in your own writing, I feel in others when they have it. [...]

So I am on a reading orgy. And again trying to diet. Spending long quiet hours alone, writing a little, answering letters, doing errands, mowing the lawn, and as of today joined the Y and intend to swim daily in their outdoor pool. Soon I'll plant snapdragons and sweet william for next summer. Your shrub is thriving — I mean the one you hefted out and in the earth for me. I de-dandelioned (hopefully the stuff will work) the lawn. It is pretty here, quiet, not too hot, sun and wind. Not such rain as you seem to be having. Heard you had sun today.

I went to a movie earlier — A Taste of Honey a very fine touching film. I'm a sucker for the young and adolescent — my heart always goes out to them.

My neck is stiff and more painful that after the accident; also my car is not yet finished — but I drive a V. from the garage and don't drive much. I am reluctant to go away weekends, feel I must work, but fritter quite a lot too. Working up to it gradually.

Saw Mickey Fainstat — he goes to Fr. so reminded him to look you up — a very good man — he forgot about you, that's why you did not hear from him. We discovered a nice place for after O'Keefe coffee — Oak Room at King Edward — there is dancing and orchestra for free. But we did not dance. Always my regret — that you and I did not either.

Anyway, you did get my other letter? Thank you for your lovely witty

exposition; in your last. My love — and in case you are on holiday, have a
good one.

>   Your,
>   Miriam

•••

Roy Kiyooka to Monica Dealtry Barker
Halifax, Nova Scotia
August 31, 1971
age 45

Dear Monica

>   this is a birthday letter: i believe
>   Sept 3rd is your birthday. as they say many
>   happy returns, etc.
>
>   halifax stinks of the atlantic.
>   the dead find sanctuary in the city's heart.
>   the living do their thing aware
>   of both.
>
>   here on sun lit tobin street
>   one small child beats on a old tin can.
>   two stories up i tap out another
>   rhythm. across 4000 miles our silences measure
>   both ocean's depths.

*

>   you could phone the lawyer re the divorce.
>   ask him (if he hasn't) to read you my letter it
>   explains why nothing has happened.
>
>   if there's anything i can do from this distance
>   to help you and the children let me know —

i intend to write to all of you regularly. and
do keep me informed (if you want to .

— not into my thing yet. it's as tho i had depend'd
on a compass for so long that without it i don't
know what direction to face. i am in that sense almost
faceless. nonetheless, the itch is there and
when the time comes…i shall do what i have to.

*

ah, my 45th yr —
which i've worn like a shroud
— what have you in store for me
in halifax?

.

Roy Kiyooka to Monica Dealtry Barker
November, 1971
dear Monica

I've sent Deano another fucken cheque which should pay for a divorce
and a half. I never thought I would have to pay-through-the-nose for *the pain*
of our parting, but that we might, separately, go on sharing familiarities.
Further back when we were very much together, I thought only death could
utterly part us. That is "if" I ever thought about the matter, then.

I just want to say that after all the hassles we have had with dimwit
you shouldn't have any more to do with him the way he flaps his lard over
nothings. As for his disreputable partner, I hope the Law throws the book
at him. p/s have deposited all of S's cheques in your acct. check it out the
next time you're in.

Our PM after the stale/mated general elections said: "…no doubt the
universe will continue to unfold as it should, etc…" if so, it surely includes
all of our mutual vicissitudes, together with, whatever Beatitudes we have
had together

take good care of yourself &
our children

···

Milton Acorn to Gwendolyn MacEwen
65 Confederation Street, Parkdale, Prince Edward Island
August 16, 1968
age 45

Dear Gwen;

I've never stopped thinking of you and I miss you awfully. Perhaps you realize by now that when you tell a man he doesn't make it because he is <u>too good</u> you are bound to get a most ferocious explosion —

What a thing to tell me!

I saw your poem in "Penguin" and got the reference to a poem of mine. Well, you were hurt, but I wonder if you can imagine how much you hurt me with those letters and that phone call?

I met Gail out on the coast and got some insight into certain women's fascination with the hurt and ugly. But for heavens sake don't <u>good</u> men deserve some pity? Must I always be being punished for telling the truth, and trying to take the wisest course in everything I do?

What happened between us was no "<u>mistake</u>," Gwen. You may have forgotten a lot. And you've been up against men who tried to take over your soul, as I refused to do. That's a game men play which I refuse to play. What I saw in you was real, Gwen —

And that first book (unpublished yet) which I read of yours — I mean that book of poems around the Hebrew alphabet — was good, and should have been published...

I'd like to hear from you

Love

Milton

My "Selected Poems" are soon to come out, with Ryerson...

So I'm "making it"

whatever making it means...

Well, I wouldn't have consented if I didn't know what "making it" means for me —

That is that I can give some hope and encouragement to others —

···

Jane Eaton Hamilton to Joy Masuhara
12:45:05, Friday, July 14, 2000
age 45

...I know what you mean about this incredible love. It doesn't matter how furious we are with each other — look how we light up when the other person comes into the room. Our eyes are aglow — ridiculous — and then one of us (usually me) smiles, and the other can't help smiling and then one of us (usually you) says, "Jerk! You jerk!" and the other one says, "Jerk! You jerk!" and then somehow, even if the fight goes on, we can't help laughing and we've got some perspective...

Seven years and still this helpless melting, all our emotional insides turning to syrup just thinking about each other. And even when we're finally ensconced in the everyday, as long as we're together we're so happy. I mean that without exaggeration: Happy! I know what the expression filled with happiness means, because it feels like that — pleasure tip to toe. Satisfaction. Contentment. But also glee.

I think that I have never been as sweet on you as when I told you I'd bought chocolate ice cream to go with the raspberries and you wagged your tail. Just like a dog — your whole body wriggling in pure strains of pleasure. And I thought: Yes. Just yes. Yes yes and yes all through me. Yes to you, Joy. Yes to you who have brought me such joy.

J.

•••

Robin Skelton, 1971
age 46

The language of love is impossible

The language of love is impossible
to a century

so completely obsessed
with the language of love.

I take my mirror
into the hall of mirrors

only because it cannot
    contain your face.

•••

Dennis Lee, 1985
age 46

Coming Becomes You

        Coming be-
    comes you,
            little one:
    rockabye world as you lie, and the great pang takes you in
            waves.   Coming
    becomes you.

        With horses you come, with arabian
                slather with jugular grunts and in
    fretwork, in fistfuls, on Fridays we come in the
                    danger and midnight of horses.
            Coming you come like a spill, like a
    spell, like a spoonful of flesh in the
            roaring, high on blood
    ocean, come with your horses, you come to be played.

        In after-
            come, you nuzzle;
    you nestle and noodle and nest.
                        And the ghosts in your eyes
        do their long-legged, chaste parade.
            Each time such sadness
                    hushes me: slow
        ache in your gaze — nostalgia for
                now, for now as it
        goes away.   You're
    beautiful, small

queen of the pillow drowse, and
rockabye world in my arms.
Coming becomes you.

•••

Ian Ferrier, 2007
mid-forties

Exile's Letter
*An imitation of a poem by Li Bai, 9th century Chinese poet;
based on Ezra Pound's translation*

To Soo Kyin, old high school girlfriend,
now star musician on the stages of Europe
I think of when you found me that night club to run
south side of the levee in New Orleans. With royalties and record deals
we paid for months of song and laughter.
And we were drunk for whole seasons
forgetting money, career, family. Famous singers and poets
drifted in from New York and from the Coast.
And they made nothing of sea-crossing or of mountain crossing,
if only they could be of that fellowship.
And we all spoke out our hearts and minds, and without regret.

Then the hurricane, and everything so ruined. I set out for Texas,
& night clubs in California. And you for Scandinavia and beyond,
till we had nothing but thoughts and memories in common.
And then, when separation had come to its worst,
we met in Austin, and touring together travelled
up from the New Mexico desert, high up into the clouded mountains
to that stunning, high green valley of Pagosa Springs.

That valley at sunset, if ever I saw Shangri-La:
fields fading to coniferous green,
then amber in the honey light
of late afternoon, bathing.

That was the first valley, and when we turned north out of Durango
into the roads twisting to follow each mountain fold,
and the route so laden with snow only the plowmen went forward.
To the heart of avalanche country
where the milestones mark the road crews
swept off to destruction, and the van skidding slow as mules.

Until the road finally cleared and all the trails fell downward.
And hurtling out of Climax we landed at the festival in Boulder
with the blues players of the Delta all come calling,
and the ghostly inhabitants of the School
of Disembodied Poetics. Words shouted from balconies,
endless riffs on guitar, evenings never ending.
And all of us drunk, our thoughts so clouded
with cheap wine and good pot we danced
till we fell exhausted in each others' arms,
and even then we didn't sleep.

And my spirit so high it had flown all over heaven.
And before the end of the day we were scattered like stars or rain.
I was gone to Europe trying to make the tour last the winter. And you
    back down to Austin to record. I remember you said your father
cashed in half his pension to back that project.
And when it all went platinum he sent us first class tickets from
    Europe.
And despite all that distance
we broke tour to catch you, launch it on City Limits.
And what with insurance and cancellations
I won't say we didn't get yelled at. Manager on the tarmac
saying we'd never work again if we didn't turn around.
And the cost that high, and all of us willing to pay it.

And when we heard that amazing music (we still all talk about it)
it was as if all the aspirations of our youth had been achieved.
We were giddy and drunk for days, and had no thought of returning.
And you would walk out with me, to the fountains
of that magic park beside the capital,

with the water about it as clear as blue jade.
Boats floating and the sound of blues harps
and drums rumbling up from the music clubs along the river,
music rippling the water like dragon scales, the green grass of the park,
and pleasure lasting long past midnight.
Amazing, tragic girls followed that band,
girls from Iceland and Hong Kong, naked on ganja and champagne.
Veuve Cliquot in crystal glasses, and laughing
as if love had not one consequence. And none as beautiful as you,
whose eyes were dark blue and a hundred feet deep
and me still lost in them. And the girls chanting back at each other,
dancing in transparent brocade…

I would never have gone home, because that was my home.
The wind still lifts those songs up, high above the trees,
melodies floating me back to those unending August days.
And all of this comes to an end. And is not again to be met with.

I went up to LA to audition, but it was all too strange,
the men who heard our songs, we had nothing in common.
So I packed my voice and guitar and drove back to the Vermont
    mountains.
White headed now, you would think the days less
valuable for being so many. The opposite is true.
I have not a moment to give away, except to you.

And once again, later, we met at Mardi Gras.
And then the crowds broke up and you went back to the forests of the
    West Coast. And if you ask me how I regret that parting: It is like
    the flowers falling at spring's end, confused, whirled in a tangle.
What is the use of talking, and there is no end of talking.
There is no end of things in the heart.

And I wonder what roads you walk down
whether you still carry the same
craziness made it so much fun and dangerous to tour with you
and I think of taking time to stalk the stage with you again.

Soo Kyin is it all too late? I sit back at the keyboard,
attach my latest song to seal this message; press a key
and feel it fly three thousand miles.

So far away. You used to always hear.
Do you hear now? Do you hear me?

•••

Jeevan Bhagwat to Anna ———
December, 2013
age 46

My love, the first snows of winter have fallen. The trees are silent and
the north wind wails for want of company. Cracked December sky bleeds
sunlight unto the fields long emptied of the cricket's song. All is cold and
white.

My love, I wanted to let you know that in the midst of this desolation,
the thought of you is like the first sweet blossom of Spring that awakens my
heart to the beauty of life. Today, it sings for you. Have a great day Anna.
Your Jeevan

•

Jeevan Bhagwat to Anna ———
January, 2014

Beautiful Dreamer, all is quiet in this tender hour. Up high, the Night
wears a necklace of stars while the moon, her pendant, glimmers in gold.
The streets are desolate as the winter wind sweeps by, collecting dreams
upon his outstretched wings to carry into the heavens. Not a sound emerges
from the houses whose window lighted eyes grow drowsy in the downy
snowfall.

All is still and with whispering breath, I say a prayer for blessed dreams
to take my spirit into your arms that I may gaze upon the blue roses that
bloom in your eyes. Beautiful Anna, my dreams are stars that lie scattered
before your feet. Goodnight. I love you.
Your Jeevan

George Elliott Clarke, 2006
age 46

À Geeta

  Call yourself, glancingly,
"A small, brown woman,"
For the phrase is exact.
You are diminutive, Indian, and *une femme*,
An expert in xviii-century French erotica —
All that revolutionary Romanticism,
The pillow talk of *philosophes*,
Setting Crébillon against and over Diderot,
For you prefer common-sense cotton to slinky silk,
And value sassy erudition over easy seduction.
  True: you stand just five feet tall,
But your mind encompasses God
And your heart compasses the world,
And you overwhelm even towering fools.
  Say you're pure-blooded, a Brahmin,
A Hindu whose eyes glorify Africa, cradle of light,
And whose skin is alive with night-undressing sun:
That would be truth too.
  Ah, Pomona of Mauritius,
Kali of Île Maurice —
Honey surges in all your body's canals,
Plies gold-leaf liqueur upon your limbs,
Sears henna into your eyes,
Becomes copper igniting velvet night,
And bronzes you, spiting Canada's white desert.
To embrace you is to embrace *colour* —
Pungent spice, piquant speechifying —
And raise sari arias of cinnamon and cayenne.
  Are you talkative? A chatterbox? Yes!
Well, consider the gourmet meal
Your voluptuous lips make of words,

Even your English errors are erotic!
Remember the time you called the hotel
And told the switchboard operator,
"I want to sleep with —
I mean, speak to —
The guest in room 61"?
And though you scan Cixous, *sans souci*,
The only travel writing you admire
Is restaurant reviews —
For you sip those *Godiva* chocolates
That I, swinish, gobble,
While your indulgence of distant India
Adheres to a glowing scripture of curry.
   I have roamed with you along beaches —
In North Carolina, Barbados, and Mauritius —
Plastered by the foam-stucco'd sea,
While sun splintered through palm fronds,
And some crimson bird-of-paradise erupted
From amid slippery greenery,
And your dress was sometimes just a breeze,
Or the look of moonlight after rain,
Or the green scent of the wind —
The liberty of the Mauritian Republic,
While your tutoring tongue
Lectured away libertinage,
Erasing my unspeakable lies
With enviable truth.
   O wife, so tawny, never naughty,
Excepting the verve of your eyes —
Or the lick of *brio* on your tongue —
To hold you like the ocean holds the sun,
That is love —
And you must be clasped as closely
As a country no one has colonized.
   "A small, brown woman"?
No.
You are a fifth element, feelings, and an epoch.

•••

Christine Lowther to ———
2014
Tofino, British Columbia
age 46

Dear Lover,

You used to enjoy reading aloud to me. The entire *Odyssey*, followed directly by that beer book. How we laughed at the sprightly bachelors, the worthy henchmen, every rosy-fingered dawn and something I misheard near the end: "immortal seagulls" — followed swiftly with beer tasting and brewery tours around the world. Then Alain de Botton. When you read his line "'I love you' can only ever be taken to mean '*for now*,'" I knew how utterly appropriate it was to us. But you kept reading and I didn't speak up. That must be why you read to me in the first place: to keep me quiet.

When you barely knew me you gazed. We were turned toward one another, gazing and gazing. I ask you to remember. Then our bodies moved away from one another, the inevitable parting that begins even with the first kiss. I only reinforced your passivity by tearing open your shirt, the dehiscent spray of the buttons scattering, not seeding, our connection. Do you remember the surprise of cold chain waking the warm skin of your body? You had asked me to run its hard links down your back.

Your friends walk past me now, not knowing you send me texts since your other conquest failed. No touch from a parent since I was eight, while you were adored and served by a mother and a sister. What hope did we have? I would warn of hedonic adaptation, the plague of all couples. You would not hear a sound when I spoke.

We move: toward and away. Burning and consumed. Arrest that progression, I dare you: *rage against the dying.* Let us face each other once more. What were we seeing before? Who were you looking for? Turn to me again. Meet this gaze.

Christine

•••

Steven Heighton, 2007
age 46

Breathe like this

"He was in a terrible state — that of consciousness.
Some while ago in his life he had lost the knack
of choosing what to think about."
— *Martin Amis,* The Information

Each day an hour in heaven, an hour in hell.
First: peopled scenes, how even our quarrels
or stalemate silences are coupling of a kind
and parole from the hellself: cellblock walls
are balsa compared. Pry me open. The skull
a chatroom run by monkeys, chittering, stoned,
a roach hotel, round-the-clock arcade, a gym
for obsessives, shadow boxing. And in the end:
that haiku helm where fields' last cricket grieves
summer in a voice faint as a codicil.

Then comes that other hour, when my love revives —
when rain falls like a ransom through the hymn-
soft stillness of a mind waking to wonders small
as the ounce of breath Alison Krauss sighs in
before she sings *As I went down to the river*
to pray, or prayer itself, or the horizon
of desire your bedded body makes in cool
silhouette, deep nights, dispelling hell. Sever
nothing from here on — couple this to that. Unselved
is unsplit,
       and to breathe like this is to be absolved.

• • •

Malcolm Lowry to Margerie Bonner Lowry
The White Cottage, Ripe, England
to Atkison Morley's Hospital
Monday, October 22, 1956
age 47

Dearest dearest
　　Dearest duck — am overjoyed to get a letter from you, more than overjoyed to hear that your nurses are kind and sweet & that you've got a private
private room. This is just an interim letter to tell you how overjoyed I am:
I've rung every day & I was getting worried, not by the reports, which were
non-committal optimistic contradictory, & generally uninformative, as
is always inevitably the case (though sometimes I can't exactly see why)
but by the implication, on my calling last night anyway, that your main
trouble was that you were still "nagging at yourself something awful" about
me — this (though it was probably my imagination) in Gauntlesque tones
in which the sensitive soul seemed to detect the implied rebuke that had
one availed oneself of the priceless opportunity (& I have no doubt at all it
would have been priceless, in more senses than one) to enter Virginia Water
as an undergraduate then you wouldn't be worrying so *much*. Be that as it
may, I think *we'll* always be glad of that two or three weeks we had together
with the "heavy heavy hanging over our head" — weeks of sweetness &
even light despite the bitterness & even total dark that might more appro-
priately have been thought to be their accompaniment. Just the same, short
of getting myself stuffed & putting myself in the rectory window like one of
those local immortal Sussexian poodles, I can't think of an existence more
harmless & less productive of your worry than the one I am leading, which
is positively Jane Austen-like in its stern devotion to duty right down to
the last (missing) fly-button; moreover, although of course I miss you like
hell, in so far as this existence is tolerable, I can also find amusement in its
solitude, in its rectorish rectitude, — your plants & the garden and even
the tragedy-making Cat prove real compensations, and it need be anything
but a waste of time. Rev. El Leon immured in the vicarage is a concept that
never fails to divert me. [...] But it is also a godsent opportunity to resume
work at high pressure and break a lot of difficult ground in a hurry all of
which would be much easier - & after all it can only gratify you — it is what
you yourself want — if I could somehow feel you were making an effort to

stop worrying about me. In fact, I'm trusting you to do so. Of course I'd probably be hurt if you *didn't* worry at *all* but for god's sake lay off the heavy self-nagging & you'll find it may be an important step in your recovery. Mind you in your sweet letter there's absolutely no mumbling word or hint about worry but I scent it just the same: For let me tell you honey ah feed the plants and ah water the cat, and what do you think I get for that? Worry blues. Miaoww. Miserere Worry Blues. And instead of getting high as a kite ah lock up those cottage doors all tight at night. All right? No. Bang. Crash. Worry Blues. Miaoww! Miserere Worry Blues. Now I'm giving it to you straight honey if you got to worry, worry over something worth worrying over worry over Worrying because I'm telling you I aint worrying over you half so much as I am about worrying about you worrying about *me*, and further, are you still with me sister? Still there? If you can't stop those old birds of worry flying over your head you can sure enough stop them nesting in yo' hair! — Bang. Crash. Miaoww! Banish those Worry Blues. To banish those old Miserere quite Contrary Jelly-roll rock and rhythm Worry Blue-ue-ues!…Goddamn. […]

And the cat. Bang. Crash. Miaoww! Banish those Worry Blues. 4:15 Duck Time.

Consider thy tea brought with appropriate menu, & all dear love from
Your doting husband
Malcolm

•

Malcolm Lowry to Margerie Bonner Lowry
from The White Cottage, Ripe, England
to Atkison Morley's Hospital
November 10, 1956

Dearest sweet strong hartebeest — ma Glucose Baby, (Tennessee would have just loved to call you that, honey): — Am absolutely all in a dither of adolescent love at hearing your voice: and I took your last sweet letter out of its envelope — the words "I love you" just peeping out of the envelope, so that I half pushed the letter back again, with all the secretive self-satis-faction, religious shrine, and thrilling thunderings of heart, and heroic determination concerning juicy dragons to be laid at your feet, of a lovesick swain of 13 1/2 about to have his first date under the village elm tree. But though I'm longing — as I have been longing — to see you, I'm in a small flap about coming to see you and what day, for there is much to be usefully done here — oh, what a scurrying of little animals and brushing of rugs and mowing machines as the hot bricks are taken out of mothballs and dusted off in preparation for the Harteebeeste's Great return! We should have our minds made up to-night as we should have last night when & if I should come but that's exactly what we won't have done because we'll have too much else to talk about. If I should come, I lean at present towards Tuesday (1.30 – 3.30 pm) — maybe I can even catch the 6.20 bus back, not that we need exactly lick our chops over our saved ducats like dirty old Nasserwasser gloating over a convey of M.I.G's. I held this news back, as I did the world news, (I asked at the outset that it be kept from you, or you might just have gone into your ordeal with the invasion by Israel on you mind, and other Armageddon-like evil-bodings, by no means over as you can see, though I take an optimistic view, for us anyway. [...] Would you like me to come on Friday & get you, or both? However I don't want to act from emotion, I want to do what is useful and sensible. I have done a little nagging at myself about not having put myself in the way of having been directly consulted over this whole business: i.e. asking myself whether it was not accepting, and somewhat humiliatingly, a certain position of irresponsibility not to have placed myself in the same position vis-à-vis your doctor, as at least you were vis-à-vis Raymond etc. But I'm inclined to think that my motives here may have partly an ego-saving basis, & be irrelevant to your recovery; after all a little deflation of ego is a small price to pay for your getting well again. So I'll rule that out as a further motive for coming to the hospital perhaps, unless your doc really wants to see me on your account, but that still leaves the question as to when & if I should come at all, especially as I am working hard, & there is much to be done here. Perhaps a compromise, & a meeting at Victoria on Friday? Please try to make up your mind what will please *you* best, if you know, & I will do it. Hugehugsandkisses — Soon!

Bless you
Malc [...]

...

Robert Hilles to Pearl Luke
1998
age 47

Pearl Sweetheart —

It startled me to wake and not find you there. It reminded me how much I look forward to waking beside you. I was glad to see your note downstairs and went to bed happy. I loved your note at work too. I'm so scrambled these days it's wonderful to receive those, it's like a soft kiss in the middle of the night — makes me happy to be alive. I love you so much. I'll call you tonight or call me if you like I'll be home after 8:00pm.

Love, Robert

•

Reply

Robert,

Outside the windows, it's a cold grey day, greyer because you're not here, because we didn't cling to each other last night but only to small angers stacked carefully through the day, like kindling. Four photos of you surround me, all of them in black and white, as if you've lived your life in grayscale, uneasy about getting too caught up with color. I'm drawn to the image that avoids the camera's gaze, either doesn't know it's there, or refuses to look. Your hair — overdue for a cut — curls damp at your temple. Your lips are slightly apart, top teeth showing. You've raised the collar of your coat against the cold, and you wear no scarf. Deep lines circle your throat like an invitation to count the years and, under your jaw, flesh hangs in a soft pouch. Behind you, branches tangle and arch while dead leaves, like old cups, fill with snow. It is not a sexy photo. Yet there is intensity there, caught in the eyes that refuse me, in the furrow between them, and I know that soon you'll step out of the chill, papers spilling from arms and case. Your eyes will find me, and the colors between us will be warm.

I thought of you all day!

Pearl

• • •

Fern G.Z. Carr to Al Carr (on his 60th birthday)
August 29, 2004
age 48

Dear Al

My secret   fear is that
I will outlive   you — our lives
are so inextricably bound that to undo
a single strand would unravel the entire
fabric: the lost intimacy of a solitary bed,
unwhispered secrets, a stolen future. We
are a melding of essences; without you
there would be nothing but a clang-
ing emptiness so I offer
you this, my gift of words,
and thank you for
being your
gift to
me.
Love,
Fern

•••

Howard White, 1993
age 48

The Made Bed

When we were first married and
lived in a pink trailer
we made love in the morning
with the opening of day
the burst of birdsong
the sun fresh and damp like

a newly opened bud
    it was good to start the day
    in love
then came the kids
and our mornings were gone
our delicate and sustaining love
moved over
and another kind took its place
Silas slept in our bed
until he was three; Patrick,
whose appetite for warmth is greater,
was still there at five.

I stroke the curve of your morning hip
under the remoteness of the cloth
we never used to wear
and it seems to me the
miraculous innocence is still there
although our love has become
like an untended appletree
whose fruit are fewer and smaller
brilliant in their rarity
but less than the leafy abundance
that once was there.

    This is a loss:
        there is no avoiding it,
for all that the small shape
snuggled against your back
is a wonder our young lives
never knew. His desperate
affection cannot be denied
or resented
            and yet our loss
can never, save in these
catch-as-catch-can moments
be recovered.

I suppose the reason
I have never tried to force
our own way is a neutral
satisfaction that life
doesn't always give
as it takes away.

•••

Patrick Lane
1987
age 48

Small Love Song

Syllable of stone, the lizard lies prone
under the bright dome of the moon.
His patience lasts forever.
I know I am almost old and my bed is made of sand
but even among stones love is possible.
The lizard waits forever in the ruins.
Come to me.
I will wait for you at least one more night.

•••

Weyman Chan, 2012
age 49

Monologues and their Instruments of Torture

One week ago:
Me: What have you to say for yourself
You: Roses are ibuprofen
          Red as bald assholes
          Upon which you, oh nerve, are
          The benefactor of poofs and nevi

Me: What have you to say for yourself
When outpourings ween
The Apple bearer from her adoration
You: click
I pick myself up every morning like a fallen radius
Me: I'm reading Jane Eyre and listening to the Memphis soundtrack.
You: I'm looking for that Energizer battery charger for the triple As
on my graphing calculator. Fuck this jumbotron over pastor
Witt. I thought it was in that ceramic thing on the fireplace, and
it's open, I know, we agreed on that. You see who you want but
Me: yeah, and all the baritones and their wives and girlfriends baked
cupcakes. Remember what it was like to be an alto? You did it
all yourself!
Spiritual shock and awe, says carpet bomb of American prayer
over cleansing obliterations, you pray but what do you cry for?
A god that prompts us to remember will open the nationwide
coverage lacking beatnik loiter.
You: aren't you scared? Those who would insist. Those colonials of a
jacked up dissuasion being at the art of center —
Me: by acidosis you learn to create.
You: shouldn't we at least to try watching season 3 of Mad Men
together? Go to sidereel.com. Maybe not right away.
Me: you mean synchronize our watching of it. Okay, I'm busy
and I love you. Isn't it sad you don't underwhelm, oh bilious
isotherm. French fries are a known inquisitor. Victory's food
has unlimited 4G coverage
You: and love left me in Kobe. Broken strap doorstop knocker all off
garden gaze knitters. Elector of elevators. Left me in Kobe. Love
occiput to insinuate, corrected curtains sashimi say currently.
Ariosto Suharto fundamentally 94% Arigato. What assays
bough and needle. Swish goodbye.
Me: that's why it's so hard and I love you for what is that if not for
your black folds of glory. You're blonde, you win at prayer, praise
and pizza.
You: Pork me back like a giant salami with wings, you lacey beatnik
Me: no one talks that way. No one says things like that these days,
for god's sake, my girl. Go misc very hell lunch much miss plz

pity loiter moll pi wetter Fred ok sec Zac cad Greg green ugh book

One year ago:

Me: hi Tweetie, hope you are having a super lovely day, surely the world must adore your large feet as much as I adore them

You: ( )

Me: in case you don't recognize this cell, I might as well come out and say it…it's me!

You: ( )

Me: again from the land of text. Hoping you're having a super duper day out there. It's versatile by that I mean I can say to you wherever and whenever I please. Flywheel reading at Pages tonite as well, last night, so so. Left right away so the groceries wouldn't fly away, prior to metaphor I mean. One is considered real. Then tightness, facial entanglements in the mummed sense, scale our behavior, coffee to cloud.

You: okay, now I know how to work this thing. I'd asked your brother how this thing worked, he was on the roof again. Flew off it before showing me the send options settings. Forgot to tell you. It was nice of him to drop by.

Me: he promised me his old cell, so gave it to you, really, I didn't know

You: was this the turbidity Ellington and Ella bargained for? pajamas aren't the worst of it, though you might judge how one tries to Master the psychology of fact and concern by placing before us the interval of distance. Realm of the bomb and its rendered sorrows, you are contained.

Me: I luv (have always luved) the way your mind works its language, just cuz

You: caw caw
as for the object of presentation as a thing of earth, the accident of technology advances a state of correctness that everything from Aristotle to a Starfrit can-opener must conform to. The maze must bind its minotaur. If the eye doesn't see the bomb go off, if the word isn't the promised thing, then on whose scale is our seeing decidedly fractured?

Me: caw caw diddly caw / fuckin' caw caw caww
      Tie down the spring layers, fennel, neocortical transepts, the
      el-Hallaj of Rumi, with this pitch-perfect scythe. pour the drink
      of dew such that you, eyeing the curved pomme of this poem,
      smallest of consecrations, will figure the offer that lasts. But
      then art determines the concealment of signs, sound starts
      contesting its speak, opening the unspeakable, for what? An
      inquisition to determine trust, though knowledge, skeptically
      convinced, tries to paralyze radiance through negation in this
      regard. The negations are what ratify fiction. and fiction is the
      brain's haiku.
You: really, Said, you are too much.
Me: why up so late? Packing for yet another new adventure
You: you said it, yup. Caw caw the raw raw. Taw taw
Me: Tweetie, where snouts abouts are yea on gods green earth?
      Myself, I'm reading otolithically at the Auburn tonite.
You: I bee in the Okanagan with my manboy, chattin' and
      rat-a-tat-tat'in
Me: Ta ta to you for now, then my dear. Goodnite and safe journeys.
You: thinking of you and sending much luv.

•••

R.C. Weslowski, 2014
age 49

It's Good to Be Here

It's so good to be here.
Right here, no here,

Right   *here*

With you

Basting in Buddha's belly juices
A third nipple cripple no longer

Spinning muse tricks and soul licks
As quick as Jimi Hendrix
Pounding rocks and stone free flow
Into the afterglow of the sweet bliss
Of an aurora borealis star kiss
So in love with this moment
We don't have to say excuse me
When we kiss the sky
Oh yeah

It's so good

To be   *here*

Voila! C'est bon d'etre ici, maintenant
Je suis comme un voyageur dans la sang de dieu
La creation tout autour de moi
Copuler, coaguler, consumer, une par une
Pure exuberance, pure horreur, pure joie
C'est quoi que je dis? Je ne parle pas francais.
Eh, c'est la vie.
C'est bon d'etre ici, maintenant

Whoa
Yum, yum, yum, yum, yum
It's good

To be   *here*

With you

   Among my hard rock heroes
My home made people
In the middle of this madness
In the beauty and the gloom
The ones the angels went to war over
The reason Lucifer fell

Maybe that's why we're all so quick to anger
And follow heaven's example
To pick up a weapon
Or have a drone drop a bomb
We're all insignificant from a distance
So come closer, come closer
Be my carnival mirror
Let me see my absurdity
And I'll show you yours
We can laugh at ourselves
The biggest joke that there is
We are all just awkward clowns
Scaring each other at children's parties
So let's take off our make up
Let me see the shape of your invisible face
The glory shining through you
See you leading by example
My holy conundrums pounding
Your hearts unabashed
It's taken so long to find you
I was lacking in the vastness
Addicted to divisiveness
I couldn't see you in the shadows
I wanted a darker mythology
But now I choose a different story
You're my happy ending
We get to kiss and hold hands
Don't worry I'll ask permission
You are loved more than you will ever imagine
More beautiful than you think you are
And I just wanted to say thank you
Thank you for waiting
The detour nearly killed me
I have trouble reading maps
But you were my GPS out of the sorrow
The trail of crumbs I left behind
And I just wanted to let you know

There's no place I'd rather be
Than in this world right here beside you
Oh yeah,

It's so good

To be   *here*

With you

• • •

Frederick Philip Grove to Catherine Grove
Moosomin, Saskatchewan
10 a.m., September 10, 1928
age 49

Well my dear, here I am; and the rain is pouring down outside. When I arrived, committee was waiting, as usual; and I had to allow myself to be "entertained" till midnight. Speak to-night. This is a large club — 200 members, 3/4 of them farmers. Well…

I hope you got home all right?

I am sending *Disraeli* — read it. The latter half, from the accession to power on, is very good. Perhaps a bit superficial, but fundamentally true. A new novel is shaping itself in my head.

Please convey my thanks to the Gardiners for the ride — I am afraid I did not say very much. I was preoccupied with worry about leaving you alone. I am at bottom too old for this sort of thing. I don't want to influence life directly any longer. I want to sit back and look on. However…

It started to rain soon after I arrived; and it has been raining all night. I am glad in a way; they wanted to show me the country in the afternoon. That, at all events, I escape.

Crops here are very heavy; but most of them frozen. I enquired about price of wheat: 90c for #1 Northern. 35c for frozen wheat — that means quite a loss to the farmer. Tell John if you write. He may not be so very badly off after all. For 35c a bu does not pay for the seeding, harvesting, and threshing.

Harvest hands cannot get more than $2 a day — in threshing time. Pretty bad.

Well, as I said, keep your spirit up. This has got to be gone through.

Bye-bye
F.P.

•

Frederick Philip Grove to Catherine Grove
En route Kamloops–Jasper
October 13, 1928

I'm getting tired of this. Travelling 300 mi a day — in day coaches, so as to save a little money. The distances are enormous; and the trains so slow, climbing the mountains. It would all be very interesting and beautiful, could a person look at things with different eyes. As it is…Yet, at the end of it I hope to have $1000 in the bank — and that, of course, is something.

Yes, it's a good piece of book making. But, as you say, the cover, with the huge yellow print, is ugly. However…[…]

I see all sorts of things now and then. Strange visions. This travelling over dizzy viaducts affects me: I must be getting old. At Vancouver I could not sleep because my room was on the 12th floor. But it's all nonsense, of course.

I'd be quite satisfied to stay at Rapid City — on that hill-side we've been looking at. I suppose I'll have to go east again early next year. The sooner the better — so as to get through with it. Money, money, money!

Don't forget to tell the Zilzes that I'm spending the week-end in Jasper National Park, and that there is *no* motor-road in: and even near it you can get only from the east and by very poor prairie trails. I'd like to run down to Edmonton in daytime, too. But there is no train apart from the night train. The C.N. runs only 1 train between east and west in winter; and *it* isn't crowded.

On the island, I was thrown, for a day or so with a couple who reminded me of ourselves. The man (County Court Judge Barker) 60 or 65; the woman, 20 yrs his younger. And both still in love with each other — she, not merely his wife, but his mistress. I liked both of them.

Well, next week-end at Peace River.

Cheer up, old girl; 4 weeks from now: home!

Phil

•

Frederick Philip Grove to Catherine Grove
En route Sarnia–Toronto
February 15, 1929

(neighbourhood of Paris, Ont., you remember?)

Well, this sheet will probably reach you ahead of one or two letters mailed yesterday and today at Sarnia, farther west whence they will have to come back to Toronto for the long run. If my letters don't arrive in the right order, the reason is that I hop about this province, east and west, never adhering to one direction.

I have really nothing to say. I merely write to relieve your feeling of loneliness. The first few lines were written while stopped. Now we are hopping: and you can see it in the writing, I suppose. On the whole, we have better road-beds in the west. Next stop Brantford. In a little over 2 hrs we'll be in Toronto.

By the way, if E.S.G. is silly enough to be disagreeable about that report of yours, why not answer by resigning? RESIGNING? We'll manage. Though, of course, the salary would be welcome. But no. I can't write with this train trying to make up for lost time. So bye-bye

P

And this is Brantford whence I started yesterday morning for Sarnia. Hopping like a flea all over the country. Well, bye-bye. She is starting again.

•••

Robert Hilles to Pearl Luke
2000
age 49

Pearl:
Today waiting at the dentist I wrote this poem. I love you completely and I want this relationship to work more than anything.

with all my love a thousand, million times over:

Beloved
  (*for Pearl*)

It drizzles all day in Sooke.
By the window of our new house,
I watch the sea
take back the rain.
Your hand on my neck
rubs through pain.
Last night I turned to you in sleep
and you warmed all the places night chilled.
Rain drummed the roof
and our empty house murmured.

Today waves crest rocks
and my thoughts
follow your fingers as they travel.
Winter stays frozen to the peaks of mountains
across the Strait of Juan de Fuca and the sea
repeats the sky's delicate, worn tones.
I worry that I can describe the ocean
but not your face.
Beloved, your eyes wear
the blues and greens of spring.
You heat muffins in the oven
and walk between empty rooms
planning a future
my heart races toward.

Yesterday a seal poked its face
out of pale water.
We walked to the edge of the rocks
seeking its animal attention.
Patient as the sea, it bobbed
for an usually long time
and watched us with moist, steady eyes.

Today I scan the ocean for that seal
but the water reigns alone.

My thoughts shift from sea
to the tip of your tongue pausing between whispers.
My ears shut out all but the sounds
of us coming home.
I trace a line along the uneven surface
of the strait out into the channel
where a lone freighter
snails toward the open sea.
From our house it looks small
and insignificant just as we must
to anyone on board looking back.
I let this love slip tighter into me.
I turn away from the sea
and kiss you once
as the empty house
settles more firmly into place.

Love Robert

•••

Elizabeth Rainer and Michael Blouin
Selections from 2011 e-mails
mean age 49

Michael,
     want is nothing\ but I found a note on the library floor at the university
the other night fluorescent lights pale lines *come home Angel* it said *my heart
aches and the sex is just no good without you* I picked it up already knowing
that I would use it that I would copy it down and place it here and as I walked
away steadfast and secure the paper crumpled in my hand the acid of my
confidence could have eaten the world and then did I say my heart aches no
that was someone else feel eyes hard on me you watching me leaving one

foot in front of the other I know you're here even when you are not I feel where you are your eyes on my ass and my black boots

Elizabeth,

thought you should\ and pregnant and won't tell anyone the father's name that's just the way it is it was some guy at a dance in a t-shirt that said Coca-Cola he was sweet to her and then he just left I said that I'd pray for her and I did this morning with the sun just starting to creep the snow in the yard and the air crisp I prayed hard I gave it all I had I hope that she lands on her feet and that she finds her way inside finally and that the baby is okay I am all compassion no one should be alone

Michael,

hands just go\ where they want paper to skin to paper to skin me I not alone me I tangent to your rough me I wanting to be suddenly just now slow snow light under drawn curtain alone I if you're going to write this shit down you must first feel some of it on your hands look you're going to be a writer my father said what will you eat where will you go I believe my next life will go better my car will start there is no other way to move the sheets just now blinking digital numbers cold apostles I am moving primarily out of fear and what you think is never going to happen is road maps and fast food wrappers in the back seat a blanket cold hands accelerate I'm sorry I just wanted your hands on me

Elizabeth,

one that's almost\ we argued about Don Quixote whether to take it or leave it behind where it fits in relation to post-colonial theory we are within the one per cent of couples who can argue this and not amongst the ninety nine who have better things to do it was my father's favourite book and he won't be reading it anymore no more windmill tilting you thought it would depress me having it around the warm night at the window just the night the bed this life so strange he clung to it though this life that he had and finally we gave up arguing it was pointless anyway your close breath I can't get it clear of my mind

so just listen\ just a note to reach you and to tell you when you were painting your nails on the porch all that red polish and the stains on your arm like you had been cut and wounded as I know that you have been just to let you know all these little ragged lies of mine will just return to the earth in the end there's an old war movie on in the other room and the fella just said; *"there'll be no heroes this time"* yeah

Michael,

    hand it over\ the usual soliloquy since I was a girl I have lain on the bathroom floor next to the roaring tub wall as the bath filled almost every time I have chosen full immersion over splash and wipe I have done this always but recently I have curled into a ball I have covered myself with towels ceased to care when the water reaches the top ceased to try to stop it refused to acknowledge that as a role for me until it is too late until I am flooded but never carried away nor doved nor olive branched nor rainbowed all I do is forget with the tile floor I fall to my face refuse to get up these days the weather outside is fuck these days the weather outside is close the door I do not believe in spinal cords in the shift of nerves I do believe in cold I believe in this damp hair curled to me plastered in this I believe in nothing that I can ever hold onto

Elizabeth,

    onto every surface\ I've left this message stitched to your sheets polished on your skin transmitted carefully in all of the things I've failed to do and I've placed it carefully into your mouth while you were sleeping tied it to your forehead I've carved it into the fridge door scratched it in with a fork I've chalked the driveway written into the November frost tapped it in morse onto your soft warmth drummed it into this steering wheel my sleeves are torn I've left this message I've left the girls alone untie it now give up the world and run with me

Michael,

    that's the way\ it goes it goes mm hmm mm hmm da…mm hmm mm hmm da…something about the ocean de de de de mm hmm and being pulled from the wreckage you hardly ever hear it on the radio anymore you told me once my vagina was like a small bird and I never asked you how it doesn't forage for food in the forest in the winter nor does it sing from the trees in the spring I sometimes wonder if you had any idea what you were saying half the time you said anything at all there's a part in the middle that goes nan a na naa in the middle of the song I mean not in the middle of my vagina and a part that goes yeah yeah yeah yeah yeah *yeah* sometimes the truth is just the ceiling coming down just the ashes left see you're carrying that look on your face if you want to make love to me take off your pants and if you want to go just do it just go but either way like men say when they throw the football go long

Elizabeth,

long fingers like\ a dancer's legs around the neck of the bottle and said that she would leave him announced that you know he's a drunk and one day we will all die anyway nonsense what nonsense I don't care of course will always carry that little piece of her with me anyway white ankles red socks fingers turning she says he trips over everything and doesn't hear me he never hears me he never listens like many men this is not unusual I think maybe I don't know it's okay that I am many men but some of them really want to hurt me pretty bad I'm sorry did I scare you I didn't mean it I'm fine forget it but it's true

Michael,

true that I\ might make you sad but joy is unstable by nature and is really just asking for it that's why I'll take your keys take your car run up your bills leave you stranded that darling is why

Elizabeth,

why do you\ admire me why because I stand on hot coals and survive it's true I have done that if only figuratively and I am still here because I have survived an addiction to painkillers sweated out the withdrawal my life has been threatened with guns the cold steel at the back of my head with knives with violence of a variety rolled my jeep lost most of my blood and I am still here I have eaten the darkness suffered the loss deeply appreciated the light the sun on my arms you admire me for my tattoos or because of what I have done or what I have not and there was the time I took on the Amazon single handed in a dugout canoe or wait that was someone else we saw that on tv I think you see this is why I stopped watching television I am too ready to absorb (that one about the addiction I'm pretty sure that was an episode of House) but the rest is all true and you admire me why is it is it because I am still here I'm ready to believe that I think I think I could make the decision to fall in love with anyone I think provided they were beautiful provided they had eyes like yours and little green shoes like yours and you admire me maybe because I'm still here well me too

Michael,
    too hard for\ me if I had the right hat there would be no question if I had the right shoes if my thoughts and my desires added up to action if my human body were not so filled with uncertainty but that's just the way of it the body wants hard when it wants and can't be trusted can you?

Elizabeth,
    you may trust\ jesusallahvishnubuddhaorjudas any of them but not me your heart stretched out in the field on its own netted down spiked down alone in the sun and the crows why did you let me I never said you did that I did that and I said I wouldn't I said I wouldn't and then then seeing everything blanket slowly pulled down sheet slowly pulled down everything slowly pulled down and circus carnival streaming light see the distance slide sun on the line and everyone is a winner baby that's a fact

Michael,
    laughter fascinates me\ and everything that is at the extreme end of emotion where the wires are cut and capped or left to sputter out tears screams people who've ransacked their own lives the lives of others I do know one thing however it is better to love in spite of instead of because

Elizabeth,
    for the longest\ time I had this line in my head he's busy playing the bad man and I knew it was supposed to fit in somewhere but the characters in the novel I was writing then didn't like it and wore it like a bad suit of clothes and I tried to fit it in here but this book has no characters and it was the longest time before I realized that it was just me

Michael,
    dear heart I\ wanted to tell you I don't think that not wanting to be near danger makes me any less of a man particularly since I am a woman and anyway I'm going to buy an old car and drive across the continent sleep under a blanket in the ditch I suppose I could sleep in the car okay I'll sleep in the car but that's the only concession I'll make otherwise why start out

otherwise what would I even make this journey for I think the perfect man is pure spirit think the perfect man does not leave his shoes by the bed think the perfect man is quiet because he's always certain

Elizabeth,
   if you fall\ in love with a poet you're going to take your lumps it is a certainty it's not that they mean to do it it's just in the nature of who they are or who they've let themselves become I suppose as robert lowell once said they are always in love and that is so but the truth is that most of the time it's with themselves and most of the time they'll cut you like Christmas and leave you lying

Michael,
   now you ask\ what time it is it's late and what I've learned: nothing, you ask me whose fault this is it's nobody's turn a blind eye try the one with the stick in it

Elizabeth,
   now I mostly\ live in words and images in thoughts and what I once saw I am visual pretty much but remember those days and nights in mont-real there was a sinkhole in quebec on the news tonight a whole family swallowed up nothing is missing everything is already here and Jesus in his starry crown sorry to go away from you like this love I love you at burger king they were handing out paper crowns there are plums cold in the fridge it is very late I do and we'll see maybe we'll see in the dark I do in the night no stars light from the fridge falling now I do look at your ass in the lamp-light pulling down soft sliding down white and over tight your skirt your knees bending up and now I'm in you now and how you were made someone oughta get a medal there's chaos and there's this and move in me you say and I do I am learning to dream you am learning you now again bones under skin shift and hard pressed hard

Michael,
   hard pressed to\ come up with anything like a poem today that's what I'm supposed to do aren't I darling come up with a poem if I skip today will a species flicker out or will it matter in the end

Elizabeth,

 in the end\ I could write of your fairly perfect breast sway your falling pajamas but that's too easy and just a way of not writing that if you died the best part of me would be gone do don't I'm telling you I drove past the house I grew up in today and the concrete steps have shifted the shingles are lifting in patches but I can't write it out because something so true is not going to look true at all on this paper my effort to get things right will be vain and people will laugh at my scrumbling bricks and the haggardy yard I used to in which I used to play

Michael,

 you let me\ carry on and ramble I loved you for that hold my hand and save me from the deep end

Elizabeth,

 the deep end\ of the lake we walked around for hours in the hills and we found a little cat when we'd been lovers less than a month it had nowhere to go cold autumn gave it the tuna from your sandwich it slept next to you in the car wrapped in your sweater gave it away to someone who wanted it more and let's lie right here tell me anything quick I'll listen wax paper blowing on the floor of the backseat one hand on the wheel speeding tell me now let's lie wet fur small pink tongue darting and I wish I could still stand in the desert watch you walk away sugar sweet tattoo in the sun you are what pulls me up He doesn't always do that it's okay it's not His job all the time you always do you see what I'm saying you always do it's in you somehow to do that

Michael,

 be quiet be\ the man you should have been too late I come from a small town small enough to see that you're all gravy and no meat remember the first time I saw you what could I have done though your arm in the sun your steady gaze you smelled like a bonfire yes is what I told you just yes

Elizabeth,

 I told you\ your breath hot and damp and close to me I told you how my father described his stroke a sudden warm flowering in his head a realignment of everything he'd known and all the bartenders knew our order and I never did and I never have and I probably never will lie to you I mean it would be nice for me if you were someone else for a change someone who didn't know me so well my tremors hopes then when we were making love it would all be different once more your ankles up around and there wouldn't be that look on your face oh *him, again*

Elizabeth,
  are you there

•••

Betsy Warland and Daphne Marlatt, 1994
ages 48 and 52

March 7

breaking out, you said
muscles working together in
leading you on
                    — more that than precedence

a kind of birthing
womb the body's largest muscle
making room in the language

                with the heart
                the next

where's the mind?

where's mine?

quack, quack retort of ducks nesting

            saving our queens?
              face cards close to
                your heart?

struggle?
re-enactment?

we do not birth ourselves

       under the micro
       scope insects
       writhe

in sects
       you've left

March 7

Do you want me to add another line? i've got one

do

           *

you're not going to take off on "language"?

you can do it

[repeated searching through dictionary]

      *

i don't know what the fucking queens are doing in there

are you stuck?

   Well, this poem seems to be going in two opposite directions and i can't figure out how to re-unite them. i was really excited about something up here and we just keep getting further away
     from it

what are you doing?

i'm making notes of what i was trying to get to

March 7

the cat purred, walked all over the page, lay down on it. we stroked him. he purred (silky fur) then began to bite. us too. fight. your feeling it isn't a poem — just "blather," and that i wasn't picking up on what you were writing. my feeling your frustration, anger, and wanting to be true to the reader and our struggle for "mine." beginning too late in the day part of the problem — our minds needing their own idiosyncratic directions, the quotidian's power, even on our "day off."

missing each other's signals. my thinking your impatience is partly due to your anger at not having time to do your **own** writing (your novel) but having to respond to other deadlines (like this one). i felt betrayed as your impatience increased. felt it as early as when i wrote "where's mine"? why i wrote it. and then felt angry when you began writing, on another page. you left. i accuse you of wanting a "perfect poem," and of not wanting to make yourself vulnerable to the reader. you say it "isn't working." it's "blather."

i say it's being true to the process. i don't only want to present the reader with "perfect poems" but also the back & forth. the struggle for mine **and** the relaxing into, moving with each other into, something more than mine. that intoxicating doubling of anticipation and revelation. i didn't only intend "mine" as a possessive but also in the sense of mining. mining the mind throughout our whole bodies.

you say it's not poetry. i'm ok with that. don't want to feel controlled by form. "But people will look at lines on the page and expect poetry." i suggest we could write about this, these short lines, these unpredictable spaces — our riding the currents of one another's associative and symbolic thought. for me — that's what we're doing, and sometimes — not doing. both are equally of interest. both have the potential for meaning.

March 7

where's mine? where's mine?

territory — & the terror at the edges of losing our way in the mind-direction of the other.

we talk angrily. you accuse me of leaving the collaboration because it isn't going the way i want it to. i accuse you of judgement when you say i'm getting too theoretical.

"where's mine?" the axe split in the poem.

i want to follow the drift evolving through earlier entries, words, thoughts we nudge up to in various ways. the same and different, changing as they recur. i have a sense of something moving into focus in & through the drift & when we approach it i get excited, connections leap, though there's always the strain of contiguity — how much more that is disparate can touch on what's already there & nudge it forward?

you want to document the struggle our wandering, our mind-blather makes along with the flights when we soar together. for you, resistance to flying together is as important as flying together. all part of the process — nothing insignificant. although you still use the word "significant" when you talk about the actions, the body-shifts you choose to record in the margin. you say i want to write a perfect poem. we have a different understanding of form & process — form is more organic for you, what happens. for me form is something we make in collaboration with the poem, a 3rd entity which develops its own process as we continue. for you the poem is the trace of our collaboration, the record of our ins & outs. for me the poem is something we collaborate with. it doesn't have to be a poem you say, just because it's in lines on the page — form isn't holy. form is holy, in the sense that it is what gets revealed — and what it tells us then.

we didn't talk about this before we started. i thought we were writing a poem together with documentary asides in the margin. you thought we were documenting our writing together. the question of which takes precedence — & can we agree? or do we have to?

March 7
afterthoughts

up till now when we've collaborated we've each had individual control of our individual pieces so we could shape them according to our own sense of form. it's

surprising that we should have difficulty collaborating on such a microscopic
level — it's the first time our senses of form have collided with each other and
we've had to give up individual control.

our forms like our fingerprints? the bodies we live in. even more indelible
in their idiosyncrasies than our words?

giving each other the gears we are still engaged

March 9

timing
    & the chiming words do
lead us on
    beyond our intentions

tending inwards, vortical —

    let's give it a whirl

how to keep our centres
in each other's motion?

  mouths?

    all of them

a flight of lips
    that balance
    the top or bottom heavy
    leading somewhere?

currents aren't maps

but they **move**
    sometimes barely —

eagle floating almost still
in high sky
    seeing the duck
will plummet rapidly

stillness sharpening vision

tai chi: intention behind each
    movement turning circles

  red

tulip's dropping head against the table
breast of House Finch
have we read

    what?
    ?

— whether there's an object to the verb —

subject
   to change

March 9

are we not writing in the margin anymore? we have up until now —

do we have to be consistent?

well, i feel intimidated about it now

i feel intimidated by you — you were writing everything *down*

i wasn't writing everything down

let's not do this all the time

but then we need to indicate why we're not

we can add a note, besides, we might not even use it

we don't know that yet

well, let's write this down

March 11

collaboration on this micro-creative level is meditation. it insists on our sustained presence to the page and each other. when we did break away and write our own statements, our writing kept us in close contact, pulled us back to the same meditative page once again.

this process exposed our collaboration to also be a form of mediation "…an intervention between two disputing parties in order to effect a peaceful settlement or compromise through the benevolent intervention of *a neutral power*." but as lesbians and feminists, we know form and language are not neutral, and when up against the wall — they vie even more fiercely than we. there is no neutral, benevolent mediator — we must also assume this role. after fear and fight, there is our love. there is our paired flight.

March 12

first there is not we but i + i. starting off on different sides (of the same coin), tossing our idiosyncratic perceptions into the ring (sand, circle, performance space, these various animals — read birds — the smell of fear and applause). these perceptions that perform almost arbitrarily it seems (will she see what i mean?) (does it matter if it means something else to her?) meaning, the elusive bird, dies into dust only to rise again in a further line afllare with connections.

connections: (we): breathtaking, when thought leaps the gap between two idiosyncratic fields of association tow lives have accumulated in their separate dialects, diverse cultural origins, private value systems, unconscious dreams hordes. we still argue about the pronunciation of certain words — not the same as mis-reading **reed** *or* **lead**. *And is* **mis**-*reading the word? everything entered* *subject to change, subject to transformation in the reader's imaginary, the reader being she, after all, who constructs meaning.*

so i fears being misread, the flagrant will (raptor) wants her field day, takes off on the wing to pursue **her** *meaning. and we desires connection, (rapt) lead away, to wider horizons of each other's making, beyond limits (that first take) taken apart and given to possibility. this does not mean death, though i fears it, fears losing her way.*

March 13

yes, i + i. i for an i and i to i. my handwritten i looking very much like a semi-colon, "…punctuation indicating a degree of separation intermediate in value between the comma and the period." ii — the Roman numeral for 2 or ;; a double semicolon, where the separation between the comma and the period is amplified. double ambiguity. doubled possibility.

changing the subject — our feminist project. yet, the subject is always subject to change. from one perspective, we saw an eagle and duck. from the other, we saw a red-tailed hawk and crow. the difference a hundred feet makes.

how we sleep deep in trust. one side then the other, fetal fit 'round each other like quotation marks

"   "

"   "

book-ending one another's *unconscious dream hordes.*
buttressing each other's night-floating i.

the relief, delight of i being only part of (i)t all. the very real difference in this from how we are absented by the dominators. letting go of the notion of misreading is dependent upon our knowing the difference. "collabōrāre, com-, to-gether _labōrāre, to work." i abandons her introductory clause for a being between comma and illusory period. she needs the their double jeopardy of discovery more than her differentiating declarations, but she knows old habits die hard.

March 15

yours reads in the shape of a sandwich (toasted), the soft intimate part in the middle "egg shelly" actually what we had for lunch in the cafeteria yesterday. our day off together a gap in the text. intimate, to intimate, a movement inwards from publish. though i don't know that our bodies bookend the hordes which ride on regardless:

unlimited scope for mayhem watching her body move. egg Shelley. maybe a-hem, without hemming in the fertile urge fiction is, re-reading everything...

dreamwork: (to work) reality.

so that the object transforms into subject and back again. i being part of (i) t — the delight as you say, lighting up as perspective shifts, illuminating. the quicksilver way connection leaps the gap between subject and object in desire. she broke the thermometer; we are degrees of thumb and forefinger pooling of liquidities. a figure of telling,

egg shelley actually the name in play,

yours,

March 16 & 17

a telling figure, the seduction of — she(')ll

intimate / intimate. (p)art of each other. y — ours?
generative power of our intimacy — this too must have a life on the page.
degrees of desire — what we hold in our fingertips! yet, not to idealize.
something in between lesbian pulp romance and politically correct silence
(each puritanical in impulse). the reader needs more. we read these words
with a double voraciousness. coming out

of our shells. the writer lesbian, the reader lesbian shell shocked? sexing the
page lesbian. in our profound plurality.

"i, yōdh, hand." this is a gamble. (the roll of…) possibly a do or die. egging one another on — sandwiches originated so gamblers could stay at the table.

doubling the stakes at our tables of chance. "obsession, obsidere, to sit down before" each other's writing presence is to risk each other's inherent chaos — for here the erotic is endlessly born.

you/r bet

March 19

so, letters (safe on the other side). you write downstairs on your computer. i type upstairs. we pass the pages back and forth in the kitchen. not the same as sitting at the same table, writing on the one page. we are not the same, not one, sitting side by side, sam, together. not is where desire enters…

knotting it together, as something different (to collaborate) in a body (of work), seductive, and resistant. currents at play. combating old habits, shifting ground where we meet, quick tongue, sweet wit, cl- : not closing it.

each the other to each in our reach together. oxymoronic no doubt, in excess. yet, yes.

FOUR

Hiring Omniscient Narrators

Poets in their Fifties

Brian Fawcett to Sharon Thesen
Toronto, Ontario
May 9, 1994
age 50

Dear Sharon,

Just four days before fifty arrives. It's a very strange feeling, particularly with the book out. So far everything's fine on that count. It's beautiful, no glaring typos, and no terrible reviews. Thursday I get the cover of NOW magazine, with what I already know is a favourable profile with Susan Cole, who's a hardline radical lesbian, and likes my attitude toward sexual violence. Strange...

Speaking of strange, I had something of a heart-shock today walking down Bloor Street. A large, heavy-set man with steel-gray hair stopped me and asked if I was Brian Fawcett. I said yes, and he introduced himself as Michael Boughn. He said he'd just moved to Toronto with his wife, and I politely asked where. Turns out he's living across the street from me.

It was a curious, unpleasant sensation. Michael was the last human being I hit with my fists, and the only person I ever wanted to kill, if only for a few seconds. And even though that was more than 25 years ago, half a lifetime gone, damned if I didn't experience a pang of precisely the same pain and terror — and rage. I've been spooked out ever since, actually, trying to reset my bearings as who I am now, but with memory replaying the recaptured loop of that young man I was then.

Hence, I guess, this letter. Absurdly, I want to apologize to you for having been such an asshole, then. Because, of course, I was one — hysterical with fear and jealousy, overprotective, self-concerned, almost paranoid with (at once) self-love and self-loathing.

But on the other side (25 years later) thankful for your presence in the world, thankful for our son (who I'll see in a few days!!) and for an awful lot of the things both around me and distant. I guess I can live with Michael Boughn across the street, given all that...

love,
BF

•••

Roy Kiyooka to Daphne Marlatt
August 5, 1976
age 50

dearest Daphne
    Kit's up in Robt's Creek Jan who had gone with them said he's bored
and wants to come home and be just with his mommy i've started to fix
up our bedroom — won't tell you what i'm into but think it will please you
and phase three of SPOTA's project has begun with a vengeance between
the time i left for Yellowknife and got back they've trencht the vacant lot
across the alley and have already put the foundations floor and walls up
and the big two-storey clapboard next to the one on the other side of the
church has been torn down and the ground trencht the vacant lot across
from Benny's is heapt with lumber and a "johnny-on-the-spot" fibreglass
portable toilet with all the racket going on all around you couldn't have done
any work anyhow so you might as well enjoy Penang which almost sounds
like a doppelganger of Miss Daphne Buckle's fairy godmother's crenulated
hauntings your mother sits in a photographic alembic behind me she listens to everything on CBC and knows what's going on in Malaysia o my
own mother can't be deceived either and as far as fathers go — i speak for
myself they all 'ave a bit of the fool in them penned caged routine-ridden
driven scrivened or whatever we all need a woman to abide our fool-hearted
propensities etc your pa likewise i stared at my own father's visage on
mother's dining area wall and could only hear my own heart's stammer-
ings a man of few words we had even less to say now that he's dead and
i'm as they say going and i feel i have already had my too too brief summer
had it in Yellowknife already the scents of fall are shorter the nights grow
longer and sunshine dwindles autumn must be the dwarf's prime season
or is it my own time of life? As you have come into summer a crystalline
Yellowknife summer like the one i've just come back from was i up there
was i as a twenty-year-old lad up there — only the northland's vast silences
and that brilliant sun my body remembers tell me yes yes yes you were there
you saw Gros Cap and told the pilot where to circle the skeletal remains of
an old fishing camp too bad we couldn't have landed on water but there
were others along who had their own thots and so we circle-dippt a wing and
passed on and around back towards Yellowknife i thank Bill Padgham for
that i who had spent so much of his time up there on land and water thot

that the means of locomotion defines our knowledge of the elements and so it was that even as we flew high up above that rock and water immensity i could imagine my self laved by water best   Daphne my small tree my water maiden we're very much united despite the awesome distances   I mean what's love all about if it ain't a telegram

•••

Renée Sarojini Saklikar to ————
Hotel X, Vancouver, British Columbia
Evening, May 14, 2013
age 51

Aftermath

Dear —

Everyone writes epistolary.
Share. Embed. Report.
The poet declaiming to his goddess
warned against the month of May
Expand. Collapse. View.
where grows the rowan tree, the unlucky.

You will see I have titled this letter
as if my writing to you were one long poem
and the hour it began was the hour of The Knot,
tightened memory,
          moment when we waited backstage,
          two people at the end of what is called
          Campaign. World within words, a provincial election.
          Politics. On the internet, Anonymous
          calls himself, herself, Polly Tics,
          writing online unaware that letters have this way
          of finding out
          the reader, absent
          still present

What I mean to say, is,
much has been written
about us, when you were once—

and I, too.

     *

Dear—

before the date inscribed
inside
there was the falling away—

     Dear R,
          I have been meaning to write
          all this past year the falling away
          you and your husband
          must be experiencing,
          all that is—

     Dear R,
          I couldn't believe
          what happened:

…

there was within my brown skinned self not
that butter-soft, margarine pelleted
exploded orange-red courage to say:
Everything will fall away, the way
man and woman fall, out from the Tarot Tower
when some hapless lover draws depiction
and senses the tension these sentences meant
for your eyes only. All clichés, all popular songs

eventually we find them on this path
letter-writing a circle of leaves
strange wood: oak, catalpa, beech and fir,
shimmering aspen, a wife to her husband.
Only, I am not brave enough, so send them to a stranger.

Up ahead, as if traffic sign in yellow,
the date
this letter began,
the time of it, not anything, really.
To the many to whom such things are nothing,
them in the streets of the city
them in the long rumble-roar of the sky-train
them in the Safeway-Sobeys line: packaged carrots, packaged
    tomatoes,
them in the mall, whom I join, we imbibe stale air, clutching our
    plastic bags.
Each day is stitched. Expand. Collapse. View. Share. Embed. Report.
Pebble lodged in a boot,
       crushed conch shell blown way-side
       pristine beach never visited.

Dear —

Each day is a train at evening.
Down by the river, bed of railway ties, oil soaked,
still owned by the C.P.R.
The Train known as Lonesome, long and full of its own verboten
    nostalgia
       home is history is ownership is excluded is song of a song.
Although our readers may not credit those hands of ownership
powerful enough to find their way
       inside, wife to husband:
       rejection is that which feeds the wild green flower,
       my brown skinned
and opened heart. Wife,

who sent you letters,
the silence not hearing,
could not begin. Betrayal
just by writing. Who could blame you
for not responding—

        Dear R,
            It must be
            surreal

Dear—

Always
the falling
away is
this man
and woman
inside
a downtown
hotel.   Let words begin some other way:
Everything stands in for something else. Embed. Report.
Behind black drapery,
husband and wife, side by side.
His suit is dark. Her dress is orange lace.
They wait their cue to address a crowd.
The man will concede defeat, alone on the stage.
Head bent, eyes downcast, gesture known to any athlete, any
    opponent.
The man and woman will kiss, the kiss next day will meta-morph-ize
pixelated dots. Newspaper, you also emerge as Persona. And weapon.
The print stock owned by the owners of the words, the words
    stacked, pointed, thrust, rubbed, jolted. Laughing Prince George-
    Keremeos-all the towns to list. All the owners to bow before—

Dear R,
                    What is the worst? Question
                    posing as rhetoric:
                    to be remembered or
                    forgotten—Dear reader,

                    you whom I cannot reach.
I am not at liberty. I am locked inside.
Aftermath is a place.

Dear — as you are not near
these words be hearth to welcome
Reader, find here this chair, this fireplace,
                    even those of us against description,
                    together. We lean
                    against the mantle painted white
                              dusty surface,
                              objects
                              as found probably in a thousand households:
                              Brass vase, faded rose, petals.
                              Details create the where:
                              once,
                              a husband and his wife: dear reader,
silence is its own stand-in,

                    days pass, yellow and lined—

Dear —

The future is a black box on an oak table.
To be opened, shut. And again, presence factored
by word-edges

sharp-scald,
hurled against
you, who are joined to me,
Time finds us again—
to the hotel, night to the city, embrace of drapery.

Photograph as survivor.
The vanquished kiss in public.

Andrasta, goddess of victory:
your sword, thin shadow, long reach. Come,
stand before this table bare of anything—

Scornful one, if only you would make each word of mine
a pinpoint so poison,
        letters would as nail-heads
           fly and land on those filled with the love of Haram.

        Dear Reader, words were all over us.
        Stigma, a runnel where flows jest,
        scars there may feel their wounds.
        You will see how public infests
        private, the hearth now an empty grate,
        remains of a T.V. dinner. I sit alone before the machine
        and call to image. His green eyes.
        Let the record show an absence of tears.
        Not that May night. Perhaps the next day.
        I neither confirm nor deny. Wikipedia sparse.
        Our reader might find it deplorable,
        the love of a good cry. I have fact-checked this story.
        Lament, another way of saying yearning.
        The gory self, a fetish, busy writing.

Mistress Mockery can take unshed,
any water from my eyes,
a piss on her bastards!

Dear—

Words sharpen, their jewel encrusted ways form an edge
        the one I am running from
lance, bleed, scar and pucker
        hate burrows into expression
Twitter feeds, Facebook posts, words coagulate
Concerned Citizens, where are they? Unselected.

I took a snapshot. *Thems that were the ones that did it.*
Brought inside our home.

My heart is a wild word-stalker.
Who will read it?

Obscenity is a hunt drafted in red.
This chronicle compulsion.

Nowhere to run to, baby,
Dear—
you will know how the song ends, popular.

Let that woman's face, seen dozens of times on the Expo line,
        Billboard Mistress,
Muse-anti-Muse,
        her pearly whites,
her long legs stocking shiny
        her blonde hair,
her made in B.C. Breakfast Television: be graced—

All my unsent letters.

She don't even know me.

None of my curse tablets in the end proved any good at all.

...

Di Brandt, 2003
age 51

Songs for a divorce
"Who shall revoke jubilance?" — *Rainer Maria Rilke*

1

Reaching round
the brick walls
at last,
we found
ashes and raging
hot flame

It was too late then,
dear heart,
wasn't it,
though we cried
and tried,
furiously,
for many furious
months,
to save
the smoking wreckage

(heroically,
not thinking of
ourselves)

2

though I'm
puzzled now
to contemplate

breakfast plates
thrown across
kitchens and
doors slammed,
and windows,
old, bevelled,
the original
irreplaceable glass,
smashed

as a method
to save anything,
let alone
everything

3

Loving each other
beautifully
we thought
would, grandly
and single-
handedly,
take on

our unreasonable fathers,
our helpless mothers,
the war,
the Capitalist System,
environmental pollution,

and save us from
boredom,
suffocation,
indignation,
and mediocre economic destinies

4

You sang me,
O husband of forests
with beaches,

with your eyes,
and lips,
and hands,

bright coloured
canvasses,
your unreasonable joy,

your castles of sticks
in sand,

irreverent
jester's bells,

airplane tickets,
dreamer,

into life

5

At night I lay
naked
in your dark arms,

naked

6

Forgive me, beloved,
for loving
the hero I made
of you,

cradling your
knife wounds
as children

7

When I think
about it:
nearly killing
each other

for love.

8

How could we
have known,

    lost children
floundering,
with the flimsiest
of life jackets,
   in that cold sea?

9

She walks these hills
in a long dark veil,
She visits my grave
when the dark winds wail.

I love you, I love you not.

I told you once,
but you forgot.

10

Our dark bellies
Opening

      in each other's faces, spinning

to black

        space

11

keeping forever lit,
shining,
through regret

disguised as border hostilities, war

12

Whatever there is in me
that is singing,
whatever there is in me,

you are there too

•••

Mark Sinnett, 2014
age 51

Art History

I've tried in any number of complicated and winding ways
to get down a little of what it is, this happening's core.
Tortured myself two days with dull metaphor, duller
and anxious nights. I've staggered back in rooms well-lit
and populated, demanding, and others not so bright,
from your knowing and significant image looming in
alarmingly. That buzzy vision is embroidered,
I realize, with other more quick-cut details of our passing
through each other's orbit; the back of your arm reaching up,
breath catching in you sharply, then less so, the small
and warm small of your back, your arching at planets
unnamed as the long night comes strangely unhooked
from time's needle. I have even made monkish passage
through libraries, haunting, for a morning, the work
of others similarly afflicted. And discovered in Modigliani's
Reclining Nude, 1917, for instance, a similar abandon,
or if not that, then a slow dissolving of resolve, the presence
of something of-camera that might be welcomed, however
briefly, into the invisible frame. (Though his couch is dark
rather than light, and the woman, to be honest, not even
your pale imitation, possessing none of the disarming gestures,
nor your fleet route into memory.) Somewhere
further along was Turner's *Woman Reclining on a Couch*.
It is a far remove from his massed and blazing skies
of London, but I understood in fragments (without ever
believing I could put that knowledge down, entrap it)
what he was after with that frumpy interior. And how
some mornings even grey smoke pouring under, piling up
this side of his door, wouldn't interest him, such wild
conflagration was there in his blind and thumping heart.

...

Jennifer Londry to ——————
Autumn, 2013
age 51

Dear Nineteen-ninety-three,
    *Do you remember the night we gave your brother the bed while we slept on
the black leather pull-out in the living room. Panties on the floor in the morning
— back then, when you were married briefly to that American girl?*

                      ...it was a transition year. You left her. I left him —

    *Schoolgirl crush confirmed. Kids lumped together in the gymnasium, boy-
girl-boy, while I ate at home and penned your name to my headboard. Picture
day, I'd forgotten to look pretty. Went home and cut my bangs in the mirror,
crooked. I wore lip-gloss and denim to the dance. My words a helium balloon
barely tethered to, Will you dance with me? Vinyl's slow spin after the hired band
smoked their sound system and left. Do you remember m?*

                                  ...post high —

    *Invitation to a friend's wedding; the follow-up phone call the Thursday
before; how you said you thought it had been cancelled, how you'd made other
plans. Boy I took slightly embarrassed when the bride said, It's nice to finally
meet you, m ~*

                 ...I wanted to die, vomit all over the bathroom floor —

    *The car I struck while driving past your house. I missed the brake lights in
front of me entirely. I got fined for not wearing a seat belt.*

                               ...I left town —

    *After America, you moved to Ottawa. Unemployable you arrived at the job
interview a little inebriated, not enough courage, a speck of dirty on the rear
of your dress-pants. When you did finally land a job you'd slip out at noon,*

down a few pint sized vodkas, the ones they no longer sell on airplanes. Do you remember, m?

                    …saturday morning jog to the LCBO —

The company party I left early, because you were belligerent. Cold in my silver sandals I walked through snow until some sympathetic stranger offered me a ride. You never came home.

                    …cops did nothing, impending danger is not a crime —

The steps to our apartment building on Richmond Road, you splayed in the August heat like an exhumation. The day's soiled clothes dripped from shower rod. You cried yourself to sleep. Thought you were alone, I was on the balcony crying too.

                    …a move to the countryside sombre —

Sundays spent ambling in back road antique shops in a bumpy blue Ford pickup. The obese woman you made feel interesting because you asked all sorts of questions about her collection. We talked for hours while the potatoes she had on the stove bubbled over. And later, the chair you were going to re-finish, perched in the rain. Do you remember, m?

                    …three-hundred bucks rent on the kitchen table,
                                        front door wide open —

How I tossed your white shirts and blue jeans down the stairs. How you made me pick them up, return them to the closet, align the hangers proper.

                    …hands on my throat, liquor down the sink —

Sad trip to Boston, ticket change, a stand-in, better in Cape Cod. So quiet there, waves upon waves, little motel by the ocean tea lights at my feet miles between us.

                    …sixty-two days sober —

Dear December,

The telephone call I made to mum and dad in Florida to say, Merry Christmas. You passed out on the sofa not going anywhere. The long drive to my brother's house, late, because tears kept me circling the block. My sister-in-law, pregnant, served us potato chips for dinner.

I left quietly. I took the licence plates off the truck. It didn't matter. You drove it anyway. It was gone six days later when I returned bleary eyed and steering into a new year. Do you remember, m?

Love is complicated,

j

•

Dear September,

The call to tell me you'd broken a lampshade while at an auction. How you laughed and said it reminded you of me. Stairway to Heaven, Step nine: make amends with those whom you have harmed. I remember.

Life is complicated,

j

•

Dear m,

Thank you for crossing the street that day to say, "Hello, I'm eighteen years sober. I'm remarried, I have two kids."

You wed my brother's best friend's sister.

"You did the right thing," you said. How I'd laid out everything you owned neatly on the lawn, careful to attach remote to television set with duct tape.

Be sober still, m.

Love,

Two-thousand-thirteen

•••

William Wilfred Campbell to Mary DeBelle
En route Montreal – Quebec
May 12, 1911
ALLAN ROYAL MAIL LINE, R.M.S. Virginian
age 52

Dear Mary,

We are comfortable on board. My stateroom right opposite the girls. But I expect to be very sea-sick. I find it hard to get the girls to put on any wraps and hope they won't get cold in the Gulf.

In my last letter, I told you to write Lord Grey and keep in touch with him and have nothing to do with F.G. who is not to be trusted. I warn you of this again. You will see how intensely those people hate us.

Keep the children off the street. Also look after Dorothy. Be careful who she goes with. Don't let her go out alone to Britannia or other places — and don't have that fellow Fleming around her. I do not trust him. I can say no more on those questions.

Faith is awfully restless and has already made up to a Mrs. Paley and has deserted Margery who needs rest and looking after. It is all very well for you to scold me, but if you were here you would see what I mean. You might say something to Faith in your letter. She would mind you but do not say that I have complained. I am very tired and do not want to bother them.

I have written to Dr. Gibson thanking him and Mrs. Gibson also to Acland and King and Mr. Fealleston. I must close now.

I have just remembered that you have no money for fresh [illegible] if you are low give some portion for yourself.

With love to all — Dot, Basil and Di.

Yours affectionately,
Will

•••

John Glassco to Elma Koolmer
Royal Edward Laurentian Hospital
Ste-Agathe-des-Monts, Quebec
Thursday, April 13, 1961
age 51

My dearest Tweet,

It was as usual so lovely hearing your voice last night: it will be wonderful when you come up here, — for me that is, but it will be very dull for you, I'm afraid: *nothing* in Ste. A!

I am actually beginning to like it here. It's such a relief to have one's own room, in the first place, & then all the staff are very nice — not at all bossy & dictatorial like the ones in Montreal. The head-nurse on this floor is a Miss Fraser, who is about sixty-five & absolutely charming. Everybody is very deferential to me, because it seems the word has gone around that I am a sizeable Canadian poet, & the old ladies (the staff are all *bien mûres*) like that. This helps enormously!

Look, tweet, will you buy me a pair of really *nice* pyjamas (white preferably, though sand or pale-green will do) in light material, at about $7 or $8, & send them up here? My others wore out in Montreal & the only pair I could get in Ste. Agathe are sort of paisley-figured — nice but rather too fussy.

Here, I can read as late as I want: but I've made it a rule to turn out the light at 11:00 p.m. Then, ah what a relief — no snoring, hawking, farting, groaning. And at meals I am blissfully alone: those two Jews in room 501 in Montreal made more noise eating than a well-behaved dog. The Chinaman was allright, but he ground his teeth all night long — the sound was like scratching a kitchen-match on the box.

Sweetheart, there are robins here & I wish there weren't: they make me think of you & home. Thank God there are no shopping-birds…

Do you recognize the man in this clipping from the *Star*? We met him on the continuation of the dup road that day when we stole the apples — those apples tasted better than any apples I've ever had. You remember, when we filled our pockets & carried some off in the back of the car?

Those days will return — I mean that *kind* of days — for you & me. We could find them *anywhere*. I only realized last year that one can make poetry out of *anything* — now I see one can make happiness out of anything also.

Darling, I miss you & kiss you all over.

John

•

John Glassco to Elma Koolmer
Royal Edward Laurentian Hospital
Ste-Agathe-des-Monts, Quebec
May 4, 1961

Dearest,

All the books, papers, *Observer*, carbons etc. arrived safely yesterday afternoon & today your nice letter.

I'm feeling so much better these days — eating & sleeping well, much less *irritable*, not comparing the present with the past, resigned to being bored, just living from day to day (the way the doctors advise!) & how fast the days are going! In about a week I will have another sputum test & (I think) x-ray: there is just a chance the first may be negative, & then the culture grown from this will take six weeks to show up either negative or positive — but of course if it's positive they do not make a culture.

I only had an hour or so to look quickly over *Lady Chatterley*: & my reaction was unchanged after many years: then Miss Fraser, the head nurse on the floor, borrowed it with shining eyes! (I'm glad to do her favours like this, as we already get along very well & this is very handy on the floor.) I'll read it over more carefully, but I think my original ideas on it are still valid. Of course Lady C. is "unreal," as you say: she is Lawrence's projection of himself into a woman; his real love-object is Mellors (whom I find suitably irritating, then silly, and finally simply a bore — and all the time there is something squishy & eunuch-like about him), who is simply another in the series of Laurentian *heroes* (not protagonists) who are all the same, all simply former husbands or lovers of the leading female figures, & standing *behind* them. I mean that *women* are only attractive to Lawrence as a way of making contact with men: it is the men who really interest him physically. — You might try reading his two best books, *Sons & Lovers* and *The Rainbow*: they're both in the library there. Note the curious recurrence of the picture of the white-skinned man *washing himself* in all L.'s books! This seems to have some fetishistic attraction for him.

I'm so glad to hear you went out with Milton & Jimmy & Mrs. K. You mustn't become too much of a hermit! — I wish I had some news for you from here — but nothing happens in this place, which is I suppose as it should be. — There is a man about 40 who runs the canteen here who has only 31% breathing capacity: he drives, walks, drinks, smokes, etc. And I have 54%! But he eats 3 meals a day and goes to sleep at 11 p.m. every night: I suppose I could do that too: anyway, I'll probably have to!

Did you see Tight Fit's father died the other day. It was in the *Gazette*.

I find it hard not to be sad & bored in this miserable place: but that does not interfere with the cure — only fatigue, worry & excitement do that, they say.

Oh, dearest I am so anxious to get back to you & home & freedom…away from this nightmare linoleum passage. And I will, I will.

Always your tweet,
John

P.S. Would you send me the sheets marked "Inventory" & "Capital Acc't with Royal Trust"? There are 3 or 4 of them in the big file under "I."
Tweet

P.P.S. Miss F. had just returned *Lady Chat*. She disapproves: "In the nursing profession, you see so much of the nasty side of life that you don't want to read about it as well." The *nasty side* — isn't that marvellous!

•

John Glassco to Elma Koolmer
Royal Edward Laurentian Hospital
Ste-Agathe-des-Monts, Quebec
June 19, 1961

Dearest tweet,

Sorry for being so upset over the telephone about the bat situation, also over conditions generally for you. Perhaps these things don't matter so much after all, and I'm inclined to magnify them now that I'm up here and helpless to do anything. With regard to Bay, however: allow him nothing more of any kind, that will only lead to further demands. If he asks for anything, say you will have to ask me, and I will write or telephone him if you would prefer not to have to speak to him yourself.

You must not let these hicks get you down. I know how hard and efficiently they can try (and they have years of practice at chiselling), but forgetting and rebuffing them is just a part of living in the country.

As for the "maid" remark, I don't think you understand that country women have absolutely no choice or sense of words. *Meanings* are conveyed by looks, smiles, tones, nods, twitchings of the head etc. Never by words. The word "maid" was probably the only one that came into her head. And don't forget that this word has no connotation of domestic service in the E.T. as it has in Montreal or larger centres. It simply means an unmarried woman living *au pair* in a household to whose members she is not related by blood or marriage. For "servant" the word "hired girl" is used, and for "mistress" the beautiful term "girl-friend." And as far as tactlessness and stupidity goes (and these were probably a part of the remark's make-up), there are presumably intelligent men in Knowlton, Foster and Waterloo who still think that my name is "Taylor" and have gotten so used to believing it that they will even argue the point at great length.

Look sweetest, would you wrap up Byron's Goose (first looking into it to see there are not any odd papers or memoranda in the flyleaf or end-leaf), put the enclosed label on it, and send it 1st class mail, *registered* (this is important when sending to agents) to Mead Company. Find out the postal charges first of all, and buy a mail-order for the same amount payable to Mead Co. and tuck it into the front of the play before wrapping it. (Charges won't amount to more than $1.00). Try and mail it on Monday the 26th, or the preceding Friday; and then be sure to mail the enclosed letter on the 26th. I haven't much hope of this lead, but it should be followed up. The other "Agency" is just a sucker trap, with their "reading fees." I have heard again and again that the only way to peddle a play is to get on one's horse and *pester* agents personally. But I can't do that from here.

Mairobert is almost finished, with its new chapter fitted in.

Did you notice in *Tamarack* that Anne Wilkinson has just died. It was at her place that Art and Jeannie and I had tea after the Oxford party. I think I told you how charming she was. What a pity this is: a woman with beauty, great talent, wealth and unfailing kindness and generosity should have to die when she was barely 45. — Incidentally, I hope to heaven this doesn't mean the end of *Tamarack Review*: she practically maintained it out of her own purse.

I saw the movie *From the Terrace* last Friday night. The substance of the book was reproduced perfectly: an incredible amount of drinking, fornication and sentiment carried out against a background of tasteful luxury, and with no meaning at all. I have never seen such beautiful backgrounds, furniture, décor, automobiles, gowns, beautiful women, handsome and well-bred men before. The period was advanced to the late '30s, and the story telescoped and given a happy ending; but that did not matter. It was charming:

very good direction (*Citizen Kane* influence most noticeable), well-nigh perfect acting, beautiful attention to detail and all in colour. The patients didn't like it at all. By the time it was half-way through almost everyone had left the theatre: only Ingram and I left at the end. This is a wonderful way to see a movie, it made us feel like a pair of kings at a private performance. The others had their treat last Saturday with *Jet Pilot*, which had the attraction of an absolutely endless roaring of aeroplane engines and sex-play dealing with ladies' drawers being handed by a bare arm through a bathroom door (oh, boy-y-y!) That was when Ingram and I slipped out, in our turn.

Otherwise no news at all. I'm still waiting for my next sputum-test on June 30th. The days are going by like telegraph-poles from a railway-car.

Must rush to get this in the mail.

I love you so much, so much,

Your own tweet

•

John Glassco to Elma Koolmer
Royal Edward Laurentian Hospital
Ste-Agathe-des-Monts, Quebec
November 3, 1961

Dear tweet,

The news around my Cavity closing has somehow gotten around, and all the student nurses are so excited, you've no idea. There is a dear little girl called Miss Lightbody (from Ahuntsic or somewhere) who comes in every evening now and "supper." She is the breathy type, rather sweet and idealistic. She says she has never spoken to a Poet before: all agog. Good God, that I should ever figure in an infant's dreams. She seems to get all choked up when she's taking my pulse. I know these symptoms of infatuation, the mindless, brainless visionary stare, the little dew of perspiration on the upper lip. It's awful, I know what she's going through. The Older Man…Well, to hell with it: I'm through with *amours passagers*.

Now that I'm getting ready to leave I'm casting a selective eye on the books in the library. There's just so much stuff here I'd like to opt (*organizieren*) that no one has ever read or will ever read. But I'd better not: that's bad medicine. Only two: Robert Elie's *La fin des songes* (there are three copies, all untouched) and Madame Ellis' book on Garneau. They'll none of them be missed, as Gilbert says. Any way, I'd like to give them a good home.

Later. Miss Lightbody just came in, and has just gone. I'm afraid she has it badly. It's simply absurd, a pretty girl about 20 getting all exercised about a man of almost 52. The worst thing about it is that it's not me at all, I'm just some kind of kindly father-figure: don't they teach any psychology to nurses? No, that's not the worst thing, for me: the fact is, she gets me all excited. It's her smell, I think: a blend of hand-soap and javel-water, and her breath is like clover. On top of that, her breasts are lovely, you can see them pouting behind the starched student bib. And the way the little golden uncut curls on her neck grow. Oh dear darling, I did get excited when she took my pulse. I suppose this is a good sign, as far as my health is concerned!

Oh I do so want to get home to my own darling pussycat. Everything in life seems to take so long, and I have the feeling, more and more, of "time's winged chariot." Well, we shall make up for lost time very soon.

Goodnight, my dearest love,

John

·

John Glassco to Elma Koolmer
Royal Edward Laurentian Hospital
Ste-Agathe-des-Monts, Quebec
November 15, 1961

Dearest tweet,

There's something that's been on my conscience for the last week. I know you won't really mind, but on the last night of the little-girl-from-Ahuntsic's period of duty up here or whatever they call it, she came in at 9 o'clock and bared her virgin heart. That would have been allright, but the fact is things didn't stop there. God forgive me, she was a virgin and she isn't anymore. It was all so fast I really don't know how it happened: it was sort of primitive, if you know what I mean. Dearest, there's nothing to worry about: I didn't *finish*, though I pretended to, with gasps.

I don't really feel I did anything wrong. And I hope you won't feel I did either…The poor child was just all pepped up about leaving. She has gone now, and I hope she feels better — better than I do anyway. I'm really feeling wretched.

Otherwise no news.

Goodnight, my one & only love,

John

•••

Bliss Carman to Gladys Baldwin
New Canaan, Connecticut
November 22, 1913
age 52

O Dearest! [...] You say you are haunted by Rio. But I don't believe much in that Rio scare. It would be too ridiculous. He isn't worth it at all. Nice enough no doubt to make up one of the crowd, but — Heavens! A terrible bore! Nothing in his cosmos but Ego! You would be ready to jump over-board before the voyage was half over. This sounds very mean; but it isn't. And *I* don't have to go to Rio with him — thank the Lord! The other man I didn't see. But don't try to manage too many at once. It is very difficult and doesn't yield any satisfactory results. "And who is that one to be?" say you in your heart. Why who but EGO!! — your own these many years? Too old, too poor, too homely, too dull, too selfish, too stick-in-the-mud? Tush, tush, child! [...]

I think I am a brave man not to write you truly love-letters. Am I not? [...]

Your own D.

P.S. These lines are not good at all. I cannot write. I can only love you — Now as I finish it is a most wonderful soft purple evening, all marvel and mist, as soft as a Puvis painting, and as full of soul as my Atom — whom ever and ever I adore. — Ah, soon, soon, soon! Write *soon* again and be glad.

•••

Ken Norris, 2003
age 52

Funny Valentine
for Stefani

My love, my love, I am here at the doctor's office
in the ruins of late January, in the prime of life,

with pink petalled flowers, and green plants and sunshine
and sick people, and with a gentle determination
to be true to you, the ice, the winter
and to the sometimes grim silly mission of poetry.
The ticking clock counts the minutes
with no mind of its own, the Christmas wreath
has yet to come down, and I am carving
two hearts with an arrow running through them
as a valentine, as an arcane emblem of love.

I am remembering the time you almost fell off the balcony,
the strength of your hands, the warm strength of your eyes,
and how you could yell so well in your native Spanish
that the take-out food from across the street was soon delivered.
And if I did not like the Spaghetti Bolognese
there was always the rice and the res and the dark insalata.
What didn't we accomplish in that room?
And it was so hard to leave it, and you,
the warm breeze, the curlings of your hair,
and the Caribbean Sea whispering to us all night long.

The night the dead came to wake you
you were high as a kite anyway, grinding your teeth
in the spirit of coca, and my dreams
were passing strange as well.
If we fell headlong into the mirror
it was only to become better lovers,
to leave our different languages, like shoes,
at the foot of the bed.

And now you inhabit the warm world
and I the cold, your flowers are lusher
and better than mine, and your day is far more welcoming.
I wish I could once again enter
the harbour of your slender arms and lose all sense
of the afternoon's officey Moonlight Sonata.
The radio turns me off

with its digressive formal melodies,
I long for the salsa and merengue
that are you. Soon it will be
the day of love, and I am writing
this funny valentine that you will never read,
the post office of the heart having been suspended.

Doctor Love is crazy if he thinks
I can be treated with the standard regimen of antibiotics,
or be impressed by his dark glasses.
You're in my blood for all time,
and you counteract the chirpy nurses
who never could reach me
with their meticulous blow jobs and their bedside manner.

My love,
you were the flowers and the waves rocking them,
you were the ache of a cool dawn,
you were the bold embodiment of love, mi amor.

•••

Irving Layton to Aviva Layton
December 14, 1964
age 52

My Darling Little One:

I'm taking a moment out from correcting exam papers to write you. A light snow has been falling all evening, covering the pigeon shit on the storm windows. Bach is being played on the FM, and the house is beautifully tranquil, enveloped by the snow and music. From time to time I look up from my mess of papers, imagining you coming toward me with a "schwartze cavale," imagining you reclining kitten-like on the sofa with a book in your hand, a smile on your mouth I should have kissed more often than I did.

Yes, the honours are coming thick and fast. But I see plainly I'm destined to live a solitary life. I'm unfit for living with anyone, though you know how strong the domestic side in me really is, and that I have the normal cravings for affection and companionship. Right now, I'd toss my whole achievement out of the window for one of your smiles, or one of the Pope's[3] ecstatic shrieks.

Did you receive my cheque? I'll be sending you another for $120 very shortly. Write me a long letter. Kiss my son a thousand times for me.

•••

Elizabeth Brewster, 1974
age 52

Chill

Like all the women who sleep alone
in Chinese poems,
I shiver with the cold.

I would rather have you to warm me
than either a blanket or a poem,
but what can I do?
I pull both poem and blanket
over me now
but neither of them breathes.

•••

Bliss Carman to Gladys Baldwin
Twilight Park, Haines Falls, New York
August 5, 1914
age 53

Dearest girl: Your note of yesterday still keeps a smile hovering over my heart — so glad I am to hear from you again, and to have those unmitigated epithets! Dancing is my true expression under the circumstances, and as I don't dance, I can only beam upon the world. Not even the horrible war news can quite depress my soul when you write so. [...] Only I could wish

---

3   The Laytons' nickname for their son, David.

you here in the more bracing air. [...] Dear one, take always my gentle loving wishes. And remember where you can run to, if Maryland proves too unbearable in August. As I think I told you I am shamefully well.

This war news! We hardly begin to realize what the war will mean yet. It is all too pitiable and shameful. I feel much as H.G. Wells does about it, according to his statement quoted in today's *Times* — no dislike of the German people, who are so nearly akin to ourselves, but a deep detestation of that insane imperialism and militarism imposed on them by the ruthless Iron Chancellor — enemy of mankind. [...]

Tell your Nan not to worry. Even little Canada will do what she can. Why I am not there, to be shot down if necessary, I don't know. I suppose I should be. It is a very disgusting episode in civilization, but will do good in the end I fancy.

Do write more when you can, for I am more and more your own Everybody.

•

Bliss Carman to Gladys Baldwin
Twilight Park, Haines Falls, New York
August 28, 1914

O my dearest: What a constant surprise you are, and what a stay and solace! Always there seems to be new vistas of wide and pure spiritual outlook opened up by your words. Whenever you write to me my heart is renewed with ecstasy. [...]

I still miss you here and wish you had come. For, like you, I long to avoid this stifling atmosphere of misery which hangs over the world. [...] Grieve not, dearest, but abide and be strong as ever. I shall never leave you. Poor as I am and of no worth in this mad vast world, here there always be one human being at least to smile and understand and speak gently to you. Yes, and to love you always all that you will. [...]

O my love, D

•

Bliss Carman to Gladys Baldwin
New Canaan, Connecticut
March 22, 1915

My dear Atom: [...] I have been horribly upset of late; all the springs gone dry, with nothing to bring you or to say; a dreary desolation of spirit, with rather a distraction of things.

Maybe you have not noticed how *long* Lent is! I shall be glad of Easter, and some day you must take me to St. Mary's or Saint Somebody's to smell the incense of peace, and I shall become as one of your little children. Then nothing will matter, and if I cannot find any standing room in the great "House of Truth" I shall not care. I can sit outside on the steps of the House of Love, and be happy in the dust and rain and sun.

And Saint Atom will lay her hand on my head as she passes there.

This sounds rather crazy to me, but you may find some meaning in it.

It is horrible trying to do without you.

Deedie

•

Bliss Carman to Gladys Baldwin
Richmond, Virginia
Monday, April 5, 1915

My dear Atom: Very spunky of you to turn up in the storm on Saturday. I am sure you acquired some merit thereby, and hope you were none the worse.

I woke up to the Easter sun, looking out a car window, running down through Virginia, said to myself "Christ is risen," and smiled as I thought of you. [...]

I had a very happy dinner at your favorite "Alps." You were most dear and loveable-er than ever, if that could be. We seemed to be nearer than before to knowing ourselves. You were altogether lovely and sainted, so playful and emancipated yet so delicate. It was a joy.

[...] Love is terribly sincere and great. I suppose that is why so many people are afraid of it, and so few can live up to it.

Be happy, O beloved and most-loving heart, with all the Easter joy you know so well!

With deathless tenderness, Your Deedie

Bliss Carman to Gladys Baldwin
New Canaan, Connecticut
April 9, 1915

My dearest Atom: Left today to sole possession of Sunshine House, I write to you from out of doors, in sound of the brook and the spring birds, looking down on that bit of woods where we walked and sat a year ago. Now in the warm spring air I have long thoughts about you. Not unhappy, but not gay, and rather wistful. Why? Because serious things are always touched with sadness, and because you are in trouble of spirit to some extent. I was very happy to be with you last evening, even though our serious talk was not in key with the crowded dinner room. I would gladly see you gay, but I know as well as you do that one cannot be gay always, and that one must often go through lonely places of thought and feeling — deserts of personal experience. It is some consolation to learn that one comes out of them stronger.

You go to your St. Mary's for your strength, and not for anything would I decry that refuge. I also have been there and have walked dutifully in the code of the law for many years, holding all the beliefs of the church almost as firmly as any devotee. It is not so now, of course. If I were asked to state my faith, I suppose I should be adjudged worse than a heretic. Yet I claim the right to worship in the church of my fathers, not because I assent to its doctrines, but because it claims to be universal, and I am a human being.

If you find all you need in the church, then I can only be glad. And if I cannot find all I need in the church, but must find other truth outside of the church to satisfy my need, then you must in turn be glad for me. I do not think we are far apart. It cannot be. Love brings people together, and I am not argumentative. [...] I would so gladly take away all your childish sorrow and sense of futility, and leave you with nothing but smiles. Also I am keenly and most humbly sensitive of your fondness for me.

All this is sort of a meditation on religion. It is not a love letter. I am not going to afflict your dear worried spirit with any personalities today. I fear you think I have sometimes been light or insincere in that regard. No. I don't think I am ever frivolous. But I admire gaiety, and sometimes attempt to be playful. Of this we can talk when you come out here! For is this not April?

I must say, though, that the thought of any possibility of your entering a Sisterhood gives me a revulsion of feeling. I quite respect all such associations, as I respect the rights of others to act for themselves; also I see that their lives of toilsome self-denial are to be reverenced. Their devotion to the service of humanity is beautiful to me. But that such an estate, either for men or women, is holier or more worthy than an equally self-denying life in the world, I eternally disbelieve. The less restricted and more human an Order is, the more I reverence it. I think I have more respect for the Salvation Army than for other religious Orders, because it is nearer Christ's ideal and does not separate itself from the world.

But then many of the notions of the church seem to me very horrible and heathenish and far removed from the teaching of the Gospel. Don't let this distress you. Your Deedie may quite be mistaken, and the chief thing is that he has only the lovingest wishes and tenderness for you.

Don't be sad, dear one, *don't*.

Carman

...

Irving Layton to Aviva Layton
Nice, France
July, 1966
age 54

Dearest Pussypants:

Your letter with clippings, etc. came a couple of days ago, but I was in the middle of a creative splurge so couldn't take the time off to answer it. [...] I am having the most wonderful time in the world, doing nothing else but what I seem to be exceptionally gifted for doing — writing poems. And what poems! Do you know the stuff is fairly running out of me like water and I write two, three, four poems a day! Nothing like this has ever happened to me before. It's the sun, the water, the complete isolation. No monk could lead a more industrious or abstemious life than myself.

It's as I long ago suspected. I am not for this world with its silly nonsense that with the years I'm finding it more and more difficult to have anything to do with. I never have been more happy in my life than in the past two and a half weeks during which I have led the life of a hermit, either going to the park to write my poems or staying in my room smoking a Schimmelpenninck and reading. I've never really wanted anything else from life though of course there's a side to me that's fascinated by the insane, cruel, or amusing things my fellow-creatures do. Most of my troubles have come about because I tried to live the sort of life for which I was never intended. I don't regret my past life — in any case, regret would be foolish — and indeed I would probably do it all over again, doing exactly the same mad, bad, sad things and in the same chronological order too. Because there's quite plainly some kind of connection between the man and the poet, and the one has been feeding the other all these years: giving him the guts to lay out in the beautiful or interesting patterns.

Mystery

> How is it that I,
> a pilgrim
> should have acquired
> three wives and three children?

Don't try to answer that question. Don't try to answer anything. I'm not very interested any more in anything anyone has to tell me. How could I have been so blind? Why couldn't I see the stumps where the wings had been? What in hell did I ever have to do with the mawkish, the weak, and the stupid? What magnificent poems I've written these past few weeks. Incredible, even to me who knew what powers lay within me. I'm mad with happiness. Mad with sunlight and peace and the strength of self-discovery and self-affirmation. Little people, little things — go away from me.

God — when I compare this summer with last year's! Do you know that now that my mind and heart are clear I've even begun to write poems about Greece? Terrific ones! Aviva, Aviva, how could you have done it to me? Stupid question from the old Irving. How could I have let you do it?

Don't get alarmed. I'm being my rapturous self, enjoying the ecstasy the gods have reserved for their favourite few. When I come down I'll embrace you as the one companion I wish for, and my dearest son, David, whom I long to hold in my arms.

...

Barry Dempster, 2007
age 55

Come Live with Me

Come live with me, I'd like to share
this watch that doesn't tick, this
TV set that takes the sickness
of the world and wraps it
in sex and show, this chimney
growing taller with each blast of heat.

I want to live closer to the core of
all my things, the springs and screws,
the blinking lights, the seams that separate
the *do's* from *don't's*, the gleam
within the shine. I want to be right here
when you find the perfect word
strayed across the line and learn
the courage it takes to face a brand new story.

Please, come live with me, the sun
with its hundred arms, the steam of tea
floating from lips, the damp spot on the pillow
where soul squeezed through. I want
the marrow, the stretch, the stirrings of green
deep within your eyes. I want the house
to catch your flame, to soak in your perfume,
to surrender its bones to the creak
only your feet can play.

Come live with me, I'd like to share
this life, this breathing that aims
to outlast desire, this wholeness
belonging to the both of us, like the loops
and straggles of a conversation,
or the soft babble of a kiss.

···

Richard Harrison to Lisa ——————
March 13, 2012
age 55

I love you. Did I mention that? Do I mention that enough? I just talked
with a student who tells me his life expectancy is 15 years shorter than I'm
old now, and I'm thinking about all we've done, you and I, in 15 years. This
student and I, we've worked for several terms together on his poetry and
we're here because he's seen the missing thing that you can only see when
you've been hiding what you need to say for a long time in your work, and
you've understood that you've written yourself to the limit of your hiding.
I'm feeling the kind of jolt for him that happens when I miss the step on
the flight and the floor is a punch in the heart, though it does him no good.
This is not about pity, but pity is the first fall I cannot help taking. Our son
is at home, I can see him, with the same mouth tightening around what he
feels; and it feels like all three of us are born with the instructions on how
to be men the way birds are born both naked and with the feathers they will
eventually grow. All we need is the air and enough time. I've told him that
the more he moves to speak of the life he's actually living, the more powerful
and reaching his poems will be, how much more meaningful the experience
he's going to go through will be for himself and others, that when he talks
about speaking, he will teach everyone who thinks they've got the whole
long world ahead of them how sacred words truly are, and isn't this the
point of poetry? I'm thinking of our son, talking on Skype with his friends
connected to each other across an electric city, and my father, now dead
lying there dying with his open mouth and the special moaning sound the
dying make that he made until the drugs settled him down to die quiet. I
told him it's time to let go, it's okay to let go. I want to hug the guy, but he's
a shy one, contained, and so I let him leave the office without a touch. This
job is something else; I wouldn't trade it for the world whose weight I feel
right now in my flooded arms. Did I mention how much I love you? I don't
mention it enough.

···

Ronald Everson, 1958
age 55

Cold Weather Love

Expanding in the chill,
lake ice elbows itself
and presses down the water.
I hear ice split;
Water sprays up in pressure ridges.

Cold squeezes my blood
to run faster.
Remember the rape outside Drumheller
at fifty below?
Canadians are hardy.

Beware of me, my love,
in an eternity of cold;
my death makes me more active.

...

Heather Haley to John ———
Subject: Planning
10:33 a.m., Friday, February 19, 2010
age 55

Saturday-tomorrow-or Monday in the afternoon, 1:30? Can you meet me at Lonsdale Quay? You could take the Seabus over, I'll pick you up, we can go for a drive, maybe a walk in Lynn Canyon Park. As I said before, I'd rather spend the time alone with you rather be stuck on Lions Gate Bridge. Or I could visit you at the hotel though it's not likely you'll find a reasonably priced room there until the fucking Olympics are over. Maybe you could check anyway, you never know. Maybe nobody wants to stay there but it seems there are tourists everywhere!

Agenda: if, how to proceed, bottom line, right? I know I don't want a fleeting affair and I will not invoke cataclysmic change into my life unless our relationship is substantial, meaningful. That's the only approach that makes sense to me anyway. So, if we aren't on the same page, forget the meeting I guess.

TTYS
H

•

John ——— to Heather Haley
Subject: Planning
1:14 p.m., Friday, February 19, 2010

Tomorrow. North Shore. We could hypothetically walk, if walk we must, to the Best Western at 1634 Capilano Rd., where I accidentally booked a room for some obscure reason. Name a time, baby. You can call me.

Eagerly,
Yr Impulsive Pup,
J.

P.S. Lynn Canyon Park, huh? You make me laugh, sweetie.
P.P.S. Two queen beds! You can take the left one, I the right, and we'll discuss our platonic relationship.
P.P.P.S.I wrote this horrible little poem. I need some cheer, fun, affection, room service, &c. I think it may be you I need.

His Reply to Her Lawyer

Because I'm the neighbour of nothing,
so far have I dwindled. Because no son
needs an unlit satellite for a father,
nor a speck of debris the worms laugh at,
nor a misprint comma in the stupidest
book ever. Because my son doesn't need
a ruin who's like a parody of ruin,
who's the cunt of the litter.
Oh, don't signal me. The wire is broken.
Don't wave. I'm blind as a cancer.

Don't try to summon me with tokens
of power; God, like me, hates a dancer.
Don't call, don't smile, don't even offer.
Take this knife for your answer.

•

John ——— to Heather Haley
Subject: I dunno what's next, gorgeous
3:55 a.m., Thursday, February 25, 2010

OK. To be real clear. When I was running my hand between your legs at
the Best Western and whispering dirty talk in your ear — "How do you want
to come, Heather Haley?" — and when you froze a bit and said, oh, this is all
too fast, wait, wait — and when I waited a bit before slipping deliciously into
you, my hot lacey-black disaster and nervous child, part of me was thinking,
I don't deserve such riches. Another part of me was thinking, I can't get
enough of Heather's pink stiff nipples and the way she cries out when we
fuck. Another part of me was thinking, fucking condoms, what I really want
to do is pull out and come on her pretty belly. But the largest part of me,
baby, was not thinking at all: not the first time, nor the second. And when
you swallowed me a bit, and then straddled me and guided me into your
pretty cunt, well…

•

Heather Haley to John ———
Subject: I dunno what's next, gorgeous
9:32 a.m., Thursday, February 25, 2010

I remember that! I did get overwhelmed for a moment, asked the music
be turned down, my nerves so jangled. I can't help it, I'm swept up, thank
Christ. Long hard road for me babe, to becoming orgasmic, accepting that
I love to be fucked,
    You're so cute, my manly man. I loved it when you said, "I'll take that,"
hung up my leather coat, then pulled me to you on the edge of the bed to
revel in the moment, the luxury of being face to face, indulging our hungers
via frenzied, deep kisses galore, maulings, the brainlessness of lace, skin.
You trying to tug my boots off sans zippers, my leggings. The wine-bottle

debate-Screw it!-before falling onto the bed in a tangle. You gazing down upon me, employing the word "joy" in some context. My gimpy shoulder, your cutting scars. Sorry I ripped off your band aid, I was confused. Swooning! You *are* deserving, as am I. We deserve each other, to follow desire, out of bounds, if necessary. Thinking is definitely overrated. Here's to sweet surrender.

·

John ——— to Heather Haley
Subject: Mrs Respectable
4:10 a.m., Saturday, February 27, 2010

Heather Susan, I am almost a titch embarrassed at the pseudo-porn nature of my last couple telegraphs. To be clear, while we do have a triumphant and sexual fever which I love, I firstly like *you*: the towering girl at the microphone, the tough chick from bacon-munching nowheresville, the near-American who came back, the knowledgeable rock fan, the motherly hand on the Volvo gearshift…my admirable Haley, in short, with the perma-busted shoulder under her sinner's black bra. (It moves me, that shattered outcrop…) I don't only want to lay you down and grip you and get in you, HH; I'm ready to compare mythologies, to show you my real face and look on yours, in the careful, careful limited way of a pair of adulterers, one of whom is somewhat busted (that would be me). Are you in town tomorrow (today)? Call me anytime after 3, I'd be happy to go up Lynn Canyon and hold hands and talk, and not pull down your panties at all unless requested.

I have been job-hunting and Olympicking these past couple of days, also doing Dad duty for Lisa 'cos she's been ill. Anyway you know I am not much of a phone chatter, nor even much of a correspondent really. Bed's where I like to talk, on paper's where I like to write, and face to face is where I like to kiss your murmuring mouth, my Heather,
      Happily,
      J.

·

Heather Haley to John ———
Subject: Mrs Respectable
1:30 p.m., Saturday, February 27, 2010

Ahem, that would be "Ms." Respectable to you, the irony being that I'm far too respectable, domesticated these days and though still a feminist, no longer raging. I like men, love men. Perhaps it would be more accurate to say "humanist." Ironic too that I bore a son, after longing for a daughter because he has helped to demystify you guys for me.

What a lovely morning, to wake to your message, eat my oats and blueberries, walk my hounds in the wet woods. I love how they embrace the earth, not surprisingly as "terrier" is from the Latin *terrārius, of the earth*. Not only do they sniff the ground, they rub, scratch, paw at it, devour it. Brinda eats muck and SamIAm must think he's a beaver too because he picks up rotting chunks of cedar and chews on them. They relish getting soaked and muddy and drinking freshly fallen rainwater from the various ponds and streams on the property. They make me smile and laugh and definitely earn their kibble.

Hey Pup, you can talk dirty to me anytime though it's equally arousing to hear the exquisitely sweet, romantic things that roll off your tongue, to know I am held in high esteem for all my attributes. I wouldn't be here otherwise. [...]

Shall I call later?

> TTFN Luv,
> Your natural woman

•

John ——— to Heather Haley
Subject: Just a Dream
9:07 a.m., Friday, March 12, 2010

I'm not trying to be cryptic, poet, but have you heard of the Red Shift?

It's the scientific discovery that, not only is the universe expanding, but it's expanding *faster* — we always knew everything was far apart, but the Red Shift shows everything is getting farther apart at an *accelerated pace*. So, no aliens. No contact. Less of a chance every day.

I don't want you to be lonely, baby. But how are the stars ever going to align for us, at this late date? Call me tomorrow and let's have crab cakes and fleeting kisses, if that's all the fuckin' cosmos allows. Beats the void. The *expanding* void.

I'll wear your Fluevogs if req'd, Galactic Red. I am near, I am near, I am near,

Kiss,

J.

•

Heather Haley to John ———
Subject: Just a Dream
4:49 a.m., Saturday, March 13, 2010

I've never believed in fucking aliens.

I'm really glad you made contact when you did this morning. Kinda spooky. I'd just and only finally retired to my lair, disgusted and thoroughly infuriated. I might have jumped out the window.

I think I should stay here tomorrow, behind, to bask in a rare spot of solitude. Ruminate. Rail. But I will have the luxury of calling and talking on the phone if you want to and when you're available. It will still serve to beat the void and you can wear my Fluevogs anyway, if so inclined. ;-) I am here, I am here, I am here.

Kisses,

H

P.S. I'm having erotic dreams! That's hasn't happened in sooooo long. I think I only have you to blame/thank.

•

John ——— to Heather Haley
Subject: Just a Dream
11:36 p.m., Monday, Mar 15, 2010

A scene from grade 7 "health" class, as taught by the red-faced Mr Jackson, who assured us no question was too stupid.

YOUNG JOHN: Umm, do girls have, umm, nocturnal emissions? Wet
    dreams? Thank you.
MR JACKSON: Well, John, that's —

GRADE 7 HEALTH CLASS: Boo! Titter! Sneer! Wet! Shut up!
    Goof! Tumult! Fuckin!
(Curtain.)

Wink,

J.

·

John ———— to Heather Haley
Subject: The fucking robins…
8:54 p.m., Monday, April 12, 2010

…are hard at it outside. I don't know why birdcalls are ever called song.
It's obviously delirious bellowing that just comes out as peep-peep-peep.
And not only am I too dumb to be your boyfriend, I'm too weak and sickly
as well. The symptoms thereof are callousness and cruelty, you get me?

Not to wallow in the harm I've done these past few explosive months.
Not to repudiate the kindness and beauty you've shown me, goddammit,
Heather. But I'm not the Rothian hard man I thought I was, in fact I'm soft. I
grieve and grieve and snivel over my appalling waste and stupidity; blabbing
incontinently to moron Phil, which rips up the innocent bystander Tom's
life, like my family's lives got ripped up; jesus christ, I've got to call a halt to
this. What about your innocent son, shall we smash him up next? And I've
got to stop drinking.

I'm drinking right now.

Heather Susan, you are superb and pretty and enjoyable and wild. I
cannot not speak to you again, I've just got to rest and hide for maybe a long
while. I'm going to excel at my job, which is going to take many dedicated
hours. (I need money, lots of it). I can't really go out (can I stay in? I've lost
some good friends recently too, through bloody-minded recklessness; never
told you 'cos it's humiliating). I will stay in my hutch watching vampire
movies and eating Cheerios until I've thought things through. I have to be
alone.

Can you get this, baby? I can barely imagine your fury. (Your sexy fury.) But go to your husband. Keep what you've got. Give me some time. I don't want to do this. I care about you, I admire you, I lust for you. I don't know how much Red regret you might have, none of mine is about you.

Kiss,

J.

•

Heather Haley to John ———
Subject: The fucking robins…
9:59 p.m., Monday, April 12, 2010

Dear Pup, yes, rest. Please. Repair. Be alone. Lick your wounds. Take time. Halt the drinking. Take care, get stronger. I understand, or at least I'm trying to.

I miss you is all. Nobody calls me "Baby" or "Red" or "Kitten" or kisses me the way you do. As painful as this has been at times, I don't regret one moment.

Till whenever-you're-ready,

xxx

H

P.S. Please don't show that picture of me preggers to anyone. It's embarrassing. I wish Lincoln had used the other pose.

•

Heather Haley to John ———
Subject: What We Are
9:55 p.m., Friday, April 16, 2010

Dear John;

I can hear you sniggering. I know you don't believe in *our* common destiny, my fellow skeptic, but there's something going on we're both having difficulty assimilating. The part that resonates most though is "all paths lead to the same goal: to convey to others what we are."

I spent last weekend in a quandary, trying to figure out how best to confront Tom with the truth before it was too late, before he found out from someone else, which I still maintain would have been far more humiliating, to be the-husband-is-the-last-to-know dupe.

Bottom line; this is my life and I want to be free. I was working toward to that end but your blabbermouth forced my hand. I started by reassuring T that I love him and always will. Most people are not going to give me credit for upsetting sacred equilibrium by doing the right thing, the right thing for me. It's one of the hardest things I've ever had to do in my life, injure an exceptional human like Tom by conveying what I am, who I am, by finally being honest with him and true to myself.

By now he knows, understands that I wasn't on the prowl, wasn't seeking a connection with anyone. He knows me, knows I'm not a malicious person. And to hell with hell and damnation. I am proudly atheist and refuse to think in terms of sin and punishment despite my Catholic indoctrination and your dirty talk; hotly, sweetly calling me "sinner" and "bad girl." It just happened. This thing between us.

As I've confessed to you, I've been forced to reflect, to examine this precious life of mine and variously felt torn, miserable and largely alone in my struggle. I pleaded with T not to view this as something I was doing to him for ultimately it can provide an opportunity for happiness. It constitutes a kind of abundance, this audacious proposal I've dared to propose.

I've tried to shun you Pup, but it never feels right. Why should I have to cut myself off from you? From anyone? I just want to see you sometimes, enjoy the pleasure of your company. We're consenting adults, why the shame? I don't want to sneak around, go behind T's back, disrespect him, deceive him. Why do I have to forsake one person for another? Why is giving to one person equated with taking from another? What am I, chattel? I asked Tom to look at this with an open mind, with compassion, and you know what? He has. He's upset, struggling, fighting despair, fear, but he's listening. We're talking it through.

I explained that this thing with you has caused an identity crisis of sorts, forced me to look within, to question my choices. Tom and I drifted along, quite happily for the most part, but with everything left unstated. Now I'm tripping over those unexamined presumptions and realizing people change, things change, usually when you least expect it.

I'm not duplicitous by nature. Neither am I monogamous. It's just the way I am — not normal — another thing Tom and I never really discussed. I am not a conventional person who wanted a traditional life. I was a veritable hostage as a child — abused and terrorized and vowed that when I grew up I would be free. I'm also an artist. I know you abhor such pretensions but I do push boundaries; cannot abide deeply rooted stereotypes, conformity, cultural bans, taboos or stagnation. There are so many ways to think, move, live! I don't think I can be domesticated. God knows I've tried.

I've tried to be stoic too but the past five years or so years or so have been tough. I've been very depressed — even suicidal at times. My *mental pause* has been brutal. I felt isolated, cloistered, frustrated. Lately, even before you, I'd been gaining strength though, and feeling better, like I was coming out the other side, maybe even, and finally, coming into my own, as an artist, but more importantly, as an individual.

I've shared the theory with you, that though I was forced to surrender my fertility, fight a waning libido, the upside was I didn't have to worry about birth control anymore, was free of sexual intrigue. I could revert back to the girl, the tomboy I was before life was ruled by hormones and nature. Ha! Nothing is so simple. This awakening, my Prince, has made me susceptible to urges, impulses, the wind and rain on my face. You.

So then after all my scrambling, damage control, diplomacy and hard work, you take off, tail between your legs; telling me you're calling it quits via voice mail. I am to be punished after all. I wanted to throttle you! You didn't even have the decency to discuss with it me, just lowered the boom. That hurt worse than anything. I cried bitter tears. I was so angry and disappointed to see you at Cafe Montmarte after you said that by not seeing me, or anyone, you were able to do the work you needed to do. You know, I possess a well-oiled bullshit detector — one perk of getting older. I knew your "I vant to be alone"-Greta Garbo routine was a ploy, a way to make everything easier on yourself, but I consciously took the high road and took you at your word.

So, yes, you and I can keep our relationship on the down-low. I presume it's because you hope to reconcile with your wife, want to keep all your options open? If that's not the case, I would love to hear your reasoning on this. Hmm, I wonder, does she think you're celibate, saving yourself for her? Doing penance? I think you should grow a pair and be honest about who you're seeing, what you're doing, who you are. Why should she dictate whom you see, considering she doesn't want you anymore? Man, this really is a soap opera!

I received a lovely compliment today. I was in the ferry lineup in Horseshoe Bay and saw an island friend and neighbour, who motioned me over. She said, "Does Tom tell you how beautiful you are? "Ah, well, honestly, I can't remember the last time he said that." "Well, he should! Your beauty always astounds me." Only on Bowen Island I thought and thanked her for the compliment. "It's nice to hear." Come to think of it, I'm not sure T ever has said that. As I explained, he's a nerd, gets choked up even when professing to love me though I know that he's sincere. So excuse me for living, I have come to relish my lover telling me I'm "gorgeous, sexy, girlish."

One final note. We discussed this briefly last night but I will remind you that it was you who used the "L" word first. You said you loved me, in a voice mail. Go ahead and take back if you want. It's only a word. I know how you feel. It's obvious, especially when we fuck, when you are your most eloquent. So I won't say I love you, if it's so distressing to hear, but I adore you. Okay? I first muttered those words long ago and you didn't protest. So I suppose idolatry is acceptable. ;-)

I can't go back John, pretend nothing has happened. I am assimilating this change into my life no matter what the future holds. I've been forced to name what it is that I want, to advocate for my needs. I won't bury them, be complacent or coast any longer. Perhaps we're both struggling with how to balance desire with societal pressures. Mostly, I want to be myself, accepted for who I am, flawed and only human, exactly how I feel when I'm with you.

Kisses,

H

•

John ——— to Heather Haley
Subject: What We Are
7:58 a.m., Sunday, April 18, 2010

I think you're a brat, dancing around the Mariot Pinnacle to "Poets" like the most indifferent teenage girl ever. Himalayas of the mind, sure, baby. But there's something squalid about our lusty operation, too, and all the innocents we've sideswiped. I feel like your Tom is lying in the gutter with a skull fracture and I'm screaming at him above the sirens, "Why can't you be more *open??*" But go to, you overthinker. [...]

•

Heather Haley to John ———
Subject: Suck on Me
12:10 a.m., Thursday, May 6, 2010

I guess by now, you've made up half your mind. — *Beat Farmers*

Hey Pup, no pressure, don't mind me — just musing, ruminating, alright? I know you withhold; won't, or can't tell me many things but as garrulous as I may be at times, I am selective in what I tell you, tell anyone. I am amused though by a thought I woke to this morning, that I am beginning to think in terms of BY and AY, *Before You* and *After You*. Don't worry, I don't expect anything. That way I won't be disappointed. Yeah, it sounds like hubris, doesn't it? Well dear, I'm trying.

In any case and no matter what the future holds, Before You, Before November 16, 2009,

before you changed my rhythms, life was simple, practically clean living. After You, after the Gibsons shenanigans, After the flirtation we toyed with became something more, life is

complicated, messy. Help, I'm alive! After Heather? After the moment you were fed by three words of praise, here we are.

Are we dangerous? Bent on self-destruction or merely hungry? Deviant? A pair of deviants

defiantly separating ourselves from the herd? Stupid? Can we outwit the pain? I know we're

fucken brilliant but smart people do dumb things all the time. Certainly there is danger in the search for satiety. I can be reckless, constant, roaming, bruises all over my body to prove it. Do you have a death wish? Do I? Is that the name of this struggle? If so, it appears it isn't separate from the joy we take. Be advised, I am no longer in over my head. I may be a lightweight in an altered state but in the guts and blood of reality, I rock. Rule.

This ain't no lost highway. Did you choose me to drown with you, go down with you? Sorry if I foiled your plan but I might be meant to save you, along with myself. Choose me and you're choosing Life. I'm one formidable lifesaver, baby. It's a brave new world. I'm rallying, mustering the courage to (truly) live. Can you? Will you?

You have to do write. Land on your feet, in yourself, embrace your inner scribe. Remember me saying I am what I am? Well, so are you. So what if I'm a maniac? No one is about to tell me. Not you, not anyone, so carry on I will.

You often say you don't know what you want, that you're confused. I think you do know, don't want to say what you want, name it, claim it. For then, surely there is no going back. You want freedom. Sexual and otherwise. I am familiar with this phenomenon.

I think we recognized dissimulation in each other. Clearly, we revealed only one facet of

ourselves to our respective spouses. We're too big to fuck in the Olvo, John, too big to hide. I love your voraciousness, your masculine sexual desire, commands, smooth ride-carriage, fervour, frenzy, your voice loud with clarity, your poetry, your infectious smile-buffoonery, your courage, unflappable sovereignty. I for one am grateful you are who you are.

H

•

John ——— to Heather Haley
Subject: Suck on Me
12:13 a.m., Saturday, May 8, 2010

Well, I'm not here to *edit* you, Heather Susan, good God. You make me feel good, I am so glad of you, not just your sexiness but your patience, given that I as yr BF:

1) don't much want to talk
2) don't much want to listen
3) am not very interested in reading
4) am disinterested in writing
5) don't wish to wake up mornings
6) absolutely cannot sleep nights
7) must stay employed
8) must escape my employment, and
9) am generally as paralytic as a fencepost.

Whereas you, GF, you're dynamic. As your husband has probably noticed! You sure you wanna keep pouring your unfailing energy into me? I'm an unfillable bucket, darling, maybe: gurgle gurgle gurgle etc.

J

•

John ——— to Heather Haley
Subject: Suck on Me
3:20 a.m., Thursday, May 13, 2010

Is it possible to simultaneously not give a shit, a fuck and/or a damn? I am testing the proposition. Early indications are, yes, it can be done. Whether it's advisable, that's a whole other research project, Statistical Red, from which I exclude you, a few books and songs, one small child of my acquaintance, and all the robins of Prior Street.

Meanwhile, let the fog of indifference spread; whether it's good or bad, who cares? There are a great many things we shouldn't care about; or, more scientifically, it doesn't matter whether we care about things: 'cos things don't care about us. The sophomore proposition would be: will any of our present excitements have relevance 100 years from now? Me, I'm pretty sure it'll all be ashes within a decade, or possibly by Tuesday.

Whoof. The heavy-osity, baby! To be clear, next time I see you (the May Two-Four?), I'm going to strip you naked, slip into you, come in your pretty cunt, and kiss you in the morning when we wake up together. It'll be so sweet, I am giving a hard damn just thinking about it. Very hard; all yours. Please wear your topless stockings, kitten, it's not so far away.

Loved them Stooges, btw. Here's my prezzie in return,

J.

•

Heather Haley to John ———
Subject: Question
8:51 p.m., Wednesday, September 1, 2010

Well, you've got me all excited now! I love your proposal, especially the sweet fornicating bears part but alas, darling, I am locked into previously laid plans, which could have included a sleep-over with you had I known.

Sounds like we will only have a few precious hours tomorrow and will have to play it by ear, which will be hairy but I want to see you so bad, I will do whatever it takes, come to you when you give me the signal, arrange my errands accordingly. My nieces will be visiting soon and I will have to return to orchestrate the madness.

I do wish you wouldn't be so hard on yourself. Regardless of your marital status it seems you've been punishing yourself for a long time. When will you stop eschewing your true nature and just embrace it?

"Now is the time to understand / That all your ideas of right and wrong / Were just a child's training wheels / To be laid aside / When you finally live / With veracity / And love." – Hafez, poet (1315-1390)

You don't have to love me but for chrissakes, please summon up some regard for yourself and I'll say it again, be true to yourself. (And have there really been bicycles and training wheels since 1315? Guess I've never thought about that before.)

It is something! A gift, unless you already have enough friends and "gorgeous redheads" queuing up to suck your cock. I have men hitting on me all the time but they are half-wits and hollow compared to you.

But this "rueful" business is getting tedious. You make me happy! I'm a big girl and I will decide if you're bad for me or not. I don't expect anything other than what we have. If only you would stop doubting it, questioning yourself. This ride has got its own momentum, in case you haven't noticed. You might as well climb on. Hold on, certainly, and who knows where or how it will end but for the here and now, enjoy! We only go around once. And you're wasting precious time.

So, can we plan to spend the night together, with all night to pursue afore mentioned pleasures? Soon? Next Friday maybe?

In the meantime keep me posted regarding tomorrow.

xxx

Yr "Honeyed Girl"

•••

Susan Musgrave to Stephen Reid
Haida Gwaii, British Columbia
April 9, 2007
age 56

After you hung up I went for a long walk. The beach was empty and misty and grey. An eagle sat on the beach and then flew into a tree where a raven mobbed it. I liked it there. Imagined us together, getting wood, in the rain. Not talking on cell phones across the beach to one another, like some people do.

When you call, the loneliness I feel is further emphasized. And I think that turns to anger, too. I can tell you about your day and you can tell me about mine (or the other way around!) but the fact that we are not together becomes even more apparent. The phone emphasizes our separateness. I feel I should be up, cheerful, responsive, so I put expectations upon myself which I don't live up to, then am mad at myself because I fail to live up to my own expectations. I think of my mother, who put on lipstick for when my dad came home, and poured him a drink and didn't tell him any of her day's bad news because he'd had enough problems of his own at work. Maybe that is how to make marriage work. Did theirs work? In some ways, but Mum didn't really have a life of her own (until he died). But still, she's my role model, I guess. Our parents' marriage is all we know about marriage, until we leave home and see that other people's parents live different ways. Everyone dies in the end, so what the fuck, eh? What have I become, my only friend?

Anyway, I am trying not to feel badly about our phone call(s). The times you remember me being talkable (as Sophie used to say) were probably the times when I hadn't spoken to you for a few days. Then I have something to say! I so much prefer letters where I can be reflective instead of reactive. If I didn't need the phone line for email I might chuck the thing into the sea.

I have started reading "Reading Lolita in Tehran" where the faculty at the university was concerned with how to excise the word wine from a Hemingway story, and decided not to teach Brontë because she appeared to condone adultery. I thought, I guess I am lucky that I don't live in a restrictive regime. I would have been stoned to death before I was born.

I feel old. In the sense of the important things in my life having already happened. Old in that I can't imagine being surprised by anything. That nothing astounds me, or controls me, the way it once did. My feelings, I mean. I used to feel a wild and out of control sense of endless possibility. Now I just bite the skin around my fingers and make myself bleed.

Maybe it's not old, but in between. Isn't old supposed to be wise, accepting? Or is that just another myth, another lie. Maybe old is just old. Invisible to most people, especially oneself.

Well, on that cheery note, I must sign off now (as people used to say at the end of letters when they didn't know what else to say.) I tried to weigh myself on Friday (which is the day I would go to Weight Watchers usually) and got a reading that said ERR. I checked the manual and it said that if you got an ERR reading it meant there was too much weight on the scale. Hmmm. I might as well go back to eating cake and cookies, eh?

I love you, Stephen. That doesn't change. If only I wasn't me, I would be so much happier. In my gravel pit of dis-pear.

To work. With bleeding fingers I soldier on.

Xxx

•

Susan Musgrave to Stephen Reid
Haida Gwaii, British Columbia
April 10, 2007

Feeling better today, especially after writing to you. When I write letters I can sometimes see what is bothering me. Or not.

Today I read a piece about emotions from a book Dana (my friend from Regina who comes here to give meditation retreats) had given her. Useful. How not to identify with emotions, just name them. Instead of saying, "I feel miserable and alone," say, "That is misery. That is loneliness." It really helps — if I can just remember to do it! Maybe I have been feeling "stuck" in my practice because I needed some teachings, a teacher, some outside input. Once again my body leads me where I need to go.

Did I tell you that AA joke about the doctor who tells the addict they have invented a miracle pill — one pill it cures you of everything, you will live a long and happy problem-free life, etc. etc. "What happens if I take two?"

Filling the holes in our lives. All to avoid an unpleasant feeling that we want to escape from, when, if we sit with it, stay with it, it loses its power. But I forget to sit with it, stay with it. I want a whole carrot cake instead.

Did I ever send you this, part of a poem by David Whyte, called "Sweet Darkness"? I thought of you when I read it.

> Sometimes it takes darkness and the sweet
> confinement of your aloneness
> to learn
>
> anything or anyone
> that does not bring you alive
>
> is too small for you.

I am having *déjà vu* all over again so I probably did send it to you. The two stanzas that go before are:

> You must learn one thing.
> The world was made to be free in.

> Give up all the other worlds
> except the one to which you belong.[4]

I don't know which world I belong to. Which worlds. Do you?
Love you, sweetheart.

•

Susan Musgrave to Stephen Reid
Haida Gwaii, British Columbia
November 6, 2007

Hi sweetheart:

When I get back into the habit of writing to you, it becomes like dreaming: if you don't do it all the chaos builds up in your mind and you go moth-crazy.

I liked your Butch Cassidy Personality-Recipe card. You are all the things you described Butch as being, including innovative. The day I got the card (yesterday) I ordered a new book (along with "Survival of the Sickest") about Billy the Kid. I think we must be well matched, in terms of our sharing of mythologies, etc. No wonder it is easy for you to talk about celebrity outlaw hood. I mean, easier than talking about God. Frenchy, in my novel, says, "God be just one more white muhfuh, weigh more than a secondhand Cadillac."

You wrote, "One of the things about chronic drug use is the loss of observance of holidays, rituals, occasions, these passages of ceremony that make up the stuff of our lives." I agree with you, but isn't that why we USE drugs or alcohol — because of the pressures created by the artificiality these holidays have mostly become? I listened to a good interview with an English journalist who spends his time in war zones in the Middle East. He is a

---

4   David Whyte, "Sweet Darkness," from *The House of Belonging.* (Langley, WA: Many Rivers Press, 1996.) © Many River Press and David Whyte. Reprinted by permission of the publisher.

heroin addict when he is not in a war zone. When he gets on a plane to fly to Baghdad or wherever he leaves his drugs behind, is sick for a couple of days, then never has any cravings. When his plane touches down at Heathrow he gets the urge to use again. And did, apparently, until seven years ago.

I was glad to hear him talk like that. When I get on a plane at Pat Bay I am able to leave my cravings behind as I hurtle towards the war zone that is Tow Hill Road on Haida Gwaii. No cravings whilst I hew wood and carry water, but the minute my plane touches down in Pat Bay, I am disturbed and restless and I want to escape my life.

The book is called "Another Bloody Love Letter." I think I'll order it.

I am too hot in the house, even with two windows open. Another thing about these ceremonies and rituals of our culture — they involve spending money. "Happy people don't need festivities," I once read. Not the kind that tells you to Say it with Flowers, ones grown in Colombian sweat factories where girls tear their hands plucking out thorns so that we may have our roses without thorns thereby contradicting the adage, "Every rose has its thorn."

Of course substances cost money, too. But at least you are an outsider when you use, not one of the millions of people leading lives of quiet desperation. I shouldn't be saying this to you (i.e. this is not an encouragement to use) but it's how I sometimes feel. I don't want to be connected to the festivities of this world, because I already feel disconnected from them in the first place. But of course drugs are their own kind of quiet desperation. As we know. In other words, life is a lose-lose situation.

I don't enjoy life very much, never have. I don't like the effects of alcohol, either, too depressing. If only I could find a pharmaceutical source of cocaine — in a pill, the way Freud used to describe it — (the reason we crave more is because by snorting it we are taking too much at one time) — then I could go off my other addictive medications.

Enough of that foolishness. There is nothing better than the sound of rain. You and me and a big opium bed. A blowjob here, a blowjob there, here a blow, there a job, everywhere a blowjob. A movie, and sleep.

On that salacious note I will leave you hanging. Or standing. Full mast.

•••

Gerald Hill to K.
Regina, Saskatchewan
March, 2007
age 56

Dear K.,

This is how it happened. Leaving my apartment
on Spence, I picked up my mail, a handwritten

envelope, return address I didn't know.
I remember saying to no one, *I'll open this letter*

at work and tossing it into my bag. So I get to my office,
this was a weekend. I head across the hall to take

a shit, grabbing the letter. 20 seconds later, I'm ripping
open the envelope. *Dear Gerry*, it says. *I hope*

you're sitting down when you read this and it's from you.
Re-connections have gladdened your life. I'm

supposed to be one of them and you'd like
to chat, and there's a photograph of you

with your son. Trouble is, I don't recall
the time fondly, us together or apart. You say

I was kind, and took care of you, which I don't
remember. It was mostly, as I say, humiliation.

I'm happy for you, don't get me wrong, but haven't
answered your letter until now. The other day

I walked by that townhouse where I'd breathed
a virgin's air for the last time, thanks to you

giving me my birthday present early. The City
should put up a plaque to what

happened there and I should more freely
admit the pleasures you showed me.

I'd be stealing from all my poems if
before I leave this letter I go over

how we met. At the King's Hotel
downtown. Maybe these are memories

you feel detached from. I drove you home
and we necked in front of your mom's house

till sunrise. Pretty soon we moved in together,
top floor on Smith. I have a pic of you

cooking, the smile on your face, the haircut.
Around the time you told me to bugger off.

Those were times I had to go through.
I was way too immature.

Sincerely, G.

•••

Roy Kiyooka to Daphne Marlatt
December 23, 1983
age 57

Dear Daphne
   in so far as i've been into letter writing lately, i thot yes i must write
Daphne a letter too. callit a Xmas letter. or better still the letter i owe you
for all your fecund letters thru the years. as i sit this cold clear morning with
the brief but bright sun glancing off my cheek, i'm listening to the cassette

tape i made when we were together on the Queen Charlottes a light year ago. i can hear the surf pounding the sounds of our footsteps along the wet pebbled shore, the incessant hiss of wind, the salutary mantra of my zither and, although all of this has probably become mere datum in your momentums, i go on assiduously attending to all such evocations. i mean, despite the intricate ways we came awry and yes despite the sullen moments when we travelled afar together and never quite made out — i go on being all ears, all nose, all mouth & all eyes. i don't know if i ever told you, but "this," callit, a porosity-of-being, i was told in a peyote vision (back/forward in the late '50s) is the very abdomen of any artist, irrespective of time/place. this Friday morning i thot i had better get my photo supplies for the holiday ahead and i went out to start the old Toyota and, tho it wheezed & groaned, not being used to frigid temperatures, it started up. whereupon i went back into the house to finish my cupa coffee and let it warm up. then when i came out a few minutes later i found it steaming from under the hood. well, to make a long story really short, i had blown a rubber gasket and the antifreeze etc. poured out! so much for gadding about over the holidays…unless i get it fixt. i keep on peering over my shoulder to see if Jim has come to work yet. as you can imagine, the severity of the cold has kept him at home. me too. me be, as usual, all alone at home…this my so-called "sabbatical year" goes right on being utterly amazing in all its winter solstice humdrum. & if i may be ironic, so does the rest of the hurdy-gurdy world with its awesome solar dynamics. & as i sit here wondering what will fall onto this page next, i am thinking that this brief solstice sun spins an untellable warmth and that perhaps has a lot do with abiding the very absence of intentionality. given the levity of the above, i am, to all intents and purposes, utterly emptied of, callit, the prerogative of hustling language into the shapeliness of mind's own thots. if there's such a discrete but knowable entity as a "will," I, for one, don't know where to place it in the structure of my being. if it's anything to me, it's something like these thin bones and how many layers of cloth i swathe them in these days. tell that to the erstwhile determinists and their dramaturgy of gross conflicts.

We made a Pledge at La Push to act in/upon the world as if our very lives were an utter Gift. We as much as sd to each other and the tumultuous sea outside our cabin window that we would Praise the whole extant world as it impinged upon our daily lives. Or so i thot thinking abt that long ago afternoon. You had gone off on a meditative walk while i prepared myself to "mind" the mushroom's potent inscape. It was after you returned from your perambulatory walk at the marge of the sea and i had sat thru the afternoon stript of my usual visors: we spent the twilight hours gathering the mantle of night around ourselves and barely spoke of the Gift of our lives. Now, you are stooping at the foamy edge of that wild sea with its insistent heave while i click the shutter. Cupt in my ear i can hear its distant resonances, and the lilt of our ofttimes droll laughter draws the very breath out of me. It's going to take all the fervor i've got left in me to go on praising our own time given the manifold embodiments of callit the monstrous that beset our politics. It's going to bear down heavily on our most private selves and, like it or not, the pledge we made at La Push will (for myself) stand for all that is yet-to-be-born-within-us. All that makes us a "you," a "me" and an "us." If you ever need me (wholly unconditionally) i am as close as your oh fallow ear. Love to all 3 of you from the goat-footed hermit of Keefer Street. Dear Betsy: these words don't have any real privacy in a permeable world. Nobody I know owns the language. Look! I say to myself — you've put a small net out and look at what you've caught. Season it: eat it: shit it out, but never think to own it. If it's in the New Year pack of cards I'm abt to shuffle, we'll get to talk to each other soon. Ah, Language, how it mothers all of us mercifully.

•••

David Bateman, 2013
age 57

letter to a former lover from a young drag queen on the threshold of manhood

My darling,
we are all the same, doing the same thing at the same time
coming in from other rooms and meeting
what with heavy scented blossoms flying off of hats
the dull sharp thud of your forearm
settling gently down upon my frilly groin

                    leaning into love like laps were faded cozy armchairs
                                 of the cloistered kind

as my fingers rattled up your ass-based spine
your thighs under mine
back to front and front to back
French-tips longing for a softer line

do you remember these things
these shapes and sounds, these holes and cracks
these contorted emotional ties
my wig on your bathroom floor
these distended rhymes.

I do, he said. I do.

I write you with such flower-like propensity
stamens arched and set to fire camp bred petals into open wounds
you have always inspired such raw insipid verse
pistils rife with such a stench of stemless headless bunches

                              single carpels, ovules, styles

wretching vile buds shot into vase-like urns
endless wordless odes, fallen roses, wilted heart-shaped pansies
lining floral walls of your design.

You told me you were Roman, spring-like, northern, blonde, with
     an
air of heavy beauty.

I never believed the things you said or were
but the bedside toga and the galley proofs of some earmarked bible
had me fooled for awhile.

Always wanting to believe but never really quite abreast
of how to sink so low into fresh despair
from finally admitting to being such an idiot savant
with a weakness for the duller ones among us
when the fools and folds of rented frocks could soar much higher
than your maladjusted brow,

but I could barely tell, my mascara thick with widened glee,
sullied rouge, warring cheeks among the unconverted zealots,
lipstick like the dumbed up mouths that dare not speak
thrown to lions with all those nasty Christians.

                              And that name you called me — Cushion!?

Then you wrote me out of love
with penny candy, pink erasers dark with use
primping as decline
a cheque or two blank

some wine

so now I craft epistolaric fobs
stuffing curt poetic realism through the grimy keyhole of your heart
the unreal way in which I loved you
and you returned that love with buttocks clenched
praying for self-declensive pronouns
like she or her

not me

not mine

allowing for one cruel point of view

my own

without recourse to hiring omniscient narrators
to take that leap with prose
to play with full arboreal strands,
forests of follicular debris across
your thighs
matted, oily, strewn

you thought I didn't notice.

I do, I said. I do.

My frayed lingerie has lost its flounce
and all your predilections for remorse have strayed

                                          go home

weep solemnly in that big brick cave
lie on patios shaped by gravel crosses
with ivy altars fit for barbeques, salted flavored chips
lean boneless chicken breasts.

We are all the same, doing the same thing at the same time
coming in from other rooms and meeting
what with heavy scented blossoms flying off of racks
the dull sharp thud of empty hangers, closets

forearms gently settling down upon these frilly loins
leaning into love like laps as faded armchairs of the cloistered kind

fingers rattling up your ass-based spine
entering crevasses withheld until the marble plated fountain flows
with coins
your thighs under mine
back to front and front to back.
Do you remember these things
these shapes and sounds

                                  these holes and cracks

these contorted emotional ties

my wig on your bathroom floor
my crinoline in your trunk
my bare arms

your wallet hung like Samson's hair on tiled vanities
slinging pennies into urine scented wishing wells
hoping I would strive for dimes.

I fire you out of lavender incensed drawers
into pocket histories of your own cemented filth.

You fake
you overwhelming bore.

Your truth is mine.

p.s. could you send me those encrusted pumps
the ones with eight inch heels and zirconed ankle straps
that gave me all the hope you mocked, adored

I think I left them on the kitchen floor
          those lush imported tiles and the harsh synthetic
            colours of those gorgeous cupboard drawers.
        xoxo

•••

Bruce Whiteman to Kelly M.
March, 2010
age 57

Dear Kelly,

"...And you and love are still my argument."
— Shakespeare, Sonnet 76

One is the loneliest number of all. We took the great breath of lovers
but now we breathe alone, and incomprehensibly your body in the world
is pain. Consolation drifts out of reach like music in another room, barely
recognizable before it goes *tacet*. I don't know what to say.

Eros-the-loosener-of-limbs has no advice. Permanent loss is not in his
lexicon of love. Language itself is a machine that has swallowed an alien
object and cannot go on. It will always be wet and silent out of doors, like
Christmas eve, with the moon in its first quarter coverted behind the clouds.

Mute cows haunt the gloom beyond the city. They love one another and never leave. I don't know what to say.

The Persian lovers sing of wanting the bond of love to last forever. It doesn't. Mad, intolerable determination snips it to drag on the muddy ground. It flops uncontrollably, spurting heart's blood in the air. Enough blood for lost love can never be spilt.

Your absence is everywhere. I see you disappear from all our sacred places, beds and other blessed furniture, rooms with no discernible geometry, sunny lawns and other implausible spaces made holy by your loss. Well no. They were always holy is the truth.

I don't know what to say.

•••

Katherine Lawrence to Randy Burton
Regina, Saskatchewan
May 18, 2014
age 59

My love —

How do we celebrate this milestone anniversary? I know of only one way. This is for you:

For thirty years we shared the same bed, gave birth twice, adopted a dog, pooled our money into a single bucket full of holes we stuffed with longer hours and freelance jobs that kept us running through traffic to our offices and back home every day, every month, year after year to dinner with the kids and often our friends: you across the table from me, clatter of tongues, forks, spoons. Where did the years go? How tall the crooked tower of dirty dishes and pots sticky with rice and green vegetables? Did we speak to one another about anything other than what was or wasn't in the refrigerator, the gas tank, the chequing account? Did we talk before we fell asleep, exhausted? Did you know how often I woke to the sound of the house breathing, the small cough and snuffle down the hall, the half moments of silence when all I could hear was my heart? Did you know that I used to stare into the darkness, as I do now, and wonder what path it was that led me here, to you, and all that we built with our beautiful bodies?

I love you,
Katherine

···

Jane Eaton Hamilton and Julia Balén
OKCupid Messages
Spring, 2013
age 59 (Hamilton)

JEH: Your friends say you have great ears? How could anyone resist?
Sent on 4/18/2013

JB: Well no one has nibbled on them recently. That's one hell of a list of books and films. So when is the next time you might head to California?
Sent on 4/19/2013

JEH: I was just looking up PH on a map, as I hadn't a clue where that was. But obviously — obviously — it is the location of your ears, so I don't quite know why I was wondering. I couldn't geo-locate my way out of a paper bag, but I have been known to hop planes, particularly to take in art, and as it happens, "Girl With a Pearl Earring" is in San Francisco's de Young Museum right now until June 2, the first time in N. America. I have a yen, though recognize it lands me still somewhat north of your auditory canals or the nibbly bits below them.

I enjoyed your profile. In particular, the things you most value, like thinking (clearly) and engagement with the world and good friends.

When is the next time you might be headed north? (Do your ears even travel?)

I have a cat, and I myself am somewhat taller than the cat, although still short. Tell me about your spawn. Mine are mid-30s and lovely, lovely, lovely.
Sent on 4/20/2013

JB: My ears do travel — along with the rest of me. My son is bigger than a cat and is a 35 yr old musician in LA. The dogs with the tall ears are my friends' who helped me put my profile together, though I dog-sit them now and again.

I just saw "Girl With a Pearl Earring" last month — amazing piece. Beautiful show. Don't know what's in LA at the moment, though maybe there is something there to entice you? While I may head north a bit this summer, I had not planned on going that far. Where is TO? (Down here that refers to Thousand Oaks, but I am guessing you mean Toronto.)

Your profile made me smile. Love that you start it with "out dyke activist" — especially given that I refer to myself as "professionally queer."

So what are your books about?

Sent on 4/20/2013

JEH: I have "Girl with a Pearl Earring" envy (and I suppose if you stop to think about it this might suggest a further ear fixation). I imagine crowds. Is GWPE exhibit crowded? Was it wonderful? It is such a compelling piece. I don't know what's showing in LA now, but can look..

Kids sound same vintage. Mine this year are 35 and 32.

My books are mostly short fiction and poetry, though I'm in the middle of writing a novel now. In this, my protagonist is an ornithologist who specializes in brood parasitism while her life is variously plundered. What are you reading now? I am reading (among many short story collections... Murakami etc) Sally Armstrong's *Ascent of Women*. She is of the opinion deep, good changes are happening regards women's equality around the world right now; I am more cynical, especially given much of her anecdotal evidence.

Sent on 4/20/2013

JB: GWPE envy — that's a new one. It was pretty busy. Not quite as bad as the Mona Lisa at the Louvre.

Just read "Sleepless" on my iPhone in a restaurant twitching between bites, catching my breath. Mixed blessing to read at this point in my life. Reminds me of Wittig's work a bit in its honesty. Read this after your essay on losing your beloved. I know this loss better than I would like as well. Too much to say in a parking lot on my iPhone awaiting friends.

Only fair to let you know my work too. After "rate your professor" a google search gets more interesting.[...]

Home now post movie ("Filly Brown") and just listened to you reading your poem in order to hear the grain of your voice. Sadly the audio cuts off before the end. It's a beautiful piece. I know and respect such passion, such honoring of our vulnerabilities and power with each other. I love the raw playfulness of the poem as well as your posts here.

There are very few people online who have piqued my interest much at all. You definitely have. I would be happy to move this conversation to something more direct. At least to personal email. I look forward to hearing from you.

Sent on 4/20/2013

JEH: But you don't understand. I have just started looking you up and now I am frozen with admiration and shyness.

Sent on 4/21/2013

JB: Dios mio! Please do not freeze. I was thinking how pale my writing career seems in the face of yours.

Oh, I forgot to answer the what I am reading: too many student papers at the moment, though I just finished listening to "The Last Nude" and loved it. My guess is that I would also find Armstrong's take too pollyanna-ish, though I am a little more hopeful in the last year or so based on student activism. Murakami is very interesting. Just got finished teaching "Jazz," one of my favorites of Morrison's and Hong-Kingston's "China Men."
Sent on 4/21/2013

JB: I don't have a page on Wikipedia about me…
Sent on 4/21/2013

JEH: Hello, hello;

I am half-watching a program on the National Ballet and Karen Kain while awaiting emails from my daughter — god, I love ballet. During my recent move, I stumbled across my ballet slippers, the ribbons turned yellow and crispy. This would give you the idea that I danced seriously, but that isn't true; I danced only affectionately, and, worse still, I think doing ballet in my late 30s did something permanently hinky to my left hip. Do you dance? I loved couple dancing the most — Latin and ballroom and was an avid if uncoordinated follow.

Ok, phew, kid is sorted until morning.

Je prêterai l'attention à tu maintenant [sic]. Let's see. Where were we? You, woman, have a list of accomplishments that are taller than I am (and we have already established that I am considerably higher than a cat). I am agog. To have all these successes and to have great ears, too…

Thankfully, to offset my agogery, I did go to "Rate My Professor" and there you were taken down several laughable pegs.

I will when more energetic really absorb your CV.

I have such a hard time on Cupid because, when I look at profiles, I roll my eyes and snort, and then end up falling off my chair, and then I've broken my toe or my arm and have to go to the ER. Everyone in Vancouver rides bikes, snowboards, hang-glides, runs, hikes, parachutes, rollerblades, does finger exercises, flexes their toes, pops their knees, rolls their shoulders etc etc and they do it all in Lululemon without a thought in their heads. Me, I sit in a chair all day, and that is hard enough to manage without a thought in my head. On Cupid, I decided to search "anywhere" and "atheist" or "agnostic" and see if that might shake something free, and there you were, there you were with your small and perfect ears.

I don't exactly know what I'm doing in writing to you, though I'm certainly gratified that you wrote back.

I'm sorry the audio for "Sleepless" cut off. I forget my pieces because, to me, once they're written they are just artifacts (flawed artifacts). I didn't even recall that there was audio to that poem till you mentioned it, and I definitely haven't listened to it. I remember the day I wrote the poem, though, and how long it took (about 12 hours). I challenged myself to write a poem that was strictly sexual without being either loving or pornographic, though I think some tenderness probably crept in.

As for the piece called "Bird Nights," that really is my interior life on the page and a bit of writing I'm proud of. Not that I wouldn't re-shape it if I had it back, I would, and not that I actually conceptualized a yellow bird etc except when writing, but with its metaphors, its wide fictional grasp, it manages to capture a kind of breakup truth, and I love the — phantasmagoric playfulness? m— of the writing. And riding that perilous border between poetry and prose.

Of the nitty gritty: I am out of a bad relationship for a couple years, have mucked around with dating but am not really attuned to it, being, you know, old and flabby of body and brain (see above, sitting in chair as the fit jog past), and seem to very quickly make a botch of it. It is not really helpful to spend a date thinking: I could be gardening.

I found "Remembering Wittig" on Frontiers (where I've also published) and the first page is replete with sumptuous writing, Jules, and now I am agog anew.

(But can't access more than the first page.) I feel you aching for Wittig, your nearly inchoate yearning for the writing that will take you to her when words, these words, mere strung letters, are so damnably inadequate. I can feel your writer's experience because of my own pen against paper. Yet, also, I feel awe at my reader's experience, which is your great success in evocation, your perfection of punctuation, your sensuous, poetic engagement.

I am charmed and delighted.

Well, I'm going to stop because it's crazy late. I just returned from Shanghai a few days ago and every night I've been up until 4 or 5 — cannot shake jet lag.

JB: Glad to know that things with the kid got ironed out.

You make me laugh — about the dating, especially online. UGH! There are times I think I have just read this same litany in the last profile. Spent one of the most hilarious nights recently reading my buddies some of the email exchanges I have had. Nothing like gay friends to riff on human silliness. i almost peed my pants.

You make me ache with lines like: "She is always saying goodbye with her actions while she smiles hello with her lips" or "It feels exactly like my heart is failing" or..."Bird Nights" is phenomenal in so many ways and once again reminds me of Wittig, whose work I am echoing in the poem you read. (Do you know Wittig's work?) Seems like we both return to words to work out the pleasures and pains, though you seem much easier in your wording the world than I experience myself being.

There are so many stories I could tell about the loves in my life. About a year ago I literally felt as if tectonic plates were moving inside of me and last fall I had repeated meditations during which I had images of ripping out old wiring and completely rewiring myself. What I am returning to is finding my own pleasure. Your work is further inspiration in this direction and I thank you for this.

So what did you do in Shanghai? How was it? There are so many places I have never been and that is one.

Feel free to call — though I guess the international thing could be expensive, huh? Facetime/skype? I don't know where this might lead either, but I find so few souls in the world who might actually "recognize" me that I am inclined to pursue those connections.

Listening to the birds in my garden anew,
Jb

JEH: Oh hell, let's just go for a walk on the beach now.

JB: Which beach, yours or mine?

JEH: I pick yours as it's cold and rainy here. (Though incandescently lovely with all the cherries and plums and magnolias in simultaneous bloom.)

I have a long two days now of tax prep and a walk on your no-doubt warmer beach sounds like a much better scheme. Not to mention that you'd be beside me. And that I could, you know, take secret glances at your remarked-upon ears. Which could send me to writing or reciting, per this two-minute poem composed on the spot:

Anvil stirrup semicircular canals
throbbing hammer on drum
red electrical impulses towards vestibulocochlear nerve
or just eustachan canal
just just stand closer
small whorl/d/s minute hairs dyke vibrations
stand here where whispering nothing
touches

J

FIVE

I Promise Not to Philosophize

Poets in their Sixties, Seventies, and Beyond

Susan Musgrave to Stephen Reid
October 12, 2011
age 60

Hi, love:

Feeling so sad because I haven't heard from you for so long. I got very lonely over Thanksgiving, remembering when the kids were small, our trips to Long Beach. I still get a lump in my throat, chest, all over body, and feel like crying. No good to dwell on what is past. But, still. We've known the days.

Today is our 25th wedding anniversary (I think!) Was it 1986 we got married? And you got out in 1987? And we moved into The Treehouse?

I keep having a feeling you are not with me, in your heart. The last time we spoke on the phone I felt you just wanted to get off the phone… something hurried about it all and I can't tell if it's just your involvement in the play, or what? I hope you have not fallen in love with an actress. Lorna says we shouldn't be worried about things like that at our age, but I thought it was a good sign that I still do.

Happy Anniversary. I miss you terribly.

xox

•

Susan Musgrave to Stephen Reid
October 13, 2011

Hi, love:

I forgot to date yesterday's letter, our quarter of a century anniversary. I did get four letters from you as I was posting my one saying I figured you were cheating on me…so I felt a bit better. We only get mail delivery twice a week. All your letters were written at the beginning of October, including the one where you gave me the dates of the play.

I loved all the pictures you sent. The poor guy who drank Lysol… reminds me of the photos you used to send from Millhaven: "This guy was found in the trunk of a car…" "This guy was found in Lake Ontario…" Not your usual snapshots at life. "Aunt Jean playing croquet after a glass of cooking sherry," and so on.

I am glad you re-started the letter-writing component (for lack of a better word) of our lives. I realize, writing to you now, how much I have missed doing this. In a weird way it keeps me in touch with my own life, also.

I miss having you to talk to. And to touch. My anger (over your addiction) was fear: fear of losing you. My fears came true. Though I will always find you, whether either of us is/are lost.

Love you so much.

...

Bliss Carman to Kate Eastman
New Canaan, Connecticut
June 3, 1922
age 61

Dear Sweetheart: I couldn't have you go away today. Yesterday was tremendous. I came home in a completely shot-to-pieces condition. I was not expecting it, you see. And you carried all my trenches with a rush. I had long long ago forgotten that love can have such strange reactions — to eat or sleep was next to impossible. There are persons who can carry on such mundane physical duties under spiritual excitement, but not I. It was not only that I was thinking of you, but you seemed strangely to have invaded my whole being. Every fibre seemed to be stirred as the earth must be with the coming of Spring, and there is a change taking place. I hope I did not wake you this morning, but I could not wait, and was terrified lest you go back without seeing me again — darling thing! It is very good of you to wait over until Monday. I could not well come in before then. Thank you so much, and I am very happy — how otherwise could I be?

Am I not yours?

.

Bliss Carman to Kate Eastman
Santa Cruz Inn, Haines Falls, New York
Sunday, June 11, 1922

Kate dear: [...] Twilight is beautiful as ever, and wonderful with the showers sweeping over it. From this room in the Inn I look down the Kaaterskill Clove (as it is called) a Cañnan as we would call it in the West, where the mountains come down on each side in great forested walls of green. I grieve that you are not here to see it, and *more* that you are not here to be loved. I think of our ecstatic hours and hope you are as happy as I in the memory of them. [...]

Also I miss you sorely, and dread the idea of going West so far — and so soon. It is rather dreadful, you know. Why loving hearts should be torn apart, I don't know. I think the truth is that we are a lot of miserably over-civilized creatures, and yield to the pressure of circumstances. We allow any sort of petty condition to stand in the way of love or friendship far too easily, whereas love and friendship are the greatest things in life, and other things should give way to them. We are a puny lot, we mortals! I mean *I* must be. I don't think *you* are. You know there was something tremendous, heroic, and magnificent in your visit to N.Y. A *little* woman would never have returned. I think it was glorious of you — much more than I ever deserved. But certainly you have flooded my heart with warm sunlight, most adorable dear!

> Fondly,

•

Bliss Carman to Kate Eastman
Los Angeles, California
January 4, 1923

Dear darling Kay: [...] I think of you very often and very tenderly. You are a true mystic and a true lover, because your heart knows the goodness of love. It is like the goodness of the earth, the goodness of the air, the goodness of beauty — the real virtue or strength of things; and because you have all courage of your love. So many *think* they love, and have no courage of their love. Never dream of realizing it, but keep it always divorced from sense and kindness and fondness. But in you it is all through your gentle soul and mind and senses, making the adorable thing you are —. O much too good for a distracted friend like this one, torn and confused by the perplexity of wandering incarnate through a strange world.

> Bless your heart! As ever, C.

•••

Bill Howell, 2008
age 62

Local Subtext

Inevitably, directly: constant newness.

The distance between seen & said.

From whim to whimper, Max the cat
gets the lay of the land:
the possible as it really comes over & along,
day by day.

The temper of the seasoning.

The wish to arrive without qualification,
like bees across gardens.

Cell phones
calling one another in the same location
because we choose to use them that way.

Not so much to be sure first.
Or last.

Just because
your body has another, secret name for me.

•••

Thomas Dilworth, 2008
age 63

Neither Apple Trees

nor Newfoundland,
you are more personal and temporal:

face combining Otto Dix and Modigliani,
neck entirely Burne-Jones,
at its base, between collar bones,
                    a romantic chasm;
shoulders and upper back tense
with *Strum und Drang.*

Breasts, eighteenth-century
    (consult Gainsborough and Corelli).
Belly of Renaissance Madonnas
and medieval Eves with impossible navels
    (belladonna, belissima),
the Middle Ages
arising from the Dark,
            rich time of beginning.
Linger a while at classical thighs,
            long lines and impersonality.
Knees, six-century B.C. kores, smiling
            Nausiccas for Ulysses's kisses.
Shanks, ankles, feet, and toes, prehistoric
            grooming ticklish,
            evolution in progress.
Arms extend like institutions:
aristocracy, for instance, reaching
from Marie Antoinette to the Middle Ages,
or wide for infinity.
With Christian eagerness to embrace
or Buddhist welcome of embraces.

Your head contains all these,
their literature, music, philosophies,
and their mystics, yearning, like you,
for something better.

Reading this, you will advise
greater familiarity with the subject.

•••

Lorna Crozier, 2011
age 63

Getting Used to It

Our lovemaking that day was slow and tender
as if both our childhoods crowded around our bed.
My mother, on her own now sixteen years,
had phoned. Her brother's widow two doors down
was having family over, but not her. "It's okay,"
Mom said. "I'm used to being treated this way,"
then, "Happy New Year," her loneliness
a hard salt on my skin. You moved over me like water,
old water I'd swum in for years, knowing where
the bottom fell away, where warmth became a shiver,
then warmth again, you let me weep, you left
your smell all over me as if you'd just walked
naked in our garden, juniper, rosemary, snow's
blue flowers melting on your skin, our bodies
old, now one year older. I swear I won't get used to this,
your cries muffled in my hair, the hurt and no-one touching
that my mother has to bear; a thousand miles
away from us, a single setting at her table
the first day of her eighty-eighth new year.

•••

Lillian Allen to Jay
July 10, 2014
age 63

Dear sweet and gentle heart

Hazy over here. Reaching out for u swimming out there,
    somewhere, 'way from me...
Feels like love is drowning. Know all I want is to pull u back, take
    this greedy longing

And long it with u.
Call
Whatever it is u need
from me the answer is yes
Let's talk
Desperate to keep connected.

•••

Anne Szumigalski, 1986
age 64

Desire

desire is not like a wedding which rushes relentlessly towards us from the
other end of time   it comes unexpected as a cloud inviting questions
and implying answers   *can three lovers meet as two* we ask can they
walk out of a summer's morning and roll as all true lovers must in the dewy
wayside grass without one of them feeling neglected, worse still pitied, by
the other two   can four lovers meet as three or must they remain always
two pairs as isolated from each other as we all are from the begetter of our
uncertainties   and does all this apply not only to lovers but to brothers
and sisters both secular and holy

darling we shall say to our child *you were born of our surprising ability to
couple and couple again without weariness without a thought for the garden half-
planted for the book half-read* certainly we shall never tell her of our present
condition what an effort it is to keep up an interest for the sake of our tinpot
relationship for the sake of our parenthood for the sake of the future which
while we lie here locked in each other is rapidly crumbling into the past

•••

James Deahl to Norma West Linder
June 12, 2010 — bedtime
age 65

Well, Norma, the Hamilton Public Library has none of the anthologies containing your short stories, not even the one published by Oberon.

So while I can go to bed with the poetic Norma West Linder tonight, the fictional Norma West Linder will escape my embrace.

James

•

Norma West Linder to James Deahl
June 14, 2010

Maybe the real one won't want to escape it!

Cheers!

Norma

•

James Deahl to Norma West Linder
June 14, 2010

My Dearest Norma,

I hardly know how to take your astounding e-mail of today. So I have decided to take it *seriously* because I dearly want to believe it is possible.

When I met you in 1995, and you so kindly inscribed a copy of *Morning Child* for me, I noted that you were a stunningly beautiful woman. Fourteen years later we met again at the Al Purdy celebrations in Brighton and Ameliasburgh. Through some magic I cannot understand, you had not changed. Then again this spring during National Poetry Month: the same pretty girl of 1995.

Of course not really the same — you had suffered the grief of the death of your second husband; life is not easy and sorrows collect in all our lives — but the same *beauty*. Being a heterosexual male, I cannot fail to notice how lovely you are, how breathtakingly desirable you are in every way. Being an honest male, I refuse to pretend that I have not been greatly affected by your many charms.

One does not, dearest Norma, fall in love with a pretty face, not even one as pretty as yours. One falls in love (or does not fall in love) with the woman who comes with the face. And here again you are irresistibly desirable. I need not tell you that you are charming, intelligent, creative, and kind. You surely know all that, but I simply can't resist making the list.

I never dreamed that I would ever be telling you this. (And I am sorry if you are offended.) I never dreamed a day might come when I could tell you how special you are and how strong my feelings for you truly are. So if it is possible that I could embrace the *real* Norma as I have embraced your delightful book these past few evenings…well, I can hardly permit myself such a dream.

I believe that Debbie told me that she hosts an open mic at the Lawrence House on the final Friday of the month. This month that would be Friday, June 25th. Shona will be finished with final exams by then, and I could visit Sarnia. In that way I could express my love and affection in a more direct way.

And I could visit sooner, if that would please you. I am free to travel from June 22nd through the 28th.

It strikes me that you could have meant your e-mail in a more light-hearted way. It strikes me this letter may be unwelcome. If so, I dearly hope the above will not affect our friendship.

I would love to be your *friend* for the rest of our lives. And I would love to be more than friends, too, if that would please you. Friend or boyfriend, my dear Norma, I will try to be whatever will make *you* happy.

With my deepest love. May I get to say these things in person.

James

p.s. I can't believe how nervous I am. It has taken me forever to write this brief letter. My mind is in a daze, and I can hardly spell even simple words.

I'm afraid I have lost all restraint. Forgive me, but it must be love.

•••

Charles G.D. Roberts to Constance Davies Woodrow
Moncton, New Brunswick
December 19, 1925
age 65

On train,—on the way back to my Ever Beloved wee Poet & dear Home of my Heart!

Oh, my Heart, the long long weeks that I have not written to thee. But always, always, through the silence, my love & my thoughts have been going out to thee, with such [illegible] longing & tenderness. I have *had to* trust to thy heart's understanding, Beloved. For I simply *could not* write. I had exhausted my nerve & Brain force & felt an *overwhelming* inhibition against putting words on paper. I have been staying with friends in Halifax, when not darting all over the country & speaking & being "recepted," — & in that house I had no privacy ever, & so could not commune with thee except in thought & desire, & when I would lie awake in the night, in the dark, & stretch out my arms for you. When I could snatch a few minutes alone, — & on my train journeys, — I would read and reread your adored, wonderful letters, — which *always* I carry everywhere in my pockets, & which have become very worn with travel & kissing.

Now, thank the Gods, I am on the way back to thee, Heart's Delight. And how much I have to tell thee! I have to break my journey at *Fredericton*, & at *Woodstock*, — a day in each place to settle up some family business with relations. On *Monday*, the 21st, I start straight for Toronto, via C.P.R., — through *McAdam Junction (N.B.), Sherbrooke, Montreal*; arriving Toronto, please the Gods, *Wednesday morning*, at 7:35. (I have to stop off for the day, Tuesday, at Montreal, to see the Railway Chiefs about new passes.) I will go up to the Ernescliffe with my luggage, (after a bite of breakfast in the station), then will phone my Beloved at the office, & get right down to see her, — unless she can get out for an hour to come & see me at the Ernescliffe!

Oh, to hold thee to my heart again, my Dear Delight.

I love thee, dear Heart, I love thee, ever more & more.

Thine

•

Charles G.D. Roberts to Constance Davies Woodrow
Ottawa, Ontario
Sunday, January 31, 1926

My Beloved One —
   What a dear, dear comfort it was to get your dear wee note from Montreal. Oh, indeed it was hard for both of us, that farewell. But we had to be wise & kind. That was the first thing to think of! And must be, always!
   How I worried over the fierce wind that was lashing our world when you left! But it was an off-shore wind; and now it has gone quite down & the weather is springlike. So I am trusting that my dear Love may have a fair voyage after all. My prayers & dreams & longings go with her.
   I have no news to tell you, Sweet, — things have seemed to stand still since you left, — but in any case all *news* had better come to you from other sources! This is just to take you my deep & true love, and to tell you that it will not change or weaken in your absence, — of that you must be always sure. Its foundations are too securely laid for any wavering, Beloved!
   In a few days I will write again. I shall hope for a long letter written on the voyage, telling me everything. And Oh, how earnestly I hope & pray that things may go well with you when you reach your family, — and that good fortune may soon, *soon* bring you back to me!
   I love you, dear Heart.
                              Yours

                              ·

Charles G.D. Roberts to Constance Davies Woodrow
Toronto, Ontario
March 9, 1926

Beloved Mine —
   Oh how happy & relieved I was to find thy dear, dear letter awaiting me here on my return from Lennoxville & Stanstead College. I feel once more really in touch with you, dear Heart. Before the letter came, it was like sending my letters & my dreams & desires off into the voids of space. It was comforting to know you had such a warm & loving welcome to the old home. And I am so glad to have all the intimate family details, (however sad some of them are!), because it lets me closer into your life, Beloved. How

deeply pathetic it is to think of the penitence of your poor father, coming only now, so near the end! But what a joy for you & him to be reconciled, in time!

M. came in to see me last night, — & went to the Poetry Society meeting with me. I gave him a good big drink, & it bucked him up wonderfully.

I am so busy & driven my mind is in confusion. I speak in Hamilton (for Applegath) tomorrow night. Back here Friday, — & off Saturday for the West. I will, of course, write my Darling regularly. Back here, I think, first week in May! Oh, No, Beloved, I shall not leave Canada before you return, *never fear*!!! Oh, to hold you close, close, close once more!

And indeed, indeed, I will never stop loving you. How can I? And words cannot tell you how I long for you, & need you.

Can you feel my kisses? Can you feel me hold you to my heart?

Yours

•••

Irving Layton to Sandra Beaudin
Florida
March 2, 1979
age 66

My dear, very beautiful Sandra:

Red ink is so sexy, it makes your radiant self leap from the page. Of course the dazzle makes it difficult for me to read what you have written, so I have to use all my will power to brush your lovely image aside. How's that for openers? I'm trying to imagine your face as you read those lines, how you line up the smile in your eyes with the smile on your lips before you give your royal assent. Which you do, but with such queenly grace that it appears as if you're bestowing compliments rather than receiving them. I admire that trait in you. No doubt there's royal blood flowing in your veins. It wouldn't astound me too much to learn that you're a direct descendant of one of King Solomon's less dusky paramours.

Though Leonard sent a telegram saying he'd write to explain his mysterious phone calls, or should I call them fruitless, his letter hasn't arrived and I don't think it ever will. He has other and better things on his mind, if he's courting a beautiful model. If there's a hole somewhere around, my dear friend is sure to crawl into it. Anyhow, anything that takes him away from Suzanne is a blessing. He needs a long, long rest. Maybe the model will give it to him and heal some of his psychic wounds. Or maybe the experience has knocked some wisdom into his balls and taught him that every beautiful woman is an atomic pile on which the gods have written HANDLE WITH CARE. Unfortunately it's written in invisible ink. I do not suppose you've heard from him. As for his whereabouts, he might be hiding out in a Parisian bidet for all I know. My guess is that he's in Ydra, enjoying the lusts of the spirit and wondering why an erection always heralds their onset.

So you think I fall in love with my mother each time I fall in love with a woman. You wouldn't say that, my lovely Sandra, if you had known my mother. Well, you don't exactly say that. You say I'm carting around an "anima" in my head, an idealized image of the perfect woman. I doubt that. The women whom I have loved are so different from one another that I can't think of them as reflections of the idealized Platonic form that is forever unrealizable in the flesh. I prefer my own theory to Jung's. Love is a form of self-hypnosis and nobody can predict who or what is going to begin the process. One woman waves her bra, another her scent. One woman had me enslaved because of the way she shaped her mouth when she said "Prunes." Another, because she was frail and handicapped, and my vanity was able to sublime compassion into what I thought was love. Life is much more various than analysts and Sufis have ever supposed. I get lost contemplating its fecundity and have given up trying to reduce my bafflement into a theology or a metaphysic, or into any sort of comforting theory.

My screen play is almost done. Just the final scene to be written in but since it's set in a courtroom and is the climax of the story I have to consult with a lawyer to make sure I get the details right. [...] I've written enough new poems since coming here to begin thinking of a successor to DROPPINGS FROM HEAVEN. I'll bring it out in 1980 and I'm thinking of titling it FOR MY NEIGHBOURS IN HELL. So in Toronto, at the meeting with the editors, I'll have to decide which poems finally get slotted for which book. The only thing I've decided so far is to make the former the stronger of the two, a book so finely honed it'll slice the pubic hairs of anyone who gets too close to it.

Sorry to learn that David Solway is in trouble with his college. But, like Leonard, he's not happy unless he's miserable with a worry of one sort or another. If you speak to him, tell him I mentioned him in a cassette I did for sale & distribution by the League of Poets and said he's one of the finest poets around. Which he is. If he can knock the fishhooks outa his head — or perhaps if he doesn't — he'll give all the oldtimers a run for their money. Greece might be the answer to his problems. [...]

Remember me to Bob McGee. I'd like to get to know him better. I hope you're doing your bit to inspire him. Get him mad, inflame him with love or anger. Find out what starts the adrenalin flowing: vanity, lust, moral indignation. Any one or two in combination will make a poet gush geyserlike into all the right places and he's sure to fall in love with the woman who does this to him. But I rattle on.

•••

Steven Ross Smith, 2011
age 66

Rush: Coral Bracho

       existence is binary
full of coincidence
and weather

2 hands, 4 hands, sunblast, thunder,
on / off
2 "I"s clutch, palm on palm
palm on juicy raindrops
duck beneath a gallant cloak, umbrella-arc
duck-dash for door-dark mystery
twist the slippery knob,
this way, that
left, right

step, outside 2 inside 2 inside job's compulsion
in2 the room's towel
on
      off
          rub absence, ruff

acquiescence
find
    fondle, animal
    friction
        1 to 1, 2 to 1
    loosen in the old-new room, tongue
    words uncharge, recharge
    reflect,
        deflect

each makes other
        possible
        bone holds flesh
        flesh 2 flesh
        flesh 2 god
        god 2 beyond
        bond 2 here
        hereness holds 2 tare

        holy-hands mould
        pare,
        pair 2 shape
makers or made?
"I"s come,
hand-led in shadows
blind, all-seeing hands, tip, turn, on, slip
limb-vines
        entwine
2gether
          on/off
       coil/un/coil
       incant

want that can/t-be
       hide/unhide

sill mud-clumped,

bare floor, a foot put there,
imprint bare, arch- and toe-wet
pool, 2
vapour
2 puddle of light

what's 2 be is
being done
undone

•••

Bliss Carman to Margaret Lawrence[5]
Twilight Park, Haines Falls, New York
September 10, 1927
age 66

Good morning, dear person, and thousand thanks for your last letter just here. If you had ever had the very common experience of an attempt to get a halfway prompt letter out of this pen, you would be astonished at the volume and precipitacy (if there is such a word) of all my recent chatter to you on paper. Why is it? Infatuation, of course! A new friendship must have a touch of ecstasy — O good Lord, more than a touch. It isn't worth anything if it hasn't rapture and fondness — which in its original meaning is foolishness. It is just like falling in love, which is all foolishness, as we so well know!

I am ever so grateful for all the self-revealing, and in no wise egotistic, things you say which explain the very *you*. [...] And the more I hear the more delightful and akin you seem. That very modern and truly skeptical mind which cannot be easily fooled is just like my own exactly. [...]

"Perhaps the woman feels the need of love more than the man," you say. Perhaps, I cannot say. I never needed much else. And about the mating business, I don't know the true philosophy of that either. On the physical, evolutionary side it seems to be rather casual and transient. But on the spiritual side it is anything but casual, and the one thing the spirit longs for is permanency in its friendship. The soul is terribly lonely, and cannot understand itself, and so I suppose that is why it so longs for an understanding

---

5 The following letters addressed to Margaret Lawrence are not to the iconic novelist Margaret Laurence, who was an infant at the time of their composition.

companionship. I believe there are those who find in their human lives just such suitable companions as to make them perfectly happy. But this is rare. Blessed are those who find it. It is this mixture of the permanent and the impermanent in every soul that makes such desperate unhappiness for most mortals. [...]

No, dear, I'm not through. But the flaming spirit loves the trail through the wild and rejoices in the miles, forgetting that the willing shape (heroic line or no heroic line) cannot take all the grades in high. Sometimes I run myself down and then have a break, fatigue and nerve-exhaustion, and even a touch of despondency and apprehension. Don't ever let yourself overdo to that point. It is worse than anything. I am all right now. [...]

You *are* very dear. Carman

•

Bliss Carman to Margaret Lawrence
New Canaan, Connecticut
October 7, 1927

Oh, Margaret, I do love you. [...]

First of all though [...] I must tell you how deeply I appreciate all you told me of your own most private life, and of your happy years with our great wise friend. [...] And it never occurred to me to wonder whether the relation was thus and so, or this and that. I only know it was all right, whatever way. [...] The spirit is of no age, and the greatest love is inclusive of all things. I understand so well. When there is disparity of years, it is all so confusing, but really no more confusing than all this incarnation of spirit is. The soul must condescend, to live. And the governance of the creature impulses is the dilemma of humanity. [...] Yet we have our day to day life; that is all we are asked to face at a time; and the door opens as we near the entrance. [...]

I love you dearly, and all I have to say is — whatever you do, don't love any man out of pity for his helplessness. Oh, my Lord! So many do that. The mother instinct. Just because women are so unselfish and must sacrifice themselves. [...]

The blessing of Allah and the Great Ones be with you, loving and beloved.

Ever, C.

•

Bliss Carman to Margaret Lawrence
New Canaan, Connecticut
October 13, 1927

Margaret dearest: "Poets need to write love letters," say you! Indeed it seems so. [...] Well, my dear, I have a very delightful letter to greet my returning. And I want to say at once that I am sure much of these hurried scratches and dashed-off dashes of mine should not be too gravely considered when they seem critical or didactic. Truth is I am the least censorious person imaginable. Though I often splutter quite violently and have far too quick a temper, I am very tolerant, and never voluntarily criticize others or offer advice. I seldom analyze, for in the first place I have no ability for it, and then I don't care. I have not the least innate wish to reform people or things, nor to see people grow. Too indifferent for that. [...] So never mind what I say [...] about history. [...] It is only splutter. [...]

As to the matter of incarnation — or "nations" — how should I know? As I understand the Theosophs, they say the spirit incarnates in order to redeem the animal being with which it manifests itself, or is associated. And that every time we behave in a low-down manner, or do what we are ashamed of, the spirit is crucified afresh. But whose fault is that? Certain it is that our chief task is in keeping the spirit supreme, and not giving way to our less admirable impulses. But I am not at all sure that this dualistic notion is true. I am very convinced that the *most* important thing is to *harmonize* ourselves, to think and act as a unity, to spiritualize the physical, and embody the spiritual in daily life and doing, and never to divorce body from soul, nor either one from reason (or mind). [...] To do, or say, or think anything which our inmost spirit (commonly called conscience) does not approve — that is evil. [...] I also think that evil probably works itself out, and does not persist eternally, being due to our mistakes and ignorance of the law, and not in harmony with the Goodness which is the prime cause. [...]

Now I have a great and untarnished happiness in your friendship and caring. [...] And I never have the least impulse to be other than unselfish with you [...] and to enjoy a clear glad companionship. This is almost all there is of love, except its mystic (slightly insane) side, when it becomes a possession and carries one away body and mind! A dangerous whirlpool, which ought to be marked "Danger!" but isn't.

I promise not to philosophize any more, until the next time.

Lovingly ever, C.

•

Bliss Carman to Margaret Lawrence
Twilight Park, Haines Falls, New York
July 11, 1928

Darling Margaret: Here is a glorious mountain morning, dry sweet light, cool-warm air in my heavenly Catskills. [...]

Thanks for the reviews which I am delighted to see. [...] I see Pierce's picture in the clipping too. Good old L.P. But for God Almighty's sake don't let him have any of my letters! He is like all biographers and collectors, consumed with an unholy lust of acquisitiveness. Their greed is voracious. Don't let the wolf in the door. He would gobble us up hide and hair. Lord, it's too much this peeking and keyholing and gumshoeing. Damned if I like it. I propose to *live* my biography first. [...]

A job or a husband! For the love of the dear Lord, Margaret, don't say it! Husbands! But NO! NOT! Husbands are awful things. There are men, women, and husbands. [...] They are a domestic pest and a public nuisance. Dull, thick, ignorant, and pestiferous. Kiss me on the brow in fond farewell when you commit husbandry. O horrible! All the honeymoon you will, but no wedding march! [...]

Now Margaret, sweet dear, how is this for a letter? Piffle. [...] If I can gabble away like this, I should think I might do my own biography! Ha, ha! Te-he! Not on your life. [...]

All at present from your truly loving and horribly far off C.

•••

Dave Margoshes, 2009
age 67

Polar exploration
for dee

Peary at his pole, Byrd at his,
me as far as I can go with you,
Hillary at the top of the world,
the lush valleys of Nepal falling below.

You come to the end of something
only to find you've been there before,
the footprints you've been following
your own. You circle around like a dog
intent on picking up its own trail,
a scent both familiar and frightening.
Like Peary, like Hillary, we go to extremes
to find comforts that elude us at home,
only to discover there is no comfort
beyond the idea of home, something
we carry with us. Byrd went north,
then south, the centre always one step
ahead, wondering how far
he could go, as I might struggle
to find a peace which lies within you,
within my grasp.

                    St. Peter's Abbey, Muenster, SK

                          •••

Earle Birney to Esther Birney
Saturday Night, August 21, 1971
age 67

esther dear
     how's my little wandervögeln? i guess you'll be back in london by now or
anyway when you get this   no great news from our fambly   everything
fine with marsha,bill,chris(walking almost as much as crawling now)
you'll have got a letter from her by now anyway
     i'm making steadier progress with the book now   about half way
thru, i think   still get interruptions. mail that has to be answered, people,
etc.   today sophie knocked with a letter from george to me   asking me
to read something he'd written(it was enclosed) & come & talk about it over
a drink   so i'll have to go in tomorrow   nice of them   phone
calls to me from seymour mayne, judy   copithorne, etc. but i put them off
     letter from rita   she back in toronto,at the treehouse,& loving being back
they wont come out to vanc. this summer (just as well, for me & my work)

i been lovin your cards, not to speak of yr letter of the 8th with chart of Hotel Grenzwald etc   i'm happy youve been happy & i hope the trip has continued to be just as good, and will, till you get back

did you get my birthday card, & notes to h.grenzwald?

hope you had a good birthday party somewhere — dear

hope also you are getting time and energy now to contact old friends Has the charter company agreed to let you stay longer?

i do hope you did as i advised and took your travellers cheques in British pounds when you went to europe   so you wont have suffered from the slump of the american dollar   i feel very clever that i saw it coming,but not as clever as i wish i had been,since i didnt buy pounds and make a lot of money

ive been several times over to the fambly's ,working on the garden, & getting a good mess of marsha's chow

heard from gabie that her son,bill(used to be called zuki)drove, into a car parked on a highway and is in hospital with a broken femur,facial injuries,shock   even worse news from another old friend, bet cox, who has had her womb removed to stop a cancer,which may be stopped she has come out to a cottage up at Sechelt to recuperate   i went up to see her   she's in a frail state and it's hard to know

you keep well,have fun, stay as long as you're having more of it there than you would back here   but it's getting pretty silent around here without you

        love to all, especially to you
        earle

•••

Louis Dudek, 1986
age 68

Love Words

Smoke-rings of aroma
twirl about the flesh —
the extensions of you.
The treacle tones of fiddles
like wine from fingers

explode along the scales —
as if seeing you, I heard!
A bubble bath
punctuating my body
with clean-coloured wishes;
a feathered bird
with a ruffled crown
of rainbows and winds —
images of your frail vanities.
I fall down stairways wondering
how love is a box of stars,
and how your words live in the air
like agates in a dream.
The image of your face
lights up my memory,
and the gods grin at a stumbling mortal
knocking about on feet of clay,
with a heart of amber.

•••

Henry Rappaport, 2012
age 68

Make Dead

Make dead the light
and lie with me
to touch and hear
in the dark song
we sing
how longing
sweetens sleep.

Touch the dark shore
I am for you.
In the morning

like the light,
for me, make
dead the night.

•••

Duncan Campbell Scott to Miss Elise Aylen
from Victoria, BC to 274 O'Connor St., Ottawa Ontario
Canadian Pacific Railway Company's Telegraph
Nov. 23, 1930
age 68

Arrived here saturday morning after a busy time in vancouver the minister left last night and I intend to be here until thursday and take a holiday posted a letter this evening the weather is fine and I feel rested and much better I send you all the messages you know by heart.
                         Duncan.

•

Duncan Campbell Scott to Elise Aylen
1930

DEAREST:
     WRITE DISTINCTLY, YOU COMMANDED, SO THE ONLY THING TO DO IS TO PRINT THE LOVE LETTER AS I HAVE NO TYPEWRITER WITH ME. ENOUGH OF FOOLING I THINK YOU Don't like my nonsense. I insert this apothegm "one charm of a written letter is the difficulty of reading it." Besides you will have the writer to expound any obscure passages and clear up all illegibility — that is one comforting thought that I will be soon again within easy reach of my Little Darling able to hear her voice feel her lips look into her clear eyes & know again for the hundredth time how much all that dear girl means to my happiness and & how much I love her. I realize that as I write this 400 miles away on a rainy good Friday, realize it by lonesomeness and a desperate feeling that I should like to fly away north. The white birches are stationed as usual on the hill. Just birds sing, but there are no thrushes to say "Elise" amongst the leaves or the shadows; so my heart has to say it even more sweetly than the birds,

for they were quite unconscious of the memory of beauty called up by their voices but when my heart repeats it over & over I can see the dear eyes as perfectly matched, & the eyebrows with nearly the same number of hairs in each & the sweet face so full of tenderness & the love of beautiful things. At this distance I can think of myself as the guardian & conservator of this delicate charmer one whose duty it is to love, to admire, to draw forth all the latent beauty of some body & to record it somehow somewhere. But even as I think, as this perfect Knight & his ideal, my rebel senses become confused & I begin to think of other troublesome things; learning and intellect go for naught and I say with the Monk who was also a Painter "all the Latin" no, it begins "Flower 'o the clove; all the Latin I can find is Amo I love." Well Browning knew a thing or two about Life & Love. My memory being defective & no Browning at hand. I cannot match your Chaucer quotation with a Browning — O, yes I can! — "Why not witness, calmly gazing, that Earth holds naught, speak Truth, about her- naught above this tress & this I touch but cannot praise I love so much. Where are your tresses? One must alter the lines

Naught like this dear cropped head I touch

&c&c

I read your several letters on mountains. You know I can never want for anything. I must have what I want when I want it so wanting to know what was inside your envelope I opened it the moment the prohibition was removed. I am obedient as well as impatient. too obedient I think. Fancy my being commanded & controlled by a mere child! Your short note was almost memorized before reaching me & the failure of this letter if it be a failure is because I hadn't with me the packet of <u>model</u> love letters. This does not conform to the model but it is just as full of love as any of yours — As this is almost my first love letter. I don't mean my first to you but <u>really</u> my first I feel as if I am not doing badly. I have cultivated reticence too long & I am so perfect in that kind that it does not come easily for me to speak my strongest, most secret feelings on this blue page, so when I write I love you dear Elise I feel all the restraint back of it and the confession is or seems to me richer than if I could give myself up to repetitions. It is like a flower that grows out of the rock, the granite is proud of it and you, even you, who pluck it may find some greater beauty in it because it found difficulty in blooming but you tame it root & all — this may be obscure but there is something in the idea. If I (as you say) give you the companionship that you have lacked. What Joy! For I truly believe that your heart and mind are worthy of all devotion so I give myself to that destiny in all simplicity. I have not opened the parcel — when does Easter begin? At 12:01 Sunday morning? What obedience. What self control! Although I post this Friday I'm afraid you won't get it until Monday as there is no afternoon delivery on Sat.

Now I fold you in my heart & cherish you there with all the love you can wish for

Yours devotedly
Duncan

•••

Elizabeth Greene, 2011
age 68

Per Aspera ad Astra

When I first saw Saul Steinberg's cartoon,
his roadmap *per aspera ad astra*
I thought it travel enough
for a lifetime. Even in my teens
I understood the easy travel between Lex,
Pax, Lux, Pulchram, Sanitas — fifteen minutes,
half an hour's drive over straight roads
starting from Prosperitas, the norm in 1958.
But once bitten by divine discontent, seekers
leave all that behind, trek north, over roads
increasingly remote, uncertain, whited out
with sand or snow.
                    Caritas is close
enough, the road still paved and straight.
The next town, Labor, sits by a lake or swamp —
a detour, as is Amor, on an island —
that's where we met — you working —
I lost, derailed, enswamped.

You were scared — love *is* a byway — the stars far off
and farther to the East. The road twists insanely
through Mediocritas — no one wants to stay there, but
it's on the way, more loops and curves, through Veritas, Timor
   Dei —
we've both known those — both spent time in remote Aspera.

Why didn't you take my hand — travel with me
footsore in our dusty boots?
Together, we might have found that unmarked path to Astra.
You're miles away, and I don't know if I can reach
those far stars on my own.

•••

Earle Birney to Esther Birney
August 13, 1973
age 69

Esther dear,
   i think of you often and often, & more so this week as your birthday
approaches/ you will be a very young 65 & i pray you are keeping good
health & will do so for many years yet   & I hope they are happier years
for you than many of them have been for you when living with me — but
as for myself it is happy things i remember about you & our life together
the first birthday of yours i think we were together was in '35 in ampton
st....was it the time of the British election?& the italians were taking over
ethiopia, & grant & frost had arrived, & hans & max were with us   i
remember the good nights (was our bed a mattress on the floor?) & one
night when you held me tight a long time when my nerves were bad...i guess
the next august you were in mrs. macphail's house & you were the one whose
nerves had struck & you were miserable, poor girl, but you were still putting
up a cheerful front and giving me your love and concern   the next year
we must have spent your birthday at the house we rented off Sasamat, with
probably a dinner at my mother's, just before we set off back to toronto
the next august 19 would be in new jersey — we had our troubles that month
too, you going in to the psychiatrist in washington square, me with that long

bout of poison ivy, but i remember the good cheer when the schadhtmans & the hilton moores came out weekends & we played croquet where i'd sickled the long grass, & you were the lively cheerful outgoing hostess, as you have always been / in '39 we spent august in toronto, with the shadows of the war closing around us — i remember (or am i wrong?) that we had moved into 40 hazelton, & you had a social work job or were you just graduating   & i was thick into the trotskyite preparations to go "underground"   so many augusts to remember   but all with happy things   because for all our dissension & quarrels & partings i truly believe that we have had times as intensely happy together as people can have   & so it's not possible to think of you without love and loving concern & to have the need to send you my old, inadequate but very real, love on your birthday/i hope it is a happy one with bill and marsha & the family   give them all my love...i will write them in a few days, when i know what my new address is going to be   thank you dear for sending on my mail,   i will try to make a clean sweep of address-changes when i find a new flat (the lease on this one is not renewable after august 31) & i'll drop alan crawley a line   i would have written many people before now but i haven't been well lately   — just a bout of stomach flu   which is over now, but it went on for nearly 2 weeks i hope you are avoiding all such bugs

   spend the enclosed on <u>yourself</u>, please dear
                        earle

                        •

Earle Birney to Esther Birney
September 22, 1973

   esther dear   your lovely letter has made my days much happier   it makes me feel i can write you again without reserve   i do understand dear that you had to write honestly, and that is how i want you to write so that i too may do the same   i too "do not feel changed in any fundamental way towards you"   what rejections we have given each other have come out of the necessity to be ourselves, i think and feel   i have never <u>wanted</u> you to be lonely or feel rejected or hurt, nor have you wanted to cause any such feelings in me   but i too came to the place where i had to choose separation from you in order to have enough of the kind of living i wanted, to stay alive at all   one pays for everything, and i pay daily in sad concern for you in your loneliness, and for the loss of the thousand little affections and closeness we had in our daily living, in those times when, as you say, we did achieve "a reasonable and tender atmosphere"   believe me i long to see you, hear your voice, share daily things as we did   but i would be a worse person than i am if i led you to think that my plan is to ask you to take me back in the foreseeable future   i have the kind of happiness i lacked and had grown desperate for — and i have the new responsibilities that go with it but i think i am again a well enough person and i hope a big enough one to feel that my responsibilities to you have not really lessened   i would never want to lie seriously ill or hurt or in deep spiritual misery without feeling that i could call on you for comfort   and i earnestly hope you will always feel the same about reaching out to me

as for the things of money, i feel you are reasonably provided for, but i think it would be best if Bill continued to pay you the monthly instalments on the loan for his house [...]

and i want to write you a longer letter later this week   i rush this off to tell you how grateful and loving i feel towards you still, my dear one   39 years of loving you even in my unsatisfactory way, will always stand central in my life, as i know it will in yours — it has been an achievement we should not ever depreciate   i wish that it could have gone on, but nothing ever goes on the same   i had begun to fear we would lose all love for each other and now i dont deserve that any should remain on your side   but i am glad, most grateful, most happy that you still have some love for me, as i always for you

earle

•••

Irving Layton to Harriet Bernstein
January 15, 1982
age 69

My dear Gypsy Jo:

Passion was my crime. I loved you deeply. Adored you. Read over the poems I wrote for you, poems of great affection and tenderness. Now, poems of hate and despair. Two sides of the same man, inextricably linked. I loved you and Samantha and thought I'd have you with me for the remainder of my life. It didn't turn out that way. I can understand your turning against your husband and even against the love you spent so many blissful days & nights with in Italy, St. Lucia, etc. But to turn against the poet? You... Gypsy Jo...Flower child...? Yes, I've ranted and raved and written some silly letters, but nobody ever hurt me as you have hurt me. Is it impossible for you to understand my anguish and bewilderment? Can't you at least try? O Harriet, it didn't have to end so stupidly. Our beautiful romance deserved a better ending.

Migod, madness & blackness come when I think I can't see my little girl. Where's your heart, Harriet? How can you do this to a man who loved you as greatly as I did and showed his commitment to our marriage in every way he could. The evidence is all there before you and can only be ignored through malice and vindictiveness. Why did you ignore and rebuff every single move I made towards amity & friendship — letters, phone calls.

I promise you — when I get the Nobel Prize, our daughter will receive an equal share with my other children.

•

Irving Layton to Harriet Bernstein
January 18, 1982

My dear Harriet:
What terrible things did I do to you to make you want to treat me like a leper? That I loved and doted on you for nearly seven years? That I gave you a beautiful, intelligent child three years ahead of the agreed-upon schedule? That I wrote some of the most perfect lyrics to and about you, expressing my love and devotion? That at my age I trusted you sufficiently to invest all my life savings in a marriage which you had given me every reason to hope would last longer than the two years it did? I deeply regret my love and devotion didn't come through, that I didn't fulfill all your needs, but were these sufficient reasons for heaping the abuse & humiliation upon me that you and your parents did? Did I really deserve that?

If I wasn't a poet I'd have really gone off my mind and lapsed into the silence that A.M. Klein fell into, so great was my pain and bewilderment. For I loved you with all my heart and soul. I don't suppose I can get you to believe that, nevertheless it happens to be the plain truth. The pain has eased considerably because that love has died in me and because I know there's no chance of reconciliation and I must get you out of my mind and memory. The road to get to where I am now has been long, hard and nightmarish. But I assure you that I'm once again the man you fell in love with, only much handsomer because I've lost weight and much humbler because of the devastating experience our separation has put me through. I hope to put that experience to very good use and I have some wonderful creative plans for the future.

Don't you think the time has come to put aside bitterness and recrimination and face the fact that you and I are the parents of Samantha and that whether we like it or not there's a bond that cannot be ruptured or put aside. Wouldn't amity make greater sense than hate or hostility? Don't you see that your denying me access to Samantha is what has disordered my emotions, is disordering them? Don't you see the injustice and vindictiveness in your behaviour? And that all that pain and bewilderment are unnecessary? That the pain can be lightened if we both share it? Do you really wish to make me spend additional dollars to secure a court action? Do you? I shall phone you next week for your answer, Harriet. Please consult your heart and the memory you have of me as your ravished lover in St. Lucia and Italy.

•••

Linda Rogers
2014
age 70

Anniversary Letter to the Passerine Who

1. Found Me

I say:

My mother said all humans come
from animal species, so, one night
that was twice as long, I looked up

Class: Aves
Species: Human

Maybe we imagine everything — even touch.
Yo tengo — a partner for slow dancing
across the firmament. When I was a child,
I lay awake, my left hand dreaming, the way
the Fauvist painter, Matisse, used chalk
on a stick to draw cartoons on the ceiling.
I saw crows, I drew you, the shadow outline
of you, on the windows, when I was alone

and afraid.

And later, in the morning, when I
erased your breath, your reflection,
so no one would guess what went on
in my room at night, the windows

laughed, vibrating strings,
all treble clef, your 'hood.

This is possession; isn't
it the corvid that flies
in and out, changes our
intonation? Trickster!

You say:

2. In The Dark

I say:

You were in a movie-hold the
night we met, with a cardboard

cut-out of Cher, mum of Chastity,
the shape-changer. Funny, the
film was *Dangerous Liaisons,*
but I wasn't afraid, not at all.

I'd come with a frog on a leash
and watched him swallow his
skin at the candy counter,
then turn himself inside out,
into crow, and then into you,

in a tango frame with the shape-changer's mother.

You told me the sound of popcorn
popping reminded you of catching
hail in a saucepan, the reason you
play mandolin; and your favourite
music was *Mysterious Barricades*
by Couperin, also French, and I
thought you meant The Revolution,
not iron underpants. Chastity? Bad
idea. I was living vicariously, living
with poetry. Imagine, now we have
the metaphor, women pleasured
while reading, *Hysterical Literature.*

O, everything captured in perfect circles:
orgasm, laughter, wedding rings, round
midnights that always turn into morning.

Another joke; soon I would learn everything
I'd need to know about harmonic suspension.

You say:

3. Again

I say:

This dance lasts forever:
the solstice, the crows
in the attic, imitating
our intonation, snoring,

dreaming in our world, *apilado,*
abrazo cerrado, your chest hair
grazing my nipples all night long,
makes me laugh, makes me sneeze
esposo, even when I'm running
with wolves haunting my sleep.

One night you played the *Masochism Tango,*
by Lehrer, and I whipped you, burned your
arms with cigarettes, and bruised your shins;
but still you laughed, and crow laughed too.

El eje, volcado, you never lose your centre
of balance, do you? Every morning you
make coffee with perfect crema; except
on Sunday, you add bacon sandwiches.

You say:

da/dum da/dum dadada/dum

4. And Again

I say:

Again! the child commands,
when the story ends well.

She loves to sit on the roof
and visit the birds with us.

This is our season of unrelenting
vigilance. Now we are nurse-logs
watching the sky fall, smelling of
compost and incontinence. We
wait in the rain, our perfumed
bath, dressed for redemption —
you in your red sweater and me
in feathers chosen from my closet
full of negligees — and sleep with
the crows, our eyes open, soldiers
on sentry duty, expecting ghosts,
Valkyries: maybe the Sultanahmet
spice merchant who left saffron
handprints on my dress or the tango
instructor who raptured up when
I shamed his *paradas* with my
calfskin soles. *Who will come for*
us when the morphine kicks in?

Neither of us expects the child.

We make a deal: just one last *gancho*,
the hook, and two *lustradas* before we leave.
I will polish my shoes on your shins.

We must be in love with death already.
Imagine, the feature's about to roll.
Your wings are trembling in the red
sweater as you remind yourself, *don't*
play the wrong notes, your credo, and
your heart tumbles like roller pigeons,
the good news angels we finally met
on the mountain near Kas, in London,
Havana and Goreme, and on the roof
of the old brothel in San Francisco,

and I, still breathing, my left hand
dreaming, hope you'll remember
the top note of me, the Pheromone
that made you sneeze, and find me

again, as the child insists, in the movie dark.

You say: da capo!

• • •

Richard Outram
2001
age 71

Late Love Poem

Well. Here we are. Where we have always been,
of course; and sometimes recognized as such.
I wonder that the cosmos can survive
the theme and variation of your touch.

Well, there you go, where we have never gone:
of course, but something understood at last.
I doubt that even God remembers, Dear,
the paths that we have scrambled in the past.

Well this is it. At least we think it is,
or may have been, or may be at the close
of any narrative of passion and reprieve.
My God you are redemptive in repose!

Well. Just as well. The others never got
beyond the starting gate; and if they won
the velvet pisspot, with rosette, so what?
By God Sweetheart you always jumped the gun!

Well that is that. Finito. QED.
Wrapped up in greaseproof paper. That's show biz:
"Styx nix hix pix." Okay, I know it ain't
all over till it's over. Then it is.

Well, what the Hell. Or Heaven. Which is where
we came in Love and which is where we leave.
Earth to earth, the sure and certain earth,
earth Incorruptible. I shall not grieve.

...

Earle Birney to Wailan Low
August 4, 1976
age 72

dear love, dear wife, dear soul of me
    i cant tell you all over again how miserable i feel without you & why
should i make you miserable talking about it   our letters to each other have
already said it all so many times   I wont repeat my loneliness   you know
how i feel — you had two wretched months of living alone here   & there
were the days — 3 years & more ago — when you were in toronto or in victoria & i in vancouver   it's better when one has to cope with other people
yesterday was o.k. because i worked right through till 7:30 p.m. before bobbie came for me — he'd been delayed at the office — & it was good to relax
with him & rita, & listen to rita's account of her Group — she believes the
month there this summer has changed her radically   it's possible — she
is much aware for the first time that she had been deliberately avoiding
ordinary skills (e.g. driving a car) out of dependency patterns formed in
childhood — more about that when you come back
            when you come back...the phrase is with me all the time   life
inside me is suspended till then   but outwardly I can't complain   Sunday

dinner at the jensens, mondays at maria's, tuesday's at the allens — tomorrow (thurs) the allens will pick me up & go with me to johnny rock's girl's place for dinner & fri. the laytons will pick me up in the evening to go to a party marta kurc is throwing   she phoned me today to invite me & said she'd taken a week off, accumulated leave or something, just to relax in town & see the people she wanted to see   she told me the laytons were coming & that irving had got back "at three a.m. this morning"   i asked if he had phoned her at that time but she said no no it was aviva who told her   so a little while later aviva phoned to thank me for the <u>Rugging</u> & i asked her how Irving liked his trip now that he was back   she was astounded i knew he was back so i said i had my spies out everywhere & didnt need to leave my balliol eyrie to keep tab on cdn letters & that i even knew he had arrived at 3 this morning   this really took her breath away till i told her marta had been phoning me   whereupon she offered a ride to marta's with irving & her   she also indicated things were still dicey between them   more from the gossip centre at 2201 when next i write…aviva was really ecstatic about the "6 for lan"

    & today's mail brought a surprise letter from al the purdy: "the Six for Lan are the best love poems i've ever seen of yours. As if some bars to being personal had dissolved in yourself, & I think you have had such bars. But these, now, are lovely & delicate, they care about what they say. I am struck by the differences between my own love poems & yours. I am wildly romantic, at least to myself; but you are delicate and tender, with an overlooking sort of love. See you on the 16th." The last is because he thought he was coming up on the 9th & i invited him to stay with me & he accepted. Now he's assuming it's O.K. for the 16th, damnit. I'll have to write & tell him that's the day you arrive back & he'll have to smoke on the porch I'd rather tell him not to come at all but i just cant, he'd be offended — darling we'll have our reunion nevertheless & i'll be at the airport alone & we'll have our bedrooms (i'm sleeping in yours every night — it's the nearest i can get to you just now)

    al also thinks the Shotgun Marriage piece is a wonderful found poem

    an autograph hunter in rockland, ont., sends me a newspaper photo of me with desmond pacey, to autograph   well, he cant send it to poor old des now

    & a letter from jamie Hamilton with a first mock-up of a book of my visuals — he's willing to approach McStew for rights to 7 they've printed, & has 13 others of mine, but wants to use 32 pages, so needs more   maybe i can do it

what wonderful big red radishes you found for me   & so much good food every moment in this home of ours i am aware of your thoughtful loving care and devotion   how have i ever deserved you? is it evil of me to hold you away from your own generation like this?

i love you

•

Earle Birney to Wailan Low
Sunday morning, August 8, 1976
The Round Table Steak House and Tavern, Ontario

dear loving Spirit   you are so far away in the flesh & yet so close in my heart that i feel you as Spirit   the Ghost of my best, numbed self   numbed by your absence, the cold dark rains outside, the silence & solitude inside, & in me   it's Sunday morning   sunless, made for staying in our big bed & making love or just lying talking & loving   no one to make pancakes for, so i make porridge & find it insipid...i turn on the hi-fi & the beautiful music disturbs me because there's no You to share it with   the tv has Uriah-Heep-preachers   i resent the African violets for blooming so much when you, their Benefactress, is away   i water the plants & turn them & wash up my dishes & fail to get interested in a book   & so there's nothing left but to work   even writing you is wrong because i'm depressed & my letter might depress you   o well there's always Work, or more precise, there's always Letters to Answer   here goes   (self-pity, that's all that's wrong with me)   i've not seen or spoken to another being since friday night   but only because i turned down an invitation from the Lamperts to go over there Sat nite for their annual summer-session-poet-teacher lawn-house party p.k.page was coming, but also that vicious creep, andreas Schroeder   so i stayed in the flat-(- i almost said "stayed home" but it's not a home when you arent in it) & finished a tangled job of deciding the content &the right versions of various visuals & audiovisuals for jamie hamilton's edition   he wants to put out at least 32 pages of text & is willing to include some stuff in the McStew domain if they'll make the price easy   on Monday i'll see what i can do via Lorene meantime   he'll have all my proposals, choices, etc
    i feel guilty so often when i think how little real fun, shows, concerts, we have taken together, all my fault, my lethargy &self-indulgence to my stupid leg — darling, let's go to the shows & places you want to see, these last

two precious weeks before Skool (by the way the TTC busdrivers etc are probably going to strike on August 30 — the union explains they chose the date because "it wouldn't affect the CNE, which will have finished" — they admit that the strike will make it awkward for school & college openings (but the t.u. officials, of course, dont go to school any more) it's already too late for us to subscribe to the Cdn Opera (Sep-Oct) when you come back i'll try for seats to whichever opera you most want (choice of La Boheme, Tosca, Die Walkure, & an Offenbach—Grand Duch. of Gerolstein) & there's Stratford

...the more that astronomers find out about the rest of creation, the more difficult it is to regard the importance of "future" unless i'm to give up a lifelong materialism & start believing in personal immortality, that sort of a Soul, i must be content with the sort of immortality that persists, for a few years, in the memories of others after my death & this is not a thought to bring contentment i would have done so little, considering the talents i was born with & i have done so much i would undo, i have failed so many people, failed my own best self, through most of my life & now, in my seventies, has come the greatest gift life ever brought me, the gift of you & i must not fail with you i mean this not just for my own vanity, my own wish to be well remembered no, much more, it is my knowledge, my sensing, of a greatness in you that i must help to blossom & fruit & joy in and for you & for all whom you share life with i could not possibly have held you to me this long, could not even have gained your love for a day, if there wernt something truly extraordinary in you, insight, independence, daring, sensitivity, enormous capacity to love, & beyond even that wonderful rare thing, a capacity to grow, endure, keep faith with ideals, — these are the virtues of "social" greatness / i really mean this, my love & that is mainly why i am so desperately anxious to make my loving <u>help</u>

the friday night party at marta's had a mixed bag: bill french the columnist & his wife, larry ritchie & ditto, sylvia fraser, the laytons (who brought me & took me home), one of the massey girls, & a dozen others vaguely familiar from other publisher parties her apt. is on Bathurst just above St. Clair nr the ravine surprisingly rural feeling looking from her balcony a very tiny balcony where i spent most of the time because it was the only place where i didnt get choked up & headachy from the otherwise universal cigarette-smoking i looked out at the moon & thought of you & rested my

leg & people would drift out to look at me & i'd send them away if they were
smoking   irving came out & we talked a lot   i'll post this off now
                         with all my love, dear peanut

                                   •••

Leonard Cohen, 2006
age 72

The Mist of Pornography

when you rose out of the mist
of pornography
with your talk of marriage
and orgies
I was a mere boy
of fifty-seven
trying to make a fast buck
in the slow lane

it was ten years too late
but I finally got
the most beautiful girl
on the religious left
to go with her lips
to the sunless place

the art of song
was in my bones
the coffee died for me
I never answered
any phone calls
and I said a prayer
for whoever called
and didn't leave a message

this was my life
in Los Angeles
when you slowly
removed your yellow sweater
and I slobbered over
your boyish haunches
and I tried to be
a husband
to your dark and motherly
intentions

I thank you
for the ponderous songs
I brought to completion
instead of ----ing you
more often
and the hours you allowed me
on a black meditation mat
intriguing with my failed
aristocratic pedigree
to overthrow vulgarity
and set America straight
with the barbed wire
and the regular beatings
of rhyme

and now that we are gone
I have a thousand years
to tell you how I rise
on everything that rises
how I became that lover
whom you wanted
who has no other life
but your beauty
who is naked and bent

under the quotas of your desire
I have a thousand years
to be your twin
the loving mirrored one
who was born with you

I'm free at last
to trick you into posing
for my Polaroid
while you inflame
my hearing aid
with your vigorous obscenities

your panic cannot hurry me here
and my panic and my falling
shoulders
our shameless lives
are the grains
scattered for an offering
before the staggering heights
of our love
and the other side of your anxiety
is a hammock of sweat
and moaning
and generations of the butterfly
mate and fall
as we undo the differences
and time comes down
like the smallest pet of G-d
to lick our fingers
as we sleep
in the tangle
of straps and bracelets

and Oh the sweetness of first nights
and twenty-third nights
and nights

after death and bitterness
sweetness of this very morning
the bees slamming into the broken hollyhocks
and the impeccable order
of the objects on the table
the weightless irrelevance
of all our old intentions
as we undo
as we undo
every difference

•••

Anne Marriott, 1985
age 73

July 9

The bed is narrow.
I lie
half sad
half happy hearing sea.
All my life
blood has rushed saltily through my veins
like sounds of water.
I learned currents early, wind directions
legends of rocks and sandbanks
tightening weeds, whales' deaths
and fiercer deaths of ships.
(You listened once against my ear
heard the ocean in its shell.)

The sea that bars me from you
binds me to you
with every rustle and drop.

•••

Earle Birney to Wailan Low
August 23, 1979
age 75

dearest love i am writing you letters all the time in my head as i shuffle about this apartment (trying to turn it again into our home) & then i sit at this machine & words leave me because there are so many needed to say how much i love you

& no time to say the right ones

& because the right ones are hands & arms around you

so i leave the typewriter & make myself some postum

& the letters start writing in the skull again, full of self-reproach because i am not really writing them & sending them off to you

while you, so much more articulate, really, so much more the poet than i am, your letters come breathing your warmth and love on me, this undeserving wretch

what have i been doing that's so more important than writing you? nothing, of course   the day you left i got my mailsack, as i told you, & opened letters & took laundry & drycleaning out, & took cheques into the bank, & came back & started unpacking, & had diner at the Allens...sat. morning early, more unpacking (hunting for the right files needed to answer some of the letters) & then a giant shopping spree at the Market with Bobbie & elsewhere, & phoning friends & more unpacking, & cooking

sunday, cleaning, unpacking, Jack in for "tea" in aft., in evening dashing off replies to urgent letters

monday, phoning publishers, unpacking & sorting books, files, clothing, etc. till supper time when i went by arrangement to Jack's to have dinner with him & his girl-friend-from-Oxbow-Sask. i was feeling very tired & lowspirited, but jack's cheerfulness & a scotch brought me out of it — the girl, whose name i cant remember (last name Wigmore?) was late so by the time she came we all needed another scotch   then off to a new restaurant — Greek — at Church & Esplanade   spacious, with excellent food at medium(?)prices-i had calamari, largish ones, stuffed with chestnut & wild rice — fantastic — ($8.50)   Jack, who was insisting on paying for everything, a "welcome home" to me, ordered a bottle of very tasty, slightly retsinish, white wine — & then a second bottle   i skipped desert but was persuaded into an ouzo   i was in an emotional muddle, enjoying the company, the food, the wine — & aching with longing for you, thinking how much you would have enjoyed it, trying to keep lively in spite of the sense of "bereavement" — so i had two ouzos & got "home" at eleven to the chaos in the silent flat & to the realization i was drunk something ive never really been since the heart attack — ive been high, but not soused — i was shocked & alarmed at myself & flopped around shoving orange juice down my stupid gullet, & sank on the bed into 8 hrs of oblivion

all monday morning i had the feeling my bones were melting, while my head had petrified by noon, happily, i was well enough to be picked up by robin & driven out ot the King City farm & be restored by a fine lunch Eleane gave us — after that, robin & i put in four solid hours on the Album, then i inspected their garden (much plagued by bugs this year — a grasshopper landed in my beard — wonder what he thought i was) & then they and dorothy-anne drove me down to Angelina's on Avenue Road for supper / this time i avoided all alcohol & resisted the tempting gourmet items for a little plain fare   what an eater robin is! he must have one of those metabolisms that burns up all fats and sugars!   dorothy-anne is a smouldering seventeen-year-old sex queen all legs & breasts & big waiting eyes   she is going off to Queens to take PhizzEd & live in residence   she had come down from the Northern Ont cottage to play in her school's tennis tournament — robin had had to come down because Nexus had a 2-day engagement at the CNE / i gathered they had been paid very handsome performers' fees but that the concert conditions were godawful—they were programmed between a clown act for children, & a circus band & MC-ed by Uncle Bobbie!

i got home at 9, hoping you would phone, but flopped to sleep by eleven the next day, i.e. yesterday, i worked on correspondence & unpacking from about 5 a.m. till noon, when Sue Bone phoned to say she had her pictures of us so i invited her for lunch (toasted cheese, etc) i was surprised & happy with her pictures, especially on the ones with you and me together there is one with me looking absentmindedly down at my feet while you are looking away from me with a most wonderful patient happy loving laughing face / & one where you have somehow wriggled out from under my armpit, a happy mouse beside by an enormous sheep-man   & there is a beautiful [one of] You framed in petunias, looking out to me eyes speaking tenderness and the love and devotion you have given me these many wonderful years, beyond all possible deserving…sue is having some prints made for herself and then mailing me the sheet of negatives   so that we can blow up any we want to   she is moving now to Halifax to live there again   later yesterday, after Sue left, Sharon came   she thinks the photos are lovely too   we went for a swim & i made some supper of sorts   & we talked a lot about Reuben & about her trip   Reuben insisted on paying for everything in London, & took them to shows, posh restaurants, boat trips to Greenwich & Hampton Court & Kew   today she flies off with him for a weekend in Washington, then home to Winnipeg for a week   he is still madly in love with her & though he is now willing to live with her without marriage, she feels his hope is that once she starts living with him she will want to marry him   she thinks it may work contrary but she also values his good qualities & i think is still unsure whether those qualities are enough to make such a marriage last happily for both

   & now it's Thurs. noon, & ive been phoning Lorene Wilson, & house-keeping, & unpacking books, & writing you, writing you inadequately, not saying how it is when you are 3000 miles away — it's hard to know if i'm still in jet lag, or stretched out form that Britrail week, or just descended another step into gaffericis, or maybe still hung over from ouzo   anyway, dear princess, i'm glad you resisted that Brigham Young type, that you are well housed, coping with relatives, able to see the Olympics (the rainclouds are swirling around no.200 balliol today) & still wanting to come back to me   that's what keeps me living

   sharon is also in B group, starting in afternoons

   your HBC cheque goes off this hour

   you are the most beautiful, most intelligent, most loyal, most loving giraffe in all the world's savannahs

                              keep yourself safe, well, happy — for <u>us</u>
                              Woodstock

phone me always "collect" but after 6 p.m. your time

                              •••

Joe Rosenblatt, 2008
age 75

Phantom Dog

I'm your salivating beast, a phantom dog.
From my invisible world I move toward you
stealthily like a silvery moth under starless sky.
Shivering, you've become my sparkling eyes;
my large paws weigh heavily on your thighs
brailing your body, trust me, I'm your guide dog;
follow my footsteps away from the darkness.
Metamorphosed as sunlight, let us enter my lair.

Gristle, shards of bone, and the soul, too, consumed
with its platinum feathers, truly an iridescent meal;
for love is the tiniest of briskets, and hardest to view,
mangle and chew, and absorb in lechery's saliva.

Let us ingurgitate our reckless moments together.
My paw rests on your heart; I give you my breath.

•••

George Bowering, 2010
age 75

from Knot of Light

7.

There is nothing
so much to desire
as the Montreal
smile in your
photograph.

And if there is
a problem in composition
there is still the
picture, and you
are so much in it.

8.

My eyes say we
focus, say
we folk are
large in our lives,

say something of
us, you and I
subject of our
perspective.

11.

You. I remember
are grass, we are
grass, for all we
like to think
we think.

We are under
foot, fresh as the spring,
open to love, long
natural
love.

12.

The beasts of
the field shall
honour us, the
dragons and the owls

be our familiars,
kin to speak
our new tongue
with, seemly.

15.

You are on
your new ladder.
"She paints,"
I think, another
lovely poem

woman. Making
a wall pumpkin
in colour, relative
to a world full of your hues.

17.

I wish, you
are my well,
my deep
drink, my waking.

You wake and
my wish comes
true, my Eve,
my happy morn.

22.

You hold up
at least
half the sky, I
climb under, lie
on my back.

The view, as
they say, flushes
my heart, is that
the right word, flushes
my old heart.

•••

Douglas LePan, 1990
age 76

Flames, at the Beginning

I am burning your letter, as you asked me to.
In the light through the window it flames up like a great
    gold chrysanthemum.
Our love will flourish like that, extravagant and secret.

•••

Al Purdy, 1994
age 76

To —

To the you that has been given some twenty
pounds of added flesh
— I have made room for this added you in my mind
and love that too

To the throat and neck that were once a column
of light holding up the moon
has been added little noughts and crosses of webbing
like to an earth pattern on long hot days
before the end of summer
— and the clear luminous mirror of the sky
that was your face has been examined by God
and all the gods and given shadows
here and there that the sons of men
may look upon you and not lose their vision

And the mind that is both fearful of nothing
and fearless of everything has grown and become
lovely and earthly and yet beyond our soiled planet
its innocence the wisdom of things newborn
before corruption has entered their minds and bodies
and directed them to walk toward their death

— to see everything and to realize the best and worst
of everything
is to love and not forget

•••

Charles G.D. Roberts to Joan Montgomery
Hotel Oak Manor, Oak Park, Illinois
April 13, 1938
age 78

My most loved and ever Desired —
    Imagine my fierce anxiety & worry when even this morning, six days
after leaving you, yet brings not one word from you. I think of a thousand
things, & I am tortured. And only tomorrow night you are to leave Toronto
and come to me, Beloved!
    Of course I know this will not reach thee in time. But I cannot help
sending it off, — an arrow shot into the void.

I know you would wire me in the intolerable event that you were not coming. I shall be at the Illinois Central Station at 7:45 Friday morning to meet thee, Oh, most dear and longed-for.

I love you, I love you.

> Your
> Charles

•

Charles G.D. Roberts to Joan Montgomery
Low Eaves
May 26, 1938

My Own Belovedest Ever —

Our plans have changed somewhat. Neither Lloyd nor Leila is coming up to Toronto at present. The car is more or less "on the blink." So I am bringing Edith *by train*. We will leave Ottawa at 3 o'clock *Standard* (4 daylight Saving) on Sunday afternoon, & arrive, *Deo Volente*, 9:30 Standard, *Sunday Evening*. Wilt thou, my Dearest One, be at No. 25 to receive us? Wilt thou (with our own Betty) welcome us with open arms? Oh, Sweet, how I am longing for you!

It has been, & still is, a *rush* here every minute, but I have no responsibilities, so I'm well, & more or less rested. But it is *cold* here, & I am writing in Lloyd's study with my overcoat on! But the birds are rioting cheerfully, & the blossoms have left off their overcoats, — and *someday* it will be summer here.

I'm going in to town with Lloyd right after lunch, & hope to get a line from thee at the Press Gallery; — & then on to the Royal Society meetings.

With all my heart I love you.

> Charles.

•••

George Woodcock, 1994
age 80

À Ma Belle Laide

I watch those deaf, myopic looks
when your eyes enlarge,
swim in incomprehension,
tender and soft,
yet flash
hard and steel-blue
as the mind leaps
over the body's flaws.

Then I love your ugly
beauty, all scarred
irregularity and fluid
character.

Only the French know
that the complementary
is not the
antithetical, and see
in such ugliness,
· as I do,
beauty's index.

Index of Poets and Correspondents

Contributors and Credits

Material is reprinted by permission of the authors or is
in the public domain unless otherwise noted.

Milton Acorn was born in Charlottetown, Prince Edward Island, in 1923.
After serving in the Canadian army during World War II, Acorn moved to
Montreal in 1956. Acorn received the Governor General's Award for *The Island
Means Minago* (1976). He was also awarded the Canadian Poets Award in
1970. His books of poetry include *In Love and Anger* (1956) and *I've Tasted My
Blood* (1969). He received an honorary doctorate from the University of Prince
Edward Island in 1977. Acorn died in Charlottetown in 1986. Known as "the
people's poet," he is the subject of two films produced by the National Film
Board of Canada. Acorn's letters, housed at Library and Archives Canada, are
reprinted by permission of Mary Hooper for the Estate of Milton Acorn.

Lillian Allen, dub poet, writer, performer, musician, and teacher, was born
in Jamaica in 1951. She studied at the City University of New York and York
University. Allen is the author of six books of poetry, including *Rhythm An'
Hardtimes* (1982), and the creator of half a dozen recordings. She received Juno
Awards for *Revolutionary Tea Party* (1986) and *Condition Critical* (1988). Allen
also co-produced and directed the documentary film *Blak Wi Blakk* (1994).
She was writer-in-residence at Queen's University, Kingston, and now teaches
creative writing at OCAD University in Toronto.

Tyson John Atkings is a visual artist and poet. He was born in Nipawin,
Saskatchewan, in 1989. He received a BFA in painting from the University of
Saskatchewan. His paintings have been exhibited across Canada. Atkings's
instant-messaging correspondence reproduced here first appeared in the chapbook *Exi[s]t/I* (JackPine Press, 2014), a collaboration with C. Isa Lausas.

Louise Bak was born in Kingston, Ontario, in 1972. She is a writer, editor, broadcaster, performance artist, and co-founder of SLANT, a television magazine
that explores Canadian-Asian culture. She is studying cultural studies and

women's studies at the University of Toronto, and her published books include *emeighty* (1995), *Gingko Kitchen* (1998), and *Tulpa* (2005). Bak lives in Toronto. "Restlessness" first appeared on http://halvard-johnson.blogspot.ca.

Julia Balén is a feminist scholar and a professor of English. She earned a PhD at the University of Arizona and directed the undergraduate and graduate women's studies programs at the same institution. She has published widely in the area of sexuality and social justice.

John Barton was born in Edmonton in 1957. He attended the University of Alberta, the University of Victoria, and Columbia University. He is the author of eight books of poetry and the recipient of numerous literary awards, including the CBC Literary Award. Barton also co-edited *Seminal: The Anthology of Canada's Gay-Male Poets* (2007). He was the long-time editor of *Arc Poetry Magazine* and is currently editor of *The Malahat Review*. "Sixth Letter in Autumn" was originally published as the seventh section of "Six Letters in Autumn and One Unwritten" in *Notes Toward a Family Tree* (Quarry, 1993).

Rhonda Batchelor was born in Brantford, Ontario and has lived on Vancouver Island for over thirty years. She holds a BFA from the University of Victoria. Batchelor's books of poetry include *Bearings* (1985), *Interpreting Silence* (1994), and *Weather Report* (2002). She has also published a young adult novel, *She Loves You* (2008). Batchelor has served on the editorial board for *The Malahat Review*.

David Bateman, a spoken-word poet and performance artist, was born and raised in Peterborough, Ontario. Bateman studied at the University of Calgary and has gone on to teach and perform at a variety of institutions across Canada. Bateman's *Wait Until Late Afternoon* (2009), co-authored with Hiromi Goto, was published by Frontenac House. Bateman's collections include *Impersonating Flowers* (2007) and *Invisible Foreground* (2007), short-listed for the Stephan G. Stephansson Award for Poetry. "Letter to a former lover from a former drag queen on the threshold of manhood" appeared in *Designation Youth* (Frontenac, 2014).

Derek Beaulieu, poet, theorist, publisher, and prose writer, was born in 1973. He studied at the University of Calgary. He is the founder of housepress and co-editor of *Shift & Switch: New Canadian Poetry* with Angela Rawlings and Jason Christite (2005). Beaulieu's books include *Fractal Economies* (2006) and *How to Write* (2010). His selected poems, *Please, No More Poetry*, edited by Kit Dobson (2013), appeared along with a short-fiction collection. He is poet laureate of Calgary. Beaulieu's untitled visual poems are excerpted from *KERN* (Les Figues, 2014).

Gregory Betts was born in Vancouver in 1975. He studied at Queen's University and the University of Victoria. Betts is currently a professor at Brock University. He is the author of five collections of poetry, editor and co-editor of several volumes, and the author of *Avant-Garde Canadian Literature: The Early Manifestations* (2013) and *This is Importance: A Student's Guide to Literature* (2013). Betts also writes extensively on art.

Jeevan Bhagwat lives in Toronto. His poetry has been published widely in literary magazines such as *Tower, Quills,* and *Blue Skies.* His poetry book *The Weight of Dreams* was published in 2012. Bhagwat won the Monica Ladell Prize for Poetry, sponsored by the Scarborough Arts Council Award, in 2003 and 2005.

Earle Birney, poet, novelist, teacher and scholar, was born in Calgary in 1904. He studied at the University of British Columbia, the University of Toronto, the University of California, and the University of London. Birney served in the Canadian army during World War II. He founded the first Canadian creative writing program at the University of British Columbia in 1946. Birney's novel *Turvey* was published in 1949. Among his dozens of books of poetry, Birney won the Governor General's Award for *David and Other Poems* (1942) and for *Now is Time* (1945). Birney received numerous awards, including the Lorne Pierce Medal in 1953. He was made an officer of the Order of Canada in 1970. He died in 1995. Earle Birney's letters to Esther Birney are housed in the archives of the University of British Columbia. All Birney correspondence is reprinted by permission of Wailan Low, executor of the Estate of Earle Birney.

bill bissett, born in Halifax in 1939, moved to Canada's west coast when he was seventeen. bissett studied at Dalhousie University and at the University of British Columbia with Warren Tallman. bissett is a poet, painter, lyricist, and performer. He was a leader in the small-press movement with his work on gronk and blewointment Press. bissett co-founded the cooperative art gallery, Th Mandan Ghetto. The author of innumerable books of poetry, bissett is the subject of substantial literary criticism on concrete poetry and the National Film Board documentary *Strange Grey Day This* (1963). In 1971, Dennis Lee and Margaret Atwood edited *Nobody Owns the Earth,* a first volume of bissett's collected works. bissett received the George Woodcock Lifetime Achievement Award in 2007. He received the Dorothy Livesay Poetry Prize and the Milton Acorn People's Poet Award. The selection here is from *Pomes for Yoshi* (Talon Books, 1977).

Ronna Bloom is a poet and psychotherapist. She is the author of five books of poetry. Her poems have been translated into several languages and broadcast on the CBC. Her most recent book of poetry, *Cloudy with a Fire in the Basement* (2012), was short-listed for the ReLit Award. She teaches poetry workshops and is currently the poet-in-community at the University of Toronto and poet-in-residence at Mount Sinai Hospital. Excerpts from this piece were published as poems in *Personal Effects* (Pedlar Press, 2000).

Michael Blouin has won the ReLit Award for Best Novel, been short-listed for the Amazon First Novel Award, the bpNichol Award, the CBC Literary Award, and is a winner of the Diana Brebner Award and the 2012 Lampman Award. He has collaborated on recent projects with poet Gillian Sze, film director Bruce MacDonald, and poet and artist bill bissett. He has been published in most Canadian literary magazines. He is represented internationally by Westwood Creative Artists.

Christian Bök is one of the earliest founders of conceptual literature. Bök has created artificial languages for two television shows: Gene Roddenberry's *Earth: Final Conflict*, and Peter Benchley's *Amazon*. He has earned many accolades for his virtuoso recitals of sound-poems (particularly *Die Ursonate* by Kurt Schwitters), and he has performed lectures and readings at more than 200 venues around the world in the last four years. Bök is on the verge of finishing his current project, entitled *The Xenotex*, a work that requires him to engineer the genome of an unkillable bacterium so that the DNA of such an organism might become not only a durable archive that stores a poem for eternity but also an operant machine that writes a poem in response. Bök teaches in the department of English at the University of Calgary. "Vowels" first appeared in *Eunoia* (Coach House Books, 2001), which earned Bök the Griffin Poetry Prize. It is reprinted here by permission of the publisher.

Roo Borson was born in 1952 in Berkeley, California, and studied at the University of British Columbia. Borson is the author of over a dozen books of poetry, including *A Sad Device* (1981) and *Short Journey Upriver toward Oishida* (2004), which won the Governor General's Award, the Griffin Poetry Prize, and the Pat Lowther Award. Borson is also a member of the award-winning poetry ensemble Pain Not Bread. She lives in Toronto. "You Leave the City" first appeared in *Water Memory* (McClelland & Stewart, 1996).

George Bowering, the author of over one hundred books, was born in Penticton, British Columbia, in 1935 and grew up in Oliver, British Columbia. Bowering studied at the University of British Columbia and the University of

Western Ontario. He was involved with the founding of the magazine *TISH*. His books include poetry, fiction, chapbooks, criticism, memoirs, plays, and edited volumes. Bowering was the poet laureate of Canada from 2002 to 2004. Bowering won the Governor General's Award for Poetry in 1969 (for *The Gangs of Kosmos*) and the Governor General's Award for Fiction in 1980 (for *Burning Water*). He has received many other awards, including the Order of Canada in 2002. Bowering has taught at various colleges and universities in Canada, including the University of Calgary and Simon Fraser University. "Knot of Light" from *My Darling Nellie Grey* by George Bowering, © 2010 George Bowering, Talon Books Ltd., Vancouver B.C. Reprinted by permission of the publisher

Di Brandt grew up in Reinland, Manitoba, the Mennonite farming village where she was born in 1952. She studied at the Canadian Mennonite Bible College, the University of Manitoba, and the University of Toronto. She holds a PhD from the University of Manitoba. Brandt taught at the University of Windsor and is currently at Brandon University. Brandt's books of poetry include *questions i asked my mother* (1987) and *Now You Care* (2003). She has been a finalist for the Governor General's Award and the Griffin Prize and the recipient of numerous other awards. She is also the author of two essay collections and the co-editor of two anthologies. "Songs for a Divorce" from *Now You Care* © Di Brandt, 2003. Reprinted with the permission of Coach House Books.

Elizabeth Brewster, born in 1922 in Chipman, New Brunswick, studied at various universities, including the University of New Brunswick, Radcliffe College, and Indiana University. She taught at the University of Saskatchewan. Brewster's numerous books include almost two dozen poetry collections. Her poetry book *Footnotes to the Book of Job* (1995) was short-listed for the Governor General's Award. She also received the award for Lifetime Excellence in the Arts from the Saskatchewan Arts Board. Brewster was made a member of the Order of Canada in 2001. Brewster died in 2012 in Saskatoon. "Chill" is reprinted from *Selected Poems* by permission of Oberon Press.

William Wilfred Campbell is often considered part of the Canadian Confederation Poets' group. He was born in Newmarket, Upper Canada, in 1860. Campbell studied at the University of Toronto and the Episcopal Theological School in Cambridge, Massachusetts. While living in Ottawa, Campbell collaborated with Archibald Lampman and Duncan Campbell Scott on the column "At the Mermaid Inn." Campbell began publishing his poetry around 1880. He also published fiction and non-fiction. Campbell's poetry books include *Beyond the Hills of Dream* (1899; 1900) and *The Poems of Wilfred Campbell* (1905). Campbell was elected to the Royal Society of Canada in 1938. He died in Ottawa in 1918. Campbell's letters are housed at the National Archives of Canada.

Bliss Carman was born in Fredericton, New Brunswick, in 1861. He studied at the University of New Brunswick, receiving a BA (1881) and MA (1884). Carman also studied at Oxford, the University of Edinburgh, and Harvard University. Known as one of Canada's Confederation Poets, Carman authored dozens of poetry collections beginning with *Low Tide on Grand Pre: A book of Lyrics* (1893; 1894). Carman lived much of his life in the United States; he died in New Canaan, Connecticut, in 1929. He was elected to the Royal Society of Canada in 1925. He received the Lorne Pierce Medal in 1928 and a medal from the American Academy of Arts and Letters in 1929. Raymond Souster and Douglas Lochhead edited *Windflower: Poems of Bliss Carman* (1985). Carman's letters appear in the collection edited by H. Pearson Gundy, *Letters of Bliss Carman* (McGill-Queen's University Press, 1981) and are reprinted by permission of the publisher.

Fern G. Z. Carr is a multi-lingual poet, teacher, and former lawyer. She is widely published in such places as *The Windsor Review, Magnapoets,* and *Outlook,* among others. Carr's work was nominated for a Pushcart Prize in 2013 for work in *The Worcester Review.* She has also been the featured poet in the SOPA Fine Arts gallery in Kelowna. Carr has been poet-in-residence for the League of Canadian Poets.

Weyman Chan was born in Calgary in 1963. His first book of poetry, *Before a Blue Sky Moon* (2003), won the Alberta Book Award. *Noise from the Laundry,* his second book, was a finalist for Governor General's Award and the Acorn-Plantos Award for People's Poetry (2009). He was also a finalist for the W.O. Mitchell Literary Prize in 2010 for *Hypoderm.* His latest book is *Chinese Blue* (TalonBooks, 2012).

George Elliott Clarke was born near Windsor Plains, Nova Scotia, and raised in Halifax. He studied at the University of Waterloo, Dalhousie University, and Queen's University. He is the inaugural E.J. Pratt Professor of Canadian Literature at the University of Toronto. Clarke's books of poetry include *Execution Poems,* winner of the Governor General's Award (2001); *Lush Dreams, Blue Exile: Fugitive Poems* (1994); and *Whylah Falls* (1990). He edited the two-volume anthology *Fire on the Water* (1991). His many awards include the 1998 Portia White Prize and the Dartmouth Book Award for fiction for *George & Rue* (2006), which was also longlisted for the Dublin IMPAC Award. Elliott

Clarke was appointed to the Order of Canada in 2008. "À *Geeta*" appeared in *Black* (Gaspereau, 2012) and is reprinted by permission of the publisher.

Fred Cogswell, poet, scholar, translator, editor, and teacher, was born in East Centreville, New Brunswick, in 1917. He studied at the University of New Brunswick and Edinburgh University and served in the Canadian army during World War II. Cogswell was a professor of English at the University of New Brunswick for thirty-one years. He was a founder of Fiddlehead Poetry Books, which became Goose Lane Editions. Cogswell published over thirty books of his own poetry and received numerous awards, including the Bliss Carman Award and the Alden Nowlan Award for Excellent in Literary Arts (1995). He received several Honorary Doctorates and was appointed a Member of the Order of Canada in 1981. Cogswell died in 2004. "Lost Dimension" is reprinted by permission of the Estate of Fred Cogswell.

Leonard Cohen, born in 1934 in Westmount, Quebec, is a singer, songwriter, poet, musician, and novelist. He studied at McGill University and Columbia University. His first book of poetry, *Let Us Compare Mythologies*, appeared in 1956. Since then he has published over a dozen books of poetry and the novels *The Favourite Game* (1963) and *Beautiful Losers* (1966). Cohen has been the subject of documentary films and the recipient of numerous awards and honours, including Juno Award nominations, a Grammy Lifetime Achievement Award (2010), a Governor General's Performing Arts Award, and a PEN Award for Songwriting Excellence (2010). Cohen was made an officer of the Order of Canada in 1991 and a companion of the Order of Canada in 2003. He received the Glenn Gould Prize in 2011, and in 2013 he was named the Juno Award Artist of the Year. "The Mist of Pornography" excerpted from *Book of Longing* by Leonard Cohen. Copyright © 2006 Leonard Cohen. Reprinted by permission of McClelland & Stewart, a division of Random House of Canada Limited, a Penguin Random House Company.

Ivan E. Coyote grew up in Whitehorse, Yukon. The author of eight books of short stories and one novel, Ivan is also a performer with three CDs and four short films. Coyote, the author of the bestselling book *Boys Like Her*, has received many writing awards, including the ReLit Award for *Bow Grip*. Coyote's books have been short-listed for the Ferro Grumley Award and the Danuta Gleed Award. Coyote has taught writing and mentored writers at Capilano University and Carleton University and has been writer-in-residence at the University of Winnipeg and the University of Western Ontario.

Lorna Crozier, born in 1948 in Swift Current, Saskatchewan, studied at the University of Saskatchewan and the University of Alberta. She held the post of chair of the writing department at the University of Victoria until her retirement in 2013. She is the author of more than a dozen collections of poetry and two books of non-fiction. Crozier's 1992 collection, *Inventing the Hawk*, won the Governor General's Award and the Pat Lowther Memorial Award. *Everything Arrives at the Light* (1995) received the Pat Lowther Memorial Award. *The Garden Going On without Us* (1985) and *Angels of Flesh, Angels of Silence* (1988) were nominated for the Governor General's Award. A volume of selected poems appeared in 2007 and a volume of collected poems in 1996. Crozier lives in Saanichton, British Columbia. "Getting Used to It" excerpted from *Small Mechanics* by Lorna Crozier. Copyright © 2011 Lorna Crozier. Reprinted by permission of McClelland & Stewart, a division of Random House of Canada Limited, a Penguin Random House Company.

Frank Davey was born in Vancouver in 1940. He studied at the University of British Columbia and the University of Southern California. Davey was founding editor of the journal *Open Letter* and *TISH* poetry magazine and a teacher of literature at several universities, including York University and the University of Western Ontario. Davey is a cultural critic, poet, and the author of over twenty-five books of poetry, including *The Abbotsford Guide to India* (1986) and *Bardy Google* (2010). His numerous works of literary criticism include *Surviving the Paraphrase* (1983) and *Canadian Literary Power* (1994). "The Tower" is reprinted from *Arcana* (Coach House Books, 1973).

James Deahl, poet and publisher, was born in 1945 in Pittsburgh, Pennsylvania. A founding member of the Canadian Poetry Association, he has lived in Canada since 1970. His many books include *Into This Dark Earth* (1985); *A Stand of Jackpine*, co-authored with Milton Acorn (1987); *If Ever Two Were One* (2008); and numerous others. Deahl is the publisher of Unfinished Monument Press. He lives in Hamilton.

Rocco de Giacomo, born in Toronto, is a Toronto poet. His first poetry collection, *Ten Thousand Miles Between Us*, was published in 2010 and longlisted for the ReLit Poetry Award. His book of poetry, *Every Night of Our Lives*, is forthcoming from Guernica Editions. De Giacomo is the author of five chapbooks. His writing has been published widely in magazines and journals in Canada and across the world.

Barry Dempster, poet, novelist, and editor, was born in Toronto in 1952. One of the founding editors of *Poetry Canada Review*, Dempster is now an editor with Brick Books. His work has been widely anthologized, and his more than two dozen books of poetry include *Fables for Isolated Men* (1982), short-listed for the Governor General's Award; *The Burning Alphabet* (2005), short-listed for the Governor General's Award and winner of the Jack Chalmers Poetry Award; and, most recently, *Dying a Little* (2011) and *Invisible Dogs* (2013). His published fiction includes the novel *The Outside World* (2013). Dempster lives in Holland Landing, Ontario. "Come Live with Me" appeared in *Love Outlandish* (Brick Books, 2009).

Thomas Dilworth is a poet and scholar and for many years was a professor at the University of Windsor. His poetry has been published widely in *Rampike, Ontario Review, Poetry* (Chicago), and *Notre Dame Review*, among other places. His scholarship on romantic literature and modernism has also been published widely. Dilworth has received numerous awards, including induction in the Royal Society of Canada.

Christopher Doda is a poet, critic, and editor. He is the author of two collections of poetry from Mansfield Press: *Among Ruins*, and *Aesthetic Lessons*. Doda is the series editor for *Best Canadian Essays*. He has also been an editor at *Exile: The Literary Quarterly*. He lives in Toronto.

Louis Dudek was born in Montreal in 1918 and studied at McGill University. Dudek was involved with the magazines *First Statement* and *Northern Review*. He founded Contact Press with Raymond Souster and Irving Layton in 1952. He also began his own poetry magazine, *Delta*. Dudek was a professor of English at McGill University. Dudek's own poetry was varied in form and included long poems such as *Atlantis* (1967) and prose volumes such as *Essays on Myth, Art & Reality* (1992). Dudek also edited *The Making of Modern Poetry in Canada* with Michael Gnarowski (1967). Dudek was named to the Order of Canada in 1984 and died in 2001 in Montreal. "Love Words" appeared in *Zembla's Rocks* (Véhicule Press, 1986) and is reprinted by permission of the Estate of Louis Dudek.

Nathan Dueck was born in Winnipeg in 1979. He grew up in Winkler, Manitoba, and currently lives in Calgary, where he teaches at St. Mary's University College. Dueck studied at the University of Manitoba. Dueck's book *King's(Mere)* explores the life of William Lyon Mackenzie King. His book of prose fragments, *he'll*, was published by Pedlar Press in 2014.

Jane Eaton Hamilton, born in 1954 in Hamilton, Ontario, is a poet, fiction writer, and visual artist. She has won or been a finalist for dozens of awards and has won the CBC Literary Award twice. Her work has been short-listed for the

Journey Prize, the Pat Lowther Memorial Award, the Ferro-Grumley Award, and the Ethel Wilson Prize, among others. Hamilton's books of poetry include *Body Rain* (1992) and *Steam-Cleaning Love* (1993). Her forthcoming poetry book is *Love Will Burst into a Thousand Shapes*.

Tanya Evanson is a poet, teacher, and performer. She studied creative writing and English at Concordia University. Evanson has published six books of poetry, and her work has been widely anthologized in volumes such as *The Great Black North: Contemporary African Canadian Poetry* (2013) and *WomanSpeak: A Journal of Writing and Art by Caribbean Women* (2014). She has participated widely in poetry slams and directs the Banff Centre's spoken word program. Evanson received the Poet of Honour Award at the Canadian Festival of Spoken Word in 2013. Evanson's Paris letter appears on the CD "Invisible World" (Mother Tongue Media, 2004), and the Fez letter appears in the unpublished novella "Book of Wings."

Ronald Everson was born in 1903 in Oshawa, Ontario. He studied at the University of Toronto and Upper Canada Law School. During this period he edited *Acta Victoriana*. Everson's first book of poetry, *Three Dozen Poems*, was published in 1957. A founding member of the League of Canadian Poets, he went on to publish more than a dozen books of poetry. Everson died in 1992. "Cold Weather Love" appeared in *A Lattice for Momos* (Contact Press, 1958) and is reprinted by permission of Phil Everson.

Brian Fawcett was born in 1944 in Prince George, British Columbia. He studied at Simon Fraser University. A cultural theorist, journalist, teacher, and writer of fiction and non-fiction, he is the author of numerous books, including seven volumes of poetry. His book *Virtual Clearcut: Or, the Way Things Are in My Hometown* won the 2003 Pearson Prize for Canadian Non-Fiction. Fawcett lives in Toronto. Fawcett's letters to Sharon Thesen are housed at the Simon Fraser University special collections.

Ian Ferrier is a poet, musician, and performer. He has toured his work across North America and Europe. The poetry/music label Wired on Words, co-founded by Ferrier, won a broadcasting award. Ferrier's spoken word and music creations have been produced with the dance company For Body and Light. His work has also been translated into French. Ferrier's first CD/book was *Exploding Head Man*. His CD, *What is this Place* was chosen as Best CD of 2007 by *HOUR* Magazine. He lives in Montreal and mentors writers at Concordia University.

Judith Fitzgerald, poet, musician, and journalist was born in 1952 in Toronto. She studied at York University and the University of Toronto. She is the author of over twenty books of poetry, including the four-volume *Adagios Quartet* (2003, 2004, 2006, 2007) and *26 Ways out of this World* (1999). She has also published several books of prose – two on Sarah McLachlan and one on Marshall McLuhan – and has edited several volumes. Fitzgerald's book *Rapturous Chronicles* was nominated for the Governor General's Award. Her other awards include the 2003 Poetry Fellow of the Chalmers Arts Foundation. "Harmony of Moonlight" originally appeared in *Rapturous Chronicles* (Mercury Press, 1991).

Jack Garton is a poet, singer, and songwriter. He works with Vancouver's Maria in the Shower. Garton has toured with his music through Europe, the UK, and Canada. He is also a founding member of the Dusty Flowerpot Cabaret Theatre. Garton's published poetry includes the chapbook *If Only* (2014) and *Sick Notes* (2014). He lives on Canada's west coast.

John Glassco was born in 1909 in Montreal. Glassco studied at Lower Canada College and McGill University. He travelled to Paris in the twenties, an experience that formed the basis of his book *Memoirs of Montparnasse* (1970). Glassco's poetry books include *The Deficit Made Flesh* (1958) and *Selected Poems with Three Notes on the Poetic Process* (1997). He also worked in translation and wrote pornographic texts. He received the Governor General's Award for poetry in 1971. Glassco died in 1981. John Glassco's letters appear in *The Heart Accepts It All: The Selected Letters of John Glassco*, edited by Brian Busby (Véhicule Press, 2013), and are reprinted by permission of William Toye, executor of the Estate of John Glassco.

Elizabeth Greene is a poet, scholar, and teacher. She was born in New York City in 1943 and studied at the University of Toronto. Her three collections of poetry are *The Iron Shoes* (2007), *Moving* (2010), and *Understories* (2014). Her poems have been widely anthologized. Greene's edited volume *We Who Can Fly: Poems, Essays and Memories in Honour of Adele Wiseman* won the Betty and Morris Aaron Award for Best Scholarship on a Canadian Subject. Greene taught English at Queen's University before her retirement. Her poems have twice been short-listed for the Descant/Winston Collins Prize. Greene lives in Kingston, Ontario. "Per Aspera ad Astra" originally appeared in *Understories* (Inanna, 2014).

Frederick Philip Grove was born Felix Paul Greve in Prussia. He grew up in Hamburg, Germany, and studied at the Gymnasium Johanneum. Grove's first book was a collection of poetry, *Wanderungen* (1902). In 1912, Grove moved to

Manitoba, where he worked as a teacher. Later in his life, he lived in Ontario. Grove's books include *Settlers of the Marsh* (1928), *Over Prairie Trails* (1922), and the autobiography *In Search of Myself* (1946), which won the Governor General's Award. He was awarded the Lorne Pierce Medal in 1934. Grove's poems were edited by Terrence Craig. Grove died in 1948. Grove's letters appear in *The Letters of Frederick Philip Grove*, edited by Desmond Pacey (University of Toronto Press, 1976), and are reprinted by permission of the publisher.

Heather Haley, poet, singer, teacher, and media artist, was born in Matapedia, Quebec. She has toured her music and spoken word poetry internationally. Her poetry books include *Sideways* (2003) and *Three Blocks West of Wonderland* (2009). Haley's poetry has also been published widely, including in *Geist, The Antigonish Review, The Vancouver Review*, and the anthologies *ROCKsalt: Contemporary BC Poetry* and *The Verse Map of Vancouver*.

Vivian Hansen is a poet and author of fiction and non-fiction. She studied at the University of British Columbia and the University of Calgary. Hansen co-founded the Calgary Women's Writing Project and served as the editor of that organization's journal. Hansen has received awards for her poetry and non-fiction, including the Jon Whyte Memorial Essay Prize and placements in the Odes of March Poetry Contest and the Legacy Magazine Contest. Her work has appeared in many journals and anthologies. Hansen's books of poetry include *Leylines of My Flesh* (2002).

Richard Harrison, born in Toronto in 1957, is a poet, editor, and teacher living in Calgary. He studied at Trent University and Concordia University. Harrison is the author of six books of poetry, including *Big Breath of a Wish* (1998), nominated for the Governor General's Award. He has also published two volumes of essays. The tenth anniversary edition of Harrison's *Hero of the Play* appeared in 2004.

Steven Heighton, born in Toronto in 1961, is a poet and fiction writer. He studied at Queen's University and still resides in Kingston, Ontario. His numerous books include the novel *Every Lost Country* (2010), two other novels, three collections of short stories, five books of poetry, two non-fiction books, and publications in many magazines and anthologies, including *The New Canon*, edited by Carmine Starnino, (2005) and *70 Canadian Poets* (Ed Gary Geddes, 2014). Heighton's literary awards include gold medals in the National Magazine Awards and the K.M. Hunter Award for Literature (2010). He was a finalist for the Governor General's Award for Poetry in 1995 for *The Ecstasy of Skeptics*.

"Breathe Like This" from *Patient Frame*, copyright © 2010 by Steven Heighton. Reprinted with permission of House of Anansi Press. www.houseofanansi.com.

David Helwig was born in Toronto in 1938. He studied at the University of Toronto and the University of Liverpool. He taught at Queen's University for over a decade and worked for the CBC. Helwig is the author of over a dozen books of poetry, including *Book of the Hours* (1979) and *The Sway of Otherwise* (2008). He is also the author of over twenty books of fiction. He founded and edited the series *Best Canadian Stories*. In 2007 Helwig received the Writers' Trust of Canada Matt Cohen Prize, and in 2009 he was named a member of the Order of Canada. He lives in Prince Edward Island.

Gerald Hill was born in 1951 and raised in Saskatchewan. He studied at the University of Alberta and David Thompson University Centre, among other places. Hill is the author of five poetry books. His sixth collection of poems is *Hillsdale Book* (2015); previous collections include *The Man from Saskatchewan* (2001), *My Human Comedy* (2008), and *14 Tractors* (2009). Hill is also the author of the non-fiction book *Their Names Live On: Remembering Saskatchewan's Fallen in World War II* (With Doug Chisholm, 2001). Hill lives in Regina and teaches at Luther College. His writing has received several awards, including the City of Regina Writing Award. He has been short-listed several times for a Saskatchewan Book Award.

Robert Hilles, poet, novelist, and editor, was born in Kenora, Ontario, in 1951. He currently lives on Salt Spring Island. Hilles is the author of almost twenty books of poetry, including *Cantos from a Small Room* (1993), winner of the Governor General's Award. His *Wrapped within Again: New and Selected Poems* appeared in 2003. Hilles has been short-listed for the Milton Acorn People's Poetry Prize and the Howard O'Hagan Award, among others. Hilles's poem "Beloved" appeared in *Higher Ground* (River Books, 2001). Robert Hilles's correspondence with Pearl Luke is archived at the University of Calgary's special collections.

Bill Howell was born in Liverpool, England, in 1946. He grew up in Halifax and studied at Dalhousie University. His career with CBC Radio took him to many places in Canada and the United States. Howell is one of the original Storm Warning poets. Also an award-winning playwright, his books of poetry include *The Red Fox* (1971), *Moonlight Saving Time* (1990), and *Porcupine Archery* (2009). His poetry has also appeared in a variety of journals and magazines including *Descant, Event, The Antigonish Review*, and others. "Local Subtext" first appeared in *Precipice* 16.2 (2009).

E. Pauline Johnson, also known as Tekahionwake, was the daughter of a Mohawk chief and an English mother, and was born on the Six Nations Indian Reserve near Brantford, Ontario, in 1861. She was a performer, poet, and writer of stories. Her poetry books include *The White Wampum* (1895), and *Flint and Feather* (1912). Johnson moved to Vancouver in 1909, and died there in 1913. Carole Gerson and Veronica Strong-Boag edited *Tekahionwake: Collected Poems and Selected Prose* (2002). An opera based on Johnson's life, *Pauline*, opened in May 2014.

Kai Cheng Thom was born in Vancouver in 1991. He works as a poet, performer, drag artist, and social worker in Montreal. He studied social work at McGill University and performs under the moniker Lady Sin Trayda. He has been a columnist for *The McGill Daily* and is widely published in magazines such as *Ditch, OutWrite: A Queer Review*, and *Convergence*, among others.

Penn Kemp was born in Strathroy, Ontario, in 1944. In addition to being a novelist, essayist, and poet, she is also a sound poet and multi-media performer. She studied at the University of Western Ontario, receiving degrees in English and education. She became poet laureate of London, Ontario, in 2010. She has published over twenty books of poetry and released ten CDs. In 2009-2010 she was writer-in-residence at the University of Western Ontario.

Roy Kiyooka, painter, poet, teacher, and multimedia artist, was born in Moose Jaw, Saskatchewan, in 1926. He studied at the Provincial Institute of Technology and Art from 1946 to 1949, as well as the Instituto Allende in San Miguel, Mexico. Kiyooka taught at various institutions, including the Regina College of Art, Concordia University, Nova Scotia College of Art and Design, and the University of British Columbia. His books include *Nevertheless These Eyes* (1967), *StoneDGloves* (1970, 1983), and *transcanada letters* (1975; 2004). Kiyooka's book *Pear Tree Poems* was nominated for the Governor General's Award. He died in 1994. The 1955 letters are housed at Simon Fraser University' special collections; others appear in the NeWest Press collections: *The Trans-Canada Letters*, edited by Glen Lowry (1975) and *Pacific Rim Letters*, edited by Smaro Kamboureli (2005). Kiyooka's letters are reprinted by permission of the Estate of Roy Kenzie Kiyooka.

A.M. Klein, poet and novelist, was born in Ukraine in 1909 and died in Montreal in 1972. His family moved to Montreal when he was young. Klein studied law at McGill University. Editor of *The Jewish Chronicle* from 1932 to 1955. He was involved with the McGill group of poets and *The McGill Fortnightly Review*. He is best known for his novel *The Second Scroll* (1951) and the poetry collection, *The Rocking Chair and Other Poems* (1966), which won the Governor General's Award for Poetry. He remains an important voice for Jewish-Canadian literature. The letter included here appeared in *A.M. Klein: The Letters*, edited by Elizabeth Popham (University of Toronto Press, 2011), and is reprinted by permission of the publisher.

Raymond Knister, poet, novelist, short story writer, and cultural journalist, was born in 1899 at Ruscom Station near Windsor, Ontario. He studied at the University of Toronto and took creative writing classes at Iowa State University. As a fiction writer, Knister is best known for *White Narcissus*, originally published in 1929. He was the author of three other novels. Knister wrote reviews for *Poetry* (Chicago) as well as *The Toronto Star Weekly* and *Saturday Night*. His *Selected Stories* were compiled by Michael Gnarowski in 1972, and his poems were compiled by Gregory Betts under the title *After Exile: A Raymond Knister Poetry Reader* (2003). Knister died in Stoney Point, Ontario, in 1932. His letters are housed in the special collections of McMaster University.

Robert Kroetsch was born in Heisler, Alberta, in 1927. He studied at SUNY Binghamton and taught at the University of Manitoba, among other institutions. Poet, novelist, and literary critic, Kroetsch authored nine novels and numerous poetry collections, including *The Hornbooks of Rita K*, nominated for a Governor General's Award. As a novelist he is best known for *The Studhorse Man*, awarded the Governor General's Award in 1969. His long poems, *Completed Field Notes*, were published in 1989. Kroetsch died in 2011. His letters are housed at the University of Calgary's special collection. Copyright © 2014 Robert Kroetsch. Reprinted with permission of the author's estate.

Archibald Lampman was born in Morpeth, Ontario, in 1861. He studied at Trinity College, Port Hope, Ontario, graduating in 1882. Lampman worked as a clerk for the post office in Ottawa for most of his adult life. He collaborated with William Wilfred Campbell and Duncan Campbell Scott on the column "At the Mermaid Inn" for the *Toronto Globe*. Lampman's poetry books include *Among the Millet and Other Poems* (1888) and *Lyrics of Earth: Sonnets and Ballads*, edited by Duncan Campbell Scott (1925). Lampman's books of letters and prose were published posthumously. He died in 1899 in Ottawa. Lampman's letters are housed at the special collections of Simon Fraser University.

Patrick Lane, born in 1939 in Nelson, British Columbia, is a poet, fiction writer, editor, teacher, and essayist. He is also, with bill bissett and Seymour Mayne, founder of the small press, Very Stone House (1966). Lane's dozens of poetry books include *Poems: New and Selected*, which won the Governor

General's Award in 1978; *Winter* (1989) and *Mortal Remains* (1991), both of which were nominated for Governor General's Awards; *Go Leaving Strange* (2005), nominated for the Dorothy Livesay Poetry Prize; and many others. Lane edited *The Collected Poems of Red Lane* (1968). His non-fiction book *There is a Season* (2004) was nominated for the Hubert Evans Non-Fiction Prize. He has also edited three books with Lorna Crozier. He lives in Saanichton, British Columbia.

Evelyn Lau was born in Vancouver in 1971. She left school at age fourteen and lived for a time on the streets of Vancouver. Her highly successful *Runaway: Diary of a Street Kid* was published in 1989 and released as a film in 1993. Her six books of poetry have received numerous awards, including the Milton Acorn People's Poetry Award and a nomination for the Governor General's Award. Lau, a former poet laureate of Vancouver, is also the author of essays, short stories, and a novel. "I Love You" appeared in *Treble* (Raincoast, 2005).

C. Isa Lausas was born in Tornio, Finland, in 1990. She moved to France at the age of thirteen. A visual artist and writer, Isa graduated from the École nationale de beaux-arts de Marseille in 2012. She is currently a student in the MFA in writing at the University of Saskatchewan. Her visual art has shown internationally, and she has published several collections of poetry, including *On That Border* (2012). Her chapbook *Exi[s]t/I*, a collaboration with T. J. Atkings, was published by Saskatoon's Jack Pine Press (2014).

Katherine Lawrence was raised in Hamilton, Ontario, but has lived in Saskatchewan since 1982. She studied at Carleton University. Lawrence's first book of poetry was *Ring Finger, Left Hand* (2001). She has been published steadily since then, receiving numerous writing awards, including the Brenda MacDonald Riches Award for Best First Book and nominations for the Anne Szumigalski Award and the Alfred G. Bailey Prize for Poetry. Lawrence lives in Regina.

Irving Layton was born in Romania in 1912. His family moved to Montreal in 1913. A.M. Klein published Layton's early poetry in *The McGilliad*. Layton studied at McGill University and was active in the Young People's Socialist League. He later taught at Sir George Williams University and York University. Layton's first poetry book, *Here and Now*, was published by First Statement Press in 1945. Dozens of subsequent poetry books followed, including volumes of love poems and letters. Layton was twice nominated for the Nobel Prize and was awarded the Petrach Award for Poetry and the Governor General's Award for Poetry. Layton died in 2006. Letters by Irving Layton. Originally published by Macmillan of Canada. Copyright © 1989 Irving Layton. Reprinted by permission of the Estate of Irving Layton and McClelland & Stewart, a division of Random House of Canada Limited, a Penguin Random House Company.

Dennis Lee, born in 1939 in Toronto, studied at the University of Toronto. Lee has been an English lecturer, editor, and co-founder of the House of Anansi Press. He is the author of more than twenty books, including *Civil Elegies* (1968), winner of the Governor General's Award. Lee is also a children's writer who notably created the lyrics for the TV series *Fraggle Rock*. He is the author of the best-selling children's book *Alligator Pie* (1974). Lee's many other literary awards include the Canadian Library Association Award. Lee's scholarly writing includes *Savage Fields: An Essay in Literature and Cosmology* (1977). He was Toronto's poet laureate from 2001–2004. "Coming Becomes You" appeared in *Nightwatch: New & Selected Poems 1968-1996* (McClelland & Stewart, 1996).

Douglas LePan was born in Toronto in 1914. He studied at the University of Toronto and Harvard University. He served in the Canadian army during World War II. LePan taught at Queen's University, Kingston, and the University of Toronto. LePan received many awards including a Guggenheim Fellowship, the Lorne Pierce Medal and honorary degrees. He published more than half a dozen books of poetry in addition to other works. His work appeared in *Seminal: The Anthology of Canada's Gay Male Poets*, edited by John Barton and Billeh Nickerson (2007). LePan died in 1998. "Flames at the Beginning" appeared in *Far Voyages* (McClelland & Stewart, 1990) and is reprinted by permission of Don LePan, executor for the Estate of Douglas LePan.

Charles Lillard was born in Long Beach, California, in 1944. He studied at the University of British Columbia. Lillard was the author of eight books of poetry including *Circling North* (1988), which won the Dorothy Livesay Poetry Prize, and *Shadow Weather: Poems Selected and New* (1997), short-listed for the Governor General's Award. He was also the author of several books on the history of the Pacific Northwest. He died in Victoria, British Columbia, in 1997. "Roughing the Words" printed by permission of Rhonda Batchelor, executor of the Estate of Charles Lillard.

Norma West Linder was born in Toronto in 1928. A former faculty member at Lambton College, she has published five novels, more than a dozen books of poetry, a memoir, and a biography of Pauline McGibbon.

Dorothy Livesay, poet, fiction writer, critic, activist, documentarian, and journalist, was born in Winnipeg in 1909. Her family moved to Toronto in 1920. Her first book of poetry, *Green Pitcher*, appeared in 1928. Livesay studied at the

University of Toronto and at the Sorbonne. Her poetry books *Day and Night* (1944) and *Poems for People* (1947) both won Governor General's Awards. She also won the Lorne Pierce Medal in 1947. Livesay worked for UNESCO in Paris in 1959 and taught in Zambia from 1959 – 1963. Livesay's *Collected Poems: The Two Seasons* appeared in 1972. She was made an officer of the Order of Canada in 1987. Livesay died in Victoria in 1996. Livesay's letters are housed in the University of Manitoba's special collections and reprinted by permission of the Estate of Dorothy Livesay.

Jennifer Londry is the author of two poetry collections: *After the Words* (2010), and *Life and Death in Cheap Motels* (with R.D. Roy, 2009). She has also published poetry widely in magazines and journals, including *CV2*, *Prairie Fire*, *Queen's Feminist Review*, *White Wall Review*, and *The Antigonish Review*. Londry was born in Kingston, Ontario, in 1962. She studied at Carleton University and currently lives in Kingston.

Malcolm Lowry, poet and novelist, was born in 1909 in New Brighton, England. He studied at Cambridge, worked as a deckhand on a ship, moved to Mexico in 1936, and eventually settled near Dollarton, British Columbia. Lowry's selected and collected poems were published posthumously, as were as several other books and letters. He is best known for the works of fiction *Ultramarine* (1933) and *Under the Volcano* (1947). Lowry died in 1957. Lowry's letters appear in *Sursum Corda! The Collected Letters of Malcolm Lowry*, edited by Sherrill E. Grace (University of Toronto Press, 1995), and are reprinted by permission of the publisher.

Christine Lowther is the author of three poetry collections: *My Nature* (2010), *Half-Blood Poems* (2011), and *New Power* (1999). She is co-editor of two books of essays, most recently *Living Artfully: Reflections from the Far West Coast* (2012). Her poetry appeared in *Force Field: 77 Women Poets of British Columbia* (2013). Since 1992 she has lived at Clayoquot Sound. Lowther's book, *Born Out of This*, was published in 2014 by Caitlin Press.

Pat Lowther was born in 1935 and raised in North Vancouver. She published three collections of poetry including *Milk Stone* (1974) and *This Difficult Flowering* (1968) before her death in 1975. Lowther was murdered by her husband just as her literary success was growing. Her work had begun to be anthologized in collections such as *Fifteen Winds* (1969), edited by Al Purdy. Several of Lowther's books appeared posthumously, and in 2010 Christine Wiesenthal edited *The Collected Poems of Pat Lowther*. "The Face" appeared in *Prism International* (Fall 1974) and is reprinted by permission of Beth and Christine Lowther, executors for the Estate of Pat Lowther.

Pearl Luke was born in Peace River, Alberta, in 1958. A former editor of *Dandelion*, her first novel, *Burning Ground* (2001) received the Commonwealth Writers' Prize and was short-listed for several other awards. *Madame Zee*, Luke's second novel, appeared in 2006. She teaches writing and lives on Salt Spring Island, British Columbia.

Gwendolyn MacEwen was born in 1941 in Toronto and spent most of her life in that city. Her first collection of poems, *The Drunken Clock*, appeared in 1961, and she went on to publish over twenty books, including poetry, fiction, children's books, and translations. MacEwen received many awards and accolades for her poetry, including the Governor General's Award for *The Shadowmaker* (1969) and posthumously for *Afterworlds* in 1987. Permission to reprint Gwendolyn MacEwen's letters, housed at the National Archives of Canada, is granted by David MacKinnon, executor for the Estate of Gwendolyn MacEwen.

Steve McCaffery was born in 1947 in Sheffield, England. He studied at the University of Hull. After moving to Toronto in 1968, he collaborated with bpNichol, Rafael Barretto-Rivera, and Paul Dutton to form the sound poets' group the Four Horsemen. McCaffery is the author of over a dozen books of poetry, including *Theory of Sediment*, nominated for the 1991 Governor General's Award, and *Seven Pages Missing*, nominated for the 2000 Governor General's Award. He has taught at York University and is currently the Gray Chair at the State University of New York in Buffalo.

rob mclennan was born in 1970 Ottawa, where he currently resides. He is the author of more than twenty books of poetry, fiction, and non-fiction. His poetry books include *Glengarry* (2011) and *kate street* (2011). His second novel, *missing persons*, was published in 2009. mclennan is also publisher of Chaudiere Books and above/ground press. He won the CAA/Air Canada Prize for the most promising writer under thirty in 1999. His other writing awards include the John Newlove Award; he was also short-listed a number of times for the Archibald Lampman Award. "Goldfish: studies in fine thread" originally appeared as a chapbook from above/ground press in 2012.

Kim Maltman was born in 1950 in Medicine Hat. He studied at the University of Calgary, the University of British Columbia, and the University of Toronto. He is a poet, physicist, and professor at York University. His six books include

The Sicknesses of Hats (1982) and *The Transparence of November/Snow* (1985), coauthored with Roo Borson. Maltman is also a member of the award-winning poetry ensemble Pain Not Bread. Maltman won the CBC Literary competition for his poetry. "Installation #67" first appeared in *Technologies/Installations* (Brick Books, 1990).

Dave Margoshes has published five poetry collections, among numerous other books. He holds an MFA in writing from the Iowa Writers' Workshop. In the early 1970s Margoshes moved to Canada, where he worked as a journalist and taught journalism. His most recent book of poetry, *Dimensions of an Orchard*, won the Anne Szumigalski Poetry Prize. *Wiseman's Wager*, his new novel, was published in fall 2014. He and his partner, the poet dee Hobsbawn-Smith, live on a farm west of Saskatoon.

Daphne Marlatt, founder of the West Coast Women and Words Society, was born in 1942 in Melbourne, Australia. She studied at the University of British Columbia and Indiana University. Marlatt was made a member of the Order of Canada in 2006. Her other awards include the Vancouver Mayor's Arts Award for Literary Arts. Marlatt has published poetry, novels, and numerous essays. Marlatt's many books include collaborations with Nicole Brossard and Betsy Warland. *Telling It: Women and Language Across Cultures* (1990) was a collaboration with Betsy Warland, Sky Lee, and Lee Maracle. *Opening Doors: Vancouver's East End* (1979) was an oral history collaboration with Carole Itter. Marlatt has taught in various colleges, universities, and writing programs. She lives in Vancouver. The excerpt from "Subject to Change," the collaboration between Marlatt and Betsy Warland, appeared in *Two Women in a Birth* (Guernica, 1994) and is reprinted by permission of the authors and the publisher.

Brandon Marlon is a playwright and poet living in Ottawa. He studied at the American Academy of Dramatic Arts in New York, the University of Toronto, and the University of Victoria. His poetry has been published widely in Canada, the USA, and Israel. Marlon's two poetry collections are *Inspirations of Israel: Poetry for a Land and People* (2008) and *Judean Dreams* (2009). His play, *The Bleeding Season*, was awarded the Canadian Jewish Playwriting Prize in 2007.

Anne Marriott was born in 1913 in Victoria, British Columbia. She studied at the University of British Columbia, moving to Ottawa in 1945 to work for the National Film Board. She wrote scripts for the CBC. Her long poem *The Wind Our Enemy* was published in 1939. Marriott won the Governor General's Award for *Calling Adventurers!* (1941). She also received a Women's Canadian Club Literary Award (1943) and an Ohio Award for educational broadcasting

(1958). Marriott's selected poems were published in 1981. She died in 1997 in Vancouver. "July 9" appeared in *Letters from Some Islands* (Mosaic Press, 1985) and is reprinted by permission of the publisher.

Chris Masson is a writer, performance poet, and teacher. He studied creative writing at Concordia University in his hometown of Montreal, where he is a founding member of the Throw Poetry Collective. He is the author of the poetry collection *Pants with Pockets* and, with David Eso, the co-author of the chapbook *Province of Emergency*. He has been seen on stages across the continent, either touring his solo show *Pathos, Punchlines, and Painkillers*, performing at poetry slams, or with his collaborative projects: Turtleneck, Hoorayborhood, and Death By Pedestrian.

Colin Morton was born in Ottawa in 1948. He is a poet and fiction writer and in the 1980s was a member of a poetry performance group that toured Canada. Morton has published more than ten books of poetry, reviewed books extensively, and published essays. His fiction book *The Local Cluster* (2008) was short-listed for an Ottawa Book Award in 2009.

Susan Musgrave, poet, novelist, and author of non-fiction and writing for children, was born in Santa Cruz, California, in 1951. Musgrave teaches in the University of British Columbia's MFA program. She is the author of many books of poetry, including the Governor General's Award-nominated, *A Man to Marry, A Man to Bury* (1979). Her book of fiction *The Charcoal Burners* (1980) was also nominated for a Governor General's Award. Musgrave has edited half a dozen books and written song lyrics. Her non-fiction book *You're in Canada Now...Motherfucker: A Memoir of Sorts* appeared in 2005. She lives in Sidney and Haida Gwaii.

Shane Neilson, born in 1975 in New Brunswick, is a poet, physician, literary critic, and non-fiction author. He studied at the University of New Brunswick, Dalhousie University, and Memorial University of Newfoundland. His poetry books include *Exterminate My Heart* (2008) and *Complete Physical* (2010). He is also the author of the book *Alden Nowlan and Illness* (2004). Neilson has received *Arc Poetry Magazine*'s Poem of the Year Award. The poem in Neilson's letter appeared in *Reclaim*, a self-published, single-copy chapbook designed by Frances Hunter.

John Newlove was born in 1938 in Regina. After a brief stint studying at the University of Saskatchewan, he lived in California, then Toronto, working as an editor at McClelland and Stewart. Newlove was the author of over a dozen collections of poetry, including *Lies*, which won the 1972 Governor General's Award, and *The Night the Dog Smiled*, nominated for the Governor General's Award (1986) and the Dorothy Livesay Prize. Two volumes of his selected poems have appeared, one in 1993 and one in 2007. Newlove died in Ottawa in 2003. His letters are reprinted by permission of Susan Newlove, executor of the Estate of John Newlove.

Ken Norris, born in New York City in 1951, moved to Canada in the early 1970s and was part of the Vehicule Poets in Montreal in the 1970s. Norris has published two dozen books, chapbooks of poetry, anthologies, and writing on poetics. His book, *The Better Part of Heaven*, edited by bpNichol, was published in 1984. One of his most recent books of poetry is *Rua da Felicidade* (2013). Norris taught for many years at the University of Maine. "Funny Valentine" appeared in *Fifty* (Talon Books, 2003) and is reprinted by permission of the publisher.

Alden Nowlan was born in 1933 in Stanley, Nova Scotia. A poet, playwright, and novelist, he began doing manual labour at age fourteen. He worked as a journalist in Hartland, New Brunswick, during which time his first book of poetry appeared with Fiddlehead Poetry Books. Nowlan's many books of poetry include *Bread, Wine and Salt* (1967), winner of the Governor General's Award. His books of fiction include *The Wanton Troopers* (1988) and *Will Ye Let the Mummers In* (1984). The recipient of a Guggenheim Fellowship, Nowlan was writer-in-residence at the University of New Brunswick until his death in 1983. Nowlan's drawing (Nowlan Fonds, University of Calgary, document 40.23.1.2) and the reply are printed by permission of Claudine Nowlan.

Richard Outram, born in Oshawa, Ontario, in 1930, studied at the University of Toronto. Outram worked for the CBC and then the BBC, returning to Canada in 1957. Outram's numerous books of poetry include *Dove Legend and Other Poems* (2001), *Selected Poems, 1960- 1980* (1984), and the posthumously published *South of North: Images of Canada, with drawings by Thoreau MacDonald* (2007). He also published many poems, often illustrated by his wife, Barbara Howard, under the Gauntlet Press imprint. In addition to his poetry, Outram authored numerous works of prose. He died in 2005, in Port Hope, Ontario. *The Essential Richard Outram*, edited by Amanda Jernigan, was published in 2011. "Late Love Poem" appeared in Dove Legend (Porcupine's Quill, 2001) and is reprinted by permission of the Porcupine's Quill and the Estate of Richard Outram.

P.K. Page was born in 1916 in the United Kingdom. She grew up in Calgary and Winnipeg. She worked for the National Film Board in Montreal, where she was involved with the poetry scene and *Preview* magazine. Page was also a visual artist and fiction writer. The author of numerous poetry books, beginning with *As Ten as Twenty* (1946), Page received much recognition for her writing, including the Governor General's award for poetry. Her collected poems, *The Hidden Room, Volumes One and Two* appeared in 1997, with her own artwork. Her non-fiction book *Brazilian Journal* appeared in 1986. Page died in 2010. P.K. Page's letters to F.R. Scott are housed in the F.R. Scott fonds at the National Archives of Canada and are printed by permission of the Estate of P.K. Page.

Stephen Pender studied at the University of Toronto and Queen's University. He is the co-editor of *The Common Sky: Canadian Writers Against the War in Iraq* (2003) and the author of the poetry book *Histologies* (2007) and of many scholarly articles and books on rhetoric and medicine. Pender is a faculty member in the department of English at the University of Windsor.

Marjorie Pickthall, poet, novelist, and librarian was born in London, England, in 1883. Her family moved to Toronto in 1890. Pickthall studied at the Bishop Strachan School and sold her first story while still a student there. She won two writing competitions sponsored by *The Mail and Empire*, as well as other awards. Her work was also published in *Acta Victoriana*. Her first poetry book was *The Drift of Pinions* (1913). Pickthall returned to England and tried her hand at novel writing. In 1920, she moved to British Columbia. She was widely published. She died in Vancouver in 1922 and her *Selected Poems* (edited by Lorne Pierce) appeared in 1957.

Ross Priddle was born in Calgary in 1964 and studied botany at the University of Alberta. Priddle is active in the international mail-art scene and micro-publishing through Bentspoon and his 5-copy zine project. Priddle is the founding editor of the *GAR* zine and has released several pod-books under the title *Ongoing Text*.

Robert Priest, poet, playwright, songwriter, singer, and children's and young adult writer, was born in England in 1951. He grew up in Scarborough, Ontario. His ten books of poetry include *The Visible Man* (1979), *Blue Pyramids: New and Selected Poems* (2002), and *How to Swallow a Pig* (2004). Priest has received numerous awards, including the Milton Acorn Memorial People's Poetry Award and a Chalmers Award for his musical *Minibugs and Microchips*. "Come to Me" appeared in *Blue Pyramids: New and Selected Poems* (ECW Press, 2002).

Al Purdy was born in Wooler, Ontario, in 1918. For more than fifty years, he was a publishing poet, fiction writer, memoirist, and correspondent. Purdy served in the Royal Canadian Air Force during World War II. His first book of poetry was *The Enchanted Echo* (1944). Over the following decades, he received the Governor General's Award for *The Cariboo Horses* (1965) and *The Collected Poems of Al Purdy* (1986). He was also awarded the Order of Canada (1982), among other honours. Bruce Alcock made an animated film of "At the Quinte Hotel" in 2005. Purdy died in North Saanich, British Columbia, in 2000. The Purdy home, an A-frame at Ameliasburg, Ontario, is now a writers' retreat. "To –" appeared in *Beyond Remembering: the Collected Poems of Al Purdy* (Harbour Publishing, 2000, www.harbourpublishing.com) and is reprinted by permission of the publisher and the Estate of Al Purdy.

Elizabeth Rainer is a visual artist and writer. She was shortlisted for the 2012 bpNichol Chapbook Award for *let lie* (Co-authored with Michael Blouin; above/ground press).

Henry Rappaport grew up in Monticello, New York. He studied at Syracuse University and the University of Washington. A co-founder of Intermedia Press in Vancouver, Rappaport's four poetry books include *Loose to the World* (2014). He received the Whiffen Prize for Poetry at Syracuse University. He lives in Vancouver. "Make Dead" appeared in *Love to the World* (Ronsdale Press, 2014) and is reprinted by permission of the author and publisher.

Stephen Reid was born in Massey, Ontario in 1950. Reid's first novel, *Jack Rabbit Parole*, was published in 1986. He taught writing between 1987 and 1999, when he was again incarcerated until 2008. Reid's second book, *A Crowbar in the Buddhist Garden: Writing from Prison*, received the 2013 Victoria Book Award.

Louis Riel was born in 1844. A member of a large Metis family, he was educated at Saint Boniface by Catholic priests and attended the seminary at the Collège de Montréal and the Grey Nuns' convent. He then worked as a clerk in a law office. Riel wrote poetry and stayed with the poet Louis-Honoré Fréchette. Riel returned to the Red River Settlement and became involved with the Metis National Committee in 1869 and, later, leader of the Metis Provisional Government. Riel was also instrumental in the creation of the Manitoba Act (1870). The Canadian militia pursued Riel, forcing him to flee to the Territory of Dakota. He was elected to the Canadian House of Commons, though he remained in exile in Montana. After Riel's return to Canada, he was arrested for treason during the 1885 North-West Rebellion and was hanged. Riel has been honoured by many artists, filmmakers, and writers. Riel's own *Selected Poetry* (translated by Paul Savoie and edited by Glen Campbell) was published in 2000 by Exile Editions. Riel's letters, translated by David Eso, are reprinted from the five-volume *Collected Writings of Louis Riel* (University of Alberta Press, 1985), by permission of the publisher.

Charles G.D. Roberts was born in Douglas, New Brunswick, in 1860. He grew up in the Tantramar Marsh area before his family moved to Fredericton in 1873. Roberts studied at the University of New Brunswick. His first book of poetry was *Orion and Other Poems* (1880). After a stint in Toronto at *The Week*, Roberts became a professor at University of King's College, Windsor, Nova Scotia. He moved to New York City in 1897. Roberts lived abroad until 1925. Roberts's numerous books of poetry were collected by Desmond Pacey and Graham Adams in 1985. Roberts also published non-fiction and fiction, including animal stories. His collected letters were published by Goose Lane Editions in 1989. Roberts received many honours: fellowship in the Royal Society of Canada in 1893, the Lorne Pierce Medal in 1926, and a knighthood in 1935. He died in Toronto in 1943.

Linda Rogers was born in 1944 in Port Alice, British Columbia, and currently lives in Victoria. She studied at the University of British Columbia. Rogers is the author of over a dozen books of poetry, half a dozen children's books, four works of fiction, and a non-fiction book. Rogers' work has also been widely anthologized. Rogers received the Shaunt Basmajian Chapbook Award for *Grief Sits Down* (2000). She has received a number of other awards, including the Stephen Leacock Prize for Poetry and the Hawthorne Poetry Prize.

Joe Rosenblatt was born in Toronto in 1933. He has been publishing poetry since the mid-1960s. Rosenblatt received the Governor General's Award for *Top Soil* (1976) and the Dorothy Livesay Poetry Prize *Poetry Hotel* (1985). The author of almost two dozen books of poetry and several books of fiction, Rosenblatt has also been the subject of works of literary criticism, including *The Lunatic Muse* (edited by David Berry, 2007). He lives on Vancouver Island. "Phantom Dog" originally appeared in *Dog* (Mansfield Press, 2008), a collaboration with Catherine Owen and Karen Moe.

Renée Sarojini Saklikar was born in Poona/Pune, India. She studied law, has lived across Canada, and is the author of *thecanadaproject*, a life-long poem. Saklikar is also the author of *Children of Air India: Un/Authorized Exhibits and Interjections* (2013). She has been published widely in journals and magazines such as *Geist*, *The Georgia Straight*, *CV2*, *SubTerrain*, and the anthology *Force Field: 77 Women Poets of British Columbia*, among others. Saklikar is working on a prose-poem/novel, among other projects.

Duncan Campbell Scott was born in 1862 in Ottawa. He studied at Stanstead Wesleyan College. Scott joined the civil service, to rise to the position of Deputy Superintendent of Indian Affairs. He collaborated on the newspaper column "At the Mermaid Inn" with Archibald Lampman and William Wilfred Campbell. Scott's first book of poetry was *The Magic House and Other Poems* (1893). Scott's selected poems were published in 1985 under the title *Powassan's Drum: Selected Poems of Duncan Campbell Scott*, edited by Douglas Lochhead and Raymond Souster. Scott also published a volume of stories, *In the Village of Viger* (1896), among other books of prose and edited the poetry of Archibald Lampman after Lampman's death. Scott died in 1947. His letters are housed at the National Archives of Canada.

Robert Service was born in Lancashire, England, in 1874. He attended school in Glasgow but spent much of his youth travelling. Some of Service's earliest writings were published in the *Victoria Daily Colonist*. In 1903, he began working for the Canadian Bank of Commerce. He was transferred, among other locations, to Whitehorse, where he lived until 1912. Service moved to Paris, France, in 1913. The author of dozens of books, Service is best known for poetry books such as *Songs of a Sourdough* (1907) and collections such as *The Shooting of Dan McGrew and Other Favorite Poems* (1912). His work has been reprinted many times. Service also authored six books of fiction and three books of non-fiction. He died in France in 1958. His letters are housed in the Queen's University archives.

Mark Sinnett was born in Oxford, England, in 1963 and moved to Canada in 1980. He is the author of two collections of poetry: *The Landing* (1997), which won the Gerald Lampert Memorial Award, and *Some Late Adventure of the Feelings* (2000). He has also written a collection of short stories, *Bull*, and the novels *The Border Guards* and *The Carnivore*, which won the Toronto Book Award in 2010. He is at work on a new novel about a middle-aged real-estate agent.

Robin Skelton, poet, teacher, and anthologist, was born in Yorkshire, England, in 1925. He studied at the University of Leeds and Cambridge University. In 1963 he emigrated to Canada and taught at the University of Victoria. Skelton published dozens of books of poetry, fiction, non-fiction, and scholarship. His publishing credits also include translations and dozens of anthologies and works on the occult. He was a founding editor of *The Malahat Review* and founding chair of the department of creative writing at the University of Victoria. Skelton died in 1997 in Victoria, British Columbia. "The language of love is impossible" is reprinted by permission of the Estate of Robin Skelton.

A.J.M. Smith, poet, critic, editor, anthologist, and teacher, was born in Montreal in 1902. After spending time in England, he studied at McGill University. While a student at McGill, he founded, with F.R. Scott, the *McGill Fortnightly Review*. Smith co-edited the anthology *New Provinces* (1936) with Scott and Leo Kennedy. Smith's six books of poetry include *News of the Phoenix and Other Poems* (1943) and *The Classic Shade: Selected Poems* (1978). He began teaching at Michigan State College in 1936. Smith also authored several books of literary criticism. He received the Lorne Pierce Medal in 1966. Smith died in East Lansing, Michigan, in 1980. "What Strange Enchantment" first appeared in the *McGill Fortnightly Review* (November 1925) and is reprinted here courtesy of the A.J.M. Smith Collection at Trent University Archives.

Steven Ross Smith was born in 1945 in Toronto. He studied at Ryerson University. A sound poet, journalist, and fiction writer, Smith began publishing and performing poetry in the 1970s. Smith formed his own sound poetry group, Owen Sound, in 1975. His poetry books include the fluttertongue series, one volume of which won the 2005 Book of the Year Award at the Saskatchewan Book Awards. Smith's work has been widely anthologized. He directed the Sage Hill Writing Experience for eighteen years before taking the helm of the literary arts programs at the Banff Centre. "Rush: Coral Bracho" is from the unpublished manuscript *Fluttertongue 6: Emanations*.

Raymond Souster, born in Toronto in 1921, spent most of his life in that city, working for the Canadian Imperial Bank of Commerce. Souster edited the magazine *Combustion* from 1957 to 1960 as well as several anthologies of Canadian poetry. He was the author of numerous poetry books, beginning with *When We Are Young* in 1946 and continuing until his death in 2012. Souster was a founding editor of Contact Press and a founding member of the League of Canadian Poets. "The Nest" is reprinted from *Collected Poems of Raymond Souster* by permission of Oberon Press.

Andrew Suknaski was born in 1942 near Wood Mountain, Saskatchewan. A poet and visual artist, Suknaski's books include *The Land They Gave Away* (1982), *In the Name of Narid* (edited by Dennis Cooley, 1981) and *Wood Mountain Poems* (1976). He studied at the University of Victoria, the School of Art and Design of the Montreal Museum of Fine Arts, Notre Dame University, the University of British Columbia, Simon Fraser University, and the Kootenay School of Art. Suknaski often published his work in chapbooks and limited editions. His *New and Selected Poems*, edited by Stephen Scobie, were published in 1982. In 2007, rob mclennan compiled *There Is No Mountain: Selected Poems of Andrew Suknaski*. Suknaski received the Canadian Authors Association Poetry

Award and is the subject of a National Film Board of Canada film. Suknaski died in Moose Jaw in 2012. Suknaski's work is reprinted here by permission of the Estate of Andrew Suknaski.

Fraser Sutherland, poet, critic, biographer, fiction writer, journalist, and critic, was born in Pictou County, Nova Scotia. He studied at King's College, Halifax, and Carleton University. His poetry books include *Jonestown: A Poem* (1996), *Manual for Emigrants* (2007) and *The Matuschka Case: Selected Poems* (2006). His work has been published widely and translated into numerous languages. His non-fiction books include *The Making of a Name: The Inside Story of the Brands We Buy* (2004).

Anne Szumigalski was born in London, England in 1922. She served during World War II as a medical auxiliary officer. Anne immigrated with her husband to Canada in 1951. She lived much of the rest of her life in Saskatoon. Szumigalski published over a dozen books, mostly poetry but also a memoir and a play. She was a founding member of the Saskatchewan Writers' Guild and *Grain Magazine*. Szumigalski received the Governor General's Award, the Saskatchewan Order of Merit, and numerous other awards. Her first book of poems appeared in 1971, and she published steadily until her death in 1999. Szumigalski's books include *On Glassy Wings: Poems New & Selected* (1997), *Dogstones: Selected and New Poems* (1986) and many others. Several books were published posthumously. "Desire" appeared in *Dogstones* (Fifth House, 1986) and is reprinted by permission of Fitzhenry and Whiteside Ltd.

Peter Trower moved to Canada from England, where he was born in 1930. A poet and novelist, he also worked as a logger for many years. The author of over a dozen books of poetry, he has also published four books of prose and dozens of non-fiction pieces on logging and travel, among other subjects. Trower is a musician, novelist, and editor. Trower's *There Are Many Ways: Poems New and Revised* (2002) was published by Ekstasis Editions. His book *Haunted Hills and Hanging Valleys: Selected Poems 1969-2004* was published by Harbour Publishing in 2004.

Priscila Uppal was born in Ottawa in 1974. She is the author of nine books of poetry and has also published criticism, including *We Are What We Mourn* (McGill-Queens University Press, 2009). Priscila was CANFun poet-in-residence at the Vancouver Olympics and Paralympics in 2010. Her nonfiction book *Projections: Encounters with My Runaway Mother* was nominated for the Governor General's Award and the Hilary Weston Prize. Priscila is a professor at York University, Toronto.

Miriam Waddington was born in Winnipeg in 1917. She studied at the University of Toronto and the University of Pennsylvania and was trained as a social worker. Waddington taught in the English department at York University until 1983. She was the author of fiction and non-fiction as well as poetry and also worked as an editor. Her numerous books of poetry include *The Season's Lovers* (1958), *Driving Home: Poems New and Selected* (1972), and *Collected Poems* (1986). Waddington received the Borestone Mountain Awards for Best Poetry several times, the J.J. Segal Award, and two honorary doctorates. She died in Vancouver in 2004. Waddington's letters are housed at the special collections of Simon Fraser University and are reprinted here by permission of Johnathan Waddington, executor for the Estate of Miriam Waddington.

Myna Wallin is a poet, prose writer, editor, and radio host. She is the author of *Confessions of a Reluctant Cougar* and *A Thousand Profane Pieces*. Wallin has published widely in magazines and literary journals including *Existere*, *CV2*, *Descant*, *Rampike*, *Matrix*, and many others.

Betsy Warland was born in Iowa in 1946. She studied at Luther College, Iowa. The author of eleven books of poetry and non-fiction, she emigrated to Canada in 1973. Her books include *What Holds Us Here* (1999), *Only This Blue: A Long Poem with an Essay* (2005), and *Bloodroot: Tracing the Untelling of Mother Loss* (2000). She has also authored *Breathing the Page: Reading the Act of Writing* (2010). Warland was the founder of the Toronto Women's Writing Collective (1975 – 1981). She lives in Vancouver, teaches at Simon Fraser University, and directs the Vancouver Manuscript Intensive. The excerpt from "Subject to Change," a collaboration between Warland and Daphne Marlatt, appeared in *Two Women In a Birth* (Guernica, 1994) and is reprinted by permission of the authors and the publisher.

Phyllis Webb was born in Victoria in 1927. She studied at the University of British Columbia and McGill University and went on to become a shaping force at the CBC. Webb published her first poems during her Montreal period. She has lived in Europe, the UK, Toronto, and currently lives on Salt Spring Island. Webb's first book of poems was *Even Your Right Eye* (1956). Her selected poems, *The Vision Tree* (1982), received the Governor General's Award. Her *Brush Strokes: Selected Prose* appeared in 1995. "And in Our Time" appeared in *Trio: First Poems by Gael Turnbull, Phyllis Webb, and Eli Mandel* (Contact Press, 1954).

Shannon Webb-Campbell, poet, fiction writer, and arts journalist, grew up outside Toronto and now lives in Halifax. She studied English and journalism at Dalhousie University. Currently Webb-Campbell is pursuing her MFA in creative writing at the University of British Columbia. Webb-Campbell's work has been published widely in *Riddle Fence, Quill & Quire,* and *Room,* among other places. She has served as the CWILA writer-in-residence, and recently received an Egale Canada Human Rights Trust OUT in Print Literary Award. Her first collection of poetry is forthcoming from Breakwater Books in 2015.

R.C. Weslowski, spoken word poet, storyteller, playwright, broadcaster, educator, and clown, is president of the Vancouver Poetry House. Among many awards he has received for his performances is the 2012 Canadian Poetry Slam Individual Championship. He has toured his solo shows across Canada and beyond at fringe festivals and other venues, and he has twice been a finalist in the World Cup of Poetry Slam.

Howard White, born in 1945 in Abbotsford, British Columbia, is the author of several books of poetry, including *The Men There Were Then* (1983) and *Ghost in the Gears* (1993). White studied at the University of British Columbia. He is the founder of Harbour Publishing and the periodical *Raincoast Chronicles.* His numerous awards include the Leacock Medal for Humour (1990) and induction into the Order of Canada (2007). "The Made Bed" appeared in *Ghost in the Gears* (Harbour Publishing, 1993, www.harbourpublishing.com).

Bruce Whiteman was born in 1952. He studied at Trent University and the University of Toronto. He moved to Los Angeles in 1996 and now lives in Santa Monica. Whiteman is the author of works of cultural history and numerous poetry books, including *The Invisible World Is in Decline,* Books I–VII (1981-2014) and *XXIV Love Poems* (2002). He has also done translation work. "Her Absence Filled the World" ("Dear Kelly") reprinted from *Intimate Letters: The Invisible World Is in Decline,* Book VII (Toronto: ECW Press, 2014).

George Woodcock was born in 1912 in Winnipeg. He was a biographer, historian, essayist, critic, and poet. He also founded the journal *Canadian Literature* in 1959. Woodcock joined the English department at the University of British Columbia in 1955. He was the author of dozens of books, including *Anarchy of Chaos* (1944), *Anarchism: A History of Libertarian Ideas and Movements* (1962), *Confederation Betrayed!* (1981), and *The Cherry Tree on Cherry Street and Other Poems* (1994). Woodcock died in Vancouver in 1995. A documentary film has been made of his life, and an award was founded in his honour. "À Ma Belle Laide" is reprinted from *The Cherry Tree on Cherry Street* (Quarry, 1994) by permission of the Writers' Trust of Canada, Toronto.

Lindsay Zier-Vogel studied at the University of Toronto and the School of Toronto Dance Theatre. A book binder and founder of Puddle Press, Zier-Vogel's writing has been widely published in numerous places, such as *Taddle Creek*, *Descant*, *Grain*, and *filling station*. She also founded the Love Lettering Project, a community-based arts project that has sent love letters to strangers since 2004. She is at work on a novel.

Editors

David Eso's work as scholar, poet, anthologist, and impresario unites Canadian literary heritage with its impending renaissance. His work has appeared in *Filling Station, CV2, Strangers in Paris, Canadian Literature, Arc, Freefall, Vallum, Under the Mulberry Tree*, the *Globe and Mail*, and on CBC radio. His chapbooks include *Entries from My Affair with an Escape Artist* (2003), *A Wide Path to the Narrowing Future* (2010), and *Asiarific* (2014). Charles Noble has called Eso "a force of nature and force of culture." Eso is currently a graduate student at the University of Calgary, where he is studying the letters of Robert Kroetsch.

Jeanette Lynes is the author of six collections of poetry. Her most recent book of poems, *Archive of the Undressed* (2012), was short-listed for two Saskatchewan Book Awards. Her previous work has received the Bliss Carman Award and *The New Quarterly*'s Nick Blatchford Occasional Verse Award. Lynes's seventh book of poems, *Bedlam Cowslip: The John Clare Poems*, is forthcoming from Wolsak and Wynn in 2015 under its Buckrider Books imprint. Her first novel, *The Factory Voice* (2009), was long-listed for the Scotiabank Giller Prize and a ReLit Award. She is the inaugural coordinator of the MFA in writing at the University of Saskatchewan.